COBOL PROGRAMMING

COBOL
PROGRAMMING

Nancy B. Stern

Adjunct Professor Nassau Community College

Robert A. Stern

Assistant Professor Nassau Community College

JOHN WILEY & SONS, INC.

New York • London • Sydney • Toronto

To Lori

Library of Congress Catalogue Card Number: 77-96042

SBN 471 82317 1

Printed in the United States of America

10 9 8 7 6 5 4 3 2

Preface

We have written this book with three primary objectives. We wish to provide the beginner in data processing with (1) the ability to write efficient COBOL programs, (2) an understanding of how COBOL is used effectively in commercial applications, and (3) the logical approach necessary to write sophisticated programs.

This book differs from others on COBOL in the following ways.

1. This is neither a "reference manual" nor a programmed instruction type of textbook. Instead, it combines the advantages of both, while minimizing the disadvantages. This results in a combined text-workbook approach. Thorough explanations of each topic are contained here, with illustrations, questions, and answers immediately following. (For the exercises, the student should use a sheet of paper to cover up the answers. The asterisks indicate where the answers begin.) Several topics are combined with many illustrations and questions, so that the reader can relate the information and better understand the logical approach necessary for programming in COBOL.

2. The organization of the text is most beneficial to the student. Most books on COBOL are fragmented, generally commencing with a discussion of the **PROCEDURE DIVISION** and leaving the rest for a later explanation. This makes it extremely difficult for the beginner to understand how to organize a COBOL program effectively. He may understand each segment, but the relationship of one to another is difficult for him to conceptualize. To effectively utilize COBOL as a pro-

gramming language, the programmer must understand this interrelationship. Therefore, with this book, the reader is able to write complete COBOL programs, however simple, after the first few lessons. Not only are segments of programs provided in the various explanations and illustrations, but at all points previous learning is reinforced. By giving complete illustrations and programs as answers to problems, the reader enhances his conceptual understanding of COBOL and his ability to program in the language.

3. Illustrations, questions, and programs to be written by the reader are supplied, which are totally applicable to the commercial field. Most books in this field supply examples and questions which, although relevant to the particular points being explained, do not relate effectively to the business environment. As a result, the beginner does not fully understand the total applicability of COBOL to business. We have overcome this problem by providing examples and programs to be written by the student which are realistic, in a business sense.

The student can obtain the major concepts of programming in COBOL from Chapters 1 to 19 and be able to write intermediate level programs. Chapter 20 (Disk Operations) has been provided for advanced COBOL students who would like to get an idea of some of the COBOL techniques involved when programming for mass storage devices. It is a survey chapter designed to be used in conjunction with the reference manual for the specific computer employed.

This book is divided into 5 units.

Unit 1 introduces the reader to COBOL and has him writing simplified COBOL programs. The best way to learn the language is to write complete programs, however simple, from the onset.

Unit 2 contains the basic verbs in a COBOL program which are used consistently and in depth. A thorough approach is taken, since these few statements must be understood fully to appreciate COBOL programming. At this point, the reader should program simple applications with relative ease.

Unit 3 is devoted exclusively to printed output, since the format differs slightly from other forms of output. Since much of the output from COBOL programs is printed, this unit concentrates on setting up headers and printing detailed information as efficiently as possible.

Unit 4 explains **PERFORM** statements and **OCCURS** clauses in depth. It is felt that, although difficult, this topic is necessary for programming moderately complex COBOL programs. In this unit, the logic of such applications is stressed, since difficulties encountered are usually attributable to this phase.

Unit 5 emphasizes the refinements necessary for a programmer to write good programs rather than merely adequate ones.

This book is intended primarily for junior-college and four-year college students and requires no prior exposure to programming languages. We have provided no introduction to computer equipment because this equipment varies greatly among computer centers. In addition, COBOL is designed to be basically computer independent.

We express special appreciation to Burroughs, Honeywell, and IBM for their cooperation in supplying specifications, illustrations, examples, and photographs.

Nancy B. Stern
Robert A. Stern

Acknowledgment

The following acknowledgment has been reproduced from COBOL Edition, U.S. Department of Defense, at the request of the Conference on Data Systems Languages.

"Any organization interested in reproducing the COBOL report and specifications in whole or in part, using ideas taken from this report as the basis for an instruction manual or for any other purpose is free to do so. However, all such organizations are requested to reproduce this section as part of the introduction to the document. Those using a short passage, as in a book review, are requested to mention 'COBOL' in acknowledgment of the source, but need not quote this entire section.

"COBOL is an industry language and is not the property of any company or group of companies, or of any organization or group of organizations.

"No warranty, expressed or implied, is made by any contributor or by the COBOL Committee as to the accuracy and functioning of the programming system and language. Moreover, no responsibility is assumed by any contributor, or by the committee, in connection therewith.

"Procedures have been established for the maintenance of COBOL. Inquiries concerning the procedures for proposing changes should be directed to the Executive Committee of the Conference on Data Systems Languages.

"The authors and copyright holders of the copyrighted material used herein

FLOW-MATIC (Trademark of Sperry Rand Corporation), Programming for the Univac (R) I and II, Data Automation Systems copyrighted 1958, 1959, by Sperry Rand Corporation: IBM Commercial Translator Form No. F 28-8013, copyrighted 1959 by IBM; FACT, DSI 27A5260-2760, copyrighted 1960 by Minneapolis-Honeywell

have specifically authorized the use of this material in whole or in part, in the COBOL specifications. Such authorization extends to the reproduction and use of COBOL specifications in programming manuals or similar publications."

Contents

COBOL PROGRAMMING

Unit 1

1

Introduction to COBOL Programming

A. COMPUTER PROGRAMMING

No matter how complex a computer may be, its actions are directed by individual computer instructions designed and tested by a computer **programmer.** The program consists of a set of instructions that will operate on input data and convert it to output. A computer, then, can operate only as efficiently and effectively as it is programmed.

All instructions to be operated on must be in machine-understandable form. For the programmer to code his instructions in this form is very tedious and cumbersome. Exact core storage locations must be remembered, and complex numerical computer codes must be utilized.

Since programming in a machine language is so difficult, advances in programming technology were developed to enable the programmer to write English-like instructions. These instructions, however, must be translated or **compiled** into machine language before they can be executed. The computer itself performs this translation into machine language with the use of a control program.

Among the numerous **programming languages** that can be translated into machine form is COBOL, which is the one used most often for commercial applications.

The programmer, then, writes a set of instructions, called the **source program,** in one of the programming languages. It **cannot** be executed or operated on by the computer until it has been translated into machine language.

The source program is generally punched into cards by a keypunch machine. This **source deck** enters the computer and must be translated into a machine language program called the **object program** before execution can occur. A special program called a **compiler** translates source programs into object programs.

While the computer is performing this translation, any errors detected by the compiler will be listed. That is, any violation of a programming rule is denoted as an error. For example, if the instruction to add two numbers is spelled **AD** instead of **ADD**, the computer will print an error message. If errors are of considerable magnitude, translation will be terminated. Note that the errors detected during a compilation are **not** of a logical nature. A logic error is one in which the **sequence** of programming steps is not executed properly. The machine generally has no way of judging the logic in a program, but this may be tested by executing the program in a "trial run."

If errors are not present in the source program or only minor violations of rules occur, the translation process will continue until all instructions are in machine language form. The program can then be executed, or tested, at this point. If, however, execution is not desirable at this time, the object program may be saved by punching it into cards or storing it on some other medium. Thus, this object deck may be used to execute the instructions without the necessity to recompile. Fig. 1-1 illustrates the steps involved in programming.

A program, therefore, specifies the logical sequence of computer instructions. When the logic of a program becomes complex, pictorial representations called **flowcharts** are written **prior to** the coding of the program. These pictorial representations illustrate program logic in a less complex manner, thus facilitating the writing of the program.

Such flowcharts will be illustrated throughout. For the beginner in data processing with no previous exposure to flowcharting, Appendix B provides an introduction to the basic concepts.

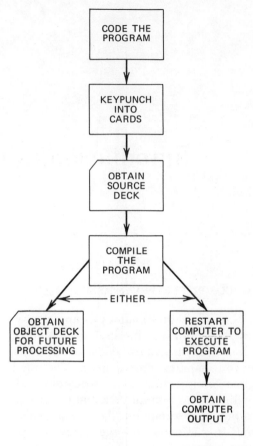

Fig. 1-1 Steps involved in programming a computer.

EXERCISES

Each question in the exercises will be followed by an asterisk which signals that the solution will follow. Use a sheet of paper to cover the solution when testing yourself.

1. A computer programmer _____.
   *****
   writes and tests computer instructions.

2. A set of instructions that will operate on input data and convert it to output data is called a _____.
   *****
   program

3. To be executed by the computer, all instructions must be in _____ language.
   *****
   machine

4. Programs are (often, seldom) written in machine language.
   *****
   seldom—too cumbersome and tedious

5. Programs written in a language other than machine language must be _____ before execution can occur.
   *****
   translated or compiled

6. _____ is an example of an Englishlike programming language.
   *****
   COBOL

7. _____ is the process of converting a COBOL program into machine language.
   *****
   Compilation

8. The program written in a language such as COBOL is called the _____ program.
   *****
   source

9. The source deck is the _____.
   *****
   set of instructions in a language such as COBOL that has been punched into cards

10. The object program is the _____.
    *****
    set of instructions that has been converted into machine language

11. A _____ converts a _____ program into a(n) _____ program.
    *****
    compiler
    source
    object

12. The errors that are detected during compilation denote _____.
    *****
    any violation of programming rules

13. The logic of a program can only be checked by _____.
    *****
    testing it or executing it in a "trial run"

14. After a program has been compiled, it may be _____ or _____.
    *****
    executed
    saved in translated form for future processing

B. THE NATURE OF COBOL

COBOL is the most widespread commercial programming language in use today. The reasons for its vast success will be discussed in this section.

The word COBOL is an abbreviation for **CO**mmon **B**usiness **O**riented **L**anguage. It is a **B**usiness **O**riented computer language designed for commercial applications. The rules governing the use of the language make it applicable for commercial problems. Thus, applications of a scientific nature cannot be adequately handled by COBOL; a scientific computer language such as FORTRAN would be more appropriate.

COBOL is a computer language that is common to many computers. That is, most computer manufacturers have designed their machines to accept a COBOL compiler, so that the same COBOL program may be compiled on an IBM s/360 and a HONEYWELL 200 with only minor variations.

The universality of COBOL, therefore, allows computer users greater flexibility. A company is free to use computers of different manufacturers while retaining a single programming language. Similarly, conversion from one model computer to a more advanced or newer one presents no great problem. Computers of a future generation will also be equipped to use COBOL.

Thus the meaning of the word COBOL suggests two of its basic advantages. It is common to most computers, and it is commercially oriented. There are, however, additional reasons why it is such a popular language.

COBOL is an Englishlike language. All instructions are coded using English words rather than complex codes. To add two numbers together, for example, we use the word **ADD**. Similarly, the rules for programming in COBOL conform to many of the rules for writing in English, making it a relatively simple language to learn. It therefore becomes significantly easier to train programmers. In addition, COBOL programs are written and tested in far less time than programs written in other computer languages.

Thus the Englishlike quality of COBOL makes it easy to **write** programs. Similarly, this quality makes COBOL programs easier to **read.** Such programs can generally be understood by nondata processing personnel. The business executive who knows little about computers can better understand the nature of a programming job simply by reading a COBOL program.

EXERCISES

1. The word COBOL is an abbreviation for _____ _____ _____ _____.

   *****

   COmmon **B**usiness **O**riented **L**anguage

2. COBOL is a common language in the sense that _____.

   *****

   it may be used on many different makes and models of computers

3. COBOL is a business-oriented language in the sense that _____.

   *****

   it makes use of ordinary business terminology

4. COBOL generally (would, would not) be used for scientific applications.

*****

would not

5. An additional feature of COBOL is that it is _____.

*****

Englishlike

C. A SAMPLE PROGRAM

Every COBOL program consists of four separate **divisions.** Each division is written in an Englishlike manner designed to decrease programming effort and to facilitate the understanding of a program by nondata processing personnel. Each of the four divisions has a specific function.

1. The **IDENTIFICATION DIVISION** serves to identify the program to the computer. It also provides pertinent documentary information which is meaningful to nondata processing personnel analyzing the program.
2. The **ENVIRONMENT DIVISION** describes the computer equipment that will be utilized by the specific program.
3. The **DATA DIVISION** describes the input and output formats to be processed by the program. It also defines any constants or work areas necessary for the processing of data.
4. The **PROCEDURE DIVISION** contains the instructions and the logic flow necessary to create output data from input.

The structure and organization of a COBOL program can best be explained by an illustration.

Definition of the Problem. A computer center of a large company is assigned the task of calculating weekly wages for all nonsalaried personnel. The hourly rate and number of hours worked are supplied for each employee, and the weekly wages figure is computed as follows:

WEEKLY-WAGES = HOURS-WORKED × HOURLY-RATE

To process any data, the incoming information, or **input,** must be in a form that is "readable" or understandable to the computer. Punched cards, magnetic tape, and magnetic disk are common forms of input to a computer system.

Thus the employee data, consisting of **EMPLOYEE-NAME, HOURS-WORKED,** and **HOURLY-RATE,** will be transcribed or **key-punched** onto a punched card so that it may be accepted as input to the data processing system. These data items are called **fields** of information. Specific columns of the card must be set aside to accept each field. The data will be entered on the card as is shown in Fig. 1-2.

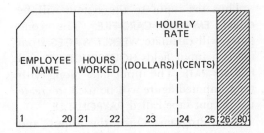

Fig. 1-2

Card Columns 1–20 are **reserved** for each **EMPLOYEE-NAME.** If any name contains less than 20 characters, the **low order,** or right-most, positions are left blank. Similarly, **HOURS-WORKED** will be placed in Columns 21-22 and **HOURLY-RATE** in Columns 23-25. The HOURLY-RATE figure, as a dollars and cents amount, is to be interpreted as a two-decimal field. That is, 125 in Columns 23-25 is to be inter-

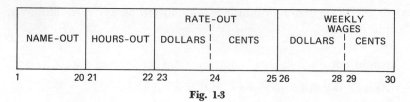

NAME-OUT	HOURS-OUT	RATE-OUT		WEEKLY WAGES	
		DOLLARS	CENTS	DOLLARS	CENTS

1   20 21   22 23   24   25 26   28 29   30

Fig. 1-3

preted by the computer as 1.25. The decimal point is **not** punched into the card, since it would waste a storage position. We will see that this method of **implying** decimal points is easily handled in COBOL.

A deck of employee cards, with the above format, will be read as input to the computer. WEEKLY-WAGES will be calculated by the computer as HOURS-WORKED multiplied by HOURLY-RATE. The computed figure, however, **cannot** be added directly to the input data. That is, we cannot create output data on an input record. Input and output must ordinarily utilize separate devices.[1]

We will create in this way an output file which contains all input data **in addition to** the computed wage figure. The output PAYROLL-FILE will be placed on a magnetic tape with the record format shown in Fig. 1-3.

Thus the input to the system will be called EMPLOYEE-CARD-FILE. The computer will calculate WEEKLY-WAGES from the two input fields HOURS-WORKED and HOURLY-RATE. The input data along with the computed figure will be used to create the output tape called PAYROLL-FILE.

The Program. Once the input and output record formats have been clearly and precisely defined as in Figs. 1-2 and 1-3, the program may be written. You will recall that a program is a set of instructions and specifications that operate on input to produce output. Fig. 1-4 is a simplified COBOL program which will operate on employee cards to create a payroll tape file with the computed wages.

Note that the program is divided into

four major divisions. The IDENTIFICATION, ENVIRONMENT, DATA, and PROCEDURE DIVISIONS are coded on lines 01, 03, 06, and 18, respectively. Every COBOL program **must** contain these four divisions in the above order.

The IDENTIFICATION DIVISION has, as its only entry, the PROGRAM-ID. That is, the IDENTIFICATION DIVISION of this program merely serves to identify the program.

The ENVIRONMENT DIVISION assigns the input and output files to specific devices. EMPLOYEE-CARDS, the name assigned to the input file, will be processed by a card reader. Similarly, PAYROLL-FILE is the output file assigned to a specific tape drive.

The DATA DIVISION describes, in detail, the field designations of the two files. The input and output areas in core storage are fully described in the DATA DIVISION. The File Description, or FD, for EMPLOYEE-CARDS defines the **record** format called EMPLOYEE-RECORD with three input fields, EMPLOYEE-NAME, HOURS-WORKED, and HOURLY-RATE. Each field has a corresponding PICTURE clause denoting the size and type of data which will appear in the field.

The EMPLOYEE-NAME field is an alphabetic data field containing 20 characters. PICTURE A(20) indicates the **size** of the field (20 characters) and the **type** of data, A denoting alphabetic information. Similarly, HOURS-WORKED is a two-position numeric field. PICTURE 9(2) indicates the type of data, 9 denoting numeric information, and (2) denoting a two-position area. HOURLY-RATE is a three-position numeric field with an **implied** decimal point. PICTURE 9V99 indicates a three-position numeric field with an implied or assumed

---

[1] An exception to this is **disk** processing, which will be discussed in Chapter 20.

IBM   COBOL Program Sheet   Form No. X28-1464-3 U/M 050
Printed in U. S. A.

| System | | Punching Instructions | Sheet 1 of 1 |

| Program | SAMPLE | Graphic | | | | | | Card | * | Identification SAMPLEOL |
| Programmer | N. STERN | Date | Punch | | | | | | Form # | | 73   80 |

```
Sequence    A  B              COBOL Statement
01  IDENTIFICATION DIVISION.
02  PROGRAM-ID. 'SAMPLE'.
03  ENVIRONMENT DIVISION.
04  FILE-CONTROL.    SELECT EMPLOYEE-CARDS ASSIGN TO READER.
05                   SELECT PAYROLL-FILE ASSIGN TO TAPE 1.
06  DATA DIVISION.
07  FD EMPLOYEE-CARDS
08  01 EMPLOYEE-RECORD.
09     02 EMPLOYEE-NAME      PICTURE A(20).
10     02 HOURS-WORKED       PICTURE 9(2).
11     02 HOURLY-RATE        PICTURE 9V99.
12  FD PAYROLL-FILE
13  01 PAYROLL-RECORD.
14     02 NAME-OUT           PICTURE A(20).
15     02 HOURS-OUT          PICTURE 9(2).
16     02 RATE-OUT           PICTURE 9V99.
17     02 WEEKLY-WAGES       PICTURE 999V99.
18  PROCEDURE DIVISION.
19  START.    READ EMPLOYEE-CARDS AT END GO TO FINISH.
20            MOVE EMPLOYEE-NAME TO NAME-OUT. MOVE HOURS-WORKED TO
21            HOURS-OUT. MOVE HOURLY-RATE TO RATE-OUT.
22            MULTIPLY HOURS-WORKED BY HOURLY-RATE GIVING WEEKLY-WAGES.
23            WRITE PAYROLL-RECORD.
24            GO TO START.
25  FINISH. STOP RUN.
```

*A standard card form, IBM electro C61897, is available for punching source statements from this form.

Fig. 1-4

decimal point after the first position. Thus 125 in this field will be interpreted by the computer as 1.25. The decimal point does **not** appear on the input document but is nonetheless implied.

Similarly, the output file called PAYROLL-FILE has a record format called PAYROLL-RECORD, which is subdivided into four fields, each with an appropriate PICTURE clause. The first three fields, NAME-OUT, HOURS-OUT, and RATE-OUT will be taken directly from each input record. The last field, WEEKLY-WAGES, must be computed.

If any constants or work areas were required in the program, they, too, would be described in the DATA DIVISION.

The PROCEDURE DIVISION contains the set of instructions or operations to be performed by the computer. Each instruction is executed in the order in which it appears unless a GO TO statement, or a **branch,** alters the sequence.

Note that the PROCEDURE DIVISION in the above program is divided into two paragraphs, START and FINISH.

The COBOL statement READ EMPLOYEE-CARDS AT END GO TO FINISH will read card data into core storage. If there are no more cards to be processed, a branch to FINISH is executed. Thus a card is read and the next instruction is processed **unless** there are no more cards, in which case a transfer to FINISH occurs.

The MOVE and MULTIPLY instructions on lines 20-22 are self-explanatory. The input data is moved to the output area. The WEEKLY-WAGES figure on the output file is calculated by multiplying HOURS-WORKED by HOURLY-RATE.

After the data is accumulated at the output area, a WRITE command is executed. The WRITE operation takes the data in the output area and places it on magnetic tape.

The above instructions will process **one**

card and create one **tape** record. To be of any significance, the program must be able to process many cards. Thus the above series of instructions must be repeated. The **GO TO START** instruction permits the program to repeat the sequence of operations.

Execution continues in this manner until there are no more input cards to be processed. Then a branch to **FINISH** is performed, and the program is terminated.

Fig. 1-4 then represents a sample COBOL program. Several steps have been omitted for the sake of clarity, but the program is essentially complete.

An analysis of the program reveals two essential points. The Englishlike manner and the structural organization of a COBOL program make it comparatively easy to learn. Similarly, the ease with which a COBOL program may be read by nontrained readers makes it a distinct asset to most data-processing installations.

EXERCISES

1. All COBOL programs are composed of _____ _____ .

   *****

   four
   divisions

2. The names of these four divisions are _____, _____, _____, and _____.

   *****

   IDENTIFICATION
   ENVIRONMENT
   DATA
   PROCEDURE

3. The function of the IDENTIFICATION DIVISION is to _____ .

   *****

   identify the program

4. The function of the ENVIRONMENT DIVISION is to _____ .

   *****

   describe the equipment to be used in the program

5. The function of the DATA DIVISION is to _____ .

   *****

   describe the input, output, constants, and work areas used in the program

6. The function of the PROCEDURE DIVISION is to _____ .

   *****

   define the instructions and operations necessary to convert input data into output

7. Incoming information is called _____.

*****

input

8. Outgoing information is called _____.

*****

output

9. _____, _____, and _____ are examples of forms of computer input.

*****

Punched cards
magnetic tape
magnetic disk

REVIEW QUESTIONS

1. Define the following terms:
(a) Program.
(b) Compiler.
(c) Source program.
(d) Object program.

2. State the differences between a compiler-generated programming language and a machine language.

3. (T or F) Compiler-generated programming languages must be converted into machine language before execution can occur.

4. (T or F) Although COBOL is a commercial programming language, it contains basic mathematical functions that can be used for complicated mathematical problems.

5. (T or F) COBOL may be used only on a small number of commercial computers.

6. (T or F) A COBOL program must contain four divisions.

7. (T or F) The sequence in which the divisions are written is IDENTIFICATION, DATA, ENVIRONMENT, PROCEDURE.

8. (T or F) The division that changes depending on the computer equipment utilized is the DATA DIVISION.

9. (T or F) The division that seems to require the least programming effort is the IDENTIFICATION DIVISION.

10. (T or F) Instructions are coded in the PROCEDURE DIVISION.

PROBLEMS

1. Fig. 1-5 is an illustration of a sample COBOL program.

Fig. 1-5

(a) Define the input.
(b) Define the output.
(c) Describe the type of processing that converts input data into output.
(d) Write a flowchart of the operation.

2. Fig. 1-6 is an illustration of a sample COBOL program.

IBM COBOL Program Sheet — Form No. X28-1464-3 U/M 050, Printed in U. S. A.

System		Punching Instructions		Sheet of
Program PROBLEM 2		Graphic	Card Form # *	Identification 73–80
Programmer STERN	Date	Punch		

```
Sequence  A   B
(PAGE)(SERIAL)                          COBOL Statement
   01  IDENTIFICATION DIVISION.
   02  PROGRAM-ID. 'PROBLEM2'.
   03  ENVIRONMENT DIVISION.
   04  FILE-CONTROL. SELECT SALES-FILE ASSIGN TO TAPE 1.
   05      SELECT PRINT-FILE ASSIGN TO PRINTER.
   06  DATA DIVISION.
   07  FD  SALES-FILE
   08  01  SALES-REC.
   09      02  SALESMAN-NAME-IN             PICTURE A(15).
   10      02  AMOUNT-OF-SALES              PICTURE 999V99.
   11  FD  PRINT-FILE
   12  01  PRINT-REC.
   13      02  SALESMAN-NAME-OUT            PICTURE A(15).
   14      02  AMOUNT-OF-COMMISSION         PICTURE 99V99.
   15  PROCEDURE DIVISION.
   16  START.  READ SALES-FILE AT END GO TO FINISH.
   17          IF AMOUNT-OF-SALES IS GREATER THAN 100.00 MULTIPLY .03
   18          BY AMOUNT-OF-SALES, GIVING AMOUNT-OF-COMMISSION, GO TO
   19          WRITE-ROUTINE.
   20          IF AMOUNT-OF-SALES IS GREATER THAN 50.00 MULTIPLY .02
               BY AMOUNT-OF-SALES GIVING AMOUNT-OF-COMMISSION, GO TO
               WRITE-ROUTINE.
               MOVE ZEROS to AMOUNT-OF-COMMISSION.
       WRITE-ROUTINE. WRITE PRINT-REC. GO TO START.
       FINISH. STOP RUN.
```

*A standard card form, IBM electro C61897, is available for punching source statements from this form.

Fig. 1-6

(a) Define the input.
(b) Define the output.
(c) Describe the type of processing that converts input data into output.
(d) Write a flowchart of the operation.

Data Organization

A. DESCRIPTION OF FILES, RECORDS, AND FIELDS

As we have seen from the program illustration, data is processed by the computer in an organized pattern. Areas are reserved in storage for **files, records,** and **fields.** Each of these terms has special significance in COBOL and must be fully understood before programs may be written.

This section will explain the above terms and their relation to each other. As we will see later, every field, record, or file used in a COBOL program must be assigned a **data-name.** The rules for forming such names will also be discussed here.

File. A **file** is the overall classification of data pertaining to a specific category. In a business environment, the term has a broad meaning. Company ABC, for example, has an inventory file, which contains **all** inventory information. Employee X's medical file contains **all** medical data on employee X.

In an electronic data processing context, a file has similar significance. It is the **major** grouping of data containing information of a specific nature. Files are generally considered the **input** and **output** to a data processing system. A file enters the computer flow as input, is processed, and an output file is produced.

A payroll card file, an accounts receivable tape file, and a transaction print file are examples of often-used data processing files.

This, then, is the major classification of data in a data processing environment. If an application uses payroll cards as input and prints a salary report as output, we say that **two** files are processed. A card file, consisting of payroll information, and a print file, containing computed salaries, constitute the two files for the application.

Most COBOL programs utilize at least one input and one output file. Except for disk[1] applications, data cannot ordinarily be updated within the same file. That is, the input must be distinct from the output. Suppose, for example, a sales-ticket file is entered as card input to the system. Price and quantity appear on each ticket and sales amount is to be computed as price $\times$ quantity. The extended sales amount figure cannot be placed on the input cards in most cases. We cannot create output data on input cards. Output data must be created independently on an output device. A new file, then, containing the input data **and** the ex-

[1] Disk applications employ unique concepts in data processing and will be discussed in Chapter 20 independently.

tended sales amount figure must be created. Thus the card-punch unit will duplicate input information and add the extended output results. Two files exist for this application—the input and the output files.

For **every** form of input and output used in a data processing application, we have **one** file. If weekly transaction cards from week 1 and a weekly transaction tape from week 2 are entered as input to a system, and a master tape file, combining the two, is created as output, we say we have **three** files. Transactions from week 1, transactions from week 2, and master transactions each constitute an independent file. Three devices are used: a card reader and two magnetic tape drives.

NAME	TRANSACTION NO.	QTY PURCHASED	UNIT PRICE	

All cards within the accounts receivable file will be credit or debit records. Thus, we say that the file contains two record formats.

A record, then, is a specific kind of data within a file. We have one file for each form of input and output that the program employs. We have one record for each format within the file.

Consider the following magnetic tape layout containing payroll data:

SALARY HISTORY			CURRENT PAYROLL					TAX RECORD				
NAME	PRES. SAL.	PAST SAL.	NAME	SAL.	NO. OF DEP.	LIFE INS. PREM.	HEALTH INS.	NAME	FED. TAX	STATE TAX	CITY TAX	

Records. A record is a unit of grouped data **within** a file which contains information of a specific nature. Consider an accounts receivable file, entered as card input to a data processing system. The file is subdivided into records. Each record contains data of a specific nature. The accounts receivable file, for example, contains **two** records, a **credit** and a **debit** record. The credit record has the following card format:

NAME	TRANSACTION NO.	AMT. OF CREDIT	

The debit record has the following card format:

Note that three types of records exist within the file: a salary history record, a current payroll record, and a tax record. Since the magnetic tape file contains three formats of data, we say that three records exist within the payroll file.

Often, however, we have only **one** record within a file. That is, all data within the file is of the same format. An inventory card file, for example, where all cards have the following form:

ITEM NAME	ITEM NO.	QTY. ON HAND	REORDER NO.	

is said to contain only one record format.

Group Items and Elementary Items.
Consider the credit record described below:

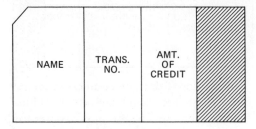

It contains the following **data fields:**

NAME, TRANSACTION-NUMBER,
AMOUNT-OF-CREDIT

You will recall that a **field** of data is a group of consecutive storage positions reserved for a specific kind of data.

Fields, in COBOL, fall into two major categories: **group items** and **elementary items.** A group item is a data field that is further subdivided. That is, a group item is a major field consisting of minor fields. A **NAME** field, for example, which contains three minor fields (**LAST-NAME, FIRST-INITIAL, SECOND-INITIAL**) is considered a group item. An **ADDRESS** field which consists of **CITY** and **STATE** is a group item. The following record format consists of three group items:

DATE		NAME		IDENT.	
MO	YR	INIT.	LAST-NAME	LEVEL	POSITION

DATE, NAME, and **IDENTIFICATION** are group items.

A data field not further subdivided is called an **elementary item. MONTH, YEAR, INITIAL, LAST-NAME, LEVEL,** and **POSITION** are elementary items in the above example.

In the credit records above, **all** fields are elementary items, since none are further subdivided. Thus group items need not exist within a record format.

The hierarchy of data may be defined as follows: **Files** contain **records.** Records contain **data fields.** Fields are described

as **group items,** if they are further subdivided, and as **elementary items,** if they are not. Group items are always further subdivided into elementary items.

Rules for Forming Data-Names. Files, records, group items, and elementary items are data groupings defined in a COBOL program. They must be given **data-names.** A data-name is a programmer-supplied name for any unit of data used in a COBOL program. The programmer must supply the names used for any item of information. Programmer-supplied data-names must conform to certain rules.

1. 1 to 30 characters may be used for any data-name.

2. Data-names may contain letters, numbers, or hyphens (-). No other special characters are permitted in a data-name. An embedded blank (a blank within a name) is considered a special character and, as such, is not valid.

3. A data-name may not begin or end with a "-".

4. A data-name must contain at least one alphabetic character.

5. The data-name assigned by the programmer must **not** be a **COBOL RESERVED WORD.** A COBOL reserved word is a word that has special significance to the COBOL compiler. Appendix A lists all COBOL reserved words which must **not** be used as data-names.

Consider the following record layout within a card file:

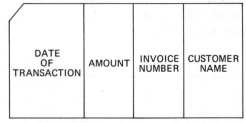

The data fields may be named as follows: **DATE-OF-TRANS, AMOUNT, INVOICE-NO, CUSTOMER-NAME.** Note that hyphens are used in place of embedded blanks.

Each file, record, and data field may be assigned a name in the COBOL program. Once a name is assigned within the program, the **same** name must be used throughout when referring to the specific unit of data. **CREDIT-AMT**, defined as a data-name in the **DATA DIVISION**, may **not** be referred to as **CR-AMT** in the **PROCEDURE DIVISION**. The same name must be used throughout the program.

Note that the data-names used in the examples suggest the type of data field. **DATE-OF-TRANS** is a more meaningful data-name than perhaps **A7**, although both names are valid. In general, use data-names that suggest the meaning of the field. This facilitates the writing of the **PROCEDURE DIVISION** and also enables noncomputer personnel to better understand the meaning of the program.

The following programmer-supplied data-names are invalid for the reasons noted:

Name	Error
EMPLOYEE NAME	Embedded blank
DISCOUNT-%	%, as a special character, is not valid
INPUT	INPUT is a COBOL reserved word

COBOL programs make extensive use of organized data. Files are assigned to specific input-output devices. Each record format within a file must be fully described by assigning data-names to the group items and to the elementary items within the file. The rules for forming programming-supplied data-names must be utilized when assigning names to files, records, and fields.

Let us consider the following program excerpt which illustrates the **DATA DIVISION** of a COBOL program:

```
DATA DIVISION.
FILE SECTION.
FD PAYROLL-FILE
   DATA RECORDS ARE SALARY-REC,
   DEDUCTIONS-REC.
01 SALARY-REC.
   02 NAME
   02 JOB-TITLE
   02 NO-OF-DEPENDENTS
   02 SALARY
01 DEDUCTIONS-REC.
   02 FICA
   02 FED-TAX
   02 STATE-TAX
   02 HEALTH-INSUR-PREMIUM
   02 LIFE-INSUR-PREMIUM
```

Data-names are defined within the **DATA DIVISION** in the above example. The **FD** entry defines the file name. The **PAYROLL-FILE**, which consists of two record formats, is the name assigned to the file. **SALARY-REC** and **DEDUCTIONS-REC** are the record names. Each is subdivided into data fields. **NAME, JOB-TITLE, NO-OF-DEPENDENTS**, and **SALARY** are elementary data fields within **SALARY-REC**. Note that the names assigned conform to the rules for forming programmer-supplied data-names. Similarly, **DEDUCTIONS-REC** is subdivided into five fields, **FICA, FED-TAX, STATE-TAX, HEALTH-INSUR-PREMIUM**, and **LIFE-INSUR-PREMIUM**. In chapter 5 you will learn the specific format of the **DATA DIVISION**. Any name which must be assigned to files, records, group items, and elementary items in this division must conform to the rules described above.

EXERCISES

1. A file is _____.
   *****
   the major grouping of data in a COBOL program

2. A record is a _____.
*****
grouping of data within a file

3. The input and output in a COBOL program are assigned _____ names.
*****
file

4. Each format within a file is assigned a _____ name.
*****
record

5. The two types of fields within a record are _____ and _____.
*****
group items
elementary items

6. A group item is a _____.
*****
field that is further subdivided into subordinate fields

7. An elementary item is a _____.
*****
field that is not further subdivided

8. If an amount field contains a code and a price, then the amount is called a _____ item and code is an _____ item.
*****
group
elementary

9. Files, records, group items, and elementary items must be given _____-names in a COBOL program.
*****
data

10. State what, if anything, is wrong with the following data-names:
    (a) DATA
    (b) RECORD 1
    (c) AMT-IN-$
    (d) ABC-123
    *****
    (a) DATA is a COBOL reserved word.
    (b) No embedded blanks: RECORD-1 may be used.
    (c) No special characters: $ is a special character.
    (d) Okay.

B. TYPES OF DATA

Thus far, we have discussed the organization of data as it appears in a COBOL program. Input and output files are described by record formats. Each record has field descriptions classified as group items or elementary items.

By defining files, records, and fields and assigning corresponding data-names in the **DATA DIVISION**, we reserve core storage for data. The File Description entry, as illustrated in the previous section, reserves core for input and output files. The area described by a File Description entry is said to contain **variable** data.

Variable data is that data which changes within the program. The contents of data fields in the input area change with each **READ** command. **READ PAYROLL-FILE** results in input data being stored in the area defined by the File Description for **PAYROLL-FILE**. This data is considered variable since it will change with each card that is read. After input fields are processed, results are placed in the output area, which is defined by another File Description. Thus we say that the contents of output fields are also variable.

By defining a data field with a data-name, we say nothing about the **contents** of the field. **AMT**, for example, is a data field within **RECORD-1**; the content of **AMT**, however, is variable. It depends upon the input record being processed, and thus changes within the program. Any field described within an input or output file contains variable data.

A **constant** is a form of data required for processing which is **not** dependent upon the input to the system. A constant, as opposed to variable data, remains unchanged in the program. Suppose, for example, we wish to multiply each amount field of the input records by .05, the tax rate. The tax rate, .05, is **not** a value on the input record but is nevertheless required for processing. We call .05 a **constant**, since it is a form of data required for processing which is not dependent upon the input to the system.

Similarly, suppose we wish to edit input cards and print the message 'INVALID RECORD' for any erroneous card. The message 'INVALID RECORD' will be part of the output, but is not entered as input to the system. It is a constant, required for processing and not part of input.

A constant may be defined directly in the **PROCEDURE DIVISION** of a COBOL program. **AMT**, a field within the input file, is to be multiplied by the tax rate, .05, to produce **TAX-AMT**, a field within the output file. The **PROCEDURE DIVISION** entry to perform this operation is as follows:

MULTIPLY AMT BY .05 GIVING TAX-AMT.

The two data fields, **AMT** and **TAX-AMT**, are described in the **DATA DIVISION**. The constant .05 is defined directly in the above **PROCEDURE DIVISION** entry and need **not** be described in the **DATA DIVISION**.

Three types of constants may be defined in the **PROCEDURE DIVISON** of a COBOL program: numeric literals, nonnumeric literals, and figurative constants. These will be discussed in detail.

NUMERIC LITERAL. A **numeric literal** is a constant defined in the **PROCEDURE DIVISION** and used for arithmetic operations. It may contain:

(a) A maximum of 18 digits.
(b) A plus or minus sign to the **left** of the number.
(c) A decimal point **within** the literal. The decimal point, however, may not be the last character of the literal.

Note that an operational plus or minus sign is **not** required within the literal but **may** be included. If it is included, it must appear to the left of the number. That is, $+16$ or -12 are valid numeric literals but $16+$ or $12-$ are not. If no sign is used, the number is assumed positive. Since a decimal point may not appear as the last character in a numeric literal, 18.2 is a valid literal but 16. is not.

The following are valid numeric literals which may be used in the **PROCEDURE DVISION** of a COBOL program:

$+15.8$
-387.58
42
.05
$-.97$

Suppose we wish to add 10.3 to an output data field, FIELDA, defined in a File Description entry in the DATA DIVISION. The following is a valid instruction:

ADD 10.3 TO FIELDA.

The numeric literal 10.3 may be used in the PROCEDURE DIVISION for arithmetic operations.

The following are **not** valid numeric literals for the reasons noted:

Invalid Numeric Literals	Error
1,000	Commas are **not** permitted
15.	A decimal point is not valid as the last character
$100.00	Dollar signs are not valid
38J	Letters are not permitted
17.45—	Operational signs must appear to the left

A numeric literal, then, is a constant that may be used in the PROCEDURE DIVISION of a COBOL program. Numeric literals are numeric constants that are used for arithmetic operations. The above rules must be employed when defining a numeric literal.

Nonnumeric Literal. A **nonnumeric literal** is a constant used in the PROCEDURE DIVISION for all operations **except** arithmetic. The following rules must be employed when defining a nonnumeric or alphanumeric literal. A nonnumeric literal may contain:

(a) A maximum of 120 characters, including spaces.
(b) Any character in the COBOL character set[2] except the quotation mark (').

[2] Characters in the COBOL character set are those characters that are permitted within a COBOL program. Appendix A lists these characters.

In addition, a nonnumeric literal must be enclosed in quotation marks. The following are valid nonnumeric literals:

    'CODE'
    'ABC 123'
    '1,000'
    'INPUT'
    '$100.00'
    'MESSAGE'

Printing any of the above literals results in those characters **within** the quotation marks; that is CODE, ABC 123, 1,000, etc. will print. Note that a nonnumeric literal may contain **all** numbers. '123' is a valid nonnumeric literal. It is to be distinguished from the numeric literal 123, which is used for arithmetic operations.

Suppose we wish to move the message INVALID RECORD to an output field, FIELD2, before we write an output record. The following is a valid COBOL instruction:

MOVE 'INVALID RECORD' TO FIELD2.

Note that 'INVALID RECORD' is a nonnumeric literal. It is defined in the PROCEDURE DIVISION and does not appear in the DATA DIVISION. FIELD2 is not a literal but a data-name. It conforms to the rules for forming programmer-supplied words. It could not be a nonnumeric literal, since it is not enclosed in quotation marks. All data-names, such as FIELD2, must be defined in the DATA DIVISION.

Therefore, a nonnumeric literal is any constant defined directly in a PROCEDURE DIVISION statement which is not used for arithmetic operations. It must conform to the rules specified above.

Figurative Constant. A **figurative constant** is a COBOL reserved word that has a special significance. We will discuss in this chapter two such figurative constants: ZEROS and SPACES.

Consider the figurative constant ZEROS. It is a COBOL reserved word meaning all zeros. To say, for example,

MOVE ZEROS TO FIELD1

results in the data field, FIELD1, being filled with all zeros. ZEROS is a figurative constant having the **value of** all zeros. ZERO, ZEROES, and ZEROS are equivalent figurative constants having the same value. They may be used interchangeably in the PROCEDURE DIVISION of a COBOL program.

SPACES is another figurative constant meaning all blanks. To say, for example,

MOVE SPACES TO FIELDA

results in blanks being placed in FIELDA. The word SPACES is a COBOL reserved word having the value of all blanks. It may be used interchangeably with the figurative constant, SPACE.

ZEROS and SPACES are the two figurative constants most frequently used. There are, however, other figurative constants which will not be discussed in this book, since they are not used by the average programmer.

Thus three types of data may be defined in the PROCEDURE DIVISION. A numeric literal, a nonnumeric literal, and a figurative constant may be defined directly in any instruction in the PROCEDURE DIVISION. Variable data fields which appear in PROCEDURE DIVISION entries must be described in the DATA DIVISION.

In future discussions of PROCEDURE DIVISION entries, the use of constants will become clearer. At this time, the reader must be able to recognize literals and to distinguish them from data fields. The specific format of ADD and MOVE statements, in which these literals were illustrated, will be discussed more fully later.

EXERCISES

1. The contents of fields defined within input and output files are _____.

   *****
   variable

2. A constant is _____.

   *****
   a form of data necessary for processing but not dependent upon the input to the system

3. A constant may be defined directly in the _____ DIVISION.

   *****
   PROCEDURE

4. Data fields that appear in PROCEDURE DIVISION statements must be defined in the _____ DIVISION.

   *****
   DATA

5. The three types of constants are _____, _____, _____.

   *****
   numeric literals
   nonnumeric literals
   figurative constants

6. What types of constants are the following?

> 'ABC'
> '123'
> 123.5
> ZERO
> 'SPACE'

*****

Nonnumeric literal.
Nonnumeric literal.
Numeric literal.
Figurative constant.
Nonnumeric literal (any group of characters enclosed in quotes is a nonnumeric literal).

7. What, if anything, is wrong with the following numeric literals?

> 123.
> 15.8—
> 1,000,000.00
> $38.90
> 58

*****

Decimal point may not be the last character.
Minus sign must be to the left of the number.
Commas not permitted.
Dollar sign not permitted.
Okay.

8. What, if anything, is wrong with the following nonnumeric literals?

> 'THE MESSAGE 'CODE' MUST BE PRINTED'
> 'INPUT'
> 'ZERO'
> '123'
> '   '

*****

Quotation marks may not be used within a nonnumeric literal.
Okay.
Okay.
Okay.
Okay.

9. The literal '   ', if printed, would result in the printing of

_____.

*****

two blanks

10. Quotation marks (are, are not) part of the literal.

*****

are not (they merely define the limits of the nonnumeric literal)

11. Two examples of figurative constants are _____ and _____.
    *****
    ZERO, ZEROES, ZEROS
    SPACE, SPACES

12. A figurative constant is a _____.
    *****
    COBOL reserved word that represents a specific value

13. Consider the following instruction:
       MOVE '1' TO FLD1
    '1' is a _____.
    FLD1 is a _____ and must be defined in the _____ DIVISION.
    *****
    nonnumeric literal—enclosed in quotes
    data-name—not enclosed in quotes
    DATA

14. To print the _____ 'ZEROS' results in _____ printing.
    To print the _____ ZEROS results in _____ printing.
    *****
    nonnumeric literal
    the word ZEROS
    figurative constant
    the value 0000

Review Questions

1. Make necessary corrections to the following data-names:
   (a) CUSTOMER NAME
   (b) AMOUNT-
   (c) INVOICE-NO.
   (d) PROCEDURE
   (e) TAX-%
   (f) QUANTITY-OF-PRODUCT-ABC-ON-HAND
   (g) AMT-OF-SALES

2. Make necessary corrections to the following literals:
   (a) '123'
   (b) 123
   (c) 'ABC'
   (d) ABC
   (e) $100.00
   (f) '$100.00'
   (g) 1,000
   (h) 100.7—
   (i) 54.

In each of the following cases, state the contents of the data field, FIELDA, after the MOVE operation:

3. MOVE 'ABC' TO FIELDA.

4. MOVE ABC TO FIELDA.

5. MOVE 100.00 TO FIELDA.

6. MOVE 'SPACES' TO FIELDA.

7. MOVE SPACES TO FIELDA.

PROBLEMS

1. Using Fig. 1-4, indicate which elements in the program are:
   (a) Files.
   (b) Records.
   (c) Fields.
   (d) Numeric literals.
   (e) Nonnumeric literals.
   (f) Figurative constants.

2. Using Fig. 1-5, indicate which elements in the program are:
   (a) Files.
   (b) Records.
   (c) Fields.
   (d) Numeric literals.
   (e) Nonnumeric literals.
   (f) Figurative constants.

3. Using Fig. 1-6, indicate which elements in the program are:
   (a) Files.
   (b) Records.
   (c) Fields.
   (d) Numeric literals.
   (e) Nonnumeric literals.
   (f) Figurative constants.

3

The Identification Division

You will recall that **all** COBOL programs consist of **four divisions.** In the next four chapters, we will discuss each division in detail. At the end of this discussion, the reader should be able to write elementary COBOL programs with no difficulty.

Before we begin, however, some basic rules for coding these programs must be understood.

A. BASIC STRUCTURE OF A COBOL PROGRAM

COBOL programs are generally written on **coding** or **program sheets** (Fig. 3-1). The coding sheet has space for 80 columns of information. Each **line** of a program sheet will be keypunched into **one** punched card. Usually the standard COBOL card is used for this purpose (Fig. 3-2).

Thus, for every line written on the coding sheet, we will obtain one punched card. The entire deck of cards keypunched from the coding sheets is called the **COBOL source program.**

Let us examine the COBOL program sheet more closely. The body of the form is subdivided into 72 positions, or columns. These positions, when coded, will be keypunched into Card Columns 1–72, respectively. In the upper righthand corner, there is a provision for the program identification number, labeled positions 73–80. The identification number will be entered into Columns 73–80 of all cards keypunched from this form.

The data recorded on the top of the form is **not** keypunched into cards. It supplies identifying information only. Fig. 3-3 illustrates the conversion of COBOL program sheets to punched cards.

The identification number, positions 73–80, and the page and serial number, positions 1–6, are optional entries in a COBOL program. Both, however, can be extremely useful.

Page and serial numbers on each line and, therefore, on each punched card are advisable, since cards are sometimes inadvertently dropped. In such cases, resequencing is necessary. If page and serial numbers are supplied, it is an easy task to insert cards in their proper place.

Page number generally refers to the number of the coding sheet. The first page is usually numbered 001, the second 002, etc. Serial number refers to the line number. The first card generally has serial number 010, the second 020, etc. They are numbered by tens, so that insertions may easily be made. If an entry is accidentally omitted and must then be inserted between serial numbers 030 and 040, for example, it may be sequenced as 031. Thus 002060 will signify page 002,

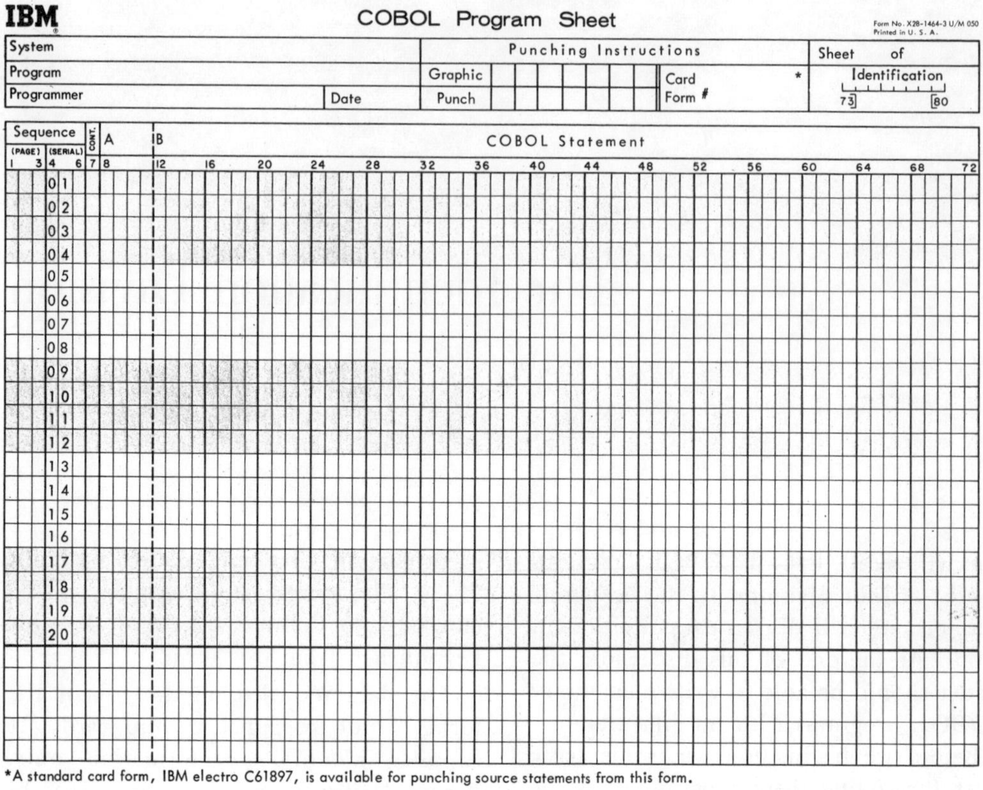

IBM   COBOL Program Sheet   Form No. X28-1464-3 U/M 050   Printed in U.S.A.

| System | | Punching Instructions | | Sheet | of |

| Program | | Graphic | | Card | * | Identification |
| Programmer | Date | Punch | | Form # | | 73   80 |

Sequence (PAGE) (SERIAL)   CONT.   A   B   COBOL Statement

(grid rows 01 through 20)

*A standard card form, IBM electro C61897, is available for punching source statements from this form.

Fig. 3-1

line 060. This method is used for sequencing of most program decks. It is, however, only a suggested method, as some applications may require other entries.

Identification numbers are also optional but are quite useful. They make it easy to distinguish one program from another.

Column 7 of the program sheet is a **continuation** position. It is used primarily for the continuation of nonnumeric literals and will not be discussed until Chapter 10.

Positions 8–72 are used for all program entries. Note, however, that Column 8 is labeled A, and Column 12 is labeled B.

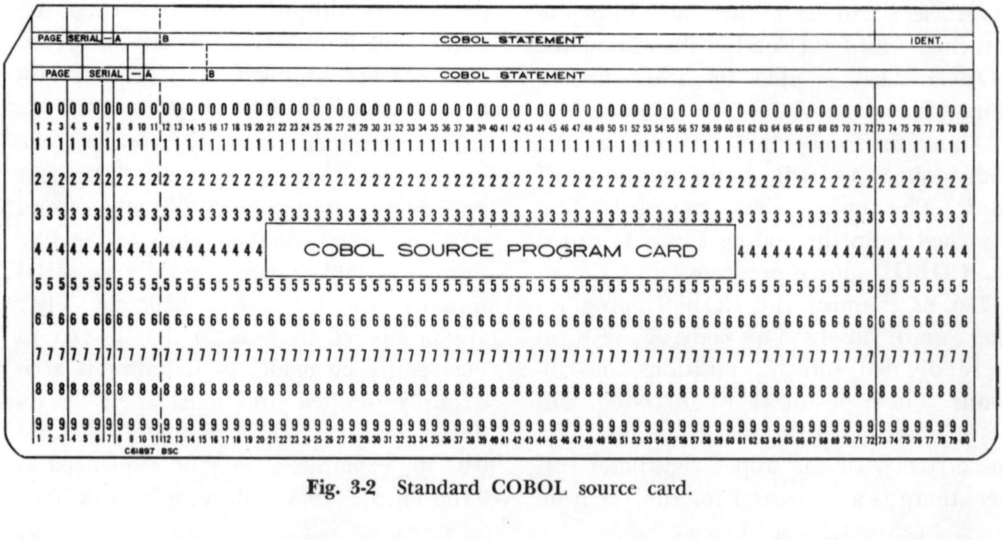

COBOL SOURCE PROGRAM CARD

Fig. 3-2 Standard COBOL source card.

Form No. X28-1464-3 U/M 050
Printed in U. S. A.

System				
Program		Punching Instructions		Sheet of
Programmer	Date	Graphic / Punch	Card / Form #	* Identification 73 80

Sequence (PAGE) (SERIAL) | CONT | A | B | COBOL Statement

```
0 1   IDENTIFICATION DIVISION.
0 2   PROGRAM-ID. 'SAMPLE'.
0 3
```

IDENTIFICATION DIVISION.

PROGRAM-ID. 'SAMPLE'.

COBOL SOURCE PROGRAM CARD

C61897 BSC

Fig. 3-3

These are **margins**. Certain entries must begin in Margin A, or position 8, and others must begin in Margin B.

If an entry is to be coded in Margin A, it **must** begin in position 8. If an entry is to be coded in Margin B, it may begin anywhere after position 11. That is, it may begin in position 12, 13, 14, etc. Note that margin rules specify the **beginning** point of entries. A word that must **begin** in Margin A may **extend** into Margin B.

Example 1: REMARKS, a paragraph name, must begin in Margin A. Any statement may then follow in Margin B.

COBOL programs are divided into **divisions**. The divisions have fixed names —IDENTIFICATION, ENVIRONMENT, DATA, and PROCEDURE. They must **always** appear in that order in a program. Divisions may be subdivided into **sections**. The DATA DIVISION, for example, which describes all storage areas needed in the program, is divided into two sections: the FILE SECTION of the DATA DIVISION describes the input and output areas, and the WORKING-STORAGE SECTION of the DATA DIVISION describes the intermediate work areas necessary to convert input to output. Each section may be further sub-

The first R of REMARKS must be placed in Column 8, or Margin A. The word itself extends into Margin B. The next entry must begin in Margin B or in any position after Column 11. In our example, the statement begins in position 17.

divided into **paragraphs**. All other entries in the program are considered COBOL statements.

Division, **section** and **paragraph** names must be coded in Margin A. All other statements are coded in Margin B. It will

27

IBM   COBOL Program Sheet   Form No. X28-1464-3 U/M 030
                                                       Printed in U. S. A.

System					Punching Instructions							Sheet	of
Program				Graphic						Card		*	Identification	
Programmer		Date		Punch						Form #			73	80

Sequence		A	B								COBOL Statement									
(PAGE) (SERIAL)																					
1 3 4 6 7 8	12	16	20	24	28	32	36	40	44	48	52	56	60	64	68	72

```
0 1   ENVIRONMENT DIVISION.
0 2   CONFIGURATION SECTION.
0 3   SOURCE-COMPUTER.
0 4       IBM-360 E30.
0 5   OBJECT-COMPUTER.
0 6       IBM-360 C40.
0 7   INPUT-OUTPUT SECTION.
0 8   FILE-CONTROL.
0 9       SELECT CARD-FILE ASSIGN TO READER.
1 0
```

Fig. 3-4

be seen that the great majority of COBOL entries are coded in Margin B.

Fig. 3-4 illustrates the above margin rules. The **ENVIRONMENT DIVISION** is coded in Margin A, as is the **CONFIGURATION SECTION**. **SOURCE-COMPUTER** and **OBJECT-COMPUTER** are **paragraph** names and, as such, must be coded in Margin A. **SOURCE-COMPUTER** and **OBJECT-COMPUTER** must have COBOL statements following them.

Each entry is followed by a period. Note that **ENVIRONMENT DIVISION, CONFIGURATION SECTION**, and **SOURCE-COMPUTER** are each followed by a period. Statements, as well, must end with a period. Where several entries appear on one line, each period will be directly followed by a space. In the **PROCEDURE DIVISION**, for example, where several statements may appear on one line, the following is permissible:

PROCEDURE DIVISION.
     MOVE TAX TO TOTAL. WRITE TAPE-1. GO TO START.

Division and section names **must** appear on a line with no other entry. That is, they must occupy independent lines. Paragraph names, however, may appear

on the same line as statements, keeping in mind, however, that each period must be followed by at least one space. The following is acceptable:

ENVIRONMENT DIVISION.
CONFIGURATION SECTION.
SOURCE-COMPUTER. H-200.
OBJECT-COMPUTER. H-200.
INPUT-OUTPUT SECTION.
FILE-CONTROL. SELECT CARD-FILE ASSIGN TO READER.

EXERCISES

1. COBOL programs are written on

    _____ .

    * * * * *

    coding or program sheets

2. Each line of the coding sheet corresponds to one _____ in the program deck.

    * * * * *

    card

3. The deck of cards keypunched from the coding sheets is called the _____ .

    COBOL source deck

4. The optional entries on the coding sheet are _____ and _____ .

    * * * * *

    identification (positions 73–80)
    page and serial number (positions 1–6)

5. Margin A begins in position _____ .
   Margin B begins in position _____ .

    * * * * *

    8
    12

6. If an entry must begin in Margin A, it _____; if an entry must begin in Margin B, it _____.

*****

must begin in position 8
may begin in position 12, 13, 14, etc.

7. COBOL programs are divided into ——— divisions.

*****

four

8. In the order in which they must appear, these divisions are _____, _____, _____, and _____.

*****

IDENTIFICATION
ENVIRONMENT
DATA
PROCEDURE

9. All _____, _____, and _____ names must be coded in Margin A.

*****

division
section
paragraph

10. Most entries are coded in _____.

*****

Margin B

11. All entries must be followed by a _____.

*****

period

12. Each period must be directly followed by a _____.

*****

space

13. _____ and _____ must each appear on a separate line. All other entries may have several statements on the same line.

*****

Divisions
sections

B. CODING REQUIREMENTS OF THE IDENTIFICATION DIVISION

The IDENTIFICATION DIVISION is the smallest, simplest, and least significant division of a COBOL program. As the name indicates, it supplies identifying data about the program.

The IDENTIFICATION DIVISION has **no** effect on the execution of the program but is, nevertheless, **required** as a means of identifying the job to the computer.

The IDENTIFICATION DIVISION is **not** divided into sections. Instead, it may consist of the following paragraphs:

    PROGRAM-ID.
    AUTHOR.
    INSTALLATION.
    DATE-WRITTEN.
    DATE-COMPILED.
    SECURITY.
    REMARKS.

As a division name, the IDENTIFICATION DIVISION is coded in Margin A. The above entries, as paragraph names, are also coded in Margin A, and each is followed by a period.

The only entry required within the IDENTIFICATION DIVISION is the PROGRAM-ID. That is, all programs must be identified by a name. The name which follows PROGRAM-ID is an external-name, and must be coded in Margin B. External-names must be enclosed in quotation marks, be eight characters or less, and consist only of letters and/or digits.

Thus the first two entries of a program must be IDENTIFICATION DIVISION and PROGRAM-ID:

IDENTIFICATION DIVISION.
PROGRAM-ID. 'SAMPLE1'.

PROGRAM-ID is followed by a period and then a space. The external-name is coded in Margin B and must conform to the rules specified above. Note that the two entries may also be coded:

IDENTIFICATION DIVISION.
PROGRAM-ID.
    'SAMPLE1'.

Since PROGRAM-ID is a paragraph name, the external-name 'SAMPLE1' may appear on the same line or on the next one. In either case, the name must be followed by a period.

The other paragraph names listed above are optional. They are useful items which provide significant facts about the nature of the program, but are not required.

Any, or all, of these paragraphs may be included in the IDENTIFICATION DIVISION. As paragraph names, these entries are coded in Margin A. Each paragraph name is generally followed by a statement, which may contain *any* character. The only requirement is that each statement is followed by a period.

The illustration below will indicate the coding of the IDENTIFICATION DIVISION.

IDENTIFICATION DIVISION.
PROGRAM-ID. 'EXHIBIT1'.
AUTHOR. R. A. STERN.
INSTALLATION. COMPANY ABC
                ACCOUNTING DEPT.
DATE-WRITTEN. JAN. 1, 1971.
DATE-COMPILED. 2/01/71.
SECURITY. THIS PROGRAM HAS TOP SECRET
                SECURITY REQUIREMENTS.
REMARKS. THIS PROGRAM WILL CREATE A
                MASTER PAYROLL SYSTEM,
                EDITING THE INPUT DATA AND
                PRODUCING AN ERROR LIST.

Note that REMARKS, as well as the other entries, may extend to several lines. Each entry within a paragraph must, however, be coded in Margin B. The last character must be a period.

In summary: (1) Paragraphs within the IDENTIFICATION DIVISION inform the reader of the nature of the program. (2) They will not affect execution of the program. (3) IDENTIFICATION DIVISION must be the first item coded. (4) It must be followed by PROGRAM-ID and a corresponding external-name. (5) This name must be enclosed in quotation marks, be eight characters or less, and contain only letters and/or digits. (6) All other identifying information in this division is optional.

EXERCISES

1. The first two entries of a COBOL program must always be
   _____ and _____.
   *****
   IDENTIFICATION DIVISION
   PROGRAM-ID

2. Each of these entries must be followed by a _____, which, in
   turn, must be followed by a _____.
   *****
   period
   space or blank

3. They are both coded in _____.
   *****
   Margin A

4. The name which follows **PROGRAM-ID** is an _____ -name.
   *****
   external

5. Code the IDENTIFICATION DIVISION for a program called **EXPENSES**
   for a corporation, Dynamic Data Devices, Inc., written July 15,
   1970. This program has a security classification and is available to
   authorized personnel only. It produces a weekly listing by department of all operating expenses.
   *****
   The following is a **suggested** solution:

   IDENTIFICATION DIVISION.
   PROGRAM-ID. 'EXPENSES'.
   AUTHOR. N. B. STERN.
   INSTALLATION. DYNAMIC DATA DEVICES INC.
   DATE-WRITTEN. 7/15/70.
   SECURITY. AUTHORIZED PERSONNEL ONLY.
   REMARKS. THIS PROGRAM PRODUCES A WEEKLY LISTING BY
                   DEPARTMENT OF ALL OPERATING EXPENSES.

   NOTE: Only the IDENTIFICATION DIVISION and PROGRAM-ID are
   required.

REVIEW QUESTIONS

Make necessary corrections to each of the following (1–5):

1. IDENTIFICATION DIVISION
   PROGRAM-ID 'SAMPLE1'.

2. IDENTIFICATION DIVISION.
   PROGRAM ID. 'SAMPLE2'
   AUTHOR.JOHN DOE

3. ENVIRONMENT DIVISION.
        CONFIGURATION SECTION.

4. IDENTIFICATION DIVISION.
   AUTHOR. MARY DOE.
   PROGRAM-ID. 'SAMPLE4'.

5. DATA DIVISION. FILE SECTION.

6. State which of the following entries are coded in Margin A:
   a. IDENTIFICATION DIVISION
   b. PROGRAM-ID
   c. (name of author)
   d. FILE SECTION
   e. (COBOL Statement) ADD TAX TO TOTAL

7. (T or F) Only one statement is permitted on a coding line.

8. (T or F) IDENTIFICATION DIVISION, PROGRAM-ID, and AUTHOR are the three required entries of the division.

9. (T or F) 'SAMPLE 12' is a valid external-name.

10. (T or F) A division name must appear as an independent item on a separate line.

11. (T or F) The IDENTIFICATION DIVISION contains instructions that significantly affect execution of the program.

12. (T or F) Information supplied in the IDENTIFICATION DIVISION makes it easier for a nondata processing employee to understand the nature of the program.

PROBLEMS

1. Code the IDENTIFICATION DIVISION for a program called UPDATE for the United Accounting Corp. The program must be written by 8/25/71 and completed by 10/25/71, and it has a top secret security classification. The program will create a new master tape each month from the previous master tape and selected detail cards.

2. Code the IDENTIFICATION DIVISION for a program that will punch out billing cards for the American Utility Co.

4

The Environment Division

The **ENVIRONMENT DIVISION** of a CO-BOL program supplies information concerning the **equipment** to be used in the program. The **ENVIRONMENT DIVISION** entries are **machine-dependent.** Unlike the other divisions of a COBOL program, the entries in this division will be dependent upon (1) the computer, and (2) the specific devices used in the program.

The **ENVIRONMENT DIVISION** is composed of two sections: the **CONFIGURATION SECTION** and the **INPUT-OUTPUT SECTION.** The **CONFIGURATION SECTION** supplies data concerning the computer on which the COBOL program will be compiled and executed. The **INPUT-OUTPUT SECTION** supplies information concerning the specific devices used in the program. The card reader, printer, card punch, tape drives, and mass storage units are devices that may be referred to in the **INPUT-OUTPUT SECTION** of the **ENVIRONMENT DIVISION.**

The **ENVIRONMENT DIVISION** is the only division of a COBOL program that will change significantly if the program is to be run on different computers. Since computer users have varied models and equipment, each data processing installation has unique **ENVIRONMENT DIVISION** specifications. The entries required in the **ENVIRONMENT DIVISION** are generally supplied to the programmer by the installation. Throughout this discussion, we will use some **sample** statements, keeping in mind that such entries are dependent upon the actual computer used, and the devices available with that computer.

A. CONFIGURATION SECTION

The **CONFIGURATION SECTION** of the **ENVIRONMENT DIVISION** indicates the computer that will be used for **compiling** the program, the **SOURCE-COMPUTER,** and the computer that will be used for **executing** the program, the **OBJECT-COMPUTER. SOURCE-COMPUTER** and **OBJECT-COMPUTER** are **required** paragraph names designated in the **CONFIGURATION SECTION.**

You will recall that all section names, in addition to division names, are coded in Margin A. Thus the **CONFIGURATION SECTION** will follow the **ENVIRONMENT DIVISION** entry, in Margin A. **SOURCE-COMPUTER** and **OBJECT-COMPUTER,** as paragraph names, are also coded in Margin A.

The **SOURCE-** and **OBJECT-COMPUTER** entries must specify: (a) the computer manufacturer, (b) the computer number, and (c) the model, if it exists. Observe the following sample entries:

```
ENVIRONMENT DIVISION.
CONFIGURATION SECTION.
SOURCE-COMPUTER.   NCR-315.
OBJECT-COMPUTER.   NCR-315.
```

Note that each paragraph name is directly followed by a period and then a space. The designated computer, NCR-315, is also followed by a period.

In the example, the source and object computers are the same. In general, this will be the case, since compilation and execution are usually performed on the same computer. If, however, the program will be compiled on one model computer and executed, at some future time, on another model computer, these entries will differ:

```
ENVIRONMENT DIVISION.
CONFIGURATION SECTION.
SOURCE-COMPUTER.    IBM-360 E30.
OBJECT-COMPUTER.    H-200.
```

In the above illustration, the program will be compiled on an IBM 360, model 30,[1] and executed on a Honeywell 200. The computer number and model is generally supplied by the installation since it will remain the same for **all** COBOL programs run at a computer center. Sample entries are illustrated in Appendix C.

B. INPUT-OUTPUT SECTION

The INPUT-OUTPUT SECTION of the ENVIRONMENT DIVISION follows the CONFIGURATION SECTION and supplies information concerning the devices used in the program. Under FILE-CONTROL, a paragraph in the INPUT-OUTPUT SECTION, a file name will be assigned to each device to be used. I-O-CONTROL, the second paragraph name of the INPUT-OUTPUT SECTION, will be discussed in Chapter 13. It is **not** a necessary entry for the coding of elementary level COBOL programs.

Thus far we have the following entries:

---

[1] The letter "E" in "IBM-360 E30" refers to core storage capacity. The meaning of each letter for IBM computers is discussed in Appendix C.

```
ENVIRONMENT DIVISION.
CONFIGURATION SECTION.
SOURCE-COMPUTER.
   (computer and model number sup-
   plied by manufacturer)
OBJECT-COMPUTER.
   (computer and model number sup-
   plied by manufacturer)
INPUT-OUTPUT SECTION.
FILE-CONTROL.
```

The FILE-CONTROL paragraph consists of SELECT clauses. Each SELECT clause defines a file name and assigns an input or output device to that file. The format may be as follows:

```
SELECT (file name) ASSIGN TO
(device specification)
```

Examples

```
SELECT FILE-1 ASSIGN TO TAPE 1.
SELECT FILE-1 ASSIGN TO READER.
```

The device specifications vary among computer manufacturers. Some specify names such as TAPE 1, READER, etc., while others require more elaborate device specifications. Consider the following format of a SELECT clause, required for some compilers[2]:

```
SELECT (file name)
ASSIGN TO (system number)
  ⎡ UNIT-RECORD  ⎤
  ⎢ UTILITY      ⎥ (device number
  ⎣ DIRECT ACCESS[3] ⎦  or name)
```

Examples

```
SELECT CARD-IN ASSIGN TO 'SYS001'
   UNIT-RECORD 2540R UNIT.
SELECT TAPE-OUT ASSIGN TO 'SYS002'
   UTILITY 2400 UNITS.
```

The FILE-CONTROL paragraph may seem unnecessarily complex at this point. The

---

[2] See Appendix C or the particular computer manual to determine whether the simplified SELECT clause or the more elaborate one is required.

[3] DIRECT ACCESS entries in the ENVIRONMENT DIVISION shall be discussed in detail in Chapter 20.

entries, however, are standard for a particular installation. The only programmer-supplied term is the file name.

The file name assigned to each **device** must conform to the rules for forming programmer-supplied names:

(a) 1 to 30 characters.
(b) No special characters except a dash.
(c) No embedded blanks.
(d) At least one alphabetic character.

In addition to conforming to these rules, the file name must be **unique:** that is, the name may not be assigned to any other data element in the program.

For each device used in the program, a **SELECT** clause must be specified. If a program requires cards as input and produces a printed report as output, two **SELECT** clauses will be specified. One file name will be assigned to the card file, and another to the print file.

When using the second format noted, each device has a designated specification in the **SELECT** clause. Every device has a (1) system number, (2) classification— **UNIT-RECORD, UTILITY,** or **DIRECT-ACCESS,** and (3) device number.

The **system number** is dependent upon the particular installation. The item will vary among data processing centers and must therefore be supplied by each particular data processing organization. Each physical device in a computer room will have a unique system number. The system number used is an external-name.

The **classifications** that may be used are standard entries. There are three types of device classifications: **UNIT-RECORD, UTILITY,** and **DIRECT-ACCESS.** Printer, punch, and card reader are **UNIT-RECORD** devices. That is, each record associated with any of these devices is of **fixed length.** A card, for example, is a **UNIT-RECORD** document, since it **always** consists of 80 positions of data. A printed form is similarly a **UNIT-RECORD** document since 132 characters always represent its size.

Tape is not a **UNIT-RECORD** document since tape records can be any size. Tape is classified as a **UTILITY** device; mass storage units such as disk, drum, and data cells are **DIRECT-ACCESS** devices.

The **device number** is designated by the computer manufacturer. IBM, for example, most often uses the following device numbers for the s/360 units:

TAPE	2400 UNITS
READER	2540R UNIT
PRINTER	1403 UNIT
PUNCH	2540P UNIT

Using arbitrary system numbers, since these will depend on the installation, let us examine the following illustrations.

Example 1: Card file, consisting of transaction data, may be assigned as follows:

SELECT TRANS-FILE ASSIGN TO 'SYS004' UNIT-RECORD 2540R UNIT.

The name, **TRANS-FILE,** is supplied by the programmer. The remaining data in the statement is necessary when utilizing the reader. The reader is a **UNIT-RECORD** device with number **2540R UNIT,** and assigned to **'SYS004',** for this installation.

Note that **SELECT** clauses are coded in Margin B.

Example 2: A tape file, consisting of employee data, may be assigned as follows:

SELECT EMPLOYEE-FILE ASSIGN TO 'SYS007' UTILITY 2400 UNITS.

EMPLOYEE-FILE is the name assigned to the tape file. All entries after the words **ASSIGN TO** are supplied by the installation to indicate a specific tape drive.

Note that the important entry in the **SELECT** clause is the file name assigned. This name is utilized in the **DATA DIVISION** to reserve the input or output area to be used by the file. It is again denoted in the **PROCEDURE DIVISION** to access the file. The other entries in the **SELECT** clause are computer dependent. An illustration of some widely used computer models and their corresponding device numbers appears in Appendix C. The system numbers, however, must be obtained from the particular installation. Any system numbers used in this book will be arbitrary assignments.

Example 1: Code the IDENTIFICATION and ENVIRONMENT DIVISION entries for the following system:

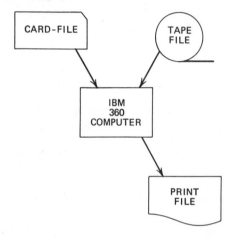

IDENTIFICATION DIVISION.
PROGRAM-ID. 'SAMPLE2'.
AUTHOR. R A STERN.
REMARKS. THE PROGRAM PRODUCES A
          PRINTED REPORT FROM A
          MASTER FILE AND SELECTED
          DETAIL CARDS.
ENVIRONMENT DIVISION.
CONFIGURATION SECTION.
SOURCE-COMPUTER.   IBM-360 E30.
OBJECT-COMPUTER.   IBM-360 E30.
INPUT-OUTPUT SECTION.
FILE-CONTROL. SELECT CARD-IN ASSIGN TO
          'SYS002' UNIT-RECORD
          2540R UNIT.
          SELECT TAPE-IN ASSIGN TO
          'SYS008' UTILITY 2400
          UNITS.
          SELECT PRINT-FILE ASSIGN
          TO 'SYS003' UNIT-RECORD
          1403 UNIT.

All SELECT clauses are coded in Margin B. The order in which the files are specified is not significant.

Exercises

1. The ENVIRONMENT DIVISION of a COBOL program supplies information about _____.
   *****
   equipment to be used

2. The entries in the ENVIRONMENT DIVISION are dependent on _____ and _____.
   *****
   the computer
   the specific devices used

3. The two sections of the ENVIRONMENT DIVISION are the _____ SECTION and the _____ SECTION.
   *****
   CONFIGURATION
   INPUT-OUTPUT

4. The entries in the ENVIRONMENT DIVISION (will, will not) change significantly if the program is run on a different computer.
   *****
   will—it is the only division that would change significantly

5. The two paragraphs required in the **CONFIGURATION SECTION** are _____ and _____.
   *****
   SOURCE-COMPUTER
   OBJECT-COMPUTER

6. The above entries are coded in Margin __ and are followed by a _____.
   *****
   A
   period

7. The **INPUT-OUTPUT SECTION** of the COBOL program supplies information about the _____.
   *****
   devices being used

8. Files are defined and assigned in the _____ paragraph of the **INPUT-OUTPUT SECTION.**
   *****
   FILE-CONTROL

9. **FILE-CONTROL** consists of a series of _____ clauses.
   *****
   SELECT

10. For every device used in the program, a _____ name must be specified.
    *****
    file

11. The file name used in the **SELECT** clause must conform to the rules for forming _____.
    *****
    programmer-supplied names

12. The **SELECT** clause assigns the file to a device having three specifications: _____, _____, and _____.
    *****
    system number
    classification
    device number

13. The three types of device classifications are _____, _____, and _____.
    *****
    UNIT-RECORD
    UTILITY
    DIRECT-ACCESS

14. A **UNIT-RECORD** device is one which _____.
    *****
    consists of records of a fixed length

15. A card reader and a printer are examples of _____ devices.
    *****
    UNIT-RECORD

16. A tape drive is a _____ device.
    *****
    UTILITY

17. The device and system number are _____ dependent entries.
    *****
    machine

18. SELECT clauses are coded in Margin __.
    *****
    B

19. Code the IDENTIFICATION and ENVIRONMENT DIVISION entries for a program that edits input cards, creates an error listing for all erroneous cards, and puts valid card data onto a tape.
    *****

```
IDENTIFICATION DIVISION.
PROGRAM-ID. 'EDIT1'.
AUTHOR. N B STERN.
REMARKS. THIS PROGRAM EDITS INPUT CARDS, CREATES A TAPE AND
          AN ERROR LISTING.
ENVIRONMENT DIVISION.
CONFIGURATION SECTION.
SOURCE-COMPUTER.  IBM-360 E40.
OBJECT-COMPUTER.  IBM-360 E40.
INPUT-OUTPUT SECTION.
FILE-CONTROL. SELECT CARD-FILE ASSIGN TO 'SYS001' UNIT-RECORD
                2540R UNIT.
              SELECT ERROR-FILE ASSIGN TO 'SYS002' UNIT-RECORD
              1403 UNIT.
              SELECT TAPE-FILE  ASSIGN TO 'SYS003' UTILITY 2400
              UNITS.
```

Review Questions

1. Indicate which entries are coded in Margin A:
   (a) ENVIRONMENT DIVISION.
   (b) CONFIGURATION SECTION.
   (c) SOURCE-COMPUTER.
   (d) FILE-CONTROL.
   (e) SELECT clause.

2. Define each of the following:
    (a) OBJECT-COMPUTER.
    (b) UTILITY.
    (c) UNIT-RECORD.
    (d) File name.
    (e) Programmer-supplied word.
    (f) CONFIGURATION SECTION.

3. (T or F) The ENVIRONMENT DIVISION of a COBOL program, like the other three divisions, is generally the same regardless of the computer on which it is run.

4. (T or F) A UTILITY device is one which may have fixed length records or variable length records.

5. (T or F) A magnetic tape may sometimes be considered a UNIT-RECORD device.

6. (T or F) The INPUT-OUTPUT SECTION of the ENVIRONMENT DIVISION assigns the file names.

Make the necessary corrections to each of the following and assume that device specification, where noted, is correct (7–10):

7. ENVIRONMENT DIVISION
   CONFIGURATION SECTION.
   SOURCE COMPUTER. MODEL-120.

8. ENVIRONMENT DIVISION.
   .
   .
   INPUT OUTPUT SECTION

9. SELECT FILE A ASSIGN TO 'SYS002' UNIT-RECORD 2540R UNIT.

10. FILE CONTROL.
    SELECT A ASSIGN TO PRINTER.

PROBLEMS

1. Code the IDENTIFICATION DIVISION and the ENVIRONMENT DIVISION for a COBOL update program which uses a detail card file and a previous master inventory tape file to create a current master inventory tape file.

2. Code the IDENTIFICATION DIVISION and the ENVIRONMENT DIVISION for a COBOL program which will use a master billing tape to punch gas-bill cards and electric-bill cards.

5

The Data Division–File Section

The **DATA DIVISION** is that part of a COBOL program which defines and describes data fields in storage. Any area of storage that is required for the processing of data must be established in the **DATA DIVISION**.

The **DATA DIVISION** consists of **two** sections. The **FILE SECTION** defines all data areas that are part of input or output files. The **WORKING-STORAGE SECTION**[1] sets up core storage for fields of data **not part** of input or output but nevertheless necessary for processing, such as constants. In this chapter, we will discuss the **FILE SECTION** only, leaving the **WORKING-STORAGE SECTION** to Chapter 10.

Any program that (1) reads data as input or (2) produces output data requires a **FILE SECTION** to describe the input and output. Since all programs read in data, operate on it, and produce output, the **FILE SECTION** will be an essential part of every program.

A. FILE DESCRIPTION

The **FILE SECTION**, as the name implies, describes all input and output files used in the program. Such files have already

[1] In this text, the **WORKING-STORAGE SECTION** will incorporate all constants; that is, the **CONSTANT SECTION**, referred to in some books, will be part of **WORKING-STORAGE**.

40

been defined in the **ENVIRONMENT DIVISION**, in a **SELECT** clause, where the file name is designated and an input-output device is assigned. Let us use the following sample statements as examples:

```
FILE-CONTROL.
    SELECT FILE-1 ASSIGN TO 'SYS005'
        UNIT-RECORD 2540R UNIT.
    SELECT FILE-2 ASSIGN TO 'SYS007'
        UNIT-RECORD 1403 UNIT.
    SELECT FILE-3 ASSIGN TO 'SYS008'
        UTILITY 2400 UNITS.
```

For every **SELECT** clause written in the **ENVIRONMENT DIVISION**, a file name is denoted. Thus, for every **SELECT** clause, we will have one file to describe in the **FILE SECTION** of the **DATA DIVISION**.

The **FILE SECTION**, as was mentioned, describes the input and output areas used in the program. An **input area** is storage reserved for an incoming file. A **READ** instruction, in the **PROCEDURE DIVISION**, will transmit data to this input area. Similarly, an **output** area is storage reserved for an outgoing file. When a **WRITE** statement is executed, any data stored in this output area is transmitted to the specified output device. The devices and file names are **assigned** in the **ENVIRONMENT DIVISION** in a **SELECT** clause. The input or output area for each file is **described** in the **FILE SECTION** of the **DATA DIVISION**.

The FILE SECTION describes each file with an FD entry. FD denotes File Description. Each FD entry will describe a file established by a SELECT clause in the ENVIRONMENT DIVISION. Thus, for the above example, we have:

```
DATA DIVISION.
FILE SECTION.
FD   FILE-1
       •
       •
FD   FILE-2
       •
       •
FD   FILE-3
       •
       •
```

Each FD entry will be followed by a file name and certain clauses, to be discussed. Since there are three SELECT clauses in our example, there must be three FD level entries in the FILE SECTION.

The two entries, DATA DIVISION and FILE SECTION, are coded in Margin A. FD is also coded in Margin A. The file name, however, is coded in Margin B. **No period follows the file name. FD PUNCH-FILE**, for example, signals the compiler that PUNCH-FILE is **about to be** described. Several entries are used to describe a file. These will follow FD (file name), and no period will be written until the last clause is specified. Observe the following examples:

```
FD   CARD-FILE
     RECORDING MODE IS F
     LABEL RECORDS ARE OMITTED
     RECORD CONTAINS 80 CHARACTERS
     DATA RECORD IS EMPLOYEE-REC.
              •
              •
FD   TAPE-FILE
     RECORDING MODE IS F
     LABEL RECORDS ARE STANDARD
     RECORD CONTAINS 50 CHARACTERS
     BLOCK CONTAINS 20 RECORDS
     DATA RECORD IS
         TRANSACTION-REC.
              •
              •
```

The preceding is a sample File Description for a card file and a tape file. We will consider the various entries cited in detail, since they are the most common. These, however, are not the only ones that may be used.

1. RECORDING MODE clause

F—fixed
V—variable
U—unspecified

The entry RECORDING MODE IS F is used when all records within a file are the same length. Several records may appear in one file; if, however, they are the same size records, the entry RECORDING MODE IS F is used.

Input data from cards and output data printed on forms or punched into cards **always consist of fixed length records.** All card records must contain 80 characters; all printed lines must contain 132 characters. Hence files assigned to unit-record devices (reader, printer, punch) must specify:

RECORDING MODE IS F

Tape and direct access files **may** have fixed length records when record layouts are the same size. Record lengths on direct access or tape files, however, may also be variable or unspecified. If a tape file, for example, has the following format:

it is considered **variable** in length. Hence RECORDING MODE IS V is specified.

When the clause RECORDING MODE IS V is part of the File Description entry, special programming techniques are required. A control field within each record, for example, must specify the size of the individual record.

The clause RECORDING MODE IS U is used when records within a file have special formats that cannot be handled by variable or fixed length designations.

Files with variable or unspecified recording mode are not often used in elementary or even intermediate level COBOL programs. Such files require special programming techniques, which will not be discussed here. Thus RECORDING MODE IS F will be considered the standard entry for this book.

The RECORDING MODE clause within the File Description is an **optional** entry. If it is omitted, however, records are assumed to be **variable** in length. Since we will be handling only **fixed** length records, we will **always** include RECORDING MODE IS F for all files.

2. LABEL RECORDS clause

LABEL RECORDS ARE	⎡ OMITTED STANDARD (nonstandard entry) ⎤

Data on a disk or a tape cannot be "read" as one reads a book or a punched card; that is, data is stored as magnetized bits which cannot be seen by the naked eye.

Label records, then, are usually created as the first and last records of a tape or disk to provide identifying information. Since the data on a tape or disk is not visible, these label records will provide a check to see if the correct file is present. Labels are created on output files so that, when the same file is later read as input, the labels may be checked. That is, labels are **created** on output files and **checked** on input files. The COBOL compiler will supply the routine for writing labels on output files or for checking labels on input files if the following entry is denoted as part of the File Description:

LABEL RECORDS ARE STANDARD

This clause signifies two things:

(a) The first record on the file is **not** a data record but a standard 80-position **header label** and, similarly, that the last record is a **trailer label.**

(b) With input files, these labels will be computer checked and, with output files, they will be computer-created.

Although no further COBOL statements are necessary to perform the label routines, a control card must be supplied when executing a program. This control card contains the information desired on the labels.

The clause LABEL RECORDS ARE STANDARD is permitted **only** for tape or direct access files. Unit-record devices do **not** utilize label records. Such identifying information is unnecessary on devices where data is visible, such as on punched cards or printed data. For unit-record files, the entry LABEL RECORDS ARE OMITTED is required.

Similarly, a tape or direct access file sometimes requires LABEL RECORDS ARE OMITTED as the entry when there is some assurance that checking for correct files is unnecessary. In that case, label records will be neither created nor checked.

When label records are to be included within a tape or direct access file, but the programmer chooses to write the routine necessary for creating them, a nonstandard LABEL RECORDS clause is included. This, again, is an advanced programming concept and will not be discussed here.

The LABEL RECORDS clause is a **required** entry for each File Description. We will generally indicate STANDARD labels for tape or disk files. The clause LABEL RECORDS ARE OMITTED **must** be used for unit-record files.

Example 1: Card files or print files **must** have the following entries:

```
FD   FILE-NAME-1
     RECORDING MODE IS F
     LABEL RECORDS ARE OMITTED
```

Example 2: Tape or direct access files usually have the following entries:

```
FD   FILE-NAME-2
     RECORDING MODE IS F
     LABEL RECORDS ARE STANDARD
```

Example 3: Variable length records on a tape with no labels may have the following entries:

```
FD   FILE-NAME-3
     RECORDING MODE IS V
     LABEL RECORDS ARE OMITTED
```

3. RECORD CONTAINS clause

```
RECORD CONTAINS (integer)
              CHARACTERS
```

The RECORD CONTAINS clause indicates the size of each record. A print file, for example, will have the following entry:

RECORD CONTAINS 132 CHARACTERS

A card file will have the following entry:

RECORD CONTAINS 80 CHARACTERS

For tape or direct access files, the RECORD CONTAINS clause varies. One of the advantages of these files is that records can be any size.

The RECORD CONTAINS clause in the File Description entry is **optional.** However, it is advisable to include it, since it provides a check on record size.

Example 4: FD entry for a card file:

```
FD   CARD-FILE
     RECORDING MODE IS F
     LABEL RECORDS ARE OMITTED
     RECORD CONTAINS 80 CHARACTERS
```

Example 5: FD entry for a disk file **may** be, for example:

```
FD   DISK-FILE
     RECORDING MODE IS F
     LABEL RECORDS ARE STANDARD
     RECORD CONTAINS 150
         CHARACTERS
```

4. BLOCK CONTAINS clause

```
BLOCK CONTAINS (integer) RECORDS
```

This clause is only included in the File Description entry for tapes or disk.

Tape or disk files often have blocked records for efficiency of operations. A specific number of logical records are included within one block to make maximum use of the tape area. Note that the programmer generally does not ascertain the most beneficial block size or **blocking factor** but obtains this data from a systems expert.

By indicating a BLOCK CONTAINS clause for an input tape or disk, the computer is able to read the correct block. By indicating BLOCK CONTAINS for an output tape or disk, the computer is able to create the correct block of records.

Thus the BLOCK CONTAINS clause of a tape or disk file is the **only** entry required to perform operations on blocked data. **No** additional COBOL statements are necessary.

When blocking of records is not specified, as on unit-record devices, the BLOCK CONTAINS clause is **omitted.**

5. DATA RECORD(S) clause

```
DATA RECORD(S)  ⎡ IS  ⎤ (record
                ⎣ ARE ⎦    name(s))
```

The DATA RECORD clause defines the record or records within the file. If there is only one record layout, DATA RECORD IS (record name) is used. Any record name may be specified. The name, however, must conform to the rules for forming programmer-supplied names. It must also be unique. Any name that appears as a file or record name may not be used for something else in the program.

If more than one record format exists for a file, specify DATA RECORDS ARE (record-1, record-2, . . .). Note that while DATA RECORDS ARE specifies more than one format for the file, it does **not** reserve additional core. To use several record descriptions within one file does **not** set up additional I-O areas; it merely redefines a **single** input or output area in several ways.

The **DATA RECORD(S)** clause is a **required** part of all File Descriptions and is followed by a period, since this is the last entry to be discussed. Note that no other period has appeared in the **FD**.

Example 6: Description of a card file that contains employee records:

```
FD   CARD-FILE
     RECORDING MODE IS F
     LABEL RECORDS ARE OMITTED
     RECORD CONTAINS 80 CHARACTERS
     DATA RECORD IS EMPLOYEE-REC.
```

Example 7: Description of a tape file containing transaction credit records and transaction debit records. Record size is 50, block size is 20:

```
FD   TAPE-FILE
     RECORDING MODE IS F
     LABEL RECORDS ARE STANDARD
     RECORD CONTAINS 50 CHARACTERS
     BLOCK CONTAINS 20 RECORDS
     DATA RECORDS ARE TRANS-DEBIT,
       TRANS-CREDIT.
```

The above five clauses in an **FD** entry are the most commonly used statements but not the only ones. For most applications in COBOL, they are quite adequate.

Several structural rules must be observed when defining files. **FD** is written in Margin A; all other entries appear in Margin B. No period is coded until the last clause is specified. In the **above** clauses, no commas were included at the end of clauses, but they are always permissible. Commas are optional anywhere in a COBOL program to separate clauses; when used, however, they must be followed by at least one space. The examples thus far placed each clause on a separate line for purposes of clarity. Fig. 5-1 illustrates the preceding two examples in a slightly different way.

The word **IS** or **ARE** in any COBOL statement may be omitted. To say **RECORDING MODE F** or **LABEL RECORDS STANDARD** is entirely appropriate.

Last, the order of these entries is **not** significant. Any clause may appear first in an **FD** entry.

Example 8:

```
FD   DISK-FILE
     LABEL RECORDS ARE OMITTED
     RECORD CONTAINS 100
       CHARACTERS
     DATA RECORD IS RECORD-1
     BLOCK CONTAINS 10 RECORDS
     RECORDING MODE IS F.
```

Therefore, each file denoted in the **SELECT** clause of the **ENVIRONMENT DIVISION** must be described by an **FD** entry and its corresponding clauses. After a file

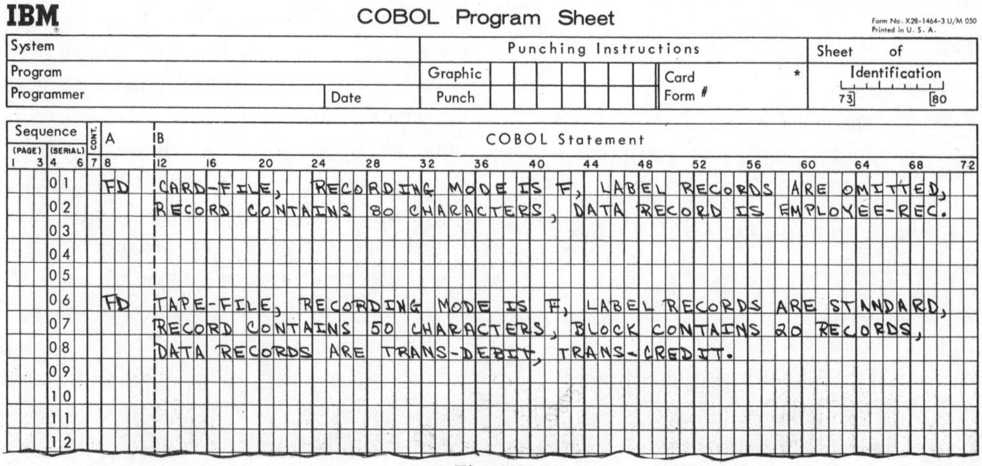

Fig. 5-1

is described and the record name or names are assigned, each record is described in detail.

Here is a summary of the entries discussed in the File Description:

1. RECORDING MODE IS $\begin{bmatrix} F \\ V \\ U \end{bmatrix}$

F—fixed in length
V—variable in length
U—unspecified

Clause Optional—if omitted, file assumed variable

2. LABEL RECORDS ARE $\begin{bmatrix} \text{OMITTED} \\ \text{STANDARD} \end{bmatrix}$

OMITTED always used for unit-record files
STANDARD usually used for tape or direct access files

Clause is required

3. RECORD CONTAINS (integer) CHARACTERS

Clause is optional

4. BLOCK CONTAINS (integer) RECORDS

Clause only used for blocked tapes or disks

5. DATA RECORDS ARE (record-1, record-2, . . .) or
DATA RECORD IS (record-name)

Clause is required

EXERCISES

1. The DATA DIVISION is that part of a COBOL program which _____.
*****
defines and describes data fields in storage

2. The two sections of a DATA DIVISION are the _____ and the _____.
*****
FILE SECTION
WORKING-STORAGE SECTION

3. The FILE SECTION defines all data areas _____.
*****
that are part of input or output

4. The first time a file name appears in a COBOL program is in a _____ clause of the _____ DIVISION.
*****
SELECT
ENVIRONMENT

5. File names must be one to _____ characters in length, contain at least one _____, and have no _____.
*****
30
alphabetic character
special characters (except -)

6. FILE 1 is not a valid file name because it _____.
   *****
   contains an embedded blank

7. File names (must, need not) be unique.
   *****
   must.

8. For every file defined in a SELECT clause, there will be one _____ entry in the FILE SECTION.
   *****
   FD

9. The five clauses that may be used with an FD entry are _____, _____, _____, _____, and _____.
   *****
   RECORDING MODE
   LABEL RECORDS
   RECORD CONTAINS
   BLOCK CONTAINS
   DATA RECORD(S)

10. RECORDING MODE must be _____ for _____ length records, _____ for _____ length records, and _____ for special conditions.
    *****
    F, fixed
    V, variable
    U (unspecified)

11. Unit-record files always have _____ length records.
    *****
    fixed

12. Tape or direct access files where records are 125 positions will have RECORDING MODE of __.
    *****
    F

13. A tape file where records may be 100 or 150 positions will have RECORDING MODE of __.
    *****
    V

14. If the RECORDING MODE clause is not included, RECORDING MODE IS __ is assumed.
    *****
    V

15. For unit-record devices, LABEL RECORDS ARE _____.
    *****
    OMITTED

16. When **LABEL RECORDS ARE STANDARD** is specified, header and trailer labels will be _____ on input files and _____ on output files.
*****
checked
created

17. The **LABEL RECORDS** clause is (optional, required).
*****
required

18. The **RECORD CONTAINS** clause is (optional, required).
*****
optional

19. The **BLOCK CONTAINS** clause is only used for _____.
*****
blocked tape or disk files

20. The **DATA RECORD(S)** clause is (optional, required) _____ and defines the _____.
*****
required
records within the file

21. Write an **FD** entry for a tape file blocked 20 with 100 position records and standard labels; one record format exists.
*****
FD   TAPE-FILE RECORDING MODE IS F LABEL RECORDS ARE STANDARD RECORD CONTAINS 100 CHARACTERS BLOCK CONTAINS 20 RECORDS DATA RECORD IS REC-1.

22. Write an **FD** entry for a print file with header and detail records.
*****
FD   PRINT-FILE
LABEL RECORDS ARE OMITTED,
RECORDING MODE IS F,
RECORD CONTAINS 132 CHARACTERS,
DATA RECORDS ARE HEADER, DETAIL.

Make any necessary corrections to the following **DATA DIVISION** entries (23, 24):

23. DATA DIVISION.
FILE-SECTION
FD   CARD-FILE.
RECORDING MODE F
LABELS ARE OMITTED
DATA RECORD IS REC-IN.
*****
No dash between **FILE** and **SECTION**; period after all Section names.
No period after **FD   CARD-FILE.**

LABEL clause should read LABEL RECORDS ARE OMITTED (assuming it is a card file).

Corrected entry:

DATA DIVISION.
FILE SECTION.
FD   CARD-FILE
     RECORDING MODE F
     LABEL RECORDS ARE OMITTED
     DATA RECORD IS REC-IN.

24. FD   PRINT-FILE
          LABEL RECORDS ARE OMITTED,
          RECORD CONTAINS 132 CHARACTERS,
          DATA RECORD IS PRINT-REC
     *****
Must have a RECORDING MODE clause for fixed length records. File Description entries must end with period.

Corrected entry:

FD   PRINT-FILE
     RECORDING MODE IS F,
     LABEL RECORDS ARE OMITTED
     RECORD CONTAINS 132 CHARACTERS
     DATA RECORD IS PRINT-REC.

B. RECORD DESCRIPTION

Level Indicators. After a file is described by an **FD**, record description entries for each record within the file follow. A record description is required for each record named in the File Description clause to illustrate the **structure** of a record. It will indicate what items appear in the record, the order in which they appear, and how these items are related to each other. Just as the file name is specified on the **FD** level, a record name is coded on the **01** level. Examine the following illustrations:

Example 1:

FD   CARD-FILE RECORDING MODE IS F,
     LABEL RECORDS ARE OMITTED,
     RECORD CONTAINS 80 CHARACTERS,
     DATA RECORD IS CARD-REC.
01   CARD-REC
     (entries to be discussed)

Example 2:

FD   TAPE-FILE RECORDING MODE IS F,
     LABEL RECORDS ARE STANDARD,
     RECORD CONTAINS 10
     CHARACTERS, BLOCK CONTAINS 50
     RECORDS, DATA RECORDS ARE
     REC-1, REC-2
01   REC-1
     (entries to be discussed)
01   REC-2
     (entries to be discussed)

Each **FD** must be followed by record description entries for the file. We have observed that records are defined on the 01 level. Now we must indicate just what is contained in each record of the file and how the items are organized.

Data is grouped in COBOL around the **level** concept. Records are considered the **highest level of data** and thus are coded on the **01** level. Any field of data within the record is coded on a level **subordinate** to 01, that is, 02, 03, etc. Any level number between 02 and 49 may be used to describe data fields within a record.

Let us examine the following card layout:

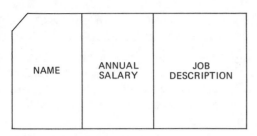

The record description entries within the FD are as follows:

Example 3:

```
01  EMPLOYEE-REC.
    02 NAME
    02 ANN-SALARY
    02 JOB-DESCRIPTION
```

The name of the record, **EMPLOYEE-REC,** is coded on the **01** level in Margin A. All fields within the record are coded on any level between **02** and **49,** anywhere in Margin B. By specifying the above fields on the **02** level, two facts are established.

1. All fields on an **02** level are **subordinate to,** or part of, the **01** level entry.

2. All fields that are coded on the same level are **independent** items.

Thus **NAME, ANN-SALARY,** and **JOB-DESCRIPTION** are fields within **EMPLOYEE-REC,** and each is independent of the other.

Let us redefine the above input:

Sometimes fields are **not** independent of one another; as in the preceding redefined input that is, a field may be subordinate to, or contained in, **another** field within a record. **MONTH** and **YEAR,** for example, may be fields within **DATE,** which itself is contained within a record. **MONTH** and **YEAR,** then, would be coded on a level subordinate to **DATE.** If **DATE** were specified on level **02, MONTH** and **YEAR** would each be specified on level **03.**

Example 4: RECORD DESCRIPTION FOR REDEFINED INPUT

```
01  EMPLOYEE-REC.
    02 NAME
        03 INITIAL1
        03 INITIAL2
        03 LAST-NAME
    02 ANN-SALARY
    02 JOB-DESCRIPTION
        03 JOB-TITLE
            04 LEVEL
            04 POSITION
        03 DUTIES
```

There are three **major** fields within the record: **NAME, ANN-SALARY,** and **JOB-DESCRIPTION,** which are still independent and coded on the **02** level. The **NAME** field, however, is further subdivided into **INITIAL1, INITIAL2,** and **LAST-NAME.** These **03** level items are independent of each other, but contained within **NAME.** Similarly, **JOB-TITLE** and **DUTIES** are independent items within **JOB-DESCRIPTION. JOB-TITLE** is further subdivided into **LEVEL** and **POSITION.**

Note that all fields are coded in Margin B. Only the highest level of organization,

NAME				JOB DESCRIPTION		
INITIAL 1	INITIAL 2	LAST NAME	ANNUAL SALARY	TITLE		DUTIES
				LEVEL	POSITION	

the record, is coded in Margin A. Note also the indentation of subordinate levels, making it clearer to read. Using this method, the fact that INITIAL1, INITIAL2, and LAST-NAME are contained within NAME is quite clear.

The names of fields (data-names), like the names of records and files, must conform to the rules for forming programmer-supplied names. One to 30 characters, no special characters (except a dash) or embedded blanks, and at least one alphabetic character.

Level numbers may vary from 02 to 49 for fields of data. Level numbers, however, need not be consecutive:

```
01   REC-A.
     03 DATE
        07 MONTH
        07 YEAR
     03 REMAINDER
```

The above is an illustration of a FILE SECTION, where level numbers are not consecutive. Note that MONTH and YEAR, on the 07 level, are contained within DATE, on the 03 level.

Observe the following illustrations:

```
01   DISK-REC.
     02 NAME
     03 LAST-NAME
     05 FIRST-NAME  ──→  inaccurate
     02 AMOUNT
```

This entry is not correct. It implies that FIRST-NAME, as an 05 level item, is contained in LAST-NAME, an 03 level item. To indicate that LAST-NAME and FIRST-NAME have equal but independent status, they both must be coded on the same level. To place them both on the 03, 04, or 05 level would be accurate.

The order in which fields are placed within the record is crucial. If NAME is the first 02 level within DISK-REC, this implies that NAME is the first data field in the record.

An item which is not further subdivided is called an elementary item. An item which is further subdivided is called a group item. In Example 4, NAME is a group item which is subdivided into two elementary items, LAST-NAME and FIRST-NAME. ANN-SALARY, on the same level as NAME, is an elementary item since it is not further subdivided.

All elementary items must be additionally described by indicating size and type of the field. A group item needs no further specification. Thus we have:

```
01  TAPE-REC.
02  CUSTOMER-NAME.
    03 LAST-NAME              (entry required)
    03 FIRST-NAME            (entry required)
02  TRANSACTION-NUMBER  (entry required)
02  DATE-OF-TRANSACTION.
    03 MONTH                   (entry required)
    03 YEAR                     (entry required)
```

Note that there is a period at the end of each group item. Elementary items require further description. We treat the record entry, on the 01 level, as a group item, since it is, in fact, a data element which is further subdivided.

EXERCISES

1. All records are coded on the ___ level.

   *****

   01

2. Levels ___ to ___ may be used to represent fields within a record.

   *****

   02
   49

3. An 03 level item may be subordinate to an ___ level item if it exists.

   *****

   02

4. What, if anything, is wrong with the following data-names:
   (a) CUSTOMER NAME.
   (b) TAX%.
   (c) DATA.

   *****

   No embedded blanks allowed.
   No special characters (%).
   DATA is a COBOL reserved word.

5. An elementary item is _____, and a group item is _____.

   *****

   one which is not further subdivided
   one which is further subdivided

6. 01 level is coded in Margin ___, 02 to 49 levels are coded in Margin ___.

   *****

   A
   B

7. Write RECORD DESCRIPTION entries for the following:

TRANSACTION RECORD					
	LOCATION			PRODUCT DESCRIPTION	
				NO. OF ITEM	ITEM NAME
INVOICE NUMBER	WARE-HOUSE	CITY	JOB LOT		
				SIZE	MODEL	

   *****

   ```
   01   TRANSACTION-REC.
        02 INVOICE-NO
        02 LOCATION.
           03 WAREHOUSE
           03 CITY
           03 JOB-LOT
   ```

```
02 PRODUCT-DESCRIPTION.
03 NO-OF-ITEM.
   04 SIZE
   04 MODEL
03 ITEM-NAME
```

Note: Period follows group items only.

Picture Clauses. Group items are defined by a level indicator. Elementary items are those fields which are not further subdivided, and they must be described in detail. We must specify:

1. The **type** of data contained within an elementary item.
2. The **size** of the field.

A PICTURE clause associated with **each** elementary item will provide the above information about a field.

There are **three** types of data fields.

ALPHABETIC. A field that may consist of letters or blanks is classified as alphabetic. A name field or a heading field will generally be considered alphabetic.

ALPHANUMERIC. A field that may contain **any** valid character is considered alphanumeric. An address field, for example, would be classified as alphanumeric, since it may contain combinations of letters, digits, or even special characters.

NUMERIC. Any field that will contain digits and plus or minus signs **only** is considered numeric.

To denote the type of data within an elementary field, a PICTURE clause will contain:

A for alphabetic
X for alphanumeric
9 for numeric

A field will contain a PICTURE of all A's, for example, if it is alphabetic. We denote the **size** of the field by the **number** of A's, X's, or 9's used in the PICTURE:

02 AMT PICTURE IS 99999.

The above field is an elementary item consisting of five positions of numeric data.

The entry:

02 ITEM PICTURE AAAA.

defines a four-position storage area called ITEM which will contain only alphabetic data or a blank. Observe the following entries:

```
01  REC-1.
    02 ITEM   PICTURE AAAA.
    02 AMT    PICTURE 99999.
    02 CODE   PICTURE XX.
```

ITEM is the first data field in the record. If REC-1, for example, defined a card record, Columns 1–4 would represent the field called ITEM. AMT, as the second entry specified, would be describing the next field of data, or Columns 5–9. That is, the five positions directly following ITEM would represent the field called AMT.

Note that a PICTURE clause may contain only one type of symbol. To define a field as 03 FLD1 PICTURE X9 is **not** valid. If a field is numeric, its PICTURE clause may contain only 9's; if a field is alphabetic, its PICTURE clause may contain only A's; if a field may contain any character or combination of digits and letters, it is defined with a PICTURE of X's.

Note that the notation

04 NAME PICTURE A(10).

is acceptable. Parentheses may be used to designate the size of a field rather than 10 A's. The word IS in the PICTURE clause, as in all COBOL statements, is optional and may always be omitted. A period will follow each PICTURE clause in the FILE SECTION.

Thus group items are those fields which are further subdivided and contain **no** PICTURE clause. Only elementary items require a **PICTURE** clause, which denotes the size of a field and its mode, that is, the type of data it will contain.

The record description entry for the following card layout is:

Examine the following card layout:

cc1-25 EMPLOYEE-NAME
cc26-30 not used
cc31-35 HOURS-WORKED
cc36-80 not used

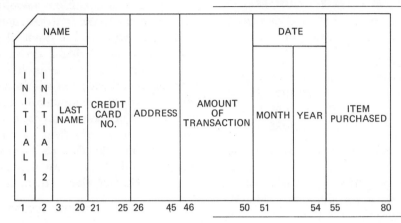

01 CREDIT-CARD-ACCT.
  02 NAME.
    03 INIT1   PICTURE A.
    03 INIT2   PICTURE A.
    03 LAST-NAME PICTURE A(18).
  02 CREDIT-CARD-NO PICTURE 9(5).
  02 ADDRESS   PICTURE X(20).
  02 AMT-OF-TRANS PICTURE 9(5).
  02 DATE-OF-TRANS.
    03 MONTH   PICTURE 99.
    03 YEAR   PICTURE 99.
  02 ITEM-PURCHASED PICTURE X(26).

The **PICTURE** clause may appear **anywhere** on the line. For purposes of clarity, each **PICTURE** clause was placed in the same position; this is not, however, required. At least one space must follow the word **PICTURE**. All A's, X's, or 9's must appear consecutively, that is, with no spaces between these characters. Similarly, if parentheses are used to denote size of a field, no spaces may appear within the clause.

The **PICTURE** clauses in a record description entry must, in total, yield the number of characters in the record. Thus, if **CREDIT-CARD-ACCT** is a card record, all **PICTURE** clauses on the elementary level must produce 80 positions of storage.

Card Columns 26–30 and 36–80 contain no pertinent data. These areas, however, must be noted as fields in the record description entry. To say **incorrectly**:

01 TIME-CARD.
  02 EMPLOYEE-NAME PICTURE A(25).
  02 HOURS-WORKED   PICTURE 9(5).

causes two major errors.

1. The computer will assume that HOURS-WORKED immediately follows NAME, since it is the next designated field. A **READ** command, then, would place card Columns 26–30 in the storage area called HOURS-WORKED.

2. The **PICTURE** clause should result in 80 positions of storage. Instead, only 25 positions are defined.

The following would then be correct:

01 TIME-CARD.
  02 EMPLOYEE-NAME PICTURE A(25).
  02 WASTE1   PICTURE XXXXX.
  02 HOURS-WORKED PICTURE 9(5).
  02 WASTE2   PICTURE X(45).

To denote a nonsignificant field of data, one which will not be utilized in the program, the COBOL word **FILLER** may be used instead of creating data-names. A

FILLER with an appropriate PICTURE clause designates an area set aside for some part of a record. As a COBOL reserved word specifying an unused area, it may not be accessed in the PROCEDURE DIVISION. To say: MOVE FILLER TO OUT-AREA, for example, is invalid. Our record description entry, then, may also read:

```
01  TIME-CARD.
    02 EMPLOYEE-NAME  PICTURE A(25).
    02 FILLER         PICTURE XXXXX.
    02 HOURS-WORKED   PICTURE 9(5).
    02 FILLER         PICTURE X(45).
```

Except for the COBOL reserved word FILLER, we will keep all other data-names unique for now; that is, we will not use the same name for different fields. We must never use a record or a file name more than once in the DATA DIVISION. We will see in Chapter 11 that one data-name may, if coded properly, be used to define several fields.

In general, a field is denoted as numeric, with PICTURE of 9's, when an arithmetic operation is to be performed. When a field is so designated, the data in the area may consist of digits and a sign only. A space, for example, is not a valid character in a numeric field. Thus, if a field is denoted as numeric, it must contain only valid numeric characters.

Note that an alphanumeric field may contain all numbers. Thus 123 in FLDA, where FLDA has PICTURE XXX, is entirely acceptable. FLDA, however, may not be used in an arithmetic operation. Only fields with numeric PICTURE clauses may be specified in computations. In short, then, fields that are to be used in calculations must be defined with PICTURE of 9's. If there is any doubt about the type of data contained in a field, define it as alphanumeric, since such fields can contain any character.

Because numeric fields may be used in arithmetic operations, their PICTURE clauses may utilize entries in addition to the basic 9. Most of these will be discussed later, since they are necessary only in higher-level COBOL programs. The symbol V, however, to denote an implied decimal, will be discussed here because of its widespread use and importance.

Suppose a five-position amount field, with contents 10000, is to be interpreted as 100.00. That is, we want the computer to "assume" that a decimal point exists. The data is five positions, and there is no decimal point within the field; but we want the computer to imply its existence. When any calculations are performed on the amount field, the computer is to consider the data as having three integer positions and two decimal positions. Its PICTURE clause, then, is

02 AMT   PICTURE 999V99.

Note that V does not occupy a core storage position. The field is five positions. We have merely indicated that data entering the field is to have three integer and two decimal positions. If 38726 is read into the area, it will be interpreted as 387.26, when the program is executed.

We have completed record description entries for the coding of elementary COBOL programs. For every record specified in the DATA RECORDS clause, an 01 level and its corresponding entries must be included.

All records within an FD are described before the next FD is defined. The following DATA DIVISION indicates the sequence in which entries are coded:

```
DATA DIVISION.
FILE SECTION.
FD  INPUT-FILE
    RECORDING MODE IS F
    LABEL RECORDS ARE OMITTED
    RECORD CONTAINS 80 CHARACTERS
    DATA RECORDS ARE REC-1, REC-2.
01  REC-1.
    02 CUSTOMER-NAME  PICTURE X(20).
    02 ADDRESS        PICTURE X(15).
    02 AMT-OF-DEBIT   PICTURE 999V99.
    02 FILLER         PICTURE X(40).
```

```
01  REC-2.                                    RECORD CONTAINS 100 CHARACTERS
     02 NAME            PICTURE  X(16).        BLOCK CONTAINS 5 RECORDS,
     02 AMT-OF-CREDIT   PICTURE  99V99.        DATA RECORD IS REC-OUT.
     02 FILLER          PICTURE  X(60).    01  REC-OUT.
FD  OUTPUT-FILE                                02 NAME-OUT        PICTURE  X(20).
     RECORDING MODE IS F,                      02 AMT-OF-TRANS    PICTURE  999V99.
     LABEL RECORDS ARE STANDARD,               02 FILLER          PICTURE  X(75).
```

EXERCISES

1. A **PICTURE** clause must be used in conjunction with each _____
_____ in a record description.

*****

elementary item

2. A **PICTURE** clause specifies the _____ and the _____ of a data
field.

*****

size

type

3. The three types of data fields are _____, _____, and _____.

*****

alphabetic

numeric

alphanumeric

4. The characters which may be included in an alphabetic field are

_____.

*****

letters and blanks

5. The characters which may be included in an alphanumeric field
are _____.

*****

any character in the COBOL character set

6. The characters which may be included in a numeric data field
are _____.

*****

digits and plus or minus sign

7. An alphanumeric **PICTURE** clause contains _____; an alphabetic
PICTURE clause contains _____; a numeric **PICTURE** clause contains

_____.

*****

X's

A's

9's

What, if anything, is wrong with the following entries (8–10):

8. 01   CARD-REC.
        02 DATE PICTURE 9999.
            03 MONTH PICTURE 99.
            03 YEAR   PICTURE 99.
    *****

    Group items, such as DATE, should not have PICTURE clauses.

9. 03 FIELDA PICTURE X9.
    *****

    Field may have either all X's to denote alphanumeric field or all 9's to denote numeric field.

10. 04 FIELDB PICTURE X (22).
    *****

    Should be: 04 FIELDB PICTURE X(22). There is no space between X and (.

11. The PICTURE clauses in a record description must, in total, indicate _____.
    *****

    the number of positions in the record

12. The word _____ is used to denote an area of a record that will not be used for processing.
    *****

    FILLER

13. The symbol __ is used to denote an implied decimal point in an arithmetic field.
    *****

    V

14. A PICTURE clause of 9V9 indicates a _____ -position data field.
    *****

    two

15. If a three-position tax field is to be interpreted as .xxx its PICTURE clause should be _____.
    *****

    V999.

REVIEW QUESTIONS

1. Which of the following entries are coded in Margin A?

    (a) FD
    (b) FILE SECTION
    (c) 01
    (d) 03
    (e) LABEL RECORDS ARE OMITTED

2. Name the clauses that are required within an **FD**.

3. Name the clauses that are optional within an **FD**.

4. How many **FD** entries are required in a COBOL program?

5. Under what conditions is the **BLOCK CONTAINS** clause required?

6. State exactly what is meant by the **PICTURE** clause **9999V9999**.

7. (T or F) There may be only one **01** level for a specific file.

8. (T or F) The order in which fields are specified in a record description is not significant.

9. (T or F) Group items must not have **PICTURE** clauses.

10. (T or F) Elementary items may or may not have **PICTURE** clauses.

11. (T or F) A **FILLER** is a COBOL reserved word that may be used in the **DATA** and **PROCEDURE DIVISIONS**.

12. (T or F) A record name is assigned in the **ENVIRONMENT DIVISION**.

13. (T or F) Two files may be assigned the same names.

14. (T or F) Levels 03, 08, 75 may be subordinate to a record level.

15. What are the rules for forming data-names?

16. How many characters must be included in the **PICTURE** clauses used to describe a card record?

17. Correct the following **DATA DIVISION**:

```
DATA DIVISION
FILE-SECTION.
FD   TAPE FILE.
        RECORDING MODE F.
        DATA RECORD IS INPUT.
01    INPUT.
        02 TRANS.NO                 PICTURE 9999.
        02 TRANSACTION-NAME         PICTURE 20X.
        02 ADDRESS
            03 NUMBER               PICTURE XXXX.
            03 STREET               PICTURE A(15).
            03 CITY                 PICTURE AAA.
        02 CREDIT-RATING            PICTURE XX.
            03 CREDIT-CODE          PICTURE X.
            03 LIMIT OF PURCHASE    X.
        02 UNIT-PRICE               PICTURE 99.9.
        02 QTY-PURCHASED            PICTURE 9(5).
        02 DISCOUNT-%               PICTURE V99.
```

PROBLEMS

1. Write the **FD** and record description entries necessary for an inventory file with the following record format:

LOCATION				PART NO.	PART NAME	REORDER LEVEL	UNIT COST	TOTAL SALES	TOTAL SALES
	WAREHOUSE								
STATE (alphabetic)	FLOOR	BIN	CITY (alphabetic)		alphanumeric		XXX·XX	2 MOS. AGO XXX·XX	LAST MO. XXX·XX
1	3 4	5 6	7 8	11 12	16 17	25 26	29 30	34 35	39 40	44

BALANCE ON HAND	QTY. SOLD	TOTAL COST	BIN CAPACITY	DESCRIPTION OF PART
		XXXXX·XX		alphanumeric
45	50 51	55 56	62 63	67 68	100

(UNLESS OTHERWISE NOTED, FIELDS ARE NUMERIC)
XXX.XX denotes a PICTURE clause of 999V99

The inventory file will be on magnetic tape with standard labels and blocked 20.

2. Write the **FD** and record description entries for the following purchase record:

Item Description	Field Type	Field Size	Positions to Right of Decimal Point
Name of item	Alphabetic	20	—
Date of order (month, day, year)	Numeric	6	0
Purchase order number	Numeric	5	0
Inventory group	Alphanumeric	10	—
Number of units	Numeric	5	0
Cost/unit	Numeric	4	0
Freight charge	Numeric	4	0
Tax percent	Numeric	2	2

3. Write **FD** entries for the following card format:

STUDENT NAME			EMPLOYER		COURSE			GRADES			
INITIAL1	INITIAL2	LAST NAME	NAME	ADDRESS	NAME	CLASS	APTITUDE TEST SCORE	DATE	FINAL EXAM SCORE	FINAL GRADE	
						SECTION ROOM					
1	2	3	20 21	40 41	50 51	60 61	63 64 66 67	69 70	75 76	78 79	80

4. Write **FD** entries for a master transaction tape file with the following two record formats:

TRANSACTION NUMBER	CUSTOMER NAME	QTY PURCHASED	COST/ITEM (Dollars and Cents)	ADDITIONAL CHARGES		DATE		
				TAX (%)	SHIPPING CHARGES (Dollars and Cents)	MO	YR	Debit record
1	5 6	20 21	25 26	30 31	32 33	36 37 38 39	40	

TRANSACTION NUMBER	CUSTOMER NAME	AMOUNT OF CREDIT (Dollars and Cents)	UNUSED	DATE		
				MO	YR	Credit record
1	5 6	20 21 25		37 38 39	40	

The master tape has standard labels and is blocked 10.

5. Write **FD** entries for the following file of records:

Account Identification
- Type of Account ↔ Alphameric, 5 positions
- Customer Name ↔ Alphabetic, 20 positions
- Acct. No.
  - Store No. ↔ Numeric, 5 positions
  - File No. ↔ Numeric, 3 positions

Account History
- Yr. Began ↔ Numeric, 2 positions
- Highest Balance ↔ Numeric, 6 positions (4 integer, 2 fractional)
- Date of Last Transaction — Numeric, 6 positions

Last Month
- Trans. No. ↔ Numeric, 5 positions
- Balance ↔ Numeric, 6 positions (4 integer, 2 fractional)

This Month
- Trans. No. ↔ Numeric, 5 positions
- Balance ↔ Numeric, 6 positions (4 integer, 2 fractional)

Last Payment
- Date ↔ Numeric, 6 positions
- Amount ↔ Numeric, 6 positions (4 integer, 2 fractional)

The file is on magnetic tape. The tape has standard labels and is blocked 50.

The Procedure Division

Thus far, we have discussed three of the four divisions of a COBOL program. The PROCEDURE DIVISION, the last to be studied, is unquestionably the most important. The PROCEDURE DIVISION contains all the instructions to be executed by the computer. All the logic of the program is contained within these instructions.

The IDENTIFICATION and ENVIRONMENT DIVISIONS supply peripheral information about the nature of the program and the specific equipment it will use. The FILE SECTION of the DATA DIVISION defines, in detail, the input and output areas. The input area is storage reserved for an incoming file. The output area is storage reserved for the accumulation of data to be produced as output by the computer. It is in the PROCEDURE DIVISION, however, that data is read and processed and output information is produced.

All instructions are written in the PROCEDURE DIVISION. The majority of chapters in this book concern themselves with executable instructions. The coding of the first three divisions is fairly straightforward; it is the manipulation of data in the PROCEDURE DIVISION that is the core of programming.

In this chapter, we will learn to:

1. Access input and output files.

2. Read and write information.
3. Perform simple move-and-branch operations.
4. Perform specific end-of-job operations.

Knowledge of these types of instructions will be sufficient for writing elementary COBOL programs in their entirety.

The PROCEDURE DIVISION is divided into **paragraphs.** Each paragraph defines an independent **routine,** or series of instructions, designed to perform a specific function.

Each paragraph is further subdivided into statements or sentences. A **statement** is a COBOL instruction to the computer. A sentence is a statement or group of statements within a paragraph. Each statement, unless it tests a condition, begins with a verb or operation. READ, MOVE, WRITE are examples of COBOL operations.

A statement usually ends with a period, which must be followed by at least one space. Several statements may be written on one line of a COBOL coding sheet, but words may not be subdivided when the end of a line is reached. Fig. 6-1 illustrates a correct coding of instructions. Fig. 6-2 is, however, incorrect since words may not be subdivided in that fashion.

Each statement may also be written on

IBM   COBOL Program Sheet   Form No. X28-1464-3 U/M 050
Printed in U.S.A.

System		Punching Instructions		Sheet of
Program		Graphic	Card	Identification
Programmer	Date	Punch	Form #	73 80

Sequence (PAGE)(SERIAL)	CONT.	A	B	COBOL Statement
0 1		PROCEDURE DIVISION.		
0 2		START.		
0 3		READ CARD-IN AT END GO TO EOJ. ADD AMT-IN TO TOTAL. MOVE		
0 4		NAME-IN TO NAME-OUT. WRITE RECORD-1.		
0 5				
0 6				

Fig. 6-1

IBM   COBOL Program Sheet   Form No. X28-1464-3 U/M 050
Printed in U.S.A.

System		Punching Instructions		Sheet of
Program		Graphic	Card	Identification
Programmer	Date	Punch	Form #	73 80

INVALID CONTINUATION

Sequence (PAGE)(SERIAL)	CONT.	A	B	COBOL Statement
0 1		PROCEDURE DIVISION.		
0 2		START.		
0 3		READ CARD-IN AT END GO TO EOJ. ADD AMT-IN TO TOTAL. MOVE NAME		
0 4		-IN TO NAME-OUT. WRITE RECORD-1.		
0 5				
0 6				

Fig. 6-2   Invalid Continuation

IBM   COBOL Program Sheet   Form No. X28-1464-3 U/M 050
Printed in U.S.A.

System		Punching Instructions		Sheet of
Program		Graphic	Card	Identification
Programmer	Date	Punch	Form #	73 80

Sequence (PAGE)(SERIAL)	CONT.	A	B	COBOL Statement
0 1		PROCEDURE DIVISION.		
0 2		START.		
0 3		READ CARD-IN AT END GO TO EOJ.		
0 4		ADD AMT-IN TO TOTAL.		
0 5		MOVE NAME-IN TO NAME-OUT.		
0 6		WRITE RECORD-1.		
0 7				
0 8				

Fig. 6-3

a separate line. For purposes of clear presentation, this method is often preferred. Fig. 6-3 illustrates this type of coding.

All statements are executed in the order written unless a branch instruction transfers control to some other part of the program:

    MOVE NAME TO NAME-OUT.
    MOVE AMT TO AMT-OUT.
    WRITE DATA-REC.

In the above routine, the **MOVE** state-ments will be executed first and then the **WRITE** statement will be performed.

All statements in the **PROCEDURE DIVISION** are coded in Margin B. Only paragraph names are written in Margin A.

A. OPEN STATEMENT

Before an input or output file can be read or written, we must first **OPEN** the file. We instruct the computer to **access** a file by an **OPEN** statement.

An **OPEN** statement in COBOL has the following format:

OPEN INPUT (file name(s)) OUTPUT (file name(s))

The format for COBOL statements will follow a particular pattern throughout this book.

1. All capitalized words are COBOL reserved words.

2. All underlined words are required elements in the statement or option specified.

3. All lowercase words are programmer supplied. The symbol (s) after a programmer-supplied word denotes that several such words are permissible.

4. The braces { } denote that the enclosed clause is optional.

5. The brackets [ ] denote that any one of the enclosed words may be used, that is,

$$\begin{bmatrix} \text{ELSE} \\ \text{OTHERWISE} \end{bmatrix}$$

denotes that either one of the two words is permissible.

6. Punctuation, when included in the format, is required.

Thus the above **OPEN** format specifies that:

(a) **OPEN, INPUT,** and **OUTPUT** are required COBOL reserved words, since they are capitalized and underlined.

(b) All input file names and output file names are programmer-supplied words.

For every **SELECT** clause in the **ENVIRONMENT DIVISION,** a file name is defined and a device is assigned.

Example

SELECT CARD-IN ASSIGN TO 'SYS005'
UNIT-RECORD 2540R UNIT.
SELECT TAPE-OUT ASSIGN TO 'SYS008'
UTILITY 2400 UNITS.

The file name **CARD-IN** is assigned to the card reader by the **SELECT** clause. For each file name specified, a file description entry in the **DATA DIVISION** is required. Thus **CARD-IN** and **TAPE-OUT** must each be described by **FD** entries.

Thus far, devices are assigned and files are described. At no point, however, have we indicated which files are input and which are output. This is accomplished by the **OPEN** statement: **OPEN INPUT CARD-IN OUTPUT TAPE-OUT.**

This instructs the computer that the storage positions assigned to **CARD-IN** in the **DATA DIVISION** will serve as an input area, and the storage positions assigned to **TAPE-OUT** will serve as an output area. Data from **CARD-IN** will be **read** by the computer and data from **TAPE-OUT** will be **written** by the computer.

An **OPEN** statement, then, designates files as input or output. It also accesses the specific devices. If **TAPE-IN,** for example, is an input tape file, the **OPEN** statement will access the specific tape drive to determine if it is ready to read data. If not, execution is suspended until the operator "readies" the device.

In addition to distinguishing input files from output files and accessing specified devices, an **OPEN** statement performs certain checking functions. If label records for an input file are indicated as **STANDARD,** for example, an **OPEN** statement checks the header label to determine if the correct tape is mounted. If label records for an output tape file are designated as **STANDARD,** the **OPEN** statement will create the header label.

In summary, two basic functions are performed by the **OPEN** statement.

1. It indicates which files will serve as input and which will serve as output.

2. It makes files available for processing.

Programs are often written using several input and output files. An **update** program, for example, may merge two input files, **TAPE-1** and **TAPE-2**, into one master output file, **TAPE-3**, and also create an error listing, **PRINT-FILE**, as well. The **OPEN** statement for such a program would read:

OPEN INPUT TAPE-1, TAPE-2, OUTPUT TAPE-3, PRINT-FILE.

All input files follow the COBOL reserved word **INPUT** and, similarly, all output files follow the COBOL word **OUTPUT**. The word **INPUT** need not be repeated for each incoming file. The word **OUTPUT** may also be omitted after the first output file is noted.

The above statement, however, may also be written as four distinct sentences:

OPEN INPUT TAPE-1.
OPEN INPUT TAPE-2.
OPEN OUTPUT TAPE-3.
OPEN OUTPUT PRINT-FILE.

When separate statements are used, the words **INPUT** or **OUTPUT** must be indicated for each file that is opened. This method is often used when files are to be opened at varying intervals throughout the program; that is, the program processes one file before it accesses the next. Unless periodic intervals are required for the opening of files, it is considered inefficient and somewhat cumbersome to issue an independent **OPEN** statement for each file.

The order in which files are opened is not significant. The only restriction is that a file must be opened before it may be read or written; a file must be **accessed** before it may be **processed.** Since the **OPEN** statement allows the accessing of files, it is generally the first instruction issued to the computer in the **PROCEDURE DIVISION.**

EXERCISES

1. The **PROCEDURE DIVISION** contains all _____ to be executed.
*****
instructions

2. The **PROCEDURE DIVISION** is divided into _____.
*****
paragraphs

3. Each paragraph defines a _____.
*****
routine

4. A routine is a _____.
*****
series of instructions designed to perform a specific function.

5. Paragraphs are divided into _____.
*****
statements or sentences

6. Statements are executed in the order _____ unless a _____ occurs.
*****
in which they appear
branch

7. An **OPEN** statement indicates _____, and it also _____ the files.

*****

which files are input and which are output

accesses

8. Before a file may be read, it must be _____.

*****

opened

9. The **OPEN** statement is coded in Margin __.

*****

B

10. The file name indicated in the **OPEN** statement also appears in a _____ clause and on the _____ level.

*****

SELECT

FD

B. READ STATEMENT

After an input file has been opened, it may be read. A **READ** statement transmits data from the input device, assigned in the **ENVIRONMENT DIVISION,** to the input storage area, defined in the **FILE SECTION** of the **DATA DIVISION.**

The following is the format for a **READ** statement:

```
READ (file name) AT END (statement).
```

The file name specified in the **READ** statement appears three other places in the program.

1. The **SELECT** clause, indicating the name and the device assigned to the file. If the card reader is the device assigned, for example, a **READ** operation transmits data from an input card to the input area.

2. The **FD** entry, describing the file.

3. The **OPEN** statement, accessing the file.

The primary function of the **READ** statement is to transmit data to core storage. It has, however, several other functions. It performs, like the **OPEN** statement, certain checks. It checks the length of each input record to insure that it corresponds to the length specified in the **DATA DIVISION.** If a discrepancy exists, a wrong length record error has occurred and execution of the program is terminated. The **READ** statement will also use the **BLOCK CONTAINS** clause, if specified, to perform a check on the blocking factor. In addition, if the **RECORDING MODE** is variable, a **READ** instruction controls the reading of the correct number of characters.

Although the primary function of the **READ** command is the transmission of data, these checking routines are essential for proper execution of the program.

The **AT END** clause in the **READ** expression tests to determine if there is no more input. An **AT END** clause together with a COBOL **READ** statement instructs the computer what to do if there is no more data to be read. The **READ** instruction is generally written in the form:

READ (file name) **AT END GO TO EOJ.**

The **GO TO EOJ** is a branch instruction which transfers control to the paragraph called **EOJ** when there is no more data.

The routine at **EOJ** performs an End Of Job function.

Thus, when there are no more input records to be processed, the **AT END** clause will be executed and a branch to the paragraph **EOJ** will occur. A more detailed discussion of branch instructions will appear later in this chapter.

Example

READ CARD-FILE AT END GO TO EOJ.

A card will be read from the specified input device, and the next sequential instruction in the program will be executed **unless there are no more cards.** If, in fact, there are no more input cards, a branch to **EOJ** occurs. If, for example, ten cards constitute the input data, the **eleventh** attempt to read a card will cause a branch to **EOJ**.

On third-generation computers, a card with a /* in the first two columns is placed at the end of data. In this case, the /* card causes an **AT END** condition to be executed.

An **AT END** clause **must be** specified for every **READ** statement.[1] The computer must be instructed what to do when there is no more data.

Examine the following **DATA DIVISION** entry:

```
FD  TAPE-FILE RECORDING MODE F, LABEL
    RECORDS ARE OMITTED, RECORD
    CONTAINS 20 CHARACTERS, BLOCK
    CONTAINS 10 RECORDS, DATA
    RECORD IS TAPE-REC.
01  TAPE-REC.
    02 NAME          PICTURE X(15).
    02 AMT-OF-TRANS PICTURE 9(5).
```

Suppose the statement **READ TAPE-FILE AT END GO TO EOJ** is executed. The first 15 positions of data from the tape will be placed in storage in the field called **NAME**. The next five tape positions will be placed in the field called **AMT-OF-TRANS**. The se-

---

[1] The AT END clause may be omitted when input is on disk. This will be discussed in Chapter 20, which describes disk operations.

quence in which entries are denoted in the **DATA DIVISION** is crucial; data is placed in the fields in the order in which the data names are specified. The **READ** command will also perform a checking function. The length of the tape block will be compared to 200 positions, or 10 records, when a record is read. Any discrepancy constitutes a wrong length record error, which would cause execution to be terminated.

Similarly, if data is read from cards, the first card columns would be placed in the first data field specified in the **DATA DIVISION**. A less elaborate checking routine would be performed, since there is no blocking of cards.

C. WRITE STATEMENT

The **WRITE** instruction takes data accumulated in the output area of the **DATA DIVISION** and transmits it to the device specified in the **ENVIRONMENT DIVISION**.

The **WRITE** statement has the following format:

```
┌──────────────────────────────────┐
│        WRITE (record name)        │
└──────────────────────────────────┘
```

One important point must be noted. Although **files** are **read,** we **write records.** The record name appears on the **01** level and is generally subdivided into fields. The record describes the **format** of the output. With each **WRITE** command, we instruct the computer to write data according to the format denoted:

```
FD  TAPE-OUT RECORDING MODE IS F,
    LABEL RECORDS ARE OMITTED,
    RECORD CONTAINS 20
    CHARACTERS, BLOCK CONTAINS 10
    RECORDS, DATA RECORDS ARE
    DEBIT, CREDIT.
01  DEBIT.
    02 NAME          PICTURE X(15).
    02 AMT-OF-DEBIT  PICTURE 9(5).
01  CREDIT.
    02 AMT-OF-CREDIT PICTURE 9(5).
    02 NAME          PICTURE X(15).
```

To write information stored in the DATA DIVISION, we say WRITE DEBIT or WRITE CREDIT, not WRITE TAPE-OUT. To say WRITE DEBIT transmits data to the output device according to the format specified in the DEBIT record; that is, the NAME will constitute the first 15 positions of tape and AMT-OF-CREDIT will constitute the last five positions of the tape record.

Each data item within the record is transmitted to the output device as it appears in the record.

The WRITE (record name) expression is used to create all output records, regardless of the assigned device. We say WRITE PUNCH-REC, WRITE TAPE-REC, or WRITE PRINT-REC. Punch and Print are not valid output instructions.

EXERCISES

1. Before a file may be read it must be _____.
   *****
   opened

2. READ FILEA AT END GO TO EOJ. FILEA appears in a _____ clause of the _____ DIVISION, an _____ level of the _____ DIVISION, and an _____ statement of the _____ DIVISION.
   *****
   SELECT
   ENVIRONMENT
   FD
   DATA
   OPEN
   PROCEDURE

3. With every READ statement, an _____ clause must be specified.
   *****
   AT END

4. READ instructions _____ data to the input area and also perform _____ functions.
   *****
   transmit
   checking

5. The AT END clause tells the computer what to do if _____.
   *****
   there is no more input data

6. In the instruction READ TAPE-IN AT END GO TO EOJ, GO TO EOJ is called a _____ instruction.
   *****
   branch

7. In the instruction READ TAPE-IN AT END GO TO EOJ, if there are 20 tape records, the _____ attempt to read a record will cause a branch to EOJ.
   *****
   21st

8. Unlike **READ** statements in which _____ are read, a **WRITE** statement writes _____.

*****

files

records

9. The record level specifies the _____.

*****

layout or record format

10. What is wrong with the following?
    (a) WRITE REC-1 AT END GO TO EOJ.
    (b) PUNCH REC-2.

*****

(a) **AT END** clause is only specified with a **READ** statement.

(b) **WRITE** command should be used, not **PUNCH**.

D. SIMPLIFIED MOVE AND GO TO STATEMENTS

Now that we are able to **OPEN** files, **READ** files, and **WRITE** records, we must learn how to manipulate input data to produce output. To say **WRITE REC-OUT** is not very effective unless there is some information in the output area. The simplest method of obtaining this data is by performing a **MOVE** operation.

A **MOVE** statement has the following format:

MOVE (data-name-1) TO (data-name-2)

Any field in storage may be moved to another field by the **MOVE** instruction.

Example Problem. To produce output tape records from input cards in the following manner:

The first three divisions of the program conform to the rules of the last three chapters. Fig. 6-4 illustrates the coding of these **DIVISIONS.**[2]

The **PROCEDURE DIVISION** may be coded as follows:

```
PROCEDURE DIVISION.
    OPEN INPUT CARD-FILE; OUTPUT
    TAPE-FILE.
    READ CARD-FILE AT END GO TO EOJ.
    MOVE NAME-IN TO NAME-OUT.
    MOVE AMT-OF-CREDIT-IN TO
    AMT-OF-CREDIT-OUT
    MOVE AMT-OF-DEBIT-IN TO
    AMT-OF-DEBIT-OUT
    WRITE TAPE-REC.
```

[2] As in all illustrations, the **ENVIRONMENT DIVISION** entries are merely samples. The **ENVIRONMENT DIVISION** is a machine-dependent division and will, therefore, vary from computer to computer. Appendix C gives sample entries for individual computers.

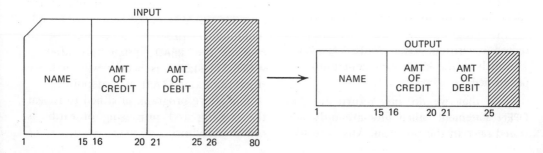

IBM COBOL Program Sheet

System		Punching Instructions				Sheet of
Program		Graphic			Card	Identification
Programmer	Date	Punch			Form #	73 80

Sequence (PAGE) (SERIAL)	CONT.	A	B	COBOL Statement
0 1		IDENTIFICATION DIVISION.		
0 2		PROGRAM-ID. 'SAMPLE'.		
0 3		ENVIRONMENT DIVISION.		
0 4		CONFIGURATION SECTION.		
0 5		SOURCE-COMPUTER. IBM-360 F40.		
0 6		OBJECT-COMPUTER. IBM-360 F40.		
0 7		INPUT-OUTPUT SECTION.		
0 8		FILE-CONTROL.		
0 9		SELECT CARD-FILE ASSIGN TO 'SYS005' UNIT-RECORD 2540R UNIT.		
1 0		SELECT TAPE-FILE ASSIGN TO 'SYS008' UTILITY 2400 UNITS.		
1 1		DATA DIVISION.		
1 2		FILE SECTION.		
1 3		FD CARD-FILE RECORDING MODE IS F, LABEL RECORDS ARE OMITTED,		
1 4		RECORD CONTAINS 80 CHARACTERS, DATA RECORD IS CARD-REC.		
1 5		01 CARD-REC.		
1 6		02 NAME-IN PICTURE X(15).		
1 7		02 AMT-OF-CREDIT-IN PICTURE 9(5).		
1 8		02 AMT-OF-DEBIT-IN PICTURE 9(5).		
1 9		02 FILLER PICTURE X(55).		
2 0		FD TAPE-FILE RECORDING MODE IS F, LABEL RECORDS OMITTED,		
2 1		RECORD CONTAINS 25 CHARACTERS, DATA RECORD IS TAPE-REC.		
2 2		01 TAPE-REC.		
2 3		02 NAME-OUT PICTURE X(15).		
2 4		02 AMT-OF-DEBIT-OUT PICTURE 9(5).		
2 5		02 AMT-OF-CREDIT-OUT PICTURE 9(5).		

*A standard card form, IBM electro C61897, is available for punching source statements from this form.

Fig. 6-4

Assuming the **PICTURE** clause of the output field is the same as the **PICTURE** clause of the input field, a **MOVE** operation duplicates input data at the output area.

The above program will access the files, read a card, process it by moving input data to the output area, and write a record. Most COBOL programs, however, operate on more than one input record. We may assume that programs are written only if there is a reasonable amount of input data to be processed.

The program, then, must be modified to accept more than one input card. In effect, we wish to repeat all the steps of the program after the first output record is written. After **WRITE TAPE-REC**, a **branch** to the **READ** statement must be performed.

Note that we do not return to the **OPEN** statement, since files are only accessed **once** in the program. After the file has been opened, data may be read or written repeatedly.

A **branch** instruction, you will recall, has the following format:

GO TO (paragraph name)

Example

GO TO START

The **GO TO** statement transfers control to the paragraph name indicated. At some point in the program, there must be a paragraph with the specified name; for example, **START** must be a paragraph name in the program. Since we wish to execute the **READ** instruction after a **WRITE TAPE-REC** has been performed, we place the name **START** at that point.

The above program, modified to repeat the reading and processing of cards, is coded as follows:

Sample

```
PROCEDURE DIVISION.
    OPEN INPUT CARD-FILE, OUTPUT
    TAPE-FILE.
START.
    READ CARD-FILE AT END GO TO EOJ.
    MOVE NAME-IN TO NAME-OUT.
    MOVE AMT-OF-CREDIT-IN TO
    AMT-OF-CREDIT-OUT
    MOVE AMT-OF-DEBIT-IN TO
    AMT-OF-DEBIT-OUT
    WRITE TAPE-REC.
    GO TO START.
```

Note that for each **GO TO** (paragraph name), there must be a corresponding line with the specified paragraph name; that is, **GO TO START** is only valid if there is a paragraph called **START** in the program.

You see that paragraph names are coded in Margin A. The rules for forming paragraph names conform to programmer-supplied word formats with one exception. A programmer-supplied word must have at least one alphabetic character; a paragraph name may contain all digits. Generally, however, paragraph names should indicate something about the statements within the paragraph. For example, **ADD-ROUTINE, EOJ, INITIALIZE-RTN** are commonly used names. Paragraph names may appear on an independent line, as in the above example, or they may be placed on a line with an instruction. In either case, a paragraph name is directly followed by a period. If it appears on the same line as an instruction, a space must follow the period. The following two routines, coded slightly differently, perform the same functions.

Method 1

Method 2

```
    OPEN INPUT CARD-FILE, OUTPUT
    PRINT-FILE.
START.
    READ CARD-FILE AT END GO TO EOJ.
    MOVE NAME-IN TO NAME-OUT.
    WRITE PRINT-REC.
    GO TO START.
```

In each case, the statement to be performed after the branch is a **READ** statement. Note that there must be only **one** paragraph called **START** in the program; that is, the paragraph name must be unique and may not appear anywhere else in the program.

Suppose an error were made and the paragraph name **START followed** the **READ** statement instead of preceding it:

```
    OPEN INPUT CARD-FILE, OUTPUT
    PRINT-FILE.
    READ CARD-FILE AT END GO TO EOJ.
START.
    MOVE NAME-IN TO NAME-OUT.
    WRITE PRINT-REC.
    GO TO START.
```

This program reads only **one** card. Note that the **READ** command is executed after the files are opened, the name is moved to the output area, and a record is printed. Since instructions are executed in the order in which they appear, the branch instruction does not transfer control to the **READ** statement but to the **MOVE** instruction. Thus **NAME-IN**, which is the name on the first card, is again moved to the output area and a record is created.

Thus we are printing the same name from the first card repeatedly. This sort of processing creates an **infinite loop**. Unless the computer operator observes the error and manually stops the run, the computer will print the same name indefinitely.

```
       OPEN  INPUT  CARD-FILE,  OUTPUT  PRINT-FILE.
START. READ  CARD-FILE  AT  END  GO  TO  EOJ.
       MOVE  NAME-IN  TO  NAME-OUT.
       WRITE  PRINT-REC.
       GO  TO  START.
```

Examine the following illustration:

READ FILE-1 AT END GO TO EOJ.
GO TO NEXT-STEP.
NEXT-STEP. MOVE NAME-IN TO NAME-OUT.

The GO TO NEXT-STEP instruction is entirely unnecessary. Without a GO TO statement, the computer will execute the next sequential instruction; that is, the MOVE statement, in our example, will be executed next. Therefore a GO TO command which transfers control to the next statement is superfluous, since the computer will proceed to that step anyway.

E. END OF JOB FUNCTIONS

We are almost ready to write **complete** COBOL programs. You will note, however, that for each GO TO statement in the program, there must be a corresponding paragraph name indicated. In the example of the last section, READ CARD-FILE AT END GO TO EOJ violates this rule. EOJ, as part of a GO TO command, must be a paragraph specified somewhere in the program. In our example, it was not. Thus we must label a paragraph EOJ and instruct the computer what to do when there are no more cards. At that point, we will have completed the sample program.

There are **two** statements which are a necessary part of every End of Job routine. We must first CLOSE all files to indicate that they are no longer needed for processing, and we must instruct the computer to STOP.

CLOSE. Files must be accessed by an OPEN statement before data may be read or written. A CLOSE statement is necessary at the end of the job to release these files. We say:

```
CLOSE (file name(s)).
```

All files that have been opened must be closed at the end of a job. The CLOSE statement, like the OPEN instruction, will perform additional functions. When creating tape records, for example, CLOSE TAPE-OUT will automatically create trailer labels and rewind the tape.

Note that a CLOSE statement, unlike an OPEN command, does **not** denote which files are input and which are output. We say, for example, OPEN INPUT TAPE-IN OUTPUT CARD-OUT to access the files but, to release them, we say CLOSE TAPE-IN, CARD-OUT. Distinguishing between input and output files is essential **before** processing commences but is not meaningful when the job is being terminated.

As with an OPEN statement, the following two routines are equivalent:

EOJ.   CLOSE CARD-IN, TAPE-1,
            PRINT-OUT.
and
EOJ.   CLOSE CARD-IN.
        CLOSE TAPE-1.
        CLOSE PRINT-OUT.

Unless files are closed at different points in the program, the latter method is considered inefficient.

STOP RUN. The STOP RUN command, as the statement implies, instructs the computer to terminate the job. All programs should end with a STOP RUN statement.

Our complete PROCEDURE DIVISION, then, is as follows (Fig. 6-4 illustrates the first three divisions):

PROCEDURE DIVISION.
        OPEN INPUT CARD-FILE, OUTPUT
        TAPE-FILE.
START.
        READ CARD-FILE AT END GO TO EOJ.
        MOVE NAME-IN TO NAME-OUT.
        MOVE AMT-OF-CREDIT-IN TO
        AMT-OF-CREDIT-OUT
        MOVE AMT-OF-DEBIT-IN TO
        AMT-OF-DEBIT-OUT
        WRITE TAPE-REC.
        GO TO START.
EOJ.
        CLOSE CARD-FILE, TAPE-FILE.
        STOP RUN.

Note that execution proceeds to the next sequential step unless a **GO TO** statement is performed. The normal flow of this program will proceed from the reading of a card to the processing of the card (**MOVE** instructions) to the writing of a record. A branch will cause the flow to be repeated. This sequence will be continued until there are no more cards, at which point a branch to **EOJ** occurs. The statements at the paragraph called **EOJ** are only performed after the last card has been processed.

We have discussed the two essential instructions of an end of job routine. They need not, however, be the only ones. If specific totals are required, for example, to indicate the number of records processed, this would be performed at **EOJ** before the files are closed.

The following illustration utilizes all the rules we have learned thus far but with a slightly different presentation.

Example Problem. To print data from a card file and then print additional information from a tape file:

```
PROCEDURE  DIVISION.
      OPEN INPUT CARD-FILE, OUTPUT
      PRINT-FILE.
START.
      READ CARD-FILE AT END GO TO EOJ1.
      MOVE NAME-IN TO NAME-OUT.
      MOVE SALARY-IN TO SALARY-OUT.
      WRITE PRINT-REC.
      GO TO START.
EOJ1.
      CLOSE CARD-FILE.
      OPEN INPUT TAPE-FILE.
START2.
      READ TAPE-FILE AT END GO TO EOJ2.
      MOVE TAPE-SALARY TO SALARY-OUT.
      MOVE TAPE-NAME TO NAME-OUT.
      WRITE PRINT-REC.
      GO TO START2.
EOJ2.
      CLOSE TAPE-FILE, PRINT-FILE.
      STOP RUN.
```

Note that there are really two separate procedures illustrated. The first major routine handles card data **only**. When there are no more cards, the **CARD-FILE** is closed and the next file, **TAPE-FILE**, is opened. Then the second routine begins, processing tape data **only**. It would have been correct to open both input files, **CARD-FILE** and **TAPE-FILE**, at the beginning and, similarly, to close them both at the end instead of treating each individually. The program flow, however, suggests that, since each file is operated upon independently, opening and closing them individually would be more meaningful.

In this chapter, we have learned how to code instructions in the **PROCEDURE DIVISION**. Operations fall into two broad categories.

Input/Output:

> OPEN
> READ
> WRITE
> CLOSE

Such statements are **necessary** in all programs that operate on input data to produce output. Note that each statement operates on the **file names,** except the **WRITE** statement which operates on the **record names.**

Processing:

> MOVE
> GO TO
> STOP RUN

These statements, although not essential in all programs, are among the operations that are the most often used. With the two categories of COBOL instructions above, complete COBOL programs, on the elementary level, may be coded.

Understanding of this chapter and the previous ones is essential for writing programs. The format or structure of such programs will now be assumed. The remainder of the book will enlarge upon the structure and the operations that may be used.

EXERCISES

1. To transmit data from one field of storage to another, the
    _____ statement is used.

    *****

    MOVE

2. To obtain the same data at the output area that appears in the
    input area, the _____ clause of both fields should be identical.

    *****

    PICTURE

3. An unconditional branch instruction in COBOL is coded by a
    _____ statement.

    *****

    GO TO

4. If GO TO STEP-5 is a statement in the program, STEP-5 is a _____,
    which must appear in Margin __.

    *****

    paragraph name
    A

5. Paragraph names (must, need not) be unique within a program.

    *****

    must

6. In general, execution will proceed to the _____ unless a _____
    statement is performed.

    *****

    next sequential step
    GO TO

7. Two statements that are a required part of the end of job routine
    are _____ and _____.

    *****

    CLOSE
    STOP RUN

8. For every file that is opened, a _____ statement must appear
    at the end of job routine.

    *****

    CLOSE

9. CLOSE INPUT CARD-IN (is, is not) valid.

    *****

    is not (**Note:** Input or output is not specified with CLOSE state-
    ments.)

10. A STOP RUN operation _____.

    *****

    terminates the job

REVIEW QUESTIONS

1. When the computer encounters a **READ** command in the **PROCE- DURE DIVISION,** how does it know which of its input units to activate?

2. Give two functions of the **OPEN** statement.

3. When are paragraph names assigned in the **PROCEDURE DIVISION?**

4. State which of the following, if any, are invalid paragraph-names:
   (a) INPUT-RTN
   (b) MOVE
   (c) 123
   (d) %-RTN

5. If a **READ** statement is used for a sequential file, what clause is required? Why?

   Make necessary corrections to each of the following (6–10). As- sume that spacing and margin use are correct:

6. OPEN MASTER-IN, MASTER-OUT.

7. PROCEDURE DIVISION
   START
      OPEN INPUT OLD-FILE, OUTPUT NEW-FILE
   UPDATE-RTN.
      READ OLD-REC AT END GO TO EOJ.
      MOVE OLD-REC TO NEW-REC.
      WRITE NEW-REC.

8. CLOSE INPUT FILE-A, OUTPUT FILE-B.

9. WRITE REC-A AT END GO TO EOJ.

10. START.
       OPEN INPUT X, OUTPUT Y.
       READ X AT END GO TO EOJ.
       MOVE FLDA TO FLDB.
       WRITE X-REC.
       GO TO START.

PROBLEMS

1. Write a program to create a master tape file from input sales records. The input is on punched card in the following format:

SALESMAN NAME	SALESMAN CODE			YEAR TO DATE FIGURES			CURRENT		
	REGION NO.	OFFICE NO.	BADGE NO.	QUOTA xxxx.xx	SALES xxxx.xx	Commission xxxx.xx	QUOTA	SALES	COMM.

```
1          20 21   22 23   24 25   26 27   32 33   38 39   44 45   50 51   56 57   62 63   80
```

The output is on magnetic tape which contains standard labels and is blocked 20. The output format is exactly the same as the input.

2. Write a program to punch output salary cards from the following input employee record card:

ccs 1–20	Employee name
21–25	Salary
26	Number of dependents
27–31	F.I.C.A. (xxx.xx)
32–37	State tax (xxxx.xx)
38–43	Federal tax (xxxx.xx)
44–80	Unused

The output contains only employee name and salary as its first two fields. The remainder of the output card should be blank. (**Hint.** You must move **SPACES** to output record to insure that the **FILLER** in the last 55 positions is blank.)

3. Write a program to print all information from the following sales card:

SALESMAN NAME	SALESMAN CODE			YEAR TO DATE FIG.			CURRENT FIGURES		
	REGION NO.	OFFICE NO.	BADGE NO.	QUOTA	SALES	COMMISION	QUOTA	SALES	COMMISSION

```
1       20 21    22 23    24 25    26 27   31 32  36 37        41 42   46 47  51 52        56 57  80
```

The printed form should contain blank spaces between fields for "readability." You may position fields in any way you choose on the output.

4. Write a program to create one master tape record for every group of two input data cards. The input consists of two types of records:

Credit Record		Debit Record	
1–20	Customer name	1–20	Customer name
21–25	Amount of credit	21–40	Address
	xxx.xx	41–45	Amount of debit
26–80	Not used		xxx.xx
		46–80	Not used

Each transaction will have both records as input. The credit record for a customer will **always** be followed by a debit record for the customer. One output record will be created from the two input records. The output format is as follows:

1–20	Customer name
21–40	Address
41–45	Amount of debit
	xxx.xx
46–50	Amount of credit
	xxx.xx

The output tape is blocked 25 and has standard labels.

5. **XYZ Utility Company** has the following master tape records:

NAME OF CUSTOMER	ADDRESS	KILOWATT HRS. OF ELECTRICITY USED	GAS USED	ELEC. BILL XXX.XX	GAS BILL XXX.XX	
1	20 21	40 41	45 46	50 51	55 56	60 61 75

The records are blocked 10 and have standard labels. Write a program to create two punched cards (bills) for each input record. The format of the two output cards is as follows:

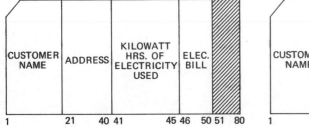
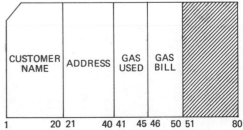

6. Two input tape files are used to create one output master tape file. The format for the two input files is as follows:

File 1		File 2	
1–20	Employee name	1–20	Employee name
21–40	Address	21–40	Address
41–43	Hours worked	41–45	Salary
44–46	Wages x.xx	46	No. of dependents
47	No. of dependents	47–51	F.I.C.A. xxx.xx
48–52	F.I.C.A. xxx.xx	52–57	Fed. tax xxxx.xx
53–58	Fed. tax xxxx.xx	58–63	State tax xxxx.xx
59–64	State tax xxxx.xx	64	Unused

The format for the output file is the same as the input files.

Write a program to write on the output file all records from file 1 and **then** all records from file 2. All files have standard labels. Blocking factor = 30.

7. Modify Problem 6 to write on tape **first** a record from file 1 and then a record from file 2. Alternate this way until records from both files are all processed. Assume that file 1 and file 2 have the same number of records.

Unit 2

7

The Move Statement

A. A BASIC APPROACH

A basic format for the **MOVE** statement is

MOVE FIELDA TO FIELDB

In the above COBOL sentence or statement, **MOVE** is called the **verb.** Every COBOL statement that appears in the **PROCEDURE DIVISION**, like every English sentence, must contain a verb. The data-name **FIELDA** is called the **sending field.** The contents of **FIELDA** will be transmitted, or sent, to another field (**FIELDB**) as a result of the **MOVE** operation. The data-name **FIELDB** is called the **receiving field.** The contents of **FIELDB** will be replaced by another field (**FIELDA**) as a result of the **MOVE** operation.

The result, then, of the **MOVE** operation is obvious. The information, or contents, stored at the sending field, **FIELDA,** will be moved to the receiving field, **FIELDB.**

Note that the **MOVE** statement is part of the **PROCEDURE DIVISION**. All COBOL operational verbs appear only in the **PROCEDURE DIVISION. FIELDA** and **FIELDB,** however, are data-names and as such must be defined in the **DATA DIVISION**. You will recall that data-names in the **DATA DIVISION** are referenced by **PICTURE** clauses to indicate the kind of data in the field (numeric, alphanumeric or alpha-

betic) and the size of the field. To perform a **MOVE** operation which replaces **FIELDB** with the **very same contents** as **FIELDA,** the **PICTURE** clauses of both fields must be identical.

Example 1

TAXA   PICTURE 999
      (numeric—three positions)
      Contents 123

TAXB   PICTURE 999
      Contents 456

If the statement **MOVE TAXA TO TAXB** is performed, **TAXB** will be replaced by 123, the contents of **TAXA.** This will occur only if **TAXA** and **TAXB** have the identical **PICTURE** clause (in this case, **999**). The original content of **TAXB,** 456, is lost during the **MOVE** operation. When moving a sending field to a receiving field, the original content of the receiving field is always destroyed.

Note, also, that data is not physically moved from the sending to the receiving field but, instead, is **transmitted** from one field to the other; that is, the content of the sending field, **TAXA,** in the above case, is duplicated at the receiving field, **TAXB.** At the end of the operation, both fields will have the same contents. Thus, the content of **TAXA** is **not** erased during the operation. **TAXA** remains unchanged;

its content is transmitted, or duplicated, at TAXB.

Example 2

FIELDA   PICTURE XXXX
        (alphanumeric—four positions)
        Contents ABCD

FIELDB   PICTURE XXXX
        Contents EFGH

If the operation MOVE FIELDA TO FIELDB is performed, FIELDB has ABCD as its contents and, also, FIELDA remains with ABCD. Since both fields have the same PICTURE clause, they are identical at the end of the operation.

EXERCISES

Use the following statement to answer Questions 1–6:

MOVE FIELD1 TO FIELD2

1. MOVE is called the _____.
   FIELD1 is called the _____.
   FIELD2 is called the _____.
   *****
   verb or operation
   sending field
   receiving field

2. The MOVE statement appears only in the _____ DIVISION while FIELD1 and FIELD2 must be defined in the _____ DIVISION, with corresponding _____ clauses.
   *****
   PROCEDURE
   DATA
   PICTURE

3. To duplicate the exact information of FIELD1 at FIELD2, both fields must have the same _____ clauses.
   *****
   PICTURE

4. A PICTURE clause indicates numeric data by _____, alphanumeric data by _____, and alphabetic data by _____.
   *****
   9's
   X's
   A's

5. The number of 9's, X's or A's in a PICTURE clause indicates the _____ of a data-field.
   *****
   size

6. Assume **FIELD1** has contents of 128, **FIELD2** has contents of 736, and both fields have the same **PICTURE** clause. At the end of the **MOVE** operation, **FIELD2** has _____ as its contents and **FIELD1** has _____ as its contents.

*****

128

128 (Note: The contents of a sending field remain unchanged in a **MOVE** operation.)

B. THE FORMATS OF THE MOVE STATEMENT

We have thus far discussed one form of the **MOVE** statement:

Format 1

MOVE (data-name-1) TO (data-name-2)

In this case, data-name-1 and data-name-2 must be given specifications in the **DATA DIVISION**. To obtain in data-name-2 the same contents as in data-name-1, the **PICTURE** clauses of both fields are assumed to be the same.

A second form of the **MOVE** statement is as follows:

Format 2

MOVE (literal) TO (data-name)

Recall that there are two kinds of literals, numeric and nonnumeric. A numeric literal is a constant consisting of all numbers, possibly a decimal point and a sign. An alphanumeric or nonnumeric literal is a constant enclosed in quotation marks and consisting of any character except a quote.

The following are examples of **MOVE** statements in Format 2:

Example 1: MOVE 123 TO FIELD1.

Example 2: MOVE 'CODE1' TO FIELD2.

Although data-names must be defined in the **DATA DIVISION**, literals need not be defined elsewhere in the COBOL program. Assuming correct **PICTURE** clauses in the receiving field, the exact form of the literal will be placed in that field. Keep in mind that the receiving field is **always** a data-name. In Example 1, the literal 123 is a numeric literal. We know that it is a literal and not a data-name because it contains all numbers, while data-names must have at least one alphabetic character. To move a numeric literal to a data-field, we require that the field have the same format as the literal, namely, that it be a numeric field. Thus, in Example 1, **FIELD1** must have a **PICTURE** of 9's. To obtain exactly 123 in **FIELD1**, **FIELD1** should have a **PICTURE** of **999**, to indicate that it is a three-position numeric field.

In Example 2, 'CODE1' is a nonnumeric literal. We know that it is not a data-name because it is enclosed in quotation marks. To move this literal to a data-field, we require that the data-field have the same format as the literal, namely, that it be an alphanumeric field. Thus, in Example 2, **FIELD2** must have a **PICTURE** of X's to indicate that it is alphanumeric. To obtain exactly 'CODE1' as the contents of **FIELD2**, **FIELD2** must have a **PICTURE** clause of X(5) to indicate that it is a five-position field.

To say: **MOVE 123 TO ADDRESS**, would be incorrect if **ADDRESS** had a **PICTURE** of **XXX**. The literal must be in the same mode as the receiving field. In the above case, the literal must be nonnumeric. Thus **MOVE '123' TO ADDRESS** would be correct.

A third form of the **MOVE** statement is as follows:

Format 3

MOVE (figurative constant) TO
(data-name)

You will recall that a figurative constant is a COBOL reserved word, such as SPACES or ZERO, having a specific value.

Example 3: MOVE ZEROS TO FIELD3.

Example 4: MOVE SPACES TO FIELD4.

In Example 4, SPACES is a figurative constant meaning all blanks. Since blanks are not valid numeric characters, the PICTURE clause of FIELD4 must be X's, indicating an alphanumeric field, or A's, indicating an alphabetic field. Again, the size of FIELD4 is unimportant since all blanks will be placed in it regardless of its length.

Thus, there are three formats for the MOVE statement:

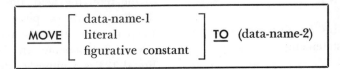

In Example 3, ZEROS is a figurative constant, meaning all 0's. Since 0 is a valid numeric character and also a valid alphanumeric character, FIELD3 may be numeric, having a PICTURE of 9's, or alphanumeric, having a PICTURE of X's. In either case, FIELD3 will be replaced with all zeros. The size of FIELD3 is unimportant; all zeros will be placed in that field regardless of its size.

The brackets indicate that any one of the three may be used as sending fields. The receiving field must always be a data name.

Note that any nonnumeric literal may be moved to an alphanumeric field. However, only those nonnumeric literals with alphabetic data or spaces may be moved to an alphabetic field.

EXERCISES

1. In a MOVE operation, the sending field may be a _____ or a _____ or a _____.
   *****
   literal
   data-name
   figurative constant

2. The two kinds of literals are _____ and _____.
   *****
   numeric
   nonnumeric

3. The receiving field in a MOVE operation is always a _____.
   *****
   data-name

   Use the statement below to answer Questions 4–6:

   MOVE A12 TO FIELD3

4. **A12** is a _____.
   *****
   data-name

5. **A12** cannot be a nonnumeric literal since it is not _____. **A12** is not a numeric literal since it _____.
   *****
   enclosed in quotation marks
   has an alphabetic character

6. If the data-name **A12** has contents of 453, _____ will be moved to **FIELD3** and **A12** will have _____ as its contents at the end of the operation.
   *****
   453
   453

   Use the statement below to answer Questions 7–11:

   MOVE 'AB1' TO FIELD6.

7. The sending field is a _____.
   *****
   nonnumeric literal

8. The sending field cannot be a data-name since it is _____.
   *****
   enclosed in quotation marks

9. Assuming a correct **PICTURE** clause in **FIELD6**, the contents of **FIELD6** will be _____ at the end of the operation.
   *****
   AB1

10. To obtain exactly AB1 in **FIELD6**, the **PICTURE** clause of the receiving field should be _____.
    *****
    XXX or **X(3)**

11. **'AB1'** (is, is not) defined in the **DATA DIVISION**.
    *****
    is not (**Note:** Literals appearing in the **PROCEDURE DIVISION** need not be defined elsewhere in the program.)

    Use the statement below to answer Questions 12–15:
    MOVE 12384 TO SAM

12. The sending field is a _____.
    *****
    numeric literal

13. The sending field must be a numeric literal and not a data-name since it _____.
    *****
    contains no alphabetic character

14. Assuming **SAM** has the correct **PICTURE** clause to accept the sending field, the contents of **SAM** at the end of the operation will be

    _____.

    *****

    12384

15. To obtain exactly 12384 in **SAM**, its **PICTURE** clause must be

    _____.

    *****

    99999 or 9(5)

16. In the operation **MOVE SPACES TO FIELDA**, SPACES is a _____,
    and **FIELDA** must have an _____ **PICTURE** clause. The contents
    of **FIELDA** will be replaced with _____ at the end of the opera-
    tion.
    *****

    figurative constant
    alphanumeric or alphabetic
    blanks or spaces

17. In the operation **MOVE ZEROS TO FIELDA**, FIELDA may have _____
    PICTURE clause. **FIELDA** will be replaced with _____.
    *****

    alphanumeric or numeric (**Note:** Zero is a valid numeric and
                              alphanumeric character.)

    0's

18. In the operation **MOVE 'SPACES' TO FIELDA**, FIELDA having a PIC-
    TURE of X(6), 'SPACES' is a _____. The contents of **FIELDA** will
    be _____ at the end of the operation.
    *****

    nonnumeric literal (**Note:** It is enclosed in quotes.)
    the word SPACES

C. NUMERIC MOVE

The relative complexity of the **MOVE** statement necessitates two classifications: numeric **MOVE** operations and alphanumeric **MOVE** operations.[1] We will leave the discussion of the alphanumeric **MOVE** until the next section.

A **numeric MOVE operation** means (1) the movement of a numeric field, defined by a **PICTURE** of 9's to another numeric field or (2) the movement of a numeric literal to a numeric field.

[1] We will not discuss the **alphabetic** moves, since they conform to the same rules as alpha-numeric move operations. The only distinction is that, in an alphabetic move, only letters or blanks may be transmitted and not special characters.

1. **MOVE** (data-name-1) **TO**
       (data-name-2).
   Both fields have numeric **PICTURE** clauses.

Assuming the size of both fields to be identical, data-name-2 will be replaced with the contents of data-name-1, without changing the sending field.

Example 1

FIELDA   PICTURE 999
         Contents 123

FIELDB   PICTURE 999
         Contents 456

Operation: MOVE FIELDA TO FIELDB

Example 2

FIELDC   PICTURE 99V99   (implied dec-
                          imal point
                          after first two
                          digits)

         Contents 12$\overset{\wedge}{3}$4   (to be inter-
                          preted as
                          12.34)

FIELDD   PICTURE 99V99
         Contents 45$\overset{\wedge}{6}$7

Operation: MOVE FIELDC TO FIELDD

The first example, as was illustrated in the previous section, places the same contents of FIELDA, 123, in FIELDB.

Although it is not quite as obvious in Example 2, the receiving field again acquires the very same contents as the sending field, 1234, to be interpreted as 12.34. (You will recall that the decimal point does not actually appear in core.) In other words, the MOVE operation maintains decimal alignment.

Often in a COBOL program, it will be necessary to move one numeric field to another, where the size of the two fields differs. You might want to move a field to a larger one to perform an arithmetic operation on it, or to move a work area field with precision of three decimal places (V999) to an output area, which requires precision of only two decimal places (V99). In both these cases, the MOVE operation will **not** produce in the receiving field the same contents as the sending field, since the size of the two fields differs.

Two rules will apply in all numeric MOVE operations—one for the movement of the integer portion of a number, and one for the decimal or fractional portion.

Rule 1: When moving an integer sending field or an integer **portion** of the sending field to the receiving field, movement is from **right** to **left**. All nonfilled high-order (leftmost) integer positions of the receiving field are filled with zeros.

Example 3

FIELD1   PICTURE 999
         Contents 123

FIELD2   PICTURE 9(4)
         Contents 4567

Operation: MOVE FIELD1 TO FIELD2

According to Rule 1, movement is from right to left:

(a) The 3 in FIELD1 replaces the 7 in FIELD2.
(b) The 2 in FIELD1 replaces the 6 in FIELD2.
(c) The 1 in FIELD1 replaces the 5 in FIELD2.

and all nonfilled high-order positions are filled with zeros:

(d) 0 replaces the 4 in FIELD2.

Thus we obtain 0123 in FIELD2. No portion of the original contents of the receiving field is maintained after the MOVE is performed.

Example 4

FIELD3   PICTURE 999
         Contents 012

FIELD4   PICTURE 99
         Contents 34

Operation: MOVE FIELD3 TO FIELD4.

(a) The 2 of FIELD3 will replace the 4 of FIELD4.
(b) The 1 of FIELD3 will replace the 3 of FIELD4.

The operation will terminate at this point, since the receiving field is thus filled. FIELD4 will have contents of 12, while FIELD3 will remain unchanged.

A good rule-of-thumb to follow in numeric MOVE operations is to be sure that the receiving field has at least as many whole number (integer) positions as the sending field. If the receiving field is **larger** than the sending field, the high-order positions of the former will be replaced with zeros, which do **not** affect the result. If, however, the receiving field is **smaller** than the sending field, you may inadvertently truncate the most significant digits.

Example 5

  TAKE-HOME-PAY   PICTURE 9(4)
                           Contents 1000

  AMT-OF-CHECK   PICTURE 999

Operation: MOVE TAKE-HOME-PAY TO AMT-OF-CHECK

In the above example, the receiving field is only three positions long. Since movement of integer positions is from right to left, 000 will be placed in **AMT-OF-CHECK**. It is clear that the check's recipient will not be pleased. To avoid such difficulties, be sure that the receiving field is at least as large as the sending field.

We will now consider the movement of fields that have fractional components, that is, numeric fields with implied decimal positions.

Rule 2: When moving a decimal or fractional portion of the sending field to the receiving field, movement is from left to right, beginning at the implied decimal point. Low-order (rightmost) nonfilled decimal positions are filled with zeros.

Example 6

  FLDA   PICTURE 99V99
           Contents 1234

  FLDB   PICTURE 99V999
           Contents 56789

Operation: MOVE FLDA TO FLDB

The integer portion of **FLDA** replaces the integer portion of **FLDB**, according to Rule 1. The decimal portion of each field is as follows:

$$\boxed{3}\boxed{4} \qquad \boxed{7}\boxed{8}\boxed{9}$$
    FLDA   FLDB

According to Rule 2, movement from the implied decimal point on is from left to right:

(a) The 3 of **FLDA** replaces the 7 of **FLDB**.

(b) The 4 of **FLDA** replaces the 8 of **FLDB**.

Low-order nonfilled decimal positions of the receiving field are zero-filled:

(c) 0 replaces the 9 of **FLDB**.

Thus we have

$$\boxed{1}\boxed{2}\boxed{3}\boxed{4}\boxed{0}$$
FLDB

Example 7

  FLDC   PICTURE V99
           Contents 12

  FLDD   PICTURE V9
           Contents 3

Operation: MOVE FLDC TO FLDD

In Example 7, movement, from the implied decimal point on, is from left to right. Thus the 1 of **FLDC** replaces the 3 of **FLDD**. The operation is terminated at this point since **FLDD** is only one position.

Example 8

  FLDE   PICTURE 999V9
           Contents 1234

  FLDF   PICTURE 99
           Contents 00

Operation: MOVE FLDE TO FLDF

Since integer movement is from right to left, the 3 of **FLDE** replaces the low-order 0 and the 2 of **FLDE** replaces the high-order zero. Since there are no more integer positions in the receiving field, that portion is terminated. The operation itself is terminated at this point, since there are no decimal positions in **FLDF**. Thus the content of **FLDF** is 23.

The second form of a numeric **MOVE** is as follows:

2. <u>MOVE</u> (literal) <u>TO</u> (data-name) where the literal and the data-name are both numeric.

The two rules specified above apply in this type of numeric move:

Example 9

FLD1   PICTURE 9(4)

Operation: MOVE 123 TO FLD1

Since we are concerned with integers in Example 9, movement is from right to left and high-order positions of the receiving field are replaced with zeros. Thus we obtain 0123 in FLD1. Treat the literal 123 as if it were FLDZ with a PICTURE of 999, contents 123, and proceed as in Case 1; that is, MOVE FLDZ TO FLD1 is performed. This can be applied to movement of all numeric literals.

Example 10

FLD2 PICTURE 99

Operation: MOVE 123 TO FLD2.

In this case, truncation occurs because the receiving field cannot accommodate the entire sending field. Since movement is from right to left, FLD2 becomes 23. This would be the same result if the operation were MOVE FLDZ TO FLD2, where FLDZ had a PICTURE of 999, contents 123. The truncation that occurs is undesirable since the most significant digit, the hundreds place, is not transmitted to the receiving field.

Example 11

FLD3   PICTURE 99V999

Operation: MOVE 12.34 TO FLD3

Note that a numeric literal is expressed with a decimal point where intended, while it is only implied in the data-field (FLD3). The integer positions of the sending field are transmitted with a result of 12 in those positions of FLD3. Movement from the implied decimal point on is from left to right, the result being 34 in the first two decimal positions of FLD3. Non-filled low-order decimal positions of FLD3 are zero-filled. Thus we obtain ⎡1⎢2⎢3⎢4⎢0⎤ in FLD3. Note again that the result is the same is if we had performed the operation MOVE FLDZ TO FLD3, where FLDZ had a PICTURE of 99V99, and contents 1234.

It should be clear at this point that the numeric MOVE operation functions exactly the same whether the sending field is a literal or a data-name. Treat a numeric literal as if it were a data field in core storage, and proceed according to Rules 1 and 2.

WORK PROBLEMS

1. When moving integer portions of sending fields to receiving fields, movement is from _____ to _____. High-order integer positions, which are not filled, are replaced with _____.
   *****
   right
   left
   zero

2. When moving decimal portions of sending fields to receiving fields, movement is from _____ to _____. Low-order decimal positions of the receiving fields are replaced with _____.
   *****
   left
   right
   zero

Use the following statement to complete Questions 3–8:

MOVE TAX TO TOTAL

	TAX PICTURE	TAX Contents	TOTAL PICTURE	TOTAL Contents (at end of operation)
3.	99V99	10ˬ35	999V999	_____
4.	99V9	37ˬ2	999	_____
5.	9(4)	1234	999	_____
6.	V99	ˬ12	V9	_____
7.	99V99	02ˬ34	9V9	_____
8.	9V9	1ˬ2	_____	2ˬ0

*****

010ˬ350
037
234
ˬ1
2ˬ3
V99

9. The particular statement or question from the above group that might give undesirable results is _____.

*****

5—truncation of the high-order significant digit occurs

10. The operation **MOVE 12.487 TO WORK** is performed. To obtain the **exact** form of the literal in the field called **WORK**, its **PICTURE** clause must be _____.

*****

99V999

Use the following statement to complete Questions 11–16:

MOVE 12.35 TO AREA-1

	AREA-1 PICTURE	AREA-1 Contents
11.	999V99	_____
12.	999V9	_____
13.	999V999	_____
14.	9V9	_____
15.	V999	_____
16.	_____	012ˬ3

*****

012ˬ35
012ˬ3
012ˬ350
2ˬ3
ˬ350
999V9

17. In a numeric **MOVE** operation, there (are, are not) instances when some **significant** portion of the receiving field is retained and not replaced with something else.

*****

are **not** (**Note: All** positions of the receiving field are replaced either with positions of the sending field or with zeros.)

D. ALPHANUMERIC MOVE

You will recall that the **MOVE** operation was separated into two categories: **numeric MOVE** and **alphanumeric MOVE**. The latter will be discussed in this section.

By an alphanumeric **MOVE** operation, we mean (1) the movement of an alphanumeric field, defined by a **PICTURE** of **X**'s, to another alphanumeric field, or (2) the movement of an alphanumeric literal to an alphanumeric field, or (3) the movement of a numeric field to an alphanumeric field. As with numeric **MOVE** operations, the rule for alphanumeric moves will encompass all of the above classifications.

Rule: In an alphanumeric move, data is transmitted from the sending field to the receiving field from **left** to **right**. Low-order positions of the receiving field, which are not filled, are replaced with spaces or blanks.

Example 1

    FLDA   PICTURE XXX
           Contents ABC

    FLDB   PICTURE X(5)
           Contents DEFGH

Operation: MOVE FLDA TO FDLB

According to the rule, data is transmitted from left to right. Thus:

(a) The A of **FLDA** replaces the D of **FLDB**.

(b) The B of **FLDA** replaces the E of **FLDB**.

(c) The C of **FLDA** replaces the F of **FLDB**.

Low-order positions of **FLDB** are replaced with spaces. Thus:

(d) A blank replaces the G of **FLDB**.

(e) A blank replaces the H of **FLDB**.

We are left with $\boxed{\text{A}|\text{B}|\text{C}|\ \ |\ \ }$ in **FLDB**. Again, no portion of the receiving field is retained after the move.

The effect of the above operation would have been the same if the following were performed: **MOVE 'ABC' TO FLDB**. We have replaced a data-name with a nonnumeric literal having the same contents, and the result is identical.

Example 2

    CODE   PICTURE X(4)
           Contents NAME

    OUT-AREA   PICTURE XXX
               Contents SPACES

Operation: MOVE CODE TO OUT-AREA.

In this case:

(a) The N of **CODE** replaces the leftmost blank of **OUT-AREA**.

(b) The A of **CODE** replaces the middle blank of **OUT-AREA**.

(c) The M of **CODE** replaces the rightmost blank of **OUT-AREA**.

The operation is terminated at this point, since the entire receiving field is filled. Again we experience truncation, but of **rightmost** characters. As in the case of numeric moves, truncation will be avoided if the receiving field is at least as large as the sending field. The result would have been the same if the following were performed: **MOVE 'NAME' TO OUT-AREA.**

Example 3

FLDA PICTURE 999
Contents 321

FLDB PICTURE XXXX
Contents DCBA

Operation: MOVE FLDA TO FLDB

Note that although FLDA is numeric, this is considered to be an alphanumeric MOVE operation. The resultant field determines the type of move.

(a) The 3 of FLDA replaces the D of FLDB.
(b) The 2 of FLDA replaces the C of FLDB.
(c) The 1 of FLDA replaces the B of FLDB.
(d) A space replaces the A of FLDB.

You may have observed that, although alphanumeric MOVE instructions encompass the movement of data from **numeric** to **alphanumeric** fields, no mention has been made of the reverse situation, the movement of alphanumeric to numeric fields. Suppose you know that FLDC, which has a PICTURE of X's, has numeric data. Can FLDC be moved to a numeric field? Similarly, can MOVE '123' TO FLDD be performed if FLDD has a picture of 9's? The question can be simplified. Is it permissible to move alphanumeric fields or literals to numeric receiving fields? The answer is unequivocably **no.** If you know that a field is numeric, define it with a PICTURE of 9's. **Never try to move alpha-**

numeric fields to numeric fields. The move will be performed by the computer, but the results will sometimes cause a "hang-up."

A matter of some importance in alphanumeric MOVE operations is the treatment of group items, or fields, that are further subdivided. It should be noted that **all** group items, even those with numeric subfields, are treated as alphanumeric fields.

Example

02 DATE.
   03 MONTH PICTURE 99.
   03 YEAR   PICTURE 99.

If MONTH or YEAR is moved to some other field, the movement is numeric. If, however, the programmer attempts to move DATE to some field, it will be treated as an alphanumeric field.

Below is a chart outlining the various MOVE operations. A check ($\sqrt{}$) denotes that the move is permissible; an X denotes that it is not.

Sending fields, you will note, are of six types. Numeric, alphabetic, and alphanumeric sending fields will denote datanames or literals. A numeric data field is moved in precisely the same manner as a numeric literal. The receiving fields are only of four types: numeric, alphabetic, alphanumeric, and group. These refer only to data fields. A literal or a figurative constant cannot serve as a receiving field.

Note that, when mixed formats appear, the MOVE operation, if permissible, is always in the mode of the receiving field.

Sending Field	Receiving Field			
	Numeric	Alphabetic	Alphanumeric	Group
Numeric	$\sqrt{}$	x	$\sqrt{}$	$\sqrt{}$
Alphabetic	x	$\sqrt{}$	$\sqrt{}$	$\sqrt{}$
Alphanumeric	x	$\sqrt{}$ᵃ	$\sqrt{}$	$\sqrt{}$
Zeros	$\sqrt{}$	x	$\sqrt{}$	$\sqrt{}$
Spaces	x	$\sqrt{}$	$\sqrt{}$	$\sqrt{}$
Group	x	$\sqrt{}$ᵃ	$\sqrt{}$	$\sqrt{}$

ᵃ Transmitting a group or alphanumeric field to an alphabetic field may produce undefined results and is definitely **not** recommended.

EXERCISES

1. In an alphanumeric move, information is transmitted from _____
to _____.
*****
left
right

2. If the receiving field is larger than the sending field, (right-, left-)
_____ most positions are replaced with _____.
*****
right-
spaces or blanks

Use the following statement to complete Questions 3–5:

MOVE FLD1 TO FLD2

	FLD1			FLD2	
	PICTURE	Contents		PICTURE	Contents
3.	X(4)	AB12		X(6)	_____
4.	X(4)	AB12		X(3)	_____
5.	XXX	ABC		_____	AB

*****
AB12ϕϕ   (ϕ denotes a blank)
AB1
XX

REVIEW QUESTIONS

In each of the following, determine the contents of the resultant
field:

	Sending Field		Receiving Field	
	PICTURE	Contents	PICTURE	Contents
1.	9(5)	12345	9(6)	
2.	99V99	12̰34	9(3)V9(3)	
3.	9V99	7̰89	9V9	
4.	999V9	678̰9	99V99	
5.	99	56	XX	
6.	99	56	XXX	
7.	XX	AB	XXX	
8.	X(4)	CODE	XXX	
9.	XXX	124	999	
10.	AAA	ABC	XXX	
11.	AAA	ABC	A(5)	

In each of the following, determine the contents of FLDX if the operation performed is:

MOVE 13.579 TO FLDX

	FLDX	
	PICTURE	Contents
12.	99V999	
13.	999V9(4)	
14.	9V99	
15.	99V9	

In each of the following determine the contents of FLDY after the following operation is performed:

MOVE 'NAME' TO FLDY

	FLDY	
	PICTURE	Contents
16.	XXXX	
17.	AAAA	
18.	AAA	
19.	A(5)	
20.	9999	

21. (T or F) Elementary items within a group item, although they are numeric, are treated as alphanumeric fields.

22. (T or F) Group items, although they contain elementary numeric items, are treated as alphanumeric fields.

PROBLEMS

1. Write a program to print data from a magnetic tape. The input is as follows:

   1–15 Customer name
   16–20 Customer number
   21–25 Amount of purchase (in dollars)

   Output should contain all input fields spaced across the line. Print heading on top of page: PURCHASE REPORT. The heading should also be spaced in the center of the form. In addition to the tape fields, print today's date (literal) on each line. The input contains standard labels and 15 records/block.

2. Using the following card record as input, print all fields on a single line. Spacing will be determined by the programmer. For readability, place a period between initials of the name, and a / between month and year of the date. Also print field headings at the top of the page. That is, print the word NAME above where the name fields will be printed, etc.

CUSTOMER NAME		DATE OF TRANSACTION		AMOUNT OF TRANS. (IN DOLLARS)	
INIT. 1	INIT. 2 LAST NAME	MONTH	YEAR		

1 2 3   20 21   22 23   24 25   30 31 80

3. Write a program to create one master tape record for every group of two input data cards. The input consists of two types of records:

Credit-record:	Debit-record:
1–20 Customer name	1–20 Customer name
21–25 Amount of credit	21–40 Address
26–80 Not used	41–45 Amount of debit xxx.xx
	46–80 Not used

Each transaction will have both records as input. One output record will be created from two input records. The output format is as follows:

1–25 Customer name
26–50 Address
51–60 Amount of debit (4 positions after implied decimal)
61–70 Amount of credit (4 positions after implied decimal)

Arithmetic Operations

A. ADD STATEMENT

A simple **ADD** statement has the following two formats:

Format 1

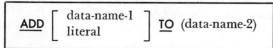

ADD [data-name-1 / literal] TO (data-name-2)

Format 2

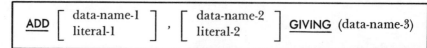

ADD [data-name-1 / literal-1] , [data-name-2 / literal-2] GIVING (data-name-3)

Examples

(1) ADD TAX TO DEDUCTIONS.
(2) ADD 15.80 TO TAX.
(3) ADD 1.20, AMOUNT GIVING TOTAL.
(4) ADD AMT1, AMT2 GIVING NET.

It is important to note that all operands (an operand is a data-field or a literal) specified must be numeric when used in an arithmetic statement. The computer will not perform an arithmetic operation on a nonnumeric field. Thus, in the examples above, all literals are numeric, and it is assumed that all data-names, when specified in the **DATA DIVISION**, have numeric **PICTURE** clauses.

The result, or sum, of an **ADD** operation is always placed in the last field specified. The **only** operand that is altered as a result of the **ADD** operation is this last field, which is the one directly following the word **TO**, when using Format 1, or **GIVING**, when using Format 2. Thus, in Example 1, the sum of **TAX** and **DEDUCTIONS** is placed in **DEDUCTIONS**. **TAX** remains with its original contents.

It is important to note at this point that **the resultant field must be a data-name**. It cannot be a literal. The statement **ADD HOURS-WORKED TO 40** is incorrect, since 40, which is the operand immediately following the word **TO** and therefore the resultant field, has an incorrect format. The word directly after **TO** or **GIVING** must be a data-name.

When using the **TO** format in an **ADD** statement, **all** the data-names and literals are added together, and the result is placed in the last field. When using the **GIVING** format, all fields and literals preceding the word **GIVING** are added together and the sum is placed in the last field. Note that, when using the **GIVING** format, the last data-field is **not** part of the **ADD** operation.

Example 5: ADD HOURS-WORKED TO WEEKLY-HOURS.

Both fields are added together; the sum is placed in WEEKLY-HOURS; HOURS-WORKED remains unchanged.

Example 6: ADD HOURS-WORKED, WEEKLY-HOURS GIVING TOTAL-HOURS.

The same addition is performed as in Example 5: HOURS-WORKED and WEEKLY-HOURS are summed. In this case, however, the result is placed in TOTAL-HOURS. The original contents of TOTAL-HOURS, preceding the ADD, is destroyed and does not in any way affect the operation.

Note that the COBOL words **TO** and **GIVING** may **not** be used in the same **ADD** operation. To say **ADD TAX TO NET GIVING TOTAL** is incorrect. The statement may be **ADD TAX TO NET**, in which case the result is placed in **NET**; or **ADD TAX, NET GIVING TOTAL**, in which case the result is placed in **TOTAL**.

The commas specified in the above statement, as all commas in a COBOL program, are available for clarity of expression but are not required. Thus **ADD TAX NET GIVING TOTAL** is also correct.

A rule-of-thumb to follow when using an **ADD** statement is to use the **GIVING** format when the contents of operands are to be retained. When you will no longer need the original contents of an operand after the addition, the **TO** format may be used.

Format 1 and Format 2, then, may be expanded:

Thus far, we have restricted ourselves to simple **ADD** statements, with a limited number of operands. However, the number of operands that may be specified in an **ADD** operation is considered to be relatively limitless, being a function only of the size of the computer and the level of the COBOL compiler.

The rules specified thus far apply.

(1) All literals and data-fields must be numeric.[1]

(2) The resultant field, following the word **TO** or the word **GIVING**, must be a data-name and may not be a literal.

(3) When using the **TO** format, all fields including data-name-n, are added together.

(4) When using the **GIVING** format, data-name-n is **not** part of the **ADD** operation and only serves as a field in which to place the sum.

(5) In no case may the words **TO** and **GIVING** be specified in the same statement.

Example 7: ADD A, B, C, GIVING D.

	A	B	C	D
Before operation:	2	4	6	15
After operation:	2	4	6	12

Note that the original content of D, the resultant field, is destroyed and has no effect on the **ADD** operation. The three operands A, B, and C are unchanged.

[1] Some compilers permit the data-name following the word GIVING to be nonnumeric; we will use the convention of requiring **all** fields to be numeric.

Format 1

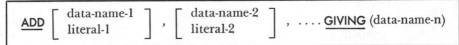

Format 2

Example 8: ADD A, B, C TO D.

	A	B	C	D
Before operation	2	4	6	15
After operation:	2	4	6	27

Note that the original content of D is added to the other three fields. The result is again placed in D, while A, B, C remain unaltered.

EXERCISES

Indicate the error, if any, in Statements 1–3:

1. ADD '12' TO FLDA.
*****
'12' is not a numeric literal.

2. ADD TAX TO 15.8.
*****
The resultant field must be a data-name.

3. ADD TAX TO TOTAL GIVING AMT.
*****
The words TO and GIVING may not appear in the same ADD statement.

4. If ADD 1, 15, 3 TO COUNTER is performed and COUNTER is initialized at 10, _____ will be placed in _____ at the end of the operation. All other fields will _____.
*****
29
COUNTER
remain unchanged

5. Without using the word TO, write a statement equivalent to the one in Question 4.
*****
ADD 1, 15, 3, COUNTER GIVING FIELDX.

6. The commas used in an ADD statement are _____.
*****
optional

7. When using a TO format, the last data-field (is, is not) part of the ADD operation. When using a GIVING format, the last data-field (is, is not) part of the ADD operation.
*****
is
is not

8. If ADD 1, 15, 3 GIVING COUNTER is performed, _____ will be the result in _____.
*****
19
COUNTER

B. SUBTRACT STATEMENT

The **SUBTRACT** operation has the following two formats:

Format 1

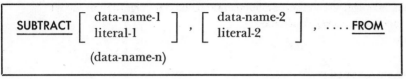

Format 2

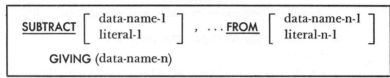

Examples

(1) SUBTRACT 25.00 FROM FLDA.

(2) SUBTRACT FLDA, FLDB, 99 FROM FLDC.

(3) SUBTRACT TAX FROM GROSS GIVING NET.

(4) SUBTRACT TAX, FICA, INSUR-PREM FROM GROSS GIVING NET.

You will note that the rules specified for addition have their counterpart in a **SUBTRACT** operation:

(1) All literals and data-names must be numeric.

(2) The word directly following **FROM** in Format 1 or **GIVING** in Format 2 must be a data-name and not a literal. The following statement is incorrect: **SUBTRACT TAX FROM 100.00.** If you want to subtract a quantity from a constant (100.00), you must use the **GIVING** format: **SUBTRACT TAX FROM 100.00 GIVING NET.**

(3) When using the **FROM** format, all data-fields and literals preceding the word **FROM** will be added together and the sum subtracted from the last data-field. The result, or difference, will be placed in this last field. All other fields will remain unchanged.

Example 5

SUBTRACT 15.40, TAX, TOTAL FROM AMT.

	TAX	TOTAL	AMT
Before operation:	3000	1000	10000
After operation:	3000	1000	4460

(4) When using the **GIVING** format, the operation performed is the same as in Rule 3 but the answer, or difference, is placed in the field following the word GIVING.

Example 6

SUBTRACT 15.40, TAX, TOTAL FROM AMT GIVING NET.

	TAX	TOTAL	AMT	NET
Before operation:	3000	1000	10000	8700
After operation:	3000	1000	10000	4460

The contents of NET before the operation are destroyed and do **not** enter into the calculation.

When the contents of an operand are not needed after the **SUBTRACT** operation, then Format 1 may be used. When the contents of operands are to be retained, use the **GIVING** format.

As in **ADD** operations, all commas are optional and are only used for clarity of expression. A space must, however, follow each comma.

Work Problems

1. In the operation **SUBTRACT 1500 FROM X GIVING Z**, the result, or difference, is placed in _____. The original contents of **X** _____. If **X** has an original value of 8500, and **Z** has an original value of 2000, the result in **Z** would be _____.

   *****

   Z
   remains unchanged
   7000

   What is wrong with the following statements?

2. **SUBTRACT $23.00 FROM AMOUNT.**

   *****

   $23.00 is an invalid numeric literal—numeric literals may not contain dollar signs.

3. **SUBTRACT A FROM 900.00.**

   *****

   The resultant field of a **SUBTRACT** operation may not be a literal.

4. Change the above statement to make it valid.

   *****

   SUBTRACT A FROM 900.00 GIVING B.

5. Use one **SUBTRACT** statement to subtract three fields, **A, B, C** from **TOTAL**, placing the answer in **AMT**.

   *****

   SUBTRACT A, B, C FROM TOTAL GIVING AMT

6. If **SUBTRACT A, B, C, 15.80 FROM D** is performed, the **PICTURE** clauses of **A, B, C,** and **D** are assumed to be _____.

   *****

   numeric

C. MULTIPLY AND DIVIDE STATEMENTS

Because of their similarities, the **MULTIPLY** and **DIVIDE** statements are covered together.

The **MULTIPLY** statement has the following two formats:

Format 1

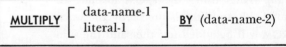

$$\text{\underline{MULTIPLY}} \begin{bmatrix} \text{data-name-1} \\ \text{literal-1} \end{bmatrix} \text{\underline{BY}} \ (\text{data-name-2})$$

Format 2

$$\text{\underline{MULTIPLY}} \begin{bmatrix} \text{data-name-1} \\ \text{literal-1} \end{bmatrix} \text{\underline{BY}} \begin{bmatrix} \text{data-name-2} \\ \text{literal-2} \end{bmatrix} \text{\underline{GIVING}} \ (\text{data-name-3})$$

Examples

MULTIPLY 100 BY FLDA.
MULTIPLY FLDA BY FLDB.
MULTIPLY TAX BY GROSS GIVING
  DEDUCTIONS.
MULTIPLY 600 BY DEPENDENTS GIVING
  STD-DED.

The **DIVIDE** statement has the following two formats:

Format 1

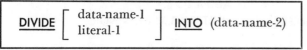

Format 2

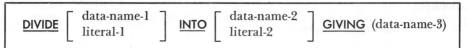

Examples

DIVIDE 12 INTO ANN-SAL.
DIVIDE N INTO SUM.
DIVIDE 12 INTO ANN-SAL GIVING
  MONTHLY-SAL.
DIVIDE N INTO SUM GIVING AVERAGE.

At this point, you know that all arithmetic statements have two basic formats. When operands are not to be destroyed during an arithmetic operation, you will always use Format 2, which specifies the **GIVING** option. If operands need not be retained, you may use Format 1. When using either format, for all arithmetic operations, the last field mentioned is the resultant field—it must always be a data-name and never a literal.

Unlike **ADD** and **SUBTRACT** operations, **MULTIPLY** and **DIVIDE** are limited in the number of operands that may be specified. With these verbs, we may perform only **one** simple multiplication or division for each statement. For example, suppose the desired product were A × B × C. **Two** operations would be necessary to perform this multiplication: **MULTIPLY A BY B.** The result, or product, is placed in B. **MULTIPLY B BY C.** The product of ABC is now in C. Hence, with each **MULTIPLY** or **DIVIDE** state-

ment specified, **two operands only** will be multiplied or divided.

The preposition used with the **MULTIPLY** verb is always **BY.** To say: **MULTIPLY A TIMES B** is incorrect. You will note that, in the **DIVIDE** operation, the preposition is **INTO.** To say **DIVIDE A INTO B** places in the resultant field, **B,** the quotient of B/A. In the example **DIVIDE 3 INTO 6 GIVING A,** the result in **A** will be 6/3 or 2. We may never use the preposition **BY** in a **DIVIDE** operation.

Let us now employ these arithmetic rules in performing some operations. We will assume that all data fields used in the following examples have the proper numeric **PICTURE** clauses in the **DATA DIVISION.** Keep in mind that the solution indicated for each example is only **one** method for solving the problem.

Example 1

Centigrade temperatures are to be converted to Fahrenheit temperatures according to the following formula:

$$F = (9/5) \, C + 32$$

C is a data field in the input area and F is a data field in the output area. Both have numeric **PICTURE** clauses in the **DATA DIVISION.**

Solution

MULTIPLY 9 BY C.
DIVIDE 5 INTO C.
ADD 32, C GIVING F.

If **C** had an initial value of 20, its value at the end of the operation would be 36 (9/5 × C) and **F** would have 68.

The routine may be reduced to two steps:

MULTIPLY 1.8 BY C.
ADD 32, C GIVING F.

Example 2

Compute the average of three fields: HRS-WEEK1, HRS-WEEK2, HRS-WEEK3. Place the answer in AVERAGE, and do not alter the contents of the three data fields.

Solution

ADD HRS-WEEK1, HRS-WEEK2, HRS-WEEK3
   GIVING AVERAGE.
DIVIDE 3 INTO AVERAGE.

Example 3

$$\text{Find } C = A^2 + B^2.$$

Again, it is assumed that **A**, **B**, and **C** are data fields defined in the **DATA DIVISION**.

Solution

MULTIPLY A BY A.
MULTIPLY B BY B.
ADD A, B GIVING C.

Note that to multiply **A** by itself places $A \times A$ or A^2 in the field A.

Observe that the following is **not** a correct solution:

ADD A TO B.
MULTIPLY B BY B GIVING C.

The **ADD** operation places in **B** the sum of $A + B$. The multiplication would then result in the product of $(A + B) \times (A + B)$, which is **not** $A^2 + B^2$.

Table 8-1 illustrates the arithmetic operations and how they are performed.

Table 8-1

Arithmetic Statement	Value *After* Execution of the Statement			
	A	B	C	D
ADD A TO B	A	$A + B$		
ADD A, B, C TO D	A	B	C	$A + B + C + D$
ADD A, B, C GIVING D	A	B	C	$A + B + C$
SUBTRACT A FROM B	A	$B - A$		
SUBTRACT A, B FROM C	A	B	$C - (A + B)$	
SUBTRACT A, B FROM C GIVING D	A	B	C	$C - (A + B)$
MULTIPLY A BY B	A	$A \times B$		
MULTIPLY A BY B GIVING C	A	B	$A \times B$	
DIVIDE A INTO B	A	B/A		
DIVIDE A INTO B GIVING C	A	B	B/A	

Work Problems

1. Using **MULTIPLY** and **DIVIDE** verbs, compute $A \times B/C$
   *****
   MULTIPLY A BY B. DIVIDE C INTO B GIVING ANS.

2. Using **MULTIPLY** and **DIVIDE** verbs, compute $(C/B + E/F) \times S$
   *****
   DIVIDE B INTO C. DIVIDE F INTO E. ADD C, E, GIVING FLD1. MULTIPLY FLD1 BY S GIVING ANS2.

What, if anything, is wrong with the following five statements?

3. DIVIDE $45.00 INTO A GIVING B.
   *****
   Dollar sign makes literal an invalid numeric field.

4. DIVIDE —35 INTO A.
   *****
   Nothing.

5. MULTIPLY A TIMES B GIVING C.
   *****
   Preposition must be BY in the MULTIPLY operation.

6. MULTIPLY A BY B BY C GIVING D.
   *****
   Only two operands may be multiplied together with one MULTIPLY verb.

7. DIVIDE A BY B GIVING C.
   *****
   Preposition used with DIVIDE verb is INTO.

D. ROUNDED OPTION

Consider the following example:

ADD A, B GIVING C.

A		B		C	
PICTURE	Contents	PICTURE	Contents	PICTURE	Contents After ADD
99V999	12857	99V999	25142	99V99	3799

This situation is not uncommon in programming. Two fields, each with three decimal positions, are added together, and the answer desired is only valid to two decimal places. In the above example, the computer adds the two fields A and B, and obtains the sum 37999 in an accumulator. It attempts to place this result into C, a field with two decimal positions. The effect is the same as performing the following MOVE operation: MOVE 37.999 TO C. The low-order decimal position is truncated. Thus C obtains the sum of 3799.

It should be clear that a more desirable result would be 3800. Generally, we consider results more accurate if answers are ROUNDED to the nearest decimal position.

To obtain rounding of results, the ROUNDED option may be specified with any arithmetic statement. The following examples serve as illustrations:

(1) ADD A TO B ROUNDED.
(2) SUBTRACT C FROM D ROUNDED
(3) MULTIPLY A BY B ROUNDED
(4) DIVIDE A INTO B ROUNDED

It is also possible to use the ROUNDED option with the GIVING format of the above verbs. The word ROUNDED directly follows the resultant data-name in all cases.

Example 5

ADD A, B GIVING C ROUNDED

If A and B have the same quantities as specified above, the computer will round the answer to 3800.

Note that using ROUNDED with any

arithmetic operator is an option only and need not be utilized. If the ROUNDED option is not specified, truncation of decimal positions, or fractional components, will occur if the resultant field cannot accommodate the decimal positions in the answer. With the ROUNDED option, the computer will always round the result to the PICTURE specification of the receiving field.

Example 6

FLDA		FLDB		FLDC	
PICTURE	Contents	P	C[2]	P	C
99V99	8723	99V99	9998	99	00

Operation A:

SUBTRACT FLDA FROM FLDB GIVING FLDC.

2 P denotes PICTURE and C denotes Contents.

In this case, 87.23 is subtracted from 99.98 and the result, 12.75, is placed in an accumulator. The computer moves this result to FLDC. Since FLDC does not allow for fractional components, truncation occurs and 12 is placed in FLDC.

Operation B:

SUBTRACT FLDA FROM FLDB GIVING FLDC ROUNDED.

In this case 12.75 is to be rounded to the PICTURE specification of the receiving field; that is, rounding to the nearest integer position will occur. 12.75 rounded to the nearest integer is 13, and thus, 13 is placed in FLDC.

EXERCISES

1. When the COBOL word ROUNDED is not specified, _____ may occur.
*****
truncation

2. ROUNDED is an _____ and therefore need only be used at the programmer's discretion.
*****
option

3. State the result in the following cases.

	A		B		C		D	
	PIC-TURE	Con-tents	PIC-TURE	Con-tents	PIC-TURE	Con-tents	PIC-TURE	Con-tents
SUBTRACT A, B FROM C GIVING D	99V9	123	99V9	456	999V9	1568	999	_____
DIVIDE A INTO B GIVING C	9V9	51	9V9	80	9	_____		
DIVIDE A INTO B GIVING C ROUNDED	9V9	51	9V9	80	9	_____		

*****
098
1
2

E. ON SIZE ERROR OPTION

Let us suppose that the following operation were performed:

ADD A, B TO C.

The fields before the operation look like this:

A			B	C		
PICTURE	Contents	PICTURE	Contents	PICTURE	Contents	
999	800	999	150	999	050	

The computer will add 800, 150, 050 in an accumulator. It will attempt to place the sum, 1000, into a three-position field. The effect would be the same as an internal MOVE operation: MOVE 1000 TO C. Since numeric MOVE operations move integer data from right to left, 000 will be placed in C. In such a case, where the resultant field is not large enough to store the accumulated sum, we say that an **overflow** or **size error** condition has occurred. It is important to note that the computer will not stop or "hang up" because of a size error condition. It will merely truncate high-order positions of the field. In our example, 000 will remain in C.

The best way to avoid a size error condition is to be absolutely certain that the receiving field is large enough to accommodate any possible result. Sometimes, however, the programmer, who must concern himself with many details, forgets to account for the rare occasion when an overflow might occur. COBOL has a built-in solution. Each time **any** arithmetic operation is performed, use an **ON SIZE ERROR** option as follows:

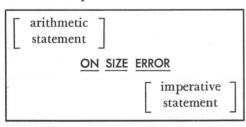

```
⎡ arithmetic ⎤
⎣ statement  ⎦
         ON SIZE ERROR
              ⎡ imperative ⎤
              ⎣ statement  ⎦
```

Examples

(1) ADD A, B TO C ON SIZE ERROR MOVE 000 TO C.

(2) MULTIPLY A BY B ON SIZE ERROR GO TO ERROR-RTN.

(3) DIVIDE A INTO C ON SIZE ERROR MOVE 'INVALID DIVIDE' TO CODE.

(4) SUBTRACT A FROM B GIVING C ON SIZE ERROR GO TO PAR1.

It is clear that **any** arithmetic statement, using either Format 1 or Format 2 may be tested for an overflow, or size error, condition. By an imperative statement, we mean any COBOL statement that gives a direct command and does not perform a test. Statements beginning with the COBOL word IF, or conditional statements, are not considered imperative statements. This concept will become clearer in the next chapter. When an imperative statement is indicated, the computer will perform the operation indicated if a size error condition is met. In Example 1, the computer will move zeros to C only if C does not contain enough integer positions to accommodate the sum of A, B, and C. If C is large enough for the result, zeros will **not** be moved to C and execution will continue with the next statement.

A size error, then, for all arithmetic operations, is a condition in which the receiving field cannot accommodate the entire result. In a divide operation, however, the size error condition has additional significance. If an attempt is made to divide by zero, a size error condition will occur.

Example 5

DIVIDE E INTO F ON SIZE ERROR
MOVE ZERO TO F.

Here are the fields before the operation:

E		F	
PICTURE	Contents	PICTURE	Contents
9999	0000	99	10

Because of the size error condition being met, **F** becomes zero. If the first operand specified in a **DIVIDE** statement contains 0, the computer will attempt to divide by zero, an impossible feat. The result of such a division is unpredictable. If **ON SIZE ERROR** is specified, the programmer does not have to worry about improper divide operations.

If the **ON SIZE ERROR** option is employed along with the **ROUNDED** option, the following format is applicable:

$$\left[\begin{array}{c} \text{arithmetic} \\ \text{statement} \end{array}\right]$$

ROUNDED ON
SIZE ERROR

$$\left[\begin{array}{c} \text{imperative} \\ \text{statement} \end{array}\right]$$

Hence the word **ROUNDED** will always precede **ON SIZE ERROR** in an arithmetic statement if both options are used.

Exercises

1. An **ON SIZE ERROR** condition occurs when _____.

   *****

   the resultant field is not large enough to store the answer

2. An **ON SIZE ERROR** condition also occurs when _____.

   *****

   an attempt is made to divide by zero

3. The word **ROUNDED** (precedes, follows) the **ON SIZE ERROR** clause in an arithmetic statement.

   *****

   precedes

4. **DIVIDE 0 INTO A GIVING B** (will, will not) result in an **ON SIZE ERROR** condition.

   *****

   will

5. **DIVIDE A INTO 0 GIVING B** (will, will not) result in an **ON SIZE ERROR** condition.

   *****

   will not (0 divided by any number = 0)

6. **ADD 50, 60 TO FLDA ON SIZE ERROR GO TO RTN-2** results in _____ if **FLDA** has a **PICTURE** of 99.

   *****

   a branch to **RTN-2**

7. **ADD 50, 60 TO FLDA ON SIZE ERROR GO TO RTN-2** results in _____ if **FLDA** has a **PICTURE** of 999.

   *****

   110 added to **FLDA**

REVIEW QUESTIONS

Fill in the missing columns (1–5):

| | | **Result if** |
| COBOL Statement | Result at | A = 3, B = 2, X = 5 |

1. SUBTRACT A FROM B

2. DIVIDE A INTO B

3. ADD A, B GIVING X

4. ADD A, B, TO X
ON SIZE ERROR
MOVE ZERO TO X

5. DIVIDE A INTO B ROUNDED

6. Write a routine to find $X = A+B/3$.

7. Write a routine to find $Y = (A+B)^2/D$.

In each of the following questions, determine the resultant field:

Operation	FLDA PICTURE	Contents	FLDB PICTURE	Contents
8. ADD A TO B	9V9	1.2	9V99	8.35
9. DIVIDE B INTO A	99V99	13.25	9	2
10. DIVIDE B INTO A ROUNDED	99V99	13.25	9	2

Determine what, if anything, is wrong with the following statements:

11. SUBTRACT A FROM 87.3 GIVING B.

12. ADD A, 10.98, B TO 100.3.

13. ADD AMT. TO TOTAL GIVING TAX.

14. DIVIDE A BY B AND MULTIPLY B BY C.

PROBLEMS

Round all results and stop the run on a size error condition.

1. Write a program to create a master sales file from input sales records (cards) with the following format:

      1–5 Salesman number
      6–11 Net price   xxxx.xx   (i.e., PICTURE 9999V99)
      12–80 Unused

The output file is created on magnetic tape with the following data fields:

1–5 Salesman number
6–11 Sales price   xxxx.xx
12–17 Commission   xxxx.xx
18–50 Unused

Notes

a. The output tape records are blocked 20 and have standard labels.

b. Output Sales price is equal to the input Net price with an added 5% Sales tax.

c. Commission is 20% of the price **exclusive** of the tax.

2. Write a program to print a weekly salary file. Input is **on** punched cards with the following format:

1–15 Employee name
16–18 Hours worked
19–21 Rate x.xx
22–80 Not used

Output is a tape with the following format:

positions   6–20 Name
31–36 Gross pay xxxx.xx
41–45 Soc. sec. tax xxx.xx
51–56 Net pay xxxx.xx

The output has standard labels, 15 records|block, and 75 characters|record.

Notes

a. Gross pay = Hours worked × Rate
b. Soc sec tax = 4.8% of Gross pay
c. Net pay = Gross pay — Soc sec tax

3. Write a program to convert British pounds to dollars and cents. The card input has the following format:

1–25 Name of British Agency
26–30 Number of pounds
31–80 Not used

Output cards are to be punched with the following format:

1–25 British Agency
26–31 Number of U.S. dollars
32–41 Unused
42–43 Number of U.S. cents
44–80 Not used

Notes

a. 1 pound = $2.40.
b. Dollars and cents are two **separate** data fields.

4. Write a program to print out each student's class average. The input records are student class cards with the following format:

> 1–20 Student name
> 21–23 Exam 1 score
> 24–26 Exam 2 score
> 27–29 Exam 3 score
> 30–32 Exam 4 score
> 33–80 Not used

Each output line should contain Student name and Class average, *& ALL FOUR SCORES* spaced anywhere on the line.

Notes

a. Class average should be rounded to nearest integer (i.e., $89.5 = 90$).

b. First line should include heading: **CLASS GRADES.**

5. Write a program to create a tape file from the following transaction card records:

> 1–5   Transaction number
> 6–20 Customer name
> 21–25 Amount 1   xxx.xx
> 26–30 Amount 2   xxx.xx
> 31–35 Amount of discount   xxx.xx
> 36–80 Not used

The output tape records are blocked 10 and contain standard labels. The format for the output tape is as follows:

> 1–15 Customer name
> 16–20 Transaction number
> 21–25 Total xxx.xx
> 26–30 Amount due xxx.xx
> 31–34 Date (month & year)
> 35–50 Not used

Notes

a. Total = Amount 1 + Amount 2.

b. Payment due = Total — Amount of discount.

c. If, through an error, Amount 1 + Amount 2 is too large for the Total field, stop the run.

d. Place today's date in the Date field. (**Hint.** Use a literal.)

Conditional Statements

A. SIMPLE CONDITION

We will define a **conditional statement** as any sentence that performs an operation dependent upon the occurrence of some condition. Such statements, in COBOL, generally begin with the word IF and, as such, are performing a specific test.

The basic format for all conditional statements is as follows:

(a) IF A IS EQUAL TO B
(b) IF A IS LESS THAN B
(c) IF A IS GREATER THAN B

These three tests are considered simple conditions.

An illustration of a simple condition is as follows:

IF A IS EQUAL TO B DIVIDE C INTO D
ELSE ADD A TO TOTAL.

$$\underline{\text{IF}} \ (\text{condition}) \left(\text{imperative statement(s)} \right) \left\{ \left[\begin{array}{c} \text{ELSE} \\ \hline \text{OTHERWISE} \end{array} \right] \left(\text{imperative statement(s)} \right) \right\} .$$

An **imperative statement,** as opposed to a conditional statement, is any COBOL expression which issues a **direct** command to the computer, regardless of any existing conditions. ADD A TO B, MOVE C TO D, OPEN INPUT MASTER-TAPE are examples of imperative statements that do not test for values but perform direct operations. Hence we say that COBOL statements are divided into two broad categories: **imperative,** which give direct operations, and **conditional,** which test for specific conditions.

A **condition** as indicated in the format above, tests for a specific relation. A **simple condition,** which is the topic discussed in this section, is a single relation test of the following form:

Note that the word OTHERWISE may be used to replace ELSE without altering the meaning of the sentence. There are really two tests performed by the above statement:

(a) IF A IS EQUAL TO B
(b) IF A IS NOT EQUAL TO B

(a) If A is equal to B, the DIVIDE operation is performed. The remainder of the statement, beginning with the ELSE option, is ignored. The program will continue execution with the very next sentence, disregarding the expression beginning with the word ELSE or OTHERWISE.

(b) If the equality, in fact, does not hold, then clearly the DIVIDE operation is not performed. Only the ELSE portion of the statement, the ADD operation, is performed. The next sentence, in either case, will be executed.

Hence with the use of the ELSE or OTHERWISE option, two tests are performed: by using the word IF, we test the initial condition and perform the instruction specified; by using ELSE, we perform an operation if the initial condition does not exist.

The ELSE or OTHERWISE option is bracketed { } which means that it may be omitted from the conditional statement. If some operation is required **only if** a condition is present and nothing different need be done if the condition is absent, the entire ELSE clause may be omitted:

MOVE NAME TO NAME-OUT. MOVE AMOUNT TO AMOUNT-OUT.
IF AMOUNT IS EQUAL TO ZEROS MOVE 'NO TRANSACTION THIS MONTH' TO OUT-AREA.
WRITE PRINT-REC.

In this case, a message NO TRANSACTION THIS MONTH is printed only if AMOUNT is zero. If not, the normal flow is continued and nothing else need be performed. Since no special operation is required if AMOUNT is not zero, the ELSE clause is unnecessary.

The mathematical notation for the three simple conditions is valid within a COBOL statement:

Notation	Meaning
<	IS LESS THAN
>	IS GREATER THAN
=	IS EQUAL TO

A COBOL conditional, then, may have the following form:

IF A > B ADD A TO C ELSE MULTIPLY B BY C.

or

IF A IS GREATER THAN B ADD A TO C ELSE MULTIPLY B BY C.

B is multiplied by C only if the relation does not hold, that is, if A equals B or A is less than B. Most COBOL compilers require a blank on each side of the relationals $<$, $>$, $=$. In coding, then, be sure you include this space.

Keep in mind that conditional statements must utilize data-fields with the same modes for proper execution. In the statement, IF A = '123' MOVE C TO D, it is assumed that A is an alphanumeric field, since it is compared to a nonnumeric literal. As in MOVE operations, the literal should be in the same form as the data-name. If B is a numeric field, with a PICTURE clause of 9's, the following conditional would be appropriate: IF B = 123 MOVE E TO F.

In the case where data-fields are compared to one another, both fields should be numeric, alphabetic, or alphanumeric. In the statement, IF A = B GO TO RTN1, both A and B are either numeric, alphabetic, or alphanumeric.

Regarding the comparisons of numeric fields, the following are considered equal:

012
12.00
12
+12

This implies that comparisons are performed **logically.** Although 12.00 does not have the same configuration as 012, their numeric values are known to be equal.

Similarly, when comparing alphanumeric or alphabetic fields, the following are considered equivalent:

ABC
ABCb̸   (b̸ denotes a blank space)

Blanks, or spaces, will not upset the balance of equivalence. Only significant positions are compared.

When performing an alphanumeric comparison, the hierarchy is as follows:

b̸ABC. . . .Z0123. . .9

Thus A is less than B which is less than

C, etc. Any letter is considered less than any digit. The comparisons are performed from left to right. Thus:

ABCD < BBCD
BBCD < ZBCD
ZBCD < 1BCD
ABCD < ACCD
ƁBCD < ABCD
ABCD < ABCE

Note that several imperative statements may appear within one conditional:

IF A < B ADD C TO D GO TO RTN5 OTHERWISE ADD E TO C GO TO RTN6.

This statement may be flowcharted as follows:

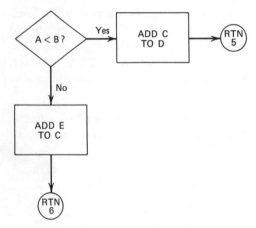

Consider these two routines:

(1) IF A = B GO TO RTN5 ELSE GO TO RTN2.
RTN2. ADD C TO D.

(2) IF A = B GO TO RTN5.
RTN2. ADD C TO D.

Observe that the two routines perform the same operations. In the first, the **ELSE** clause is unnecessary. If the condition does not exist, the program will proceed to **RTN2**, which is the next sentence, anyway. The point of this illustration is to indicate that a conditional may be written several ways and still perform the same series of operations.

Examine the following statements:

IF A = B GO TO PARA-1 ELSE ADD A TO B ADD C TO D MULTIPLY D BY F.
PARA-1. WRITE PRINT-REC.

You will note that we want to perform three arithmetic operations only if the initial condition, **A = B**, does **not** exist. There is a COBOL expression, **NEXT SENTENCE**, which eliminates the need of a GO TO statement:

IF A = B NEXT SENTENCE ELSE ADD A TO B ADD C TO D MULTIPLY D BY F.
WRITE PRINT-REC.

We do **not** say GO TO NEXT SENTENCE since that would require NEXT SENTENCE to be a paragraph name.

To say: IF A > B GO TO RTN2 ELSE NEXT SENTENCE is identical to: IF A > B GO TO RTN2.

If the condition does not exist and no **ELSE** clause is specified, the program will proceed to the next sentence anyway.

At this point, you have seen simple conditionals illustrated. Much of the logic utilized in a COBOL program is built into conditional statements and, for that reason, we will dwell on more complicated examples.

Problem: To program the following routine:

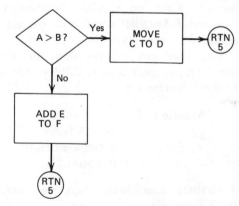

This may be coded in several ways.

(1)
IF A > B MOVE C TO D GO TO RTN5 ELSE ADD E TO F GO TO RTN5.

This is the simplest and most straightforward method. We merely write the statements as they appear on the flow-chart.

(2)
IF A > B MOVE C TO D GO TO RTN5.
ADD E TO F. GO TO RTN5.

No ELSE or OTHERWISE clause is really necessary. If A is greater than B, a branch to RTN5 will be performed, and thus the next sentence, which is the addition, is executed only if the condition does not exist.

(3)
IF A > B MOVE C TO D ELSE ADD E TO F.
GO TO RTN5.

The above flowchart may be coded with a single GO TO statement. If A is greater than B, C is moved to D. The ELSE is ignored and the program proceeds to the next sentence where it branches to RTN5. If A is not greater than B, E is added to F. The program again proceeds to the next sentence, where it branches to RTN5. By altering the sequence of operations in a flowchart, it is possible to write a more efficient program.

The conditional is often used in a **loop** —a series of operations repeatedly performed until a certain condition occurs.

Example: Suppose we want one input card of information punched into five output cards:

    MOVE ZEROS TO COUNTER1.
BEGIN.
    WRITE CARD-REC.
    ADD 1 TO COUNTER1.
    IF COUNTER1 = 5 NEXT SENTENCE
    ELSE GO TO BEGIN.
    STOP RUN.

The conditional statement determines if the routine is to be repeated or the job terminated. When writing a loop, the following operations are generally necessary:

(1) Initialize all conditions (i.e., MOVE ZEROS TO COUNTER1 where COUNTER1 is a work area, not part of the input but necessary for processing).

(2) State the operations to be repeated (i.e., WRITE CARD-REC).

(3) Change the test indicator, to eventually leave the loop (i.e., ADD 1 TO COUNTER1).

(4) Test the indicator—if the terminating condition is met, stop; if not, repeat operations (i.e., IF COUNTER1 = 5 NEXT SENTENCE ELSE GO TO BEGIN).

You will be learning a good deal more about loops but, for the most part, these four operations are usually required. The data-name COUNTER1 must be defined in the FILE SECTION, as part of the input or output area, or in the WORKING-STORAGE SECTION, as a work area. The WORKING-STORAGE SECTION will be discussed in detail in the next chapter.

Suppose we are attempting to multiply A by B by a series of successive additions. If three is added to itself four times, the result is 12, which is the product of 3×4. In COBOL this routine might look like:

    MOVE ZEROS TO TOTAL.
RTN1.
    SUBTRACT 1 FROM B.
    ADD A TO TOTAL.
    IF B = ZEROS NEXT SENTENCE ELSE
    GO TO RTN1.

The one problem with this routine is that B must be assumed to be greater than zero. It is left to the reader to determine why this is so.

EXERCISES

What is wrong with the following statements (1–6)?

1. IF A IS LESS THAN B GO TO NEXT SENTENCE ELSE GO TO PARA1.
    *****

    You cannot say: GO TO NEXT SENTENCE: IF A IS LESS THAN B NEXT SENTENCE ELSE GO TO PARA1.

2. IF A = '127' ADD A TO B.
    *****

    Since A is compared to a nonnumeric literal, it is assumed that A is an alphanumeric field. But A is **added** to another field, which implies that it is numeric. Hence a contradiction of modes exists.

3. IF A > B GO TO RTN5 ADD A TO B OTHERWISE ADD C TO D.
    *****

    If A > B, the GO TO statement is the first imperative statement encountered and thus the first executed. Once the program branches to RTN5, it will never come back to perform the addition of A to B.

4. IF A EQUALS B GO TO PARA1.
    *****

    This should be: IF A IS EQUAL TO B . . . .

5. GO TO RTN-6 IF A = C.
    *****

    The condition phrase must precede the imperative phrase: IF A = C GO TO RTN-6.

6. IF A IS LESS THEN B GO TO ERROR-RTN.
    *****

    With the words GREATER and LESS, the COBOL word that follows is THAN and not THEN—This is a **grammar** rule.

Are the following pairs of statements the same or different (7–8)?

7. IF A IS EQUAL TO C GO TO RTN5 ELSE NEXT SENTENCE.
    IF A = C GO TO RTN5.
    *****

    Same.

8.   IF A < N ADD C TO D GO TO RTN2 ELSE ADD C TO D GO TO RTN3.
    RTN2.   MOVE E TO F.
    RTN3.   MOVE G TO H.

        IF A < N NEXT SENTENCE ELSE GO TO RTN3.
    RTN2.   MOVE E TO F.
    RTN3.   ADD C TO D.
            MOVE G TO H.
    *****

    Same (only the order of operations has been changed).

9. Code the following routine:

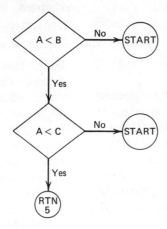

*****

IF A < B NEXT SENTENCE ELSE GO TO START.
IF A < C GO TO RTN5 ELSE GO TO START.

10. Write a routine to move the smallest of three numbers A, B, C to PRINT-SMALL.

*****

MOVE ZEROS TO PRINT-SMALL.
IF A IS LESS THAN B MOVE A TO PRINT-SMALL ELSE MOVE B TO PRINT-SMALL, GO TO RTN2.
IF A IS LESS THAN C GO TO EOJ ELSE MOVE C TO PRINT-SMALL GO TO EOJ.
RTN2.   IF B IS LESS THAN C GO TO EOJ ELSE MOVE C TO PRINT-SMALL.
EOJ.   . . . .

(Note. This is **not** the only way to write this routine.)

B. SIGN, CLASS TESTS, AND NEGATED CONDITIONALS

There are other types of conditions, besides the simple relation test, which are often used in COBOL.

Sign Test. We can test a data-field as to its relative position to zero:

Notice that saying IF A = ZERO is the same as saying IF A IS ZERO. If a numeric field contains an amount less than zero, it is considered negative. If it has an amount greater than zero, then it is considered positive:

$$\underline{\text{IF}} \text{ (data-name) IS} \left[\begin{array}{l} \text{POSITIVE} \\ \text{NEGATIVE} \\ \text{ZERO} \end{array}\right] \left(\text{imperative statement(s)}\right)$$
$$\left\{\left[\begin{array}{l}\underline{\text{ELSE}} \\ \underline{\text{OTHERWISE}}\end{array}\right] \left(\text{imperative statement(s)}\right)\right\} .$$

−387 is negative
 382 is positive
+382 is positive

0 is neither negative nor positive in this context, unless it is indicated as −0 or +0, respectively.

Example: Suppose we want to compute the distance of FIELDA from zero, regardless of its sign. For instance, if FIELDA = 2, its distance from zero is 2. If FIELDA = −2, its distance from zero is also 2, since we do not consider the sign. We call this quantity the **absolute value** of FIELDA, denoted |FIELDA|. It is mathematically formulated as follows:

If FIELDA $\geqslant$ 0, |FIELDA| = FIELDA
If FIELDA $<$ 0, |FIELDA| = −FIELDA

In other words, if FIELDA is greater than or equal to zero the absolute value of FIELDA is simply the value of FIELDA. If FIELDA is less than zero, the absolute value of FIELDA is equal to −1 times the value of FIELDA. Let us find the absolute value of FIELDA, using COBOL:

```
MOVE ZERO TO ABSA.
IF FIELDA IS POSITIVE, MOVE FIELDA TO
ABSA.
IF FIELDA IS NEGATIVE, MULTIPLY −1 BY
FIELDA GIVING ABSA.
```

Note that saying IF A IS NEGATIVE is equivalent to saying IF A $<$ 0, and IF A IS POSITIVE is the same as IF A $>$ 0. If A is

0, the contents of ABSA remain unchanged; that is, it contains zero.

Class Test. We can test the format of a field as shown in upper box (*below*).

If the ELSE or OTHERWISE option is performed with the NUMERIC class test, this implies that the data-field is either strictly alphabetic, containing only letters or a space, or it is alphanumeric, containing any possible character. If the field contains 123AB, for example, the ELSE option will be performed since the field is not strictly numeric.

Example: A one-position field in a card contains the number of dependents an employee claims. To obtain the standard deduction, we multiply the number of dependents by 600. If, however, the employee claims 10 dependents, an A is placed in the field; if he claims 11, a **B** is placed in the field, and so forth. We can only perform the multiplication if the field does not contain a letter:

```
IF NO-OF-DEPTS IS ALPHABETIC GO TO
    EXCEPTION ELSE GO TO
    CALC-RTN.
```

Negated Conditionals. All simple relation, class, or sign tests may be formed using a negated conditional as shown in lower box (*below*).

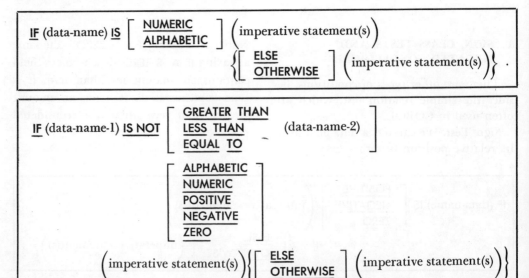

Examples

(1) IF A = B GO TO RTNX ELSE GO TO RTNY.

(2) IF A IS NOT EQUAL TO B GO TO RTNY ELSE GO TO RTNX.

The two statements above are equivalent.

To say, however, IF A IS NOT NEGATIVE, is **not** the same as saying A is positive. If A is zero, it falls into **neither** category. Thus the following two statements are **not** identical.

---

(1) IF B IS NEGATIVE GO TO RTNZ ELSE GO TO RTNQ.

(2) IF B IS NOT POSITIVE GO TO RTNZ ELSE GO TO RTNQ.

Suppose B = 0. In Case 1, a branch to RTNQ occurs; in Case 2, a branch to RTNZ is executed. Similarly; to say, IF A IS NOT ALPHABETIC, is **not** the same as saying A is numeric. If A is alphanumeric, containing combinations of letters, digits, and special characters, then it is neither. Thus the following two statements are **not** equivalent.

(1) IF C IS NOT ALPHABETIC GO TO RTNP, ELSE GO TO RTNS.

(2) IF A IS NUMERIC GO TO RTNP, ELSE GO TO RTNS.

C. COMPOUND CONDITIONAL

To be an efficient programmer, it is not enough simply to learn the rules of a programming language. We must be able to apply these rules to difficult logic problems. The **conditional statement**, as illustrated, is of prime importance in solving these logic problems. The **compound conditional** greatly extends the significance of IF statements. It enables the programmer to test for several conditions within one statement, and thus eases the difficulties in logic.

To perform an operation or a series of operations if **any one of several conditions exists**, the compound conditional may be utilized. Each condition within the statement is separated by the COBOL word OR, to imply that any one of the conditions so stated will cause execution of the imperative statement:

IF (condition-1) OR (condition-2) .... $\left(\text{imperative statement(s)}\right)$

$$\left\{\left[\begin{array}{l}\underline{\text{ELSE}} \\ \underline{\text{OTHERWISE}}\end{array}\right]\left(\text{imperative statement(s)}\right)\right\}$$

Examples

(1) IF A = B OR B > C GO TO RTN5.

(2) IF A < C OR A = D MOVE A TO B ELSE GO TO ERR-RTN.

The number of conditions that may be specified in one statement is relatively limitless, depending only upon the physical limitations of the computer.

The above format for a compound conditional illustrates that the word IF, the singular COBOL word that signals the compiler of an impending test, is needed only once in the statement. To say IF A = B OR IF B = C GO TO PARA-5 is invalid. The compound conditional is **one** test, requiring one IF, although it appears as a compound grouping.

For all compound conditionals, both operands within each condition will be specified, since most COBOL compilers will not accept **implied** operands. To say IF A = 7 OR 8 GO TO RTN5 tests two simple conditions: (1) A = 7 and (2) A = 8. Since the data-name A is omitted from the second condition test, we say that it is implied. Such statements, then, are invalid. Both operands must be indicated for each condition. Thus the above statement must read:

IF A = 7 OR A = 8 GO TO RTN5.

By using **OR** in a compound conditional, any of the conditions specified will cause execution of the imperative statement. If none of the conditions is met, either the **ELSE** option, if used, or the next sentence will be performed. Consider the following example:

IF A < D OR A = E ADD A TO B ELSE GO TO ERR-RTN.

The branch to **ERR-RTN** occurs only if **A** is greater than or equal to **D and A** is unequal to **E**. If either condition is met, **A** is added to **B**.

Example: Assume **A** is a two-position numeric field. We want to branch to **TENS-RTN** only if **A** is a multiple of 10. We may use a simple conditional, within a loop, to perform this operation:

```
    MOVE 90 TO CTR.
BEGIN.
    IF A = CTR GO TO TENS-RTN.
    SUBTRACT 10 FROM CTR.
    IF CTR = ZERO NEXT SENTENCE ELSE
        GO TO BEGIN.
```

A and **CTR** are data-names defined in the DATA DIVISION.

To program the above routine, we may also use a compound conditional:

IF A = 10 OR A = 20 OR A = 30 OR A = 40 OR A = 50 OR A = 60 OR A = 70 OR A = 80 OR A = 90 GO TO TENS-RTN.

If a statement is to be executed only when **all** of several conditions are met, then the COBOL word **AND** must be used in the compound conditional:

Note that the **ELSE** or **OTHERWISE** option will be performed if any of the stated conditions is not met.

Example: Let us code the following problem:

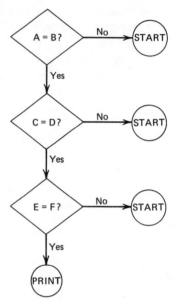

Using a simple condition, we may code this as follows:

IF A = B NEXT SENTENCE ELSE GO TO START.
IF C = D NEXT SENTENCE ELSE GO TO START.
IF E = F GO TO PRINT ELSE GO TO START.

We may, however, combine these statements into a compound conditional:

IF A = B AND C = D AND E = F GO TO PRINT ELSE GO TO START.

If **all** conditions are met, the branch to PRINT will occur. If any condition is not met, the branch to **START** occurs.

There are times when **both** the AND

IF (condition-1) AND (condition-2) ..... (imperative statement(s))

{ [ELSE / OTHERWISE] (imperative statement(s)) }

and **OR** are required within the same compound conditional:

Example: Write a routine to branch to CALC if **A** is between 10 and 20, inclusive.

On first sight, we might be inclined to use a compound conditional as follows:

IF A = 10 OR A = 11 OR A = 12 . . . OR A = 20 GO TO CALC.

This statement, however, will function properly **only if A is an integer.** The number 10.3, for instance, is between 10 and 20, but it will not pass the above tests. For the same reason, we cannot say IF A > 9 AND A < 21 GO TO CALC. If A is 9.8, it is **not** between 10 and 20 but it passes the latter test. We want to branch to CALC if:

(1) A = 10
OR (2) A > 10 AND A < 20
OR (3) A = 20

Hence the statement: IF A = 10 OR A > 10 AND A < 20 OR A = 20 GO TO CALC.

When using both **AND** and **OR** in the same compound conditional, the order of evaluation of each condition becomes extremely important. For example, look at the following illustration:

IF A = B OR C = D AND E = F GO TO PARA-1.

Suppose A = 2, B = 2, C = 3, D = 4, E = 5, F = 6.

Depending upon the order of evaluation of the above conditions, the branch may or may not occur. Suppose the statement is evaluated as follows:

I.   (a) IF A = B OR C = D
      AND (b) E = F

If this is the order of evaluation, there are two ways that the branch to PARA-1 may occur: 1) A = B and E = F or 2) C = D and E = F. Since E does not equal F this evaluation indicates that no branch will occur.

II.   (a) A = B
      OR (b) C = D AND E = F

If this is the order of evaluation, then there are two **different** ways that PARA-1 may be branched to (1) A = B or (2) C = D and E = F. Since the first condition, A = B, is met, this evaluation indicates that the branch **will** occur.

Hence, with one interpretation we obtain a branch, and with another, we do not. It should be clear, at this point, that only one of these evaluations will prove to be accurate.

Now that the significance of the order of evaluation is clear, the hierarchy rule is as follows:

Hierarchy Rule

1. Conditions surrounding the word AND are evaluated first.

2. Conditions surrounding the word OR are evaluated last.

3. When there are several AND connectors or OR connectors, the AND conditions are evaluated first, as they appear in the statement, from left to right. Then the OR conditions are evaluated, also from left to right.

In the above example, the conditions are evaluated as follows.

         (a) IF C = D AND E = F
   OR (b) A = B

Thus, with the above contents in the field, the branch to CALC will occur, since A = B.

Example: We want to print A if A is between 10 and 100, inclusive. This is often written $10 \leqslant A \leqslant 100$; 10 is less than or equal to A and, at the same time, A is less than or equal to 100.

The problem is to determine if the following statement will perform the proper test:

IF A < 100 OR A = 100 AND A = 10 OR A > 10 GO TO PRINT-RTN.

Using the hierarchy rule for evaluating compound conditionals, the first conditions to be considered are those surrounding the **AND**. Then, from left to right, those surrounding the **OR** groupings are evaluated. Thus, we have:

(1) IF A = 100 AND A = 10

OR   (2) A < 100

OR   (3) A > 10

We see that the compound expression in (1) is an impossibility: **A** can never equal 10 and, at the same time, be equal to 100. Since the first expression will never cause a branch, it can be eliminated from the statement, which reduces to:

IF A < 100 OR A > 10 GO TO
PRINT-RTN.

This, obviously, is not the solution to the original problem. In addition to the above two conditions, we want to branch to **PRINT-RTN** if the field is equal to either of the two endpoints, 10 or 100.

The original statement would have been correct if we could change the order of evaluation. If the following order of consideration were utilized, the statement would be correct:

(1) IF A < 100 OR A = 100

AND   (2) A = 10 OR A > 10

To change the normal order of evaluation, place parentheses around the conditions to be evaluated together. **Parentheses supersede the hierarchy rule**—all conditions within parentheses are evaluated together. Thus the following statement **is** correct:

IF (A < 100 OR A = 100) AND (A = 10
OR A > 10) GO TO PRINT-RTN.

When in doubt about the normal sequence of evaluation, make use of the parentheses.

A common pitfall, which is to be avoided, arises in negating compound conditionals.

Example: Write a routine to branch to **SOUTH** if **A** is not equal to 7 or 8. Otherwise branch to **NORTH**. We can write this as follows:

IF A IS EQUAL TO 7 OR A IS EQUAL TO 8
GO TO NORTH ELSE GO TO SOUTH.

But suppose we want to use the negative situation. On first thought, the following may seem appropriate:

IF A IS NOT EQUAL TO 7 OR A IS NOT
EQUAL TO 8 GO TO SOUTH ELSE GO
TO NORTH.

An evaluation of this statement will show that it is not correct. One of two conditions must exist for the branch to **SOUTH** to occur:

(a) A IS NOT EQUAL TO 7

OR   (b) A IS NOT EQUAL TO 8

Suppose A is 6; a branch to **SOUTH** occurs, which is what we want. If A = 7, however, we wish to branch to **NORTH**. In the above conditional, condition (a) is not met since **A** does equal 7. However, condition (b) is met since **A is not equal to 8**, but is equal to 7. Only one condition needs to be satisfied for the branch to **SOUTH** to occur, and since condition (b) is satisfied, we branch to **SOUTH**. Similarly, suppose A = 8. We want to branch to **NORTH**, but again we will see that the branch to **SOUTH** occurs. Condition (a) is satisfied, **A** is not equal to 7 (it is equal to 8). Since one condition is satisfied, the branch to **SOUTH** is performed. In fact, you can now see that the statement will **always** cause a branch to **SOUTH**, regardless of the contents of **A**.

The "moral" of this illustration is a lesson in **Boolean algebra**, which must be understood in negating compound conditionals. When negating conditions separated by **OR**: IF NOT (CONDITION1 OR CONDITION2. . . .), the stated conditions becomes: IF NOT CONDITION1 AND CONDITION2 AND . . . .

Hence, IF NOT (A = 7 OR A = 8 . . .) should read:

IF A IS NOT EQUAL TO 7 <u>AND</u> A IS NOT
EQUAL TO 8 GO TO SOUTH ELSE GO TO
NORTH.

EXERCISES

What, if anything, is wrong with the following entries (1–5)? Correct all errors.

1. IF A = B OR IF A = C GO TO RTN-X.

   *****

   The word IF should appear only once in the statement: IF A = B OR A = C GO TO RTN-X.

2. IF B = 3 OR 4 GO TO RTN-X.

   *****

   Implied operands are not permitted: IF B = 3 OR B = 4 GO TO RTN-X.

3. IF C < A + B GO TO STEP-5.

   *****

   Each element in a condition must be a data name. A + B is an arithmetic expression. This should be: ADD A TO B. IF C < B GO TO STEP-5.

4. IF A < 21 OR A = 21 AND A = 5 OR A > 5 GO TO RTN-1.

   *****

   There should be parentheses around elements to make statement logical: IF (A < 21 OR A = 21) AND (A = 5 OR A > 5) GO TO RTN-1.

5. IF A IS NOT EQUAL TO 3 OR A IS NOT EQUAL TO 4 GO TO RTN-X.

   *****

   A branch to RTN-X will always occur. This should read: IF A IS NOT EQUAL TO 3 <u>AND</u> A IS NOT EQUAL TO 4 GO TO RTN-X.

6. The hierarchy rule for evaluating compound conditionals states that conditions surrounding the word _____ are evaluated first, followed by the conditions surrounding the word _____.

   *****

   AND

   OR

7. Indicate whether the following two statements are equivalent:

   IF A < 2 OR A > 5 GO TO ERR-RTN.
   IF A IS NOT EQUAL TO 3 AND A IS NOT EQUAL TO 4 GO TO ERR-RTN.

   *****

   Only if A is an integer field.

8. Write a single statement to branch to PARA-5 if A is between 3 and 13, inclusive.

   *****

   IF A = 13 OR A < 13 AND A > 3 OR A = 3 GO TO PARA-5.

   (**Note.** This is **not** the only way to write the statement.)

9. Write a single statement to branch to **PARA-5** if **A** is between 3 and 13, exclusive of endpoints.

*****

IF A > 3 AND A < 13 GO TO PARA-5.

10. Write a single statement to code the following steps:

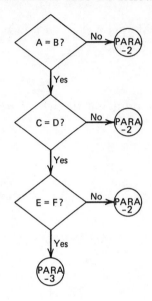

*****

IF A = B AND C = D AND E = F GO TO PARA-3 ELSE GO TO PARA-2.

REVIEW QUESTIONS

Code the following flowchart exercises with a single statement (1–3).

1.

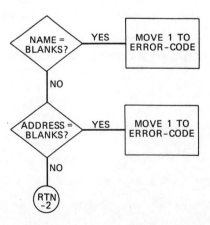

2.

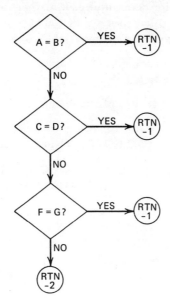

3.

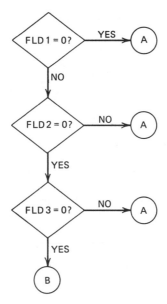

State whether FIELDA is equal to, greater than, or less than FIELDB (4–8):

	FIELDA	FIELDB
4.	012	12
5.	12.0	12
6.	−89.0	89.0
7.	ABC	ABCⱕ
8.	43	+43

9. Write a routine for determining FICA where a field called SALARY is given. FICA is equal to 4.8% of SALARY up to $7800.00. Salary in excess of $7800.00 is not taxed.

10. Find the largest of four numbers A, B, C, and D and place them in the field called HOLD.

Are the following groups of statements equivalent (11–14)?

11. (a) IF A = B ADD C TO D ELSE ADD E TO F. GO TO RTN-1.
    (b) IF A = B ADD C TO D GO TO RTN-1 ELSE ADD E TO F.

12. (a) IF A IS POSITIVE GO TO RTN-X ELSE GO TO RTN-Y.
    (b) IF A IS NOT NEGATIVE GO TO RTN-X ELSE GO TO RTN-Y.

13. (a) IF DISCOUNT IS GREATER THAN TOTAL GO TO ERR-RTN ELSE
        SUBTRACT DISCOUNT FROM TOTAL.
    (b) IF TOTAL IS GREATER THAN DISCOUNT OR TOTAL = DISCOUNT
        NEXT SENTENCE ELSE GO TO ERR-RTN. SUBTRACT DISCOUNT
        FROM TOTAL.

14. (a) IF A = B ADD C TO D GO TO RTN-5 ELSE GO TO RTN-5.
    (b) IF A = B ADD C TO D. GO TO RTN-5.

What, if anything, is wrong with the following statements:

15. IF A IS GREATER THAN OR EQUAL TO B GO TO RTN-3.

16. IF A IS NOT EQUAL TO B OR A IS NOT EQUAL TO C GO TO RTN-4.

17. IF A DOES NOT EQUAL 5 GO TO STEP-3.

18. IF A = 3 OR IF A = 4 GO TO RTN-2.

19. IF A = '123' GO TO START.

20. IF B = '23' OR B = 21 GO TO END1.

21. Write a routine to branch to a paragraph called NO-TEMP if C is between 98.6 and 100.2, inclusive.

PROBLEMS

1. Write a program to create output tape records from the following input tape:

   1–34 Identifying data
   35–39 Sales amount xxx.xx
      40 Not used

   The output record format is as follows:

   1–34 Same as input
   35–39 Sales amount xxx.xx
   40–41 Discount % .xx

42–46 Discount amount xxx.xx
47–51 Net xxx.xx
52–75 Not used

Notes

(a) Both files have standard labels and are blocked 10.
(b) If sales exceed $100.00, allow 3% discount.
      If sales are $100.00 or less, allow 2% discount.
(c) Discount amount = Sales × Discount %.
(d) Net = Sales — Discount amount.

2. Write a program to print out patient name and diagnosis for each of the following input medical cards:

1–20 Patient name
  21 Lung infection   1–if found
                                          0–if not found
  22 Temperature   1–high
                                          0–normal
  23 Sniffles   1–present
                                          0–absent
  24 Sore throat   1–present
                                        0–absent
25–80 Not used

Notes

(a) Output is a printed report with heading: **DIAGNOSIS REPORT.**
(b) If patient has lung infection and temperature, diagnosis is **PNEUMONIA.**
(c) If the patient has a combination of two or more symptoms (except the combination of lung infection and temperature), the diagnosis is **COLD.**
(d) If the patient has any single symptom, the diagnosis is **PHONY.**

3. Write a program for a dating service that uses the following format for its input data:

Card Input

 1–20 Name
21–23 Weight (in lbs.)
24–25 Height (in inches)
    26 Color of eyes 1–Blue, 2–Brown, 3–Other
    27 Color of hair 1–Blonde, 2–Brown, 3–Other
28–79 Not used
    80 Sex   M-male, F-female

Output is punched cards with the names of all:

(1) Blonde hair, blue-eyed males over 6 feet tall and weighing between 185 and 200 lbs.
(2) Brown eyed, brown hair females between 5 feet 2 inches and 5 feet 6 inches and weighing less than 120 lbs. All other combinations should **not** be printed.

4. Write a program to generate, in effect, a compiler program. Input shall be punched cards with the following format:

        ccs 1–2   Operation code
            3–12 First operand (field to be operated upon)
           13–22 Second operand
           23–80 Not used

Operation Codes

        10   corresponds to ADD
        20   corresponds to SUBTRACT
        30   corresponds to MULTIPLY
        40   corresponds to DIVIDE
        50   corresponds to STOP RUN

Program should read in each input card, perform the required operation, and print the result. For example, an input card with 20 0000010000 0000080000 as its first 22 positions should result in the printing of 0000070000. (80000-10000)

(**Hint.** Make sure that the output field is large enough to accommodate the answer.

5. Write a program to accept, as input, cards that have a date in Columns 1–6 in the form of month/day/year, i.e., 022570 refers to Feb. 25, 1970. If the date is valid, convert it to Julian date (year/day of year). (In the above example, the Julian date would be 70056.) Punch an output card with the resultant Julian date.

(**Hint.** Assume the program will be used for **20** years only, beginning with 1970. Leap years, 1972, 1976, 1980, 1984, 1988, have 29 days in FEB. All others have 28 days in FEB.)

6. Write a program to read a detail Bank Transaction Tape with the following format:

         1–19 Name of depositor
           20 Type   1–Previous balance, 2–Deposit, 3–Withdrawal
        21–25 Account number
        26–30 Amount xxxxx
        31–50 Not used

The tape records are blocked 50 and have standard labels. The tape is in sequence by account number. Type 1 records exist for each account number followed by Types 2 and 3, if they exist. Types 2 and 3 may be present for a given account number and may appear in any sequence.

   Print out the name of the depositor and his current balance (Previous Balance + Deposits — Withdrawals). Also print the heading BANK REPORT.

7. Write a program to print an inventory reorder form for each specified card input. Information on the inventory reorder form is obtained from the card record and its corresponding tape record. Input, then, consists of a detail card record and a master inventory tape record:

	Card Input		**Master Tape Input**
ccs	1–10 Product name		1–5 Product number
	11–15 Product number		6–15 Product name
	16–80 Not used		16–20 Unit price xxx.xx
			21–35 Name of vendor

block size is 10, standard
labels

If an input card for a specific product exists, find the corresponding tape record and print **PRODUCT NUMBER, PRODUCT NAME,** and **NAME OF VENDOR.** When there are no more cards, stop the run. Cards and tape are in product number sequence. Print the heading: **INVENTORY REORDER FORM.**

(**Hint.** A flowchart may be helpful before attempting to code the program.)

10

The Working-Storage Section

A. INDEPENDENT ITEMS AND VALUE CLAUSES

The DATA DIVISION is divided into two sections: the FILE SECTION and the WORKING STORAGE SECTION. Thus far, we have discussed in some depth the FILE SECTION, where all input and output files must be described in detail.

The DATA DIVISION, as a whole, contains **all defined storage areas** to be set aside for the processing of data. The WORKING-STORAGE SECTION, as part of the DATA DIVISION, contains all fields not part of input or output, which are necessary for the processing of data. Any con-

ing in some manner, are placed in the WORKING-STORAGE SECTION. This section may contain two categories of data fields: (1) independent data items and (2) group items that require subdivision. We will defer the discussion of group items to the next section.

Independent data items, defined in the WORKING-STORAGE SECTION, are individual fields, each performing a separate function and not related to any other data item. The use of independent data items will be illustrated by the following examples.

Example 1

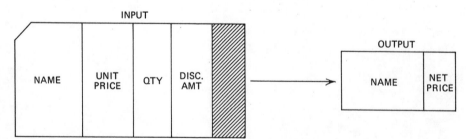

INPUT

NAME	UNIT PRICE	QTY	DISC. AMT	

OUTPUT

NAME	NET PRICE

stants,[1] intermediate totals, or work areas, not part of the files, which affect process-

---

[1] Many COBOL textbooks refer to a CONSTANT SECTION in addition to a WORKING-STORAGE SECTION. We will use the convention of placing all data fields that are not a part of files in the WORKING-STORAGE SECTION. Thus we are incorporating constants into the WORKING-STORAGE SECTION.

NET-PRICE is equal to UNIT-PRICE multiplied by QTY minus DISC-AMT.

Two steps are required to obtain NET-PRICE:

Multiplication:

MULTIPLY UNIT-PRICE BY QTY GIVING TOTAL.

TOTAL must be an independent item defined in WORKING-STORAGE. It is not part of the input and is only an intermediate result necessary for calculating NET-PRICE.

Subtraction

> SUBTRACT DISC-AMT FROM TOTAL
> GIVING NET-PRICE.

The independent item TOTAL is then an intermediate resultant field which eventually produces an output result.

Example 2: In Chapter 9, a routine to branch to TENS-RTN was coded if A, a two-position numeric input field, was a multiple of 10. The routine is as follows:

```
    MOVE 90 TO CTR.
BEGIN.
    IF A = CTR GO TO TENS-RTN.
    SUBTRACT 10 FROM CTR.
    IF CTR = ZERO NEXT SENTENCE
        ELSE GO TO BEGIN
```

CTR, a two-position field, is not part of either input or output. It is an independent item that must be specified in the WORKING-STORAGE SECTION.

Example 3: The following is a total routine that will print accumulated amount fields for cards with the same control number:

```
READ CARD-FILE AT END GO TO EOJ.
IF CONTROL-NO OF CARD-REC =
    CONTROL-NO-PREVIOUS GO TO
    ADD-RTN ELSE MOVE CONTROL-NO OF
    CARD-REC TO CONTROL-NO-PREVIOUS
    GO TO PRINT-RTN.
```

CONTROL-NO-PREVIOUS is an independent WORKING-STORAGE item that will be used to compare a current control number to that of the previous card. If they are equal, amount fields are accumulated in ADD-RTN. If they are not, the current control number is placed in CONTROL-NO-PREVIOUS and the printing of the previous totals is performed.

The WORKING-STORAGE SECTION, as all section names, is coded in Margin A. This entry follows the FILE SECTION and all its descriptions. Independent data items are given the special level number of 77 in WORKING-STORAGE. Data fields in the FILE SECTION utilize level numbers 01–49. In the WORKING-STORAGE SECTION, all independent data items use the level number of 77, which is coded in Margin A also.

The names given to items in this section conform to the rules for forming programmer-supplied words. All independent data items must have corresponding PICTURE clauses. We indicate the format or mode of a field in WORKING-STORAGE as previously specified: X denotes alphanumeric, 9 denotes numeric, and A denotes alphabetic.

Examples

```
77   INTERMEDIATE-TOTAL   PICTURE 9(5)V99.
77   CONSTANT-1           PICTURE X(4).
77   FLDA                 PICTURE AAA.
```

As in the FILE SECTION, the size of the field is indicated by the number of X's, 9's, or A's.

Independent items in the WORKING-STORAGE SECTION are generally **initialized;** that is, they are given initial contents by a VALUE clause. It is important to recall that third-generation computers **do not automatically clear storage** when reading in new programs. An area that is specified in the DATA DIVISION has an undefined quantity when a program begins execution. Unless the programmer indicates an initial value for a field, it cannot be assumed that the field is cleared with blanks or zeros.

To insure that output records or fields specified in the FILE SECTION are blank at the beginning of a program, we move SPACES to these areas in the PROCEDURE DIVISION before any processing is performed. In the WORKING-STORAGE SEC-

TION, however, we may initialize an independent item by using a **VALUE** clause.

Examples

```
77   TOTAL   PICTURE 999 VALUE ZERO.
77   CONSTANT1 PICTURE XXXX VALUE
                                SPACES.
```

A **VALUE** clause need not be specified for an independent item. If it is omitted, however, no assumption can be made about the initial contents of the field. If no **VALUE** clause is indicated, it is best to use a **MOVE** instruction in the **PROCEDURE DIVISION** to obtain an initial value in the field.

Four entries, then (the first three are required), are used to denote independent items in the **WORKING-STORAGE SECTION**.

1. Level **77**, coded in Margin A, signals the computer that an independent data item is about to be defined.

2. The programmer-supplied name defines the field.

3. The size of a field and its format or mode are defined by the **PICTURE** clause.

4. An initial value may be stored in the field by a **VALUE** clause.

The **VALUE** clause will contain a literal or figurative constant to be placed in the field. It must be in the same mode as the **PICTURE** clause. If the **PICTURE** denotes a numeric field, the value must be a numeric literal or **ZERO**.

Examples

```
77   FICA        PICTURE V999 VALUE .045.
77   CONSTANT-X  PICTURE 9(5) VALUE 07600.
77   TOTAL       PICTURE 9999 VALUE ZERO.
```

Notice that to say **77 TOTAL PICTURE 9999 VALUE ZERO** is the same as setting up the **77** level item **without** the **VALUE** clause and issuing the following instruction in the **PROCEDURE DIVISION: MOVE ZERO TO TOTAL**. Similarly, the entry **77 FICA PICTURE V999 VALUE .045** is identical to **MOVE .045 TO FICA**, where **FICA** has no **VALUE** clause.

Since the **VALUE** clause performs the same operation as a **MOVE** instruction, all rules for **MOVE** operations apply.

Example

```
77   FLDA   PICTURE 999 VALUE 12.
```

This is the same as moving **12** to **FLDA**. According to the rules for numeric **MOVE** operations (see Chapter 7), 012 will be placed in **FLDA**. In general, to obtain in the receiving field the same contents as the literal, use a **PICTURE** clause of equal specifications. To obtain exactly 12 in **FLDA**, **FLDA** should have **PICTURE 99**.

The rules for alphanumeric fields also apply to independent items in **WORKING-STORAGE**. If a field contains an alphanumeric or alphabetic **PICTURE** clause, its **VALUE** clause, if used, must contain a nonnumeric literal:

Examples

```
77   DATE PICTURE X(5) VALUE 'APRIL'.
77   FLDB PICTURE XXX VALUE SPACES.
```

It is invalid to say, for example, **77 FLD1 PICTURE X, VALUE 3**. If a field is defined with **PICTURE X** the **VALUE** clause must contain a nonnumeric literal. The value 3 is a numeric literal. The entry, therefore must read **77 FLD1 PICTURE X, VALUE '3'**. Similarly, we may not say **77 TOTAL PICTURE 99, VALUE SPACES. A space is not a valid numeric character.** Digits 0–9, decimal points, and plus or minus signs are the only characters that may be used in a numeric literal. To clear a numeric field,

we fill it with zeros and not blanks. The above entry should read **77 TOTAL PICTURE 99, VALUE ZERO**.

Note that **VALUE** clauses for initializing fields may **not** be used in the **FILE SECTION** of the **DATA DIVISION**. Only **WORKING-STORAGE** entries may have such **VALUE** clauses.

To place **ZEROS** in **TOTAL** at the onset of execution results in the initializing of the field. If information is then accumulated in **TOTAL**, it will no longer have value zero:

```
77  TOTAL PICTURE 9(5) VALUE ZERO.
PROCEDURE DIVISION.
        .
        .
        .
    ADD 5800 TO TOTAL.
```

At this point, **TOTAL** has a value of 05800 and **not** zero. If, however, we did not initialize **TOTAL**, its contents after the **ADD** would be unpredictable. When a field is not initialized, its content is unknown.

Note that we may substitute an independent data item for a literal used in the **PROCEDURE DIVISION**:

```
IF CODE OF CARD-IN = 0 MOVE 'CR' TO
    CREDIT-AREA OF TAPE-OUT.
```

is the same as

```
IF CODE OF CARD-IN = 0 MOVE CREDIT
    TO CREDIT-AREA OF TAPE-OUT.
```

where **CREDIT** is an independent item defined as follows:

```
77  CREDIT  PICTURE XX VALUE 'CR'.
```

The discretion of the programmer dictates which of the above methods to use. As a general rule, however, any literal that

18 digits in length. Thus the **VALUE** of a numeric item in the **WORKING-STORAGE SECTION** may not exceed 18 digits.

A nonnumeric **VALUE** clause, however, may contain up to 120 characters. A nonnumeric **VALUE** clause, like a nonnumeric literal, is enclosed in quotes and contains a maximum of 120 characters.

Since the **VALUE** clause for an alphanumeric field in the **WORKING-STORAGE SECTION** may contain 120 characters, it is sometimes necessary to continue a **VALUE** clause from one line of the coding sheet to another. The continuation of nonnumeric literals to two or more lines conforms to the following rules.

Rules for continuation of literals

1. Begin the literal with a quotation mark.
2. Continue the literal until the end of the line is reached (do not close with quote mark).
3. Place a dash (—) in the position marked CONTINUATION of the **next line** (position 7).
4. Continue the literal in Margin B of this next line, beginning with a quote mark.
5. End literal with a quotation mark.

Example

```
CONT.
8     12
77   HEADING     PICTURE X(36) VALUE 'MONTHLY TRANSACTIONS FOR APRI
-         'L, 1970'.
```

will be used more than once in the **PROCEDURE DIVISION** should, instead, be given an assigned storage area and a data-name in **WORKING-STORAGE**. It is more efficient to use this name several times in the program than to redefine the same literal again and again.

The **VALUE** clause of a numeric field will contain a numeric literal:

```
77  FLDA  PICTURE 99V99 VALUE 12.34.
```

12.34 is a numeric literal. You will recall that numeric literals may not exceed

Fig. 10-1 illustrates the continuation of a nonnumeric literal to three lines.

Note that a nonnumeric literal may encompass more than one line when defined in the **PROCEDURE DIVISION** as well. Consider the following **WORKING-STORAGE** entry:

```
77  FLDX  PICTURE X(50).
```

The rules for continuation of literals are the same:

IBM   COBOL Program Sheet   Form No. X28-1464-3 U/M 050
                                                                                  Printed in U. S. A.

System			Punching Instructions		Sheet	of
Program		Graphic			Card	*	Identification	
Programmer		Date	Punch		Form #		73	80

Sequence		A	B	COBOL Statement
(PAGE) (SERIAL)	CONT.			12 16 20 24 28 32 36 40 44 48 52 56 60 64 68 72
0 1		7 7	FIELD-HDGS	PICTURE X(99) VALUE \ NAME TRANSACTION N
0 2	-		UMBER DATE OF TRANSACTION AMOUNT INVOICE NUMBER
0 3	-		\ ITEM DESCRIPTION'.
0 4			
0 5			

Fig. 10-1

READ CARD-IN AT END GO TO EOJ.
    MOVE 'MONTHLY TRANSACTIONS FOR
— 'APRIL, 1970' TO FLDX

Independent **77** level items are usually an essential part of COBOL programs. Constants, intermediate totals, and work areas are generally required within a program. It is not always possible, however, to forecast their need before the **PROCE-DURE DIVISION** is written. As instructions are coded, a need for additional storage areas often arises. It is general practice, therefore, to allow space on the coding sheet for **WORKING-STORAGE** entries **prior** to beginning the **PROCEDURE DIVISION**. As independent items are needed, they may be assigned in the space provided. If it happens that no such items are required, the **WORKING-STORAGE SECTION** entry may be omitted.

EXERCISES

1. The two sections of the **DATA DIVISION** are the _____ **SECTION** and the _____ **SECTION**.
   *****
   FILE
   WORKING-STORAGE

2. Independent data items are _____, _____, or _____ defined in **WORKING-STORAGE**.
   *****
   constants
   intermediate totals
   work areas

3. Independent items in **WORKING-STORAGE** are given the special level number _____.
   *****
   77

4. **WORKING-STORAGE SECTION** and 77 are entries coded in _____.
   *****
   Margin A

5. WORKING-STORAGE SECTION and its entries follow the _____ _____ and precede the _____ _____ in a COBOL program.

*****

FILE SECTION
PROCEDURE DIVISION.

6. Independent items in WORKING-STORAGE **must** have _____, a _____, a _____ and **may** have a _____.

*****

level **77**
programmer-supplied name
PICTURE clause
VALUE clause

7. VALUE clauses to initialize fields may only be used in the _____ _____ _____.

*****

WORKING-STORAGE SECTION.

8. A VALUE clause should be used for all WORKING-STORAGE entries because _____.

*****

the computer is not automatically cleared at execution time.

9. The VALUE clause may contain a _____ or a _____.

*****

literal
figurative constant

10. The VALUE specified for a field must be in the same _____ as the _____ clause.

*****

format or mode
PICTURE

Make any necessary corrections to the following (11–16):

11. WORKING STORAGE SECTION

12. 77   FLD 1   PICTURE X VALUE SPACE.

13. 77   FLDA   PICTURE X VALUE 4.

14. 77   FLDB   PICTURE X VALUE ZERO.

15. 77   FLDC   PICTURE 99 VALUE SPACES.

16. 77   FLDD   PICTURE 99V99 VALUE 12.34.

*****

11. WORKING-STORAGE SECTION.

12. FLD-1 OR FLD1

13. **77   FLDA   PICTURE X VALUE '4'.**

14. Nothing wrong.

15. Numeric fields cannot have a value of spaces.

16. Nothing wrong.

B. GROUP ITEMS

The **DATA DIVISION**, as was emphasized in the last section, contains **all** defined storage areas, necessary for the processing of data. The **WORKING-STORAGE SECTION** of the **DATA DIVISION** contains all those storage areas which are not part of input or output.

Thus far we have discussed independent **77** level items defined in **WORKING-STORAGE**. Any **elementary** or independent item that is necessary as an intermediate work area is defined as a **77** level entry in **WORKING-STORAGE**. Such items may be assigned **values,** which initialize the fields.

In addition to elementary items, **group items** may be stored in this section. A group item, you will recall, is one which is **further subdivided** into two or more elementary fields. A name field, subdivided into first and last name, and a date field, subdivided into month, day and year, are examples of group items.

Group items requiring subdivision are **not** coded as 77 level entries in the **WORKING-STORAGE SECTION**. A **77** item is an elementary field, independent of all other entries, and may **not** be subdivided.

Group items in **WORKING-STORAGE** are coded as **records** on the **01** level. All group items follow the **77** level elementary items and are coded in Margin A, on the **01** level.

The following is a sample **WORKING-STORAGE SECTION**:

```
WORKING-STORAGE SECTION.
77   TOTAL      PICTURE 9(5), VALUE ZERO.
77   CONST    PICTURE X(4), VALUE 'CODE'.
77   SAVE-AREA   PICTURE XXX
                    VALUE SPACES.
```

```
01   ADDRESS.
     02 NUMB    PICTURE 9999.
     02 STREET  PICTURE X(20).
     02 CITY    PICTURE X(25).
     02 STATE   PICTURE XXX.
01   DATE.
     02 MONTH  PICTURE 99, VALUE 06.
     02 YEAR   PICTURE 99, VALUE 70.
```

We see that the **WORKING-STORAGE SECTION** consists of two parts. All independent items appear on the **77** level and are followed by group items, which appear on the **01** level. Both **77** and **01** level entries are coded in Margin A; **02–49** levels, if used, are coded in Margin B.

If fields within group items do not have specified values, data will be **moved** into that area. We may assume that data will be moved into the group item, **ADDRESS**, for example, since it has no **VALUE** clause. Group items may also have corresponding **VALUE** clauses that initialize the field, as **DATE** did in the above example.

Let us examine some COBOL programs that require group items in the **WORKING-STORAGE SECTION**.

Example 1: Suppose a card file consists of two records, a date card and detail transaction cards. The **FILE SECTION** entry for the card file is:

```
FD   CARD-FILE
     RECORDING MODE IS F
     LABEL RECORDS ARE OMITTED
     RECORD CONTAINS 80 CHARACTERS
     DATA RECORDS ARE DATE-REC,
     TRANS-REC.
01   DATE-REC.
     02 DATE.
        03 MONTH  PICTURE 99.
        03 YEAR   PICTURE 99.
     02 FILLER    PICTURE X(76).
```

```
01   TRANS-REC.
     02 CUSTOMER-NAME PICTURE X(20).
     02 TRANS-NO        PICTURE 9(5).
     02 AMT             PICTURE 999V99.
     02 FILLER          PICTURE X(46).
     02 DATEX.
        03 MONTHX       PICTURE 99.
        03 YEARX   '    PICTURE 99.
```

The date card will be the first card read. All succeeding cards will contain transaction data, which must be compared against the date card to determine if they are within the current period. If the date on the detail transaction card is not within the current period, an error must be indicated.

The first **READ** command will transmit the information from the date card to the input area. Unless the date is moved to some other area of storage, a second **READ** operation will **overlay** the date in the input area with the second card's data. Computers perform **destructive READ** operations. In other words, previous data in the input area is destroyed with each **READ** command.

The date, then, on the first card must be moved to some area of storage which is not part of input or output. We must move **DATE** to a **WORKING-STORAGE** entry for future processing.

We establish the **WORKING-STORAGE** entry as follows:

```
01   STORED-DATE.
     02 MONTHY   PICTURE 99.
     02 YEARY    PICTURE 99.
```

Since this is a group item, it will follow any **77** level entries required in the program.

The instruction to store the date in **WORKING-STORAGE** is coded in the **PROCEDURE DIVISION** as a **MOVE** statement:

```
MOVE DATE TO STORED-DATE.
```

Note that **STORED-DATE** is a group item which is further subdivided into two elementary fields, **MONTHY** and **YEARY**. After the date is moved to **STORED-DATE**, it is

always available for processing unless an instruction is issued to clear it.

Note that the stored date will be compared against each detail record to determine the validity of the transaction date:

```
IF YEARX < YEARY GO TO ERR-RTN.
IF YEARX = YEARY AND MONTHX <
MONTHY GO TO ERR-RTN.
```

A group item in **WORKING-STORAGE**, then, is necessary for storing input data that must be available for future processing. Such data is moved to **WORKING-STORAGE**, where it is stored unless an instruction clears it.

Example 2: Employee record cards contain salary information. Using an appropriate tax rate, which is based on salary, annual take-home pay will be computed. Since tax rates change fairly often, the **tax rate table** will be read into the computer as the first card. It will be subdivided into five 5-position tax percentages.

Thus the **FD** entry for the card file is as follows:

```
FD   CARD-IN
     RECORDING MODE IS F
     LABEL RECORDS ARE OMITTED
     RECORD CONTAINS 80 CHARACTERS
     DATA RECORDS ARE TAX-CHART,
     EMPLOYEE-REC.
01   TAX-CHART.
     02 TAX-PERCNT-FOR-SAL-BELOW-4000
                          PICTURE 9(5).
     02 TAX-PERCNT-SAL-BET-4001-8000
                          PICTURE 9(5).
     02 TAX-PERCNT-SAL-BET-8001-10000
                          PICTURE 9(5).
     02 TAX-PERCNT-SAL-BET-10001-20001
                          PICTURE 9(5).
     02 TAX-PERCNT-SAL-OVER-20001
                          PICTURE 9(5).
     02 FILLER   PICTURE X(55).
01   EMPLOYEE-REC.
     02 NAME    PICTURE X(20).
     02 SAL     PICTURE 9(5).
     02 FILLER  PICTURE X(55).
```

Since the tax data will be the **first** input card, a **READ** command will transmit the information to the input area. Unless the tax data is moved to storage, it will be destroyed by the next READ command. Thus a WORKING-STORAGE SECTION entry may appear, after any 77 level items necessary in the program, as follows:

```
01   STORED-TAX-RATES.
     02 TAX1   PICTURE 9(5).
     02 TAX2   PICTURE 9(5).
     02 TAX3   PICTURE 9(5).
     02 TAX4   PICTURE 9(5).
     02 TAX5   PICTURE 9(5).
```

To obtain the information in WORKING-STORAGE for future processing, the TAX-CHART will be read and the first 25 positions of the card will be moved:

```
READ CARD-IN AT END GO TO EOJ.
MOVE TAX-CHART TO
STORED-TAX-RATES.
```

Note that the MOVE statement denotes a group MOVE, which is always considered nonnumeric (see Chapter 7 on MOVE statements). Data in TAX-CHART is moved from left to right; since STORED-TAX-RATES is 25 positions, only the first 25 columns of card data are moved. The first 25 columns of the tax card, however, contain the desired tax data.

It is usually possible to store most fields as independent items rather than grouping them. TAX1, TAX2, TAX3, TAX4, TAX5, for example, could have been established as 77 level items. The instructions to move the input data to these fields would then require five independent MOVE statements. Since only one MOVE operation is necessary when the tax data is grouped, the above method is considered more efficient.

A major use, then, of group items in the WORKING-STORAGE SECTION is for the storage of groups of input fields that must be saved for future processing. Control cards and date cards are examples of entries that generally must be stored for further processing. In Chapter 16, we will see that group items in WORKING-STORAGE are essential for storing tables.

A second major use of group items in the WORKING-STORAGE SECTION is for the accumulation of output data. Thus far, we have written programs where output data has been accumulated in the output area of the FILE SECTION. A WRITE (record-name) instruction will transmit the stored data to the corresponding output device.

Output data may, however, be stored in WORKING-STORAGE. It must then be moved to the output area before a WRITE instruction may be executed.

A valid question, at this point, is why accumulate output data in WORKING-STORAGE. The answer is that values may be assigned to specific fields in the WORKING-STORAGE SECTION, whereas VALUE clauses cannot be used in the FILE SECTION.

Consider the following print record:

```
FD   PRINT-FILE
     RECORDING MODE IS F
     LABEL RECORDS ARE OMITTED
     RECORD CONTAINS 132 CHARACTERS
     DATA RECORD IS PRINT-REC.
01   PRINT-REC.
     02 INITIAL1    PICTURE X.
     02 CONST1      PICTURE X.
     02 INITIAL2    PICTURE X.
     02 CONST2      PICTURE X.
     02 LAST-NAME   PICTURE X(18).
     02 FILLER      PICTURE XXXX.
     02 MONTH       PICTURE 99.
     02 CONST3      PICTURE X.
     02 YEAR        PICTURE 99.
     02 FILLER      PICTURE X(101).
```

In addition to reading the first initial, the second initial, last name, month, and year from an input document and moving it to PRINT-REC, the following MOVE operations are necessary for maintaining a neat and "readable" report:

```
MOVE SPACES TO PRINT-REC.
MOVE '.' TO CONST1.
MOVE '.' TO CONST2.
MOVE '/' TO CONST3.
```

The output report would then have the appropriate constants:

```
J.E.SMITH    07/44
R.A.JONES    05/41
```

If, however, **STORED-PRINT-LINE** were defined in **WORKING-STORAGE** as follows, the above **MOVE** operations would be unnecessary:

```
01   STORED-PRINT-LINE.
     02 INITIAL1    PICTURE X.
     02 CONST1      PICTURE X,
                    VALUE '.'.
     02 INITIAL2    PICTURE X.
     02 CONST2      PICTURE X,
                    VALUE '.'.
     02 LAST-NM     PICTURE X(18).
     02 FILLER      PICTURE XXXX,
                    VALUE SPACES.
     02 MONTH       PICTURE 99.
     02 CONST3      PICTURE X,
                    VALUE '/'.
     02 YEAR        PICTURE 99.
     02 FILLER      PICTURE X(101),
                    VALUE SPACES.
```

Since **VALUE** clauses are permitted in the **WORKING-STORAGE SECTION**, the con-stants may be given initial values rather than moving the appropriate literals to these fields in the **PROCEDURE DIVISION**.

To print the data in **STORED-PRINT-LINE** after the input fields are moved to the record, we say:

> **MOVE STORED-PRINT-LINE TO PRINT-REC.**
> **WRITE PRINT-REC.**

Thus, when specified values are required in an output record, a **WORKING-STORAGE** group item may be established with the appropriate value clauses. This entry may then be moved to the output area before a record is written. The method discussed above is considered more efficient than setting up fields in the **FILE SECTION** and performing independent **MOVE** operations for each literal desired.

The use of group items in **WORKING-STORAGE** to store output data is even more significant when creating header records on the printer. This topic will be discussed more fully in Chapter 13, which treats **printed output**.

EXERCISES

1. A group item is _____.
   *****
   one which is further subdivided into elementary items

2. A group item (does, does not) have a **PICTURE** clause.
   *****
   does not (only elementary items have **PICTURE** clauses)

3. In the **WORKING-STORAGE SECTION**, all group items must _____ 77 level items.
   *****
   follow

4. Group items are coded on the __ level in Margin __.
   *****
   01
   A

5. When input data is _____, it may be stored as a group item in **WORKING-STORAGE**.
   *****
   necessary for future processing

6. Two examples of input data which must be stored for future processing are _____ and _____.

*****

date cards
control cards

7. When output data utilizes fields _____, it may be stored as a group item in **WORKING-STORAGE**.

*****

with specified values

8. To print data that is accumulated in **WORKING-STORAGE**, it must be _____ to the output area before a **WRITE** statement is executed.

*****

moved

Review Questions

Make necessary corrections to each of the following (1–8). Assume margin use and spacing are correct.

1. 77 CONSTANTA   PICTURE X VALUE 2.

2. 01 DATE.
       02 MONTH   PICTURE 99.
       02 YEAR   PICTURE 99
   77 TOTAL   PICTURE 9(5).

3. 77 CONSTANTB   PICTURE X VALUE A.

4. 77 SUM   PICTURE 999 VALUE SPACES.

5. 77 HEADER.
       02 FLDA   PICTURE X(4).
       02 FLDB   PICTURE X(4).

6. WORKING STORAGE SECTION
   77 X   PICTURE X VALUE ZERO.

7. 77 Y   VALUE 3.

8. 77 FIELDA   PICTURE X(132) VALUE SPACES.

9. (T OR F) A **VALUE** clause makes no sense in an input area.

10. (T OR F) A **VALUE** clause must be used in the **WORKING-STORAGE SECTION**.

11. (T OR F) The **WORKING-STORAGE SECTION** may either precede or follow the **FILE SECTION**.

12. Write a **WORKING-STORAGE** description of a three-position alphanumeric field called **BOB** with an initial value of zero.

13. Which of the following is coded in Margin A?

    a. **WORKING-STORAGE SECTION**
    b. **77** level
    c. **01** level
    d. **02** level

14. Write a **WORKING-STORAGE** description of a 120-position independent field with the following contents:

THIS REPORT IS RUN MONTHLY TO DETERMINE THE NAMES OF ALL EMPLOYEES WHO HAVE BEEN PROMOTED

PROBLEMS

1. Write a program for a college bursar to compute for each semester:

    (a) Tuition of each student.
    (b) Total tuition from all students.

If a student is taking 12 credits or less, tuition is $30/credit.
If a student is taking more than 12 credits, the cost is $360.

Input: Student cards
 1–20 Student name
21–22 Number of credits
23–80 Not used

Output: Magnetic tape
            Blocking factor = 50
            Record size = 40
            Standard labels

 1–20 Student name
21–22 Number of credits
23–25 Tuition
26–40 Not used

Print message **TOTAL TUITION** and the computed figure.

2. Write a program to summarize accident records to obtain the following information:

    (a) Percentage of drivers under 25.
    (b) Percentage of drivers who are female.
    (c) Percentage of drivers from New York.

There is one tape record for each driver involved in an accident in the past year:

1–4 Driver number
5   State code (1 for New York)
6–9 Birth date (Month and Year)
10   Sex (M for male, F for female)
Blocking factor = 50, standard labels

Results should be printed with constants:

% OF DRIVERS UNDER 25
% OF DRIVERS FEMALE
% OF DRIVERS FROM NY

3. Write a program to compute the number of $20, $10, $5, and $1 bills that an employee should be paid when his salary is provided as input.

Input: Cards
1–20 Employee name
21–25 Salary
26–80 Not used

Output: Printed report with name and above data (also print messages, i.e., **NO. OF 20's,** etc.).

(**Note.** Employee should be paid in **largest** denominations possible.)

4. Write a program to create a magnetic tape file from the following input card records:

1–20 Employee name
21–22 Hours worked
23–25 Rate x.xx
26–80 Not used

Output: Blocked 10, standard labels
1–20 Employee name
21–25 Gross pay
26–50 Not used

Gross pay = Reg hours $\times$ Rate + Overtime hours $\times$ 1.5 $\times$ Rate. Overtime hours are those hours exceeding 40.

5. Write a program to compute the arithmetic mean for an input file with the following format:

Card 1 for group:	1–5	Acct. no.
	6–7	Number of cards in group
Remainder of cards for group:	1–5	Acct. no.
	6–11	Amount xxx.xx

Print Acct. no. and arithmetic mean for each group.
Amount should be rounded to nearest integer.

6. Write a program to compute compound interest from the following input tape records:

1–20 Name of depositor
21–25 Principal P_0
26–27 Interest rate .xx   r
28–29 Period   n
30–35 Not used

Output is a punched card with name of depositor and principal amount after n periods of investment (p_n).

Formula: $p_n = p_o (1 + r)^n$

$$\left[\textbf{Hint.} \quad (1 + r)^n = \underbrace{(1 + r) \times (1 + r) \times (1 + r) \dots \times (1 + r)}_{n \text{ times}} \right]$$

Unit 3

Additional Data Division Entries

Thus far, we have discussed the basic entries of the **DATA DIVISION**, which would suffice for elementary level COBOL programs. There are, however, additional techniques which may be used in the **DATA DIVISION** to make coding easier and more efficient.

A. QUALIFICATION OF NAMES

You will recall that file names and record names must be unique within a COBOL program. If **XXX** is the name of a file defined in the **SELECT** clause of the **ENVIRONMENT DIVISION**, and described by an **FD** entry in the **DATA DIVISION**, then the same name, **XXX**, may **not** be used to define fields, work areas, or paragraph names. Similarly, independent **77** level items must be given unique names.

Programmer-supplied names, however, which define data fields within records, need **not** be unique. The following **DATA DIVISION** entries, for example, are correct:

```
FD   CARD-IN RECORDING MODE F LABEL
     RECORDS OMITTED, DATA RECORD IS
     CARD-REC.
01   CARD-REC.
     02 NAME    PICTURE A(10).
     02 AMT     PICTURE 9(5).
     02 CODE    PICTURE X(5).
     02 FILLER  PICTURE X(60).
```

```
FD   TAPE-OUT RECORDING MODE F,
     LABEL RECORDS ARE STANDARD,
     DATA RECORD IS TAPE-REC.
01   TAPE-REC.
     02 NAME    PICTURE A(10).
     02 AMT     PICTURE 9(5).
     02 CODE    PICTURE X(5).
```

CARD-IN and **TAPE-OUT**, as file names, must be unique, and so must **CARD-REC** and **TAPE-REC**, as record names. Note, however, that **NAME, AMT** and **CODE**, as data fields within records, need not be unique; that is, they may be used to define more than one area of storage.

In the **PROCEDURE DIVISION**, when accessing a data-name that is not unique, the name must be **qualified.** We must indicate which record is to be accessed. We cannot say, for example, **ADD AMT TO TOTAL**, since **AMT** is the name of two different data fields and it is unclear which is to be added.

When more than one field in storage has the same name, we qualify the name in the **PROCEDURE DIVISION** as follows:

$$\text{(data-name)} \left[\begin{array}{c} \underline{OF} \\ \underline{IN} \end{array} \right] \text{(record name)}$$

Examples

(1) ADD AMT OF CARD-REC TO TOTAL.
(2) MOVE NAME OF CARD-REC TO NAME OF TAPE-REC.

(3) IF NAME OF CARD-REC = SPACES MOVE 'MISSING' TO NAME IN TAPE-REC.

Whenever a name is used more than once in the **DATA DIVISION**, it must be qualified when processed in the **PROCE-DURE DIVISION**. The words **OF** or **IN** may be used interchangeably to qualify a name.

The method of using the same data-name to define several fields in separate records is a useful programming tool. **PRO-CEDURE DIVISION** entries are easier to understand for someone reading the program, and easier to debug for the programmer, when qualification of names is utilized. To say **MOVE AMT OF REC-IN TO AMT OF REC-OUT** is relatively simple to understand. To say **MOVE AMT1 TO AMT2**, where **AMT1** and **AMT2** are uniquely defined fields in the **INPUT** and **OUTPUT** areas, respectively, is less clear. Although the latter involves less coding, the reader must consult the **DATA DIVISION** entries to determine what area of storage is being transmitted and which field will receive the data. That is, the location of **AMT1** and **AMT2** in storage is unclear. With the use of qualifiers, it is quite obvious that the amount fields are part of the input and output records, respectively.

It is sometimes difficult to follow the logic of a program if its analysis requires constant referral to the **DATA DIVISION**. With the use of qualification of names, entries in the **PROCEDURE DIVISION** are often easier to follow.

In summary, file names, record names, and independent **77** level data-names must be unique. Names which define data fields within records need not be unique. The same name may define several areas in the **DATA DIVISION**. Each time these fields are accessed in the **PROCEDURE DI-VISION**, however, they must be qualified. The format:

$$\text{(data-name} \left[\begin{array}{c} \text{OF} \\ \text{IN} \end{array} \right] \text{record name)}$$

qualifies a name which is used to define more than one field.

B. JUSTIFIED RIGHT CLAUSE

Suppose we define a field in the **WORK-ING-STORAGE SECTION** as follows:

77 CODE PICTURE X(8) VALUE 'ABC'.

This entry performs the same operation as **MOVE 'ABC' TO CODE**, where **CODE** has no **VALUE** clause. Since the literal is three positions long and the field is defined as eight positions, 'ABC' will be **left justified** in the field. You will recall that, when sending fields or literals are smaller than receiving fields in alphanumeric operations, data is left justified in the receiving field and low-order positions are filled with spaces. Thus **CODE** will have contents of ABC⬚⬚⬚⬚⬚.

For specific applications, it is sometimes desirable to **right justify** data within a field. That is, we wish to obtain in **CODE** ⬚⬚⬚⬚⬚ABC.

A **JUSTIFIED RIGHT** clause, used in the **DATA DIVISION**, will produce the desired result. If **CODE** is defined as follows:

77 CODE PICTURE X(8) VALUE 'ABC' JUSTIFIED RIGHT.

the contents of **CODE** will be ⬚⬚⬚⬚⬚ABC.

Thus **JUSTIFIED RIGHT** may be used in the **DATA DIVISION** to alter the normal rules for alphanumeric move operations.[1] Normally alphanumeric fields are left justified; the above clause, used in an alphanumeric field, will cause data, which contains less characters than the receiving field, to be placed in the rightmost positions of a field, and all nonfilled high-order positions to be replaced with blanks or spaces.

The **JUSTIFIED RIGHT** clause may be specified for any elementary, **nonnumeric** data field. The clause is placed after the

---

[1] A **JUSTIFIED LEFT** clause may be used to alter the normal rules for numeric move operations. This entry, however, is not supported by all COBOL compilers.

PICTURE clause is defined, and the VALUE, if any, assigned.

To say MOVE 'C' TO FLD1, where FLD1 is defined as 02 FLD1 PICTURE XXX JUSTIFIED RIGHT, will result in ▯▯C being placed in FLD1. Thus a JUSTIFIED RIGHT clause implies that any VALUE given to the field or any data moved into the field will **not** conform to the normal alphanumeric rules. All data placed in the field will, instead, be right justified.

The JUSTIFIED RIGHT clause is often used in a print area. Let us define a print record as follows:

```
01   PRINT-REC.
     02  FILLER    PICTURE  X(60).
     02  HEADER    PICTURE  X(12).
     02  FILLER    PICTURE  X(60).
```

In the PROCEDURE DIVISION, the following instructions are coded:

```
MOVE SPACES TO PRINT-REC.
MOVE 'COMPANY ABCD' TO HEADER.
WRITE PRINT-REC.
```

In this way, we obtain the heading 'COMPANY ABCD' in the center of the form with 60 spaces on each side of it. We can, however, simplify the DATA DIVISION entries as follows:

```
01   PRINT-REC.
     02  HEADER    PICTURE  X(72)
                   JUSTIFIED RIGHT.
     02  FILLER    PICTURE  X(60).
```

Using the same PROCEDURE DIVISION as above, we obtain the identical results. 'COMPANY ABCD' will be placed in the 12 rightmost positions of HEADER, leaving 60 high-order or leftmost, blanks. Thus we have defined our record with two fields instead of three.

The JUSTIFIED RIGHT clause is used to alter the normal rules for alphanumeric move operations. The clause, therefore, may **not** be used in conjunction with fields with numeric PICTURE clauses, since such fields are normally right justified.

EXERCISES

1. Qualification of names is required in the PROCEDURE DIVISION when _____.
   * * * * *
   the same name is used to define two or more areas of storage

2. Record names and file names must be _____ but _____ need not be unique.
   * * * * *
   unique
   field or data-names

3. The words _____ and _____ may be used interchangeably to qualify a data-name.
   * * * * *
   OF
   IN

4. If an alphanumeric sending field contains less characters than an alphanumeric receiving field, the data is _____ justified in the field and remaining positions are fiiled with _____.

*****

left

blanks

5. To alter the normal rules for alphanumeric move operations, a _____ clause may be used.

*****

JUSTIFIED RIGHT

6. The JUSTIFIED RIGHT clause may not be used with _____ fields.

*****

numeric

7. The JUSTIFIED RIGHT clause follows the _____ clause and the _____ clause, if any, in the _____ DIVISION.

*****

PICTURE

VALUE

DATA

8. 77   FLDA PICTURE XXXX VALUE 'ABC' will result in _____ in FLDA.

*****

ABC⅊

9. To cause ⅊ABC to be placed in the above field, _____ will be the DATA DIVISION entry.

*****

77   FLDA PICTURE XXXX VALUE 'ABC' JUSTIFIED RIGHT.

10. 02 FLDB PICTURE XXXXX VALUE '123' JUSTIFIED RIGHT will result in _____ in FLDB.

*****

⅊⅊123

C. REDEFINES CLAUSE

It is sometimes necessary to define a single field in the DATA DIVISION in two or more distinct ways. If the same area is to be used for different purposes, it must be redefined in the DATA DIVISION.

Let us consider an example. Card columns 1–5, called AMT in the input area of the DATA DIVISION, is to be added to a field called TOTAL. To perform any arithmetic operation, the fields specified must be defined numerically, with a PICTURE of 9's. If, however, Columns 1–5 are blank, a branch to ERROR-RTN is to be executed. In the PROCEDURE DIVISION we cannot say, IF AMT = SPACES GO TO ERROR-RTN. Only nonnumeric fields may be compared to spaces. A space, you will recall, is not a valid numeric character. Since AMT is defined as numeric in order to perform the ADD operation, it may not be compared to spaces.

Thus these same five storage positions, called AMT in the input area, must be redefined as an alphanumeric field so that a valid test for blanks may be performed. Thus the area in core storage reserved for input from card columns 1–5 is to be used for **two** different purposes. A **REDEFINES** clause in the DATA DIVISION allows the programmer to employ different specifications in defining a single field in storage:

(level-no)	(data-name-1)	(PICTURE clause).
(same level)	(data-name-2)	REDEFINES data-name-1 {PICTURE}.

Example 1

```
01   CARD-REC.
     02  AMT-1   PICTURE 9(5).
     02  AMT-2   REDEFINES AMT-1
                 PICTURE X(5).
```

AMT-1 and **AMT-2** both refer to the **same** five positions of storage. When the data-name **AMT-1** is denoted, we are defining these five positions as numeric. When the data-name **AMT-2** is used, these same posi-

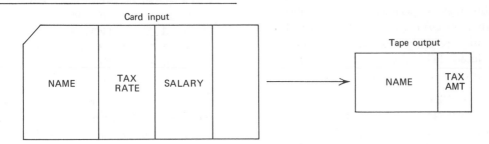

Card input / Tape output

tions are defined alphanumerically. Thus we may perform two different operations on these fields: (1) we can compare **AMT-2** to spaces, since it is defined as an alphanumeric field and (2) we can add **AMT-1** to **TOTAL** since it is defined numerically:

```
IF AMT-2 = SPACES GO TO ERROR-RTN
ELSE ADD AMT-1 TO TOTAL.
```

Note that the two **02** level items refer to the same storage area. When we refer to these positions as **AMT-2,** we are assuming it contains alphanumeric data. When we refer to the **same area** as **AMT-1,** it will contain numeric data.

A **REDEFINES** clause may be used for any item except records. That is, a **REDEFINES** clause may not be used on the **01** level.

Records are considered independent entities and may not be redefined.

If a specific level item is to be redefined, the second specification must be on the same level. **03 FLD1 PICTURE X** may be redefined only on the **03** level. A schematic for redefinition is as follows:

Value clauses may not be used in any field that is to be redefined:

Invalid:

```
02 ITEM PICTURE 99 VALUE 12.
02 ITEM-X REDEFINES ITEM PICTURE XX.
```

The above is **not** valid. A **VALUE** clause and a **REDEFINES** clause may not be used to describe the same storage area.

Example 2

$$TAX\text{-}AMT = TAX\text{-}RATE \times SALARY$$

If either **TAX-RATE** or **SALARY** contains spaces or nonnumeric data, move zeros to **TAX-AMT.**[1]

To test a field for numeric data, that field must be defined alphanumerically. A field defined numerically with a **PICTURE** of 9's must, by definition, contain numeric data. Therefore, no **numeric** test may be performed. **IF** (data-name) **IS NUMERIC** is a valid statement only if the data-name defines an alphanumeric field. The input area, then, must be defined as follows:

[1] It is obviously incorrect to have nonnumeric data in these fields. Since the input is on cards, however, the programmer must allow for keypunching errors.

```
01   REC-IN.
     02  EMPLOYEE-NAME PICTURE A(15).
     02  TAX-RATE          PICTURE V99.
     02  TAX-RATEX REDEFINES TAX-RATE
                           PICTURE XX.
     02  SALARY            PICTURE 9(5).
     02  SALARYX REDEFINES SALARY
                           PICTURE X(5).
     02  FILLER            PICTURE X(58).
```

Redefinition of **SALARY** and **TAX-RATE** is necessary, since the two fields must be (1) defined numerically to perform the arithmetic operation and (2) defined alphanumerically for comparison purposes. A valid comparison then, is: **IF SALARYX IS NOT NUMERIC OR TAX-RATEX IS NOT NUMERIC MOVE ZEROS TO TAX-AMT ELSE MULTIPLY TAX-RATE BY SALARY GIVING TAX-AMT.**

Thus a common use of the **REDEFINES** clause is to specify one area of storage in two different ways so that proper operations may be performed on the field. Another important use of **REDEFINES** clauses is in describing a record that may have different field specifications. Consider the following record layouts:

DEBIT		CREDIT	
1–20	NAME	1–20	NAME
21–25	AMT1	21–23	TOTAL1
26–30	AMT2	24–26	TOTAL2
80	CODE	27–30	TOTAL3
		80	CODE

We may define our **FD** for the card file as having two distinct record layouts:

```
FD   CARD-FILE
     RECORDING MODE IS F
     LABEL RECORDS ARE OMITTED
     RECORD CONTAINS 80 CHARACTERS
     DATA RECORDS ARE DEBIT-REC,
     CREDIT-REC.
01   DEBIT-REC.
     02  NAME       PICTURE A(20).
     02  AMTS.
         03  AMT1   PICTURE 999V99.
         03  AMT2   PICTURE 999V99.
     02  FILLER     PICTURE X(49).
     02  CODE       PICTURE X
```

```
01   CREDIT-REC.
     02  NAME       PICTURE A(20).
     02  TOTALS.
         03  TOT1   PICTURE 999.
         03  TOT2   PICTURE 999.
         03  TOT3   PICTURE 9999.
     02  FILLER     PICTURE X(49).
     02  CODE       PICTURE X.
```

With the use of a **REDEFINES** clause, however, it is also possible to consider only **one** record layout:

```
FD   CARD-FILE
     RECORDING MODE IS F
     LABEL RECORDS ARE OMITTED
     RECORD CONTAINS 80 CHARACTERS
     DATA RECORD IS REC-IN.
01   REC-IN.
     02  NAME       PICTURE A(20).
     02  AMTS.
         03  AMT1   PICTURE 999V99.
         03  AMT2   PICTURE 999V99.
     02  TOTALS     REDEFINES AMTS.
         03  TOT1   PICTURE 999.
         03  TOT2   PICTURE 999.
         03  TOT3   PICTURE 9999.
     02  FILLER     PICTURE X(49).
     02  CODE       PICTURE X.
```

In this way, only **one** record description is required. **AMTS**, within the record, is subdivided into two amount fields. We will consider that the record contains this two subfield breakdown when **CODE = 1**. If **CODE = 0**, the record contains **TOTALS**, which occupies the same storage area and is broken down into three total fields. Thus with a **REDEFINES** clause, only one record layout is required.

When the same area of storage is used for different purposes, a **REDEFINES** clause is necessary. We may redefine a field in two basic ways: (1) When specifying the mode or type of field in two different ways. For one purpose, a field may be defined numerically; for another, it may be defined alphanumerically. (2) When specifying the subfield or elementary breakdown in distinct ways. At times, for example, an area of storage contains three subfields; at other times, it contains four.

D. ADDITIONAL PICTURE SPECIFICATIONS FOR NUMERIC FIELDS

Operational Signs. Thus far, PICTURE specifications for numeric fields may contain (1) 9's to denote numeric data and (2) V to denote implied decimal points. With the above two specifications only, all numeric data will be considered **unsigned.** Unless the computer is instructed to maintain an operational sign on a field, that field will be considered unsigned and thus negative numbers will not be recognized as such.

When the possibility exists that negative numbers may be placed in a field, we must instruct the computer to maintain a sign on the field. We do this by including an S in the PICTURE clause of numeric fields. The S, which instructs the computer to retain the sign of all numbers, is always the **first** character in a PICTURE clause and does **not** add to the size of the field. 02 AMT PICTURE S999V99 is a five-position numeric field which will be considered signed, and which has an implied decimal point after the first three digits.

An S in the PICTURE clause of a numeric field is essential when data may contain signed numbers. Without the S, the operational sign of the number is dropped. Consider the following example:

```
77  WORK1  PICTURE 99.
77  WORK2  PICTURE 999.

MOVE –12 TO WORK1.
ADD WORK1, 100 GIVING WORK2.
```

Since WORK1 is not signed, 12 and not –12, is placed in the field. The negative sign is not transmitted unless an S exists in the PICTURE clause of the receiving field. Thus the ADD operation will result in 112 in WORK2. If WORK1 were defined to include the sign as:

```
77  WORK1  PICTURE S99.
```

the ADD operation would then result in 088 in WORK2.

Similarly, to say, IF (data-name) IS NEGATIVE . . . . is a valid conditional only if the data-name specified is numeric and allows for a sign in its PICTURE clause. If no S exists in the PICTURE clause, the number will always be considered unsigned and the condition would never be met. Unsigned numbers are always considered to contain positive quantities. In

```
MOVE –10 TO FLDX.
IF FLDX IS NEGATIVE GO TO RTN-1.
```

FLDX will be negative only if it has an S in its PICTURE clause.

Numeric quantities on punched cards are signed by having **zone** punches over the units, or rightmost, position of the field. To denote a minus sign on a card field, an 11-zone is placed over the units position of the field. 28J, punched in a numeric card field, will be interpreted as $28\bar{1}$ (11-zone and a 1-punch in units position). A 12-zone over the units position of a field denotes a plus sign. 28D will be interpreted as $28\overset{+}{4}$ (12-zone and 4-punch in units position). If a numeric field, on a card, contains a sign in the units position, an S must be employed in the PICTURE clause defining that field to retain that sign.

Input card data, for example, which has an amount field in card columns 1–5 that may contain a sign, must be written as:

```
01  CARD-REC.
    02 AMT  PICTURE S9(5).
```

The field will occupy the first **five** positions of the card record. Without the S, 3821K would be transmitted as 38212. With the S, 3821K would be transmitted as $3821\bar{2}$.

Thus an S in the PICTURE clause of a numeric field must be used to denote signed numbers. Without it, all data in the field will be considered unsigned. The S does not add to the size of the field. PICTURE S99 denotes a two-position signed field. It is generally more efficient to include an S in the PICTURE clause of all numeric fields.

Assumed Zeros. The character P in a PICTURE clause of a numeric field represents a digit position that is treated as if it contained a zero. Each P in the PICTURE clause denotes an assumed zero.

P's are used to position the assumed decimal point away from the actual number. Suppose we wish the computer to interpret 25 as 25000; the PICTURE clause would be as follows:

02 AMT   PICTURE 99PPP.

To say MOVE 25 TO AMT results in 25000 in the field.

Note that the above field will accept only **two** positions of numeric data. The number of 9's in a PICTURE clause of a numeric field denotes the number of characters that may be placed in that field. Since there are two 9's in the field, only two positions of data will be accepted. The computer will substitute a zero for each P in the PICTURE. Thus AMT will be considered to have 25000.

To say DIVIDE 250 INTO AMT GIVING TOTAL, where TOTAL has a PICTURE of 999, will result in 100 in the latter field.

Consider the following PICTURE clause:

77 AMT-2   PICTURE VPPP99.

To move 25 to AMT-2 would result in AMT-2 being interpreted as containing .00025. Note that P's are used to position the assumed decimal point away from the actual number being transmitted.

Example

```
DATA DIVISION.
FILE SECTION.
FD  CARD-FILE
      RECORDING MODE F
      LABEL RECORDS STANDARD
      DATA RECORD IS CARD-REC.
01   CARD-REC.
      02 CUST-NAME      PICTURE A(20).
      02 NO-OF-ITEMS    PICTURE 99PP.
      02 UNIT-PRICE     PICTURE 99V99.
      02 FILLER         PICTURE X(54).
FD  TAPE-FILE
      RECORDING MODE F
      LABEL RECORDS ARE STANDARD
      DATA RECORD IS TAPE-REC.
01   TAPE-REC.
      02 NAME           PICTURE A(20).
      02 TOTAL-PRICE    PICTURE
                            999999V99.
```

Note that NO-OF-ITEMS contains two assumed zeros. If the two-position field on the card contains 35, for example, the computer will interpret this as 3500. Since the card field denotes hundreds of items, this would be a correct interpretation.

The arithmetic operation in the PROCEDURE DIVISION would be as follows:

MULTIPLY NO-OF-ITEMS BY UNIT-PRICE GIVING TOTAL-PRICE.

E. CONDITION-NAMES

Condition-names are programmer-supplied names established in the DATA DIVISION which may facilitate processing in

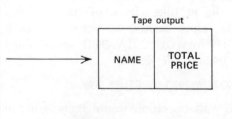

The DATA DIVISION entries are as follows:

the PROCEDURE DIVISION. A condition-name gives a name to a specific value that a data item can assume. In the **DATA DIVISION,** it is coded on the special level, **88.** All **88** level entries are condition-names which denote values of specific data items. Consider the following example:

```
02  MARITAL-STATUS  PICTURE 9.
```

Suppose that 1 in the field called **MARITAL-STATUS** denotes single status. We may use a condition-name **SINGLE** to indicate this value:

```
02  MARITAL-STATUS  PICTURE 9.
88  SINGLE          VALUE 1.
```

When the field called **MARITAL-STATUS** is equal to 1, we will call that condition **SINGLE.** The 88 level item is not the name of a **field** but the name of a **condition.** The 88 level item refers only to the elementary item directly preceding it. **SINGLE** is a condition-name applied to the field called **MARITAL-STATUS,** since **MARITAL-STATUS** directly precedes the 88 level item. The condition **SINGLE** exists if **MARITAL-STATUS** = 1.

A condition-name conforms to the rules for forming programmer-supplied names. It is always coded on the **88** level and has only a **VALUE** clause associated with it. Since a condition-name is **not** the name of a data field, it will **not** contain a **PICTURE** clause.

The following is the format for 88 level items:

```
88 (condition-name)  VALUE (literal).
```

The condition-name refers only to the elementary item preceding it and must therefore be unique. The **VALUE** of the condition-name must be a literal consistent with the data type of the preceding field:

```
02  FLDX          PICTURE XX.
88  CONDITIONA    VALUE '12'.
```

The above is a **valid** statement since the value is a **nonnumeric** literal and the field is defined alphanumerically. An **incorrect** form is:

Invalid:

```
02  FLDX          PICTURE XX.
88  CONDITIONA    VALUE 12.
```

Condition-names refer only to **elementary** items in the **DATA DIVISION.** The data item to which the condition-name refers must contain a **PICTURE** clause. **77** level items in the **WORKING-STORAGE SECTION** may have condition-names associated with them.

Condition-names are defined in the **DATA DIVISION** to facilitate processing in the **PROCEDURE DIVISION.** A condition name test is an alternative method of expressing a simple relational in the **PROCEDURE DIVISION,** using the following **DATA DIVISION** entries:

```
02  MARITAL-STATUS  PICTURE 9.
88  DIVORCED        VALUE 0.
```

we may use **either** of the following tests in the **PROCEDURE DIVISION:**

```
IF MARITAL-STATUS = 0 GO TO
    DIVORCE-RTN.
```

or

```
IF DIVORCED GO TO DIVORCE-RTN.
```

The condition-name **DIVORCED** will test to determine if **MARITAL-STATUS** does, in fact, have a value of 0.

We may use **several** condition-names for one data field:

```
02  GRADE      PICTURE X.
88  EXCELLENT  VALUE 'A'.
88  GOOD       VALUE 'B'.
88  FAIR       VALUE 'C'.
88  POOR       VALUE 'D'.
88  FAILING    VALUE 'F'.
```

Assuming that the above values are the only valid ones, a **PROCEDURE DIVISION** test may be as follows:

```
IF EXCELLENT OR GOOD OR FAIR OR
POOR OR FAILING NEXT SENTENCE ELSE
GO TO ERROR-RTN.
```

Note that we may also say, **IF NOT FAILING GO TO PASS-RTN.**

Condition-names may be used in the PROCEDURE DIVISION, at the discretion of the programmer, for ease of programming. There are some instances, however, where the use of condition-names is required. An overflow condition which tests for the end of a page, for example, may only be tested with a condition-name. This will be discussed more fully in Chapter 13.

EXERCISES

1. If the same storage area is to be used for different purposes, it must be _____ in the DATA DIVISION.
   *****
   redefined

2. Consider the following DATA DIVISION entry:

   02 AMOUNT-FIELD   PICTURE 999.

   Write a DATA DIVISION entry that will permit the above storage area to be tested for blanks in the PROCEDURE DIVISION.
   *****
   02 AMOUNT-FIELD-X   REDEFINES AMOUNT-FIELD   PICTURE XXX.

3. A REDEFINES clause may not be used on the _____ level.
   *****
   01

   Make the necessary corrections to each of the following (4–5):

4. 02 ITEM PICTURE XXX.
   03 ITEM-X REDEFINES ITEM PICTURE 999.
   *****
   should be:

   02 ITEM-X REDEFINES ITEM
              PICTURE 999.

5. 04 FLDA PICTURE XX VALUE 'AB'.
   04 FLDB REDEFINES FLDA PICTURE 99.
   *****
   cannot have a VALUE clause in an entry to be redefined

6. To retain the sign of a numeric field, an _____ must be the _____ character in the PICTURE clause.
   *****
   S
   first

7. The following is a PROCEDURE DIVISION entry: IF A IS NEGATIVE GO TO RTN-1. Write the PICTURE clause for A if it is a two-position numeric field with one decimal position.
   *****
   PICTURE S9V9.

8. +125 would be punched into a data card as _____.
*****
12E

9. —564 would be punched into a data card as _____.
*****
56M

10. S99V9 denotes a _____ -position field.
*****
three

11. S99PPPP denotes a _____ -position field.
*****
two

12. The P in the above is called an _____ _____.
*****
assumed zero

13. 34 placed in the above is interpreted by the computer as _____.
*****
(+) 340000

14. 68 placed in a field with PICTURE VPP99 is interpreted by the computer as _____.
*****
.0068

15. Condition-names are assigned in the _____ DIVISION.
*****
DATA

16. A condition-name must have a _____ clause associated with it.
*****
VALUE

17. A condition-name is always coded on the _____ level.
*****
88

18. A condition-name always refers to the data field _____.
*****
directly preceding it

19. If the following is a DATA DIVISION entry, write the PROCEDURE DIVISION entry (in two ways) to test the condition implied:

02 SALARY   PICTURE 9(5).
02 HIGHEST-SALARY   VALUE 99999.
*****
IF SALARY = 99999 GO TO . . .
IF HIGHEST-SALARY GO TO . . .

20. In the following statement, TYPE1 must be a _____ :

IF TYPE1 GO TO DEBIT-RTN.

*****

condition-name

REVIEW QUESTIONS

1. In a statement like IF MARRIED GO TO RTNX, how does the compiler know that MARRIED is a condition-name and not a data-name?

2. An independent WORKING-STORAGE item may have a code of 1 to denote MALE and a code of 2 to denote FEMALE. Write the entry and the corresponding condition-names.

3. Write a PROCEDURE DIVISION entry to branch to an error routine if the field specified above does not denote male or female (use the condition-names).

4. Write the above routine without the use of condition-names.

5. How are the following fields represented on a data card?

   (a) −358
   (b) +245
   (c)   267

6. How will the computer interpret −56 read into a field with the following PICTURE clause:

   (a) PICTURE 99.
   (b) PICTURE S99.
   (c) PICTURE 99PP.
   (d) PICTURE SVPP99.

7. Suppose ABCD is read into a 7-position alphanumeric field. Indicate the two different ways ABCD may be placed in the field. (**Hint.** Explain JUSTIFIED RIGHT.)

Make the necessary corrections to the following entries (8–17):

8. 02 AMT-1   PICTURE 99.
   88 NAME-1   VALUE ZERO.
   02 AMT-2   PICTURE 99.
   88 NAME-1   VALUE ZERO.

9. 01 ITEM-X PICTURE X(50).
   01 ITEM-Y REDEFINES ITEM-X PICTURE 9(50).

10. 02 SUB-1 PICTURE 99 VALUE ZERO.
    02 SUB-2 REDEFINES SUB-1 PICTURE XX.

11. 02 FLDX   PICTURE S99.
     02 FLDY   REDEFINES FLDX PICTURE XXX.

12. 77 X   PICTURE XX.
     88 X-ON   VALUE 12.

13. 77 SWITCHA   PICTURE 99.
     88 A-OFF   VALUE SPACES.

14. 02 TOTAL PICTURE 9(5)V9(3)S.

15. 02 FIELDA PICTURE 9999 JUSTIFIED RIGHT.

16. MOVE A TO B JUSTIFIED RIGHT.

17. 05 HEADING JUSTIFIED RIGHT PICTURE XX.

18. (T or F) A numeric field may not be compared to spaces.

19. (T or F) To test a numeric field for blanks, we must first re-
     define it.

20. (T or F) Condition-names must be unique within a COBOL pro-
     gram.

PROBLEMS

1. **Input:** Card

    1–5   Customer Number
    6–7   Number of Items Bought (in 100's)
    8–10 Cost of Each Item x.xx
    11–80 Not used

    Output: Magnetic tape; standard labels, blocked 35

    1–5   Customer Number
    6–12 Total Charge xxxxx.xx

    Notes

    1. Total Charge = Number of Items (total) × Cost/Item
    2. If Customer Number is a multiple of 10's (i.e., 00010, 00150),
       then customer has credit rating of A—allow 2% discount on
       Total Charge

    Hint. Customer number must be redefined to test for a multiple
       of 10.

2. A card file containing employee records is used to create tape files
    containing the first 20 positions of card data. One tape file is to
    be created for all females between 20 and 30 years old, under 5
    feet 6 inches but over 5 feet tall, who weigh less than 120 lbs. A
    second tape file is to be created for all male employees over 50,
    between 5 feet 6 inches and 6 feet tall who weigh more than 185

lbs and are bald. Both tape files will be blocked 20 and have standard labels. The card format is as follows:

   1–15 Name
     16 Sex   M—male, F—female
     17 Age   Y-20, M—between 20 and 30, G—between 30 and 50, E—over 50
     18 Height   X—over 6 feet, M—between 5 feet 6 inches and 6 feet, A—between 5 feet and 5 feet 6 inches
     19 Weight   H—over 185, M—between 120 and 185, N—under 120
     20 Hair   B—bald, N—not bald
   21–80 Not used

Use condition-names.

3. **Input:** tape

   1–20 Name of Employee
     21 Code   1—Wages, 2—Salary, 3—Commission
   22–26 Amt1   xxx.xx
   27–32 Amt2   xxx.xx

Output: Print name and earned amt (xxxxxx).

Notes

1. If Wages (Code = 1) multiply Amt1 by Amt2 to obtain earned amt
2. If Salary (Code = 2) earned amt is equal to Amt1
3. If Commission (Code = 3) multiply Amt1 by Amt2 and add on an additional 8%.

Use condition-names.

4. Write a program to print the name and total of all amount fields from a tape record. Before totalling the amount fields, however, make sure that they contain only numeric data.

Input: Standard labels, no blocking factor

   1–10 Name
   11–40 six amount fields each xxxxx

Print
   5–14 Name
   21–26 Total: print 'ERROR' if any input amount field is not numeric

12

Editing Printed Output

Because of the unique characteristics of printed output, we will treat it is a separate topic. Most importantly, the printed form as the primary type of computer output is used **exclusively** as an end product. It is the final result of a computer run, often to be viewed by high-level management.

Tape, disk, and punched card output is generally an intermediate product, having the ultimate function of being reentered into the computer flow as input to another job. These types of output are created for efficiency. Fields and records of this type are condensed to make maximum use of the computer and its storage capabilities. The printed report, however, is written with the businessman in mind. Since many computer-generated reports are read by company executives, such forms must be clear, neat, and easy to interpret. Several characteristics, not applicable to other forms of output, must be considered when preparing reports.

Editing of Printed Data. A punched card may have two amount fields with the following data: 00450 3872658. Although these fields are acceptable on cards or other forms of output, the printed report must contain this information in edited form to make it more meaningful. $450.00 and $38,726.58, for example, are clearer methods of presenting the data.

Editing will be considered the manipulation of fields of data to make them clearer and neater for their specific purpose. The editing of input data is of prime consideration when printing information.

Spacing of Forms. Forms, unlike other kinds of output, must be properly spaced for ease of reading. Certain entries must be single spaced, others double spaced. The printed output must have adequate margins at both the top and bottom of the form. This requires the computer to be programmed to sense the end of a form and thus to transmit the next line of information to a new page.

Alignment of Data. Reports do not have fields of information adjacent to one another as is the practice with other forms of output. Printed output is more easily interpreted when data is spaced neatly and evenly across the page.

Printing of Headers. Header information, which generally supplies job name, date, and field designations, is essential for clearness of presentation, when creating printed output.

All of the items named above, each presenting unique programming problems, must be treated individually. For that reason, we will study the printed report as a separate, and rather special, topic. The first item, editing, will be considered now. The other three items will be discussed in the next chapter.

A. THE EDITING FUNCTION

The following will be considered editing functions:

1. Suppression of leading zeros.
2. Printing of decimal points where decimal alignment is implied.
3. Printing of dollar signs and commas.
4. Printing of asterisks for check protection.
5. Printing of plus or minus signs to reflect the value of a field.
6. Printing of debit or credit symbols for accounting applications.
7. Printing of spaces or zeros as separators within a field.

The first six editing functions may only be performed on **numeric** fields, or fields with **PICTURE** clauses consisting of 9's. The last editing function, the printing of zeros or spaces as separators, may be performed on any data field.

All editing is performed by moving an elementary item to a **report-item.** An elementary item, you will recall, is a field with a **PICTURE** clause; that is, it is a data item which is not further subdivided. A **report-item** is an elementary item which has the appropriate **PICTURE** clause to perform editing functions. Note that it is the **PICTURE** clause of the receiving field, the report-item, which causes editing. The operation of editing, itself, is performed by a **MOVE** instruction.

To perform an editing function, the **PICTURE** clauses of the output area, which is the print area, must contain the appropriate symbols. Data is moved from input or work areas to these output areas. When a **WRITE** statement is executed, the information to be printed is in an edited form. As in **all** move operations, the sending fields remain unchanged after the data has been transmitted to the report-item.

EXERCISES

1. Editing is performed by a _____ operation.
   *****
   MOVE

2. Editing is performed by moving _____ to _____.
   *****
   elementary items
   report-items

3. A receiving field which has the appropriate **PICTURE** clause to perform editing is called a _____.
   *****
   report-item

4. Most editing is performed on _____ fields.
   *****
   numeric

5. When moving the contents of a data item to a report-item in order to perform editing, the contents of the data item _____ after the operation.
   *****
   remain unchanged

B. INTERPRETING EDIT CHARACTERS

Suppression of Leading Zeros. Nonsignificant or leading zeros are zeros appearing in the leftmost positions of a field and having no numerical value. For example, 00387 has two leading zeros. Nonsignificant zeros should generally be omitted when printing. 00387 should print as 387, since the two are numerically equivalent and the latter is considered better form. The operation to perform this type of editing is called **suppression of leading zeros.** Note that the number 10000 has **no** leading zeros. All zeros have numeric significance and none appear in the leftmost positions of the field. Under no circumstances would we want to suppress the printing of the zeros in 10000, since each adds value to the number.

The edit symbol $\boxed{Z}$ is used to suppress leading zeros and to replace them with blanks or spaces. **FIELDA**, with **PICTURE 999**, might be edited by moving it to **EDIT1**, with **PICTURE ZZZ.**

Each **Z** represents one storage position which may accept data from a sending field. In addition, any nonsignificant zero encountered in the sending field will be replaced with blanks. 038 will print as 38, 003 will print as 3, and 000 will print as three spaces, since all zeros lack significance. Any number which does not have leading zeros, such as 108, will print as is.

When suppressing leading zeros, the sending field must be defined as numeric. The receiving field should be the same size as the sending field. **ZZZ** indicates a three-position storage area that may accept three characters of input data, and that will suppress all leading zeros.

Often it is desirable to suppress only **some** leading zeros of a sending field. Consider the case where the content of four sending fields denoting Charity Deductions are 0020, 4325, 0003 and 0000 respectively. The output may be as follows:

NAME	SALARY	DEDUC-TIONS FOR CHARITY
A. LINCOLN	13872	20
W. WILSON	40873	4325
F. ROOSEVELT	10287	3
G. WASHINGTON	25382	

High order zeros have been suppressed. The **PICTURE** clause in the output area is **ZZZZ** or **Z(4).**

As may be evident from the above illustration, it is sometimes not advisable to leave fields blank when a zero balance is implied. Businessmen who question, at times, the accuracy of computer output, tend to regard blank fields as an indication that the computer erred or that it stopped and was restarted improperly. Perhaps **G. WASHINGTON** did, in fact, make a contribution but the computer, through an electronic error, failed to indicate it.

For this reason, it is sometimes good practice to print a **single** zero where a zero balance exists. In this way, the report will leave no doubt about the charitable inclinations of **G. WASHINGTON.**

Thus if the four-position charity field has contents 0000, we want it to print as 0. That is, we want only the three leftmost positions of the field to be zero suppressed and the last position to print **without** suppressing the zero. The **PICTURE** clause of the report-item would then be **ZZZ9.** Z's indicate numeric characters to be zero suppressed and 9's indicate numeric characters to print without zero suppression. Hence 0000 will print as 0.

The combined use of Z's and 9's in a report-item is permissible as long as all **Z**'s precede any **9**'s. Zeros may be suppressed only if they precede significant digits.

The following examples may clarify editing with the use of zero suppression. Note that edited results are obtained by the operation: **MOVE SENDING-FIELD TO REPORT-ITEM.**

Sending-Field PICTURE	Contents	Report-Item PICTURE	Edited Results
9(3)	109	ZZZ	109
9(3)	007	Z(3)	7
9(3)	000	ZZZ	
9(3)	007	Z99	07
9(4)	0082	Z999	082

Sending-Field PICTURE	Contents	Report-Item PICTURE	Edited Results
99V99	02ᴧ38	ZZ.99	2.38
99V99	00ᴧ03	ZZ.99	.03
99V99	00ᴧ05	Z9.99	0.05

Printing of Decimal Points where Decimal Alignment Is Implied. TAX, with PICTURE 99V99 and CONTENTS of 1235, should print as 12.35 when edited. The implied decimal point must, through editing, be replaced with an actual decimal point. The appropriate report-item that will print a decimal point will have a PICTURE of 99.99. The decimal point, which may **never** appear in the PICTURE clause of a numeric item, instructs the computer to place an actual decimal point where it is assumed to be in the sending field. If a sending field had PICTURE of 999V999, its report-item would have a PICTURE clause of 999.999.

Note that a sending field with PICTURE 99V99 takes **four** core storage positions since implied decimal points do not use core, while the resultant field takes **five** positions, since a real decimal point does, in fact, use core. The number 12.35, when printed, utilizes five print positions.

We can combine the two editing functions thus far discussed so that we zero suppress **and** place decimal points in the edited field. Examine the illustration at the top of the adjacent column.

Since numeric positions to the right of a decimal point have significance when they are zero, we will not perform zero suppression on these quantities. That is, .01 should **not** be edited to read .1, since the two numbers are not numerically equivalent. As a rule, then, we will not zero suppress characters to the right of a decimal point in a number.[1]

Printing of Dollar Signs and Commas. The printing of dollar signs and commas are frequent editing functions performed in conjunction with the suppression of leading zeros and the printing of decimal points, since many numeric quantities eventually appear on printed reports as dollars and cents figures. The dollar sign and comma are merely placed in the position in which they are desired, as is the case with printing decimal points. If FLDA, with PICTURE 9999V99, is to be edited as a dollars and cents figure, the dollar sign will be the first character, a digit from the sending field will follow, then a comma, three more digits, a decimal point, and two decimal positions. Thus the report-item will have a PICTURE of $9,999.99. The following examples will illustrate this point:

Sending-Field PICTURE	Contents	Report-Item PICTURE	Edited Results
1. 9(4)V99	3812ᴧ34	$9,999.99	$3,812.34
2. 99V99	05ᴧ00	$ZZ.99	$ 5.00
3. 999V99	000ᴧ05	$ZZZ.99	$ .05
4. 9(4)V99	0003ᴧ82	$Z,ZZZ.99	$ 3.82
5. 9(7)V99	0038268ᴧ45	$Z,ZZZ,ZZZ.99	$ 38,268.45

[1] There is one exception to this rule. It is permissible in COBOL to use a report-item with PICTURE ZZ.ZZ. This will suppress zeros to the right of the decimal point only if the entire field is zero, in which case spaces will print. 0003 will print as .03 but 0000 will print as blanks. Because such a PICTURE clause may be confusing, we will not use this convention.

Note that in Example 1, the sending field takes six core storage positions, while the receiving field uses nine. Dollar signs, commas, and decimal points each utilize one position of storage. A frequent result of editing is this increased use of core storage for the output area. When defining the print output record in the DATA DIVISION, be sure that nine positions are counted for the report-item.

Examples 2 through 4 illustrate the use of zero suppression in conjunction with other forms of editing. In Example 2, one leading zero is suppressed and replaced with a space. Thus there is a single blank between the inserted dollar sign and the first significant digit. Example 4 indicates that the zero suppression character Z will also eliminate or suppress leading commas. Note that the result of the edit was **not** $, 3.82 but $ 3.82. The Z will suppress both zeros and commas until it encounters the first significant digit of a field. Thus a comma will be appropriately suppressed if no significant digit precedes it. In Example 4, **four** spaces will appear between the dollar sign and the first significant digit, three for the suppressed zeros, and one for the suppressed comma.

At this point, it should be mentioned that the sending field need not allow for the same number of positions as the report-item. FLDA, with PICTURE 99 and contents 40, may be edited by moving it to EDIT1, with PICTURE $ZZ.99. As in the case of numeric move operations, the two decimal places will be filled with zeros. The result, then, in EDIT1 will be $40.00.

The Printing of Asterisks as a Check Protection Character. The suppression of zeros, by the use of Z, in conjunction with the printing of dollar signs may, at times, prove unwise.

Suppose we are using the computer to print checks. To print $ .05, as in Example 3 above, may not be advisable since the blanks between the dollar sign and the decimal point may easily be filled in by a typewriter. Some dishonest soul could conceivably collect $999.05 on what should be a five cent check.

To prevent such occurrences, a check protection symbol, the asterisk, is used in place of blanks when leading zeros are to be suppressed. Using the correct report-item, the above would print as $***.05. In this way, it is almost impossible to revise the intended figure.

To print an asterisk in place of a blank when zero suppression is to be performed, use an $\boxed{*}$ instead of a $\boxed{Z}$ in each position. Asterisks are zero-suppression characters which replace nonsignificant zeros and commas with asterisks instead of spaces.

Sending-Field		Report-Item	
PICTURE	Contents	PICTURE	Contents
9(3)V99	123∧45	$***.99	$123.45
9(3)V99	012∧34	$***.99	$**12.34
9(2)V99	00∧12	$**.99	$**.12
9(5)V99	00234∧56	$**,***.99	$***234.56

The asterisk is used most often for the printing of checks or when resultant amount fields may be tampered with. Under other conditions, the use of Z's for normal zero suppression is sufficient.

The Printing of Plus or Minus Signs to Reflect the Value of a Field. Unless the computer is instructed to do otherwise, numeric quantities will print without a sign. When reports are printed, it is customary to interpret the absence of a sign as an indication of a positive quantity.

If an amount is negative and no sign instructions are issued to the computer, it will print without a sign, which will cause it to be interpreted as positive. We must instruct the computer, with the use of editing, to print a minus sign when a negative number is read. You will recall from the previous chapter, that the PICTURE clause of the numeric sending field must contain an S if quantities are to be retained as negative or positive. Without the S, all quantities are considered unsigned.

The edit symbol, $\boxed{-}$, may be placed

either to the right **or** the left of the report-item. By placing the minus sign in one of these two positions, the computer is instructed to store the minus sign in the corresponding position if the sending field is negative, and to omit a sign when the sending field is signed positive or unsigned.

You will recall that the sign of a number is indicated by placing it above the quantity. Examine the following illustrations.

Sending-Field		Report-Item	
PICTURE	Contents	PICTURE	Contents
1. S999	$12\bar{3}$	—999	—123
2. S999	$12\bar{3}$	999—	123—
3. 999	123	—999	123
4. S999	$12\overset{+}{3}$	—999	123
5. S99V99	$02\bar{3}4$	—$ZZ.99	—$ 2.34

when the field is unsigned or signed positive, and a — sign is required when the field is signed negative. This will not be performed properly by using the edit symbol —, which generates only the minus sign if the quantity is negative and omits a sign for all other quantities.

To perform the printing of a plus sign or a minus sign for **all** fields, the edit symbol $\boxed{+}$ is used. To edit a sending field by moving it to a report-item with a + in its PICTURE clause will instruct the computer to generate a sign for each move: a + sign will be generated for positive or unsigned quantities, and a — sign will be generated for negative quantities.

Like the minus sign, the plus sign may be made to appear either to the left or to the right of a field. Examine the following illustrations.

	Sending-Field		Report-Item	
	PICTURE	Contents	PICTURE	Contents
1.	S999	$12\overset{+}{3}$	+999	+123
2.	S999	$12\overset{+}{3}$	999+	123+
3.	S999	$12\bar{3}$	+999	—123
4.	999	123	+999	+123
5.	S9999V99	$0387\bar{2}5$	+Z,ZZZ.99	—$ 387.25

Examples 1 and 2 illustrate the positioning of the minus sign within the report-item. It may appear to the right or to the left of a field and will, then, print in the corresponding position. If the sending field is negative, the edited results print with the negative sign. Examples 3 and 4 illustrate that **no** sign will print if the sending field is signed positive or unsigned. Example 5 illustrates the use of the minus sign in conjunction with other editing symbols.

There are occasions when a sign is required for both positive and negative quantities. That is, a + sign is required

The Printing of Debit and Credit Symbols for Accounting Applications. For most applications, a generated plus or minus sign to indicate positive or negative quantities is sufficient. For accountants, however, minus signs often indicate either debits or credits to particular accounts.

To facilitate the interpretation of fields specified for accounting functions, the edit symbols DB, for debit, and CR, for credit, may be used in place of the minus sign. If an amount field is to be **debited** to a specific account when it is negative, $\boxed{DB}$ will be used. If a quantity is to be **credited** to a specific account when it is negative $\boxed{CR}$ will be used.

These symbols must be specified to the right of the report-item. Unlike the minus sign itself, these symbols may **not** be used to the left of a field. If the amount is negative and **CR** or **DB** is used, then **CR** or **DB** will print, respectively. If the field is unsigned or signed positive, neither symbol will print.

It is important to note that, while a minus sign uses **one** core storage position, the **CR** and **DB** symbols use **two** each.

clause of a report-item will cause a space to be inserted in the corresponding position.

Zeros may also be inserted into fields for editing purposes. The edit symbol |0| in a **PICTURE** clause will cause a 0 to be inserted in the corresponding position of the receiving field without loss of characters from the sending field.

The following examples will illustrate the use of spaces or zeros in report-items.

| | Sending-Field | | Report-Item | |
NAME	PICTURE	Contents	PICTURE	Edited Results
SSNO	9(9)	089743456	999BB99BB9999	089 74 3456
NAME	A(10)	PASMITH	ABABA(8)	P A SMITH
DATE	X(4)	0270	XXBBXX	02 70
QTY-IN-100	999	153	99900	15300

The following examples will illustrate the use of the two symbols.

You will note that most editing is performed on numeric data. Only the last

| | Sending-Field | | Report-Item | |
	PICTURE	Contents	PICTURE	Edited Results
1.	S999	12$\bar{3}$	999CR	123CR
2.	S999	12$\bar{3}$	999DB	123DB
3.	S999	12$\overset{+}{3}$	999CR	123
4.	S999	12$\overset{+}{3}$	999DB	123
5.	S9(5)V99	0123456	\$ZZ,ZZZ.99CR	\$ 1,234.56CR

The Printing of Spaces or Zeros as Separators within a Field. Suppose a name field on a card has, in its first two positions, an employee's first two initials and in the remainder of the field, his last name. If the field is printed without editing, the following may occur: JESMITH RAJONES. For clarity of reading, J E SMITH and R A JONES would be a better representation. A space between initials, then, would add clarity.

Any field, whether alphabetic, alphanumeric, or numeric may be edited by placing blanks as separators within the field. The edit symbol |B| in a **PICTURE**

category of edit operations, the use of blanks or zeros within a field, will accept data that is not numeric. For all other editing, the sending field must be numeric—it must have a **PICTURE** clause of 9's.

Furthermore, only **elementary** numeric items may be utilized in these operations. You will recall that group items, even if they are subdivided into numeric fields, are treated as alphanumeric items by the computer. Thus, to obtain a valid numeric edit, only elementary items may be used.

It is important to understand that editing is performed by **moving** a field to a report-item, with an appropriate PICTURE clause. It is the PICTURE clause itself which determines what type of editing is to be performed. The only way to obtain edited results is by a MOVE operation. To say ADD TAX, TOTAL TO EDIT1, where EDIT1 is a report-item, will result in an error. The computer performs ADD instructions, and any other arithmetic operation, on numeric fields only. EDIT1, as a report-item, is **not** a numeric field. Data can only be moved to EDIT1, and not added to it. In the above example, a numeric area must be defined in the WORKING-STORAGE SECTION to accumulate the sum of TAX and TOTAL. This numeric area may then be moved to EDIT1, which will perform the editing function.

The Table 12-1 will serve as a review of edit operations.

Table 12-1

Sending-Field		Report-Item	
PICTURE	Contents	PICTURE	Edited Results
9(6)	123456	$ZZZ,ZZZ.99	$123,456.00
9999V99	001234	$Z,ZZZ.99	$ 12.34
9(5)V99	0000123	$**,***.99	$*****1.23
S9(6)	012345	+Z(6)	− 12345
S9(6)	123456	−Z(6)	123456
S9999V99	123456	+Z(4).99	+1234.56
S999	123	ZZZ−	123−
9(6)	123456	99BBBB9999	12 3456
S99	05	$ZZ.99BB	$ 5.00DB
999	123	999000	123000
S99V99	1234	$ZZ.99CR	$12.34CR

EXERCISES

1. The asterisk is called a _____.
   *****
   check protection edit symbol

2. The zero suppression symbol, Z, suppresses _____ and _____ up to the first significant digit.
   *****
   high order zeros or nonsignificant zeros or leading zeros
   commas

3. The asterisk replaces all _____ with _____.
   *****
   leading zeros and leading commas
   asterisks

4. To print a minus sign when an amount is negative, use a _____ symbol.

*****

—(minus sign)

5. To print a plus sign or a minus sign as appropriate with an amount field, use a _____ symbol.

*****

+sign

6. **CR** and **DB** symbols are accounting symbols used in place of a _____ sign.

*****

minus

7. All editing must be performed on _____ fields except editing using _____.

*****

numeric
zeros or blanks as field separators

8. To say **MULTIPLY A BY B GIVING C** (is, is not) correct if **C** is a report-item.

*****

is not (**Note.** All fields in an arithmetic operation must be numeric—a report-item is not numeric.)

9. A report-item is _____.

*****

an output field, which contains the appropriate symbols to perform editing

10. A plus or minus sign may be placed either to the _____ or to the _____ of a field but **CR** and **DB** must be placed to the _____ of a field.

*****

left
right
right

11. How many storage positions in the output area must be allotted for a report-item with **PICTURE $*,***.99?**

*****

Nine.

12. How many integer positions should appear in the sending field?

*****

Four.

For Questions 13–28, fill in the edited results.

	Sending-Field		Receiving-Field	
	PICTURE	Contents	PICTURE	Edited Results
13.	9(6)	000123	ZZZ,999	
14.	9(6)	000008	ZZZ,999	
15.	9(6)	123456	ZZZ,999.99	
16.	9(4)V99	1234̂56	$Z,ZZZ.99	
17.	9(4)V99	0000̂78	$Z,ZZ9.99	
18.	S9(4)V99	0000̂78⁺	$Z,ZZZ.99CR	
19.	S9(4)V99	0000̂78̄	$Z,ZZZ.99CR	
20.	S9(6)	123456̄	—999,999	
21.	9(6)	123456	—999,999	
22.	S999	123	—999	
23.	999	123	+999	
24.	S999	123⁺	+999	
25.	S999	123̄	—999	
26.	9(6)	000092	Z(6)00	
27.	X(6)	123456	XXXBBXXX	
28.	9(4)V99	0012̂34	$*,***.99	

*****

13. 123

14. 8

15. 123,456.00

16. $1,234.56

17. $ .78

18. $ .78

19. $ .78CR

20. —123,456

21. 123,456

22. 123

23. +123

24. +123

25. —123

26. 9200

27. 123   456

28. $\$***12.34$

29. NAME-FIELD PICTURE X(15) is part of an input document, with the first two positions of the field being INITIAL1 and INITIAL2, respectively. To edit this field so that a space appears between INITIAL1 and INITIAL2, and another space between INITIAL2 and LAST NAME, the report-item will have the following PICTURE clause: _____.

Redefine the input area NAME-FIELD and the output area, REPORT-ITEM, and write a routine without using editing to perform the same function.

*****

```
XBXBX(13)
02  NAME1 REDEFINES NAME-FIELD.
      03  INIT1 PICTURE X.
      03  INIT2 PICTURE X.
      03  LAST-NAME PICTURE X(13).
02  REDEFINE1 REDEFINES REPORT-ITEM.
      03  INIT1 PICTURE X.
      03  FILLER PICTURE X.
      03  INIT2 PICTURE X.
      03  FILLER PICTURE X.
      03  LAST-NAME PICTURE X(13).
MOVE SPACES TO REDEFINE1.
MOVE INIT1 OF NAME1 TO INIT1 OF REDEFINE1.
MOVE INIT2 OF NAME1 TO INIT2 OF REDEFINE1.
MOVE LAST-NAME OF NAME1 TO LAST-NAME OF REDEFINE1.
```

C. FLOATING STRINGS AND BLANK WHEN ZERO OPTION

Floating Strings. Examine the following sample output.

CUSTOMER NAME	QTY SOLD	AMT
J. SMITH	5,000	$38,725.67
A. JONES	− 2	$ 3.00

Although the fields are properly edited, the format is striking in one respect. The dollar sign of AMT and the minus sign of QTY SOLD for A. JONES appear several spaces from the numeric data. This result is a necessary consequence of the editing that we have been discussing.

The report-item must contain enough positions to accommodate the entire sending field. If the sending field, however, has many nonsignificant zeros (for example, 0000487), an appreciable number of blank positions will exist between the dollar sign and the first significant digit, or the operational sign and the first significant digit.

A leading edit character such as a plus sign, minus sign, or dollar sign may appear in the position **directly preceding** the first significant digit with the use of floating strings. A dollar sign or a plus or a minus sign may be made to "float" with the field; that is, to cause suppression of leading zeros and, at the same time, to force the respective floating character to appear in the position adjacent to the first significant digit.

With the proper use of floating strings in the PICTURE clause of the report-item, the following sample output may be produced.

Sending-Field Contents	Report-Item Edited Results
0012̧387	$123.87
0000̧400	$4.00
3876̧543̄	$38,765.43
038̄7	−387
000̄6	−6
010423	+10,423
000005	+5

You will note that the $, −, or + sign always appears in the position directly preceding the first significant digit. Only these three edit symbols may be made to float in this way.

To perform a **floating string edit**, two steps are necessary.

1. Create the report-item PICTURE clause as in the previous section. Use the floating character of +, −, or $ in conjunction with Z's, zero suppression characters.

2. Replace all Z's with the corresponding float character.

Example 1

FLDA PICTURE 9(4)V99.

Problem: To edit the field using a floating dollar sign. Resultant report-item shall be called EDIT1.

In Step 1, the PICTURE clause of the report-item is created as usual: $Z,ZZZ.99.

In Step 2, replace all Z's with the floating character, a dollar sign: $$,$$$.99.

Thus EDIT1 has a PICTURE of $$,$$$.99.

Note that there are five dollar signs. The four rightmost dollar signs are zero suppression symbols. They instruct the computer to suppress leading zeros and commas, and to place the dollar sign in the position adjacent to the first significant digit. The leftmost dollar sign signals the computer that $ will be the first character to print. In total, there is one more dollar sign than integer positions to be edited. **Four** integer positions are edited using **five** dollar signs. In general, N characters may be edited using a floating string of N + 1 characters. The explanation for the extra floating character is quite logical. In case the sending field has no nonsignificant positions, it must have some additional place to put the floating character.

Example 2

TAX PICTURE 9(4).

Problem: To edit tax using a floating minus sign. Report-item is called EDIT2.

In Step 1, the PICTURE clause of the report-item is created according to the rules of the last section, using a minus sign and zero suppression: −ZZZZ.

In Step 2, all Z's must be replaced by the appropriate floating character: − − − − −.

Thus EDIT2 will have a PICTURE of − − − − −; 003̄2 will print as −32; 048̄7 will print as −487.

Example 3

EDIT3 has a PICTURE clause of +++99.

Problem: Find the PICTURE clause of the sending field, FLD3.

Three plus signs indicate a floating-string edit that will accept **two** integer positions. The leftmost plus sign does **not** serve as a zero suppression character and is never replaced with integer data. Two characters of data will be accepted by three plus signs, and two characters of data will be accepted by two 9's. Thus the input area should have a PICTURE of 9(4). 3826 will print as +3826, 038̄2 as −382, and 0002̄ as +02.

From the above examples, it should be clear that floating-string characters may be used in conjunction with other edit symbols such as 9's, decimal points, and commas. The floating-string character, however, must be the first character in the PICTURE clause of the report-item. In addition, we may **not** use **two** floating-string characters in one report-item. If a dollar sign is to float, for example, then an operational sign may not be placed in the leftmost position of the field. You will recall, however, that signs may also appear in the rightmost position of a report-item. Thus $$,$$$.99— is a valid PICTURE clause. Only the dollar sign floats but a sign may be used in the field as well.

Blank when Zero Option. At times, it is necessary to perform elaborate editing of data fields. We have learned all the rules for performing such edits. In addition, however, it is often desirable to print spaces when a sending field consists entirely of zeros. With the use of complex editing, you may find that $.00 or —0 or + or — will print. This may detract from the clarity of a report. In such cases

the COBOL expression BLANK WHEN ZERO may be used **in conjunction with** the appropriate PICTURE clause.

Example 1: 02 EDIT1 PICTURE +++.

This report-item will accept two characters of data. 03 will print as +3, $\overline{76}$ will print as —76, and 00 will print as +. To eliminate the printing of + for a zero sending field, the BLANK WHEN ZERO option may be added:

02 EDIT1 PICTURE +++ BLANK WHEN ZERO.

When using the BLANK WHEN ZERO option in conjunction with a report-item, the normal rules of editing will be followed, depending upon the edit symbols in the PICTURE clause. If the field is zero, however, spaces will print.

Tables 12-2 and 12-3 review all the rules of editing discussed here.

Table 12-2

Sending-Field		Report-Item	
PICTURE	Contents	PICTURE	Edited Results
999V99	00$\underset{\wedge}{1}$23	$$$$.99	$1.23
S999V99	012$\underset{\wedge}{\overline{3}}$4	$$$$.99—	$12.34—
S999	12$\overset{+}{3}$	— — — —	123
S999	12$\overline{3}$	— — — —	—123
S999	00$\overline{5}$	— — — —	—5
99	37	+++	+37
S99	0$\overline{5}$	+++	—5
S99	0$\overset{+}{5}$	+++	+5
999	000	++++ BLANK WHEN ZERO	
999	000	++++	+
999V99	00000	$$$$.99	$.00
999V99	00000	$$$$.99 BLANK WHEN ZERO	

Table 12-3 Symbols that May Be Used in a PICTURE Clause

	Symbol	Meaning
	X	Alphanumeric field
	9	Numeric field
	A	Alphabetic field or space
	V	Assumed decimal point; used only in numeric fields
	S	Operational sign; used only in numeric fields
	P	Decimal scaling position; used only in numeric fields
	Z	Zero suppression character
	.	Decimal point
	+	Plus sign
	−	Minus sign
Edit Symbols	$	Dollar sign
	,	Comma
	CR	Credit symbol
	DB	Debit symbol
	*	Check protection symbol
	B	Field separator—space insertion character
	0	Zero insertion character

EXERCISES

1. Three characters that may be used in a floating string are _____, _____, _____.

   *****

   +

   −

   $

2. The edit character to "float" must be the _____ character in the field.

   *****

   first

3. If five minus signs appear in a floating string, _____ characters of the sending field may be accepted by the report-item.

*****

four

4. To print a floating dollar sign and a minus sign if a sending field with **PICTURE 999V99** is negative will require a report-item **PICTURE** clause of _____.

*****

$$$$.99—

5. The **BLANK WHEN ZERO** option has an effect on the edited output only if the sending field is _____.

*****

zero

For Questions 6–15, fill in the missing column.

	Sending-Field		Report-Item	
	PICTURE	Contents	PICTURE	Edited Results
6.	999V99	000̮05	$$$$.99	
7.	999V99	000̮05	$$$$.99—	
8.	S999V99	000̮0̄5	$$$$.99—	
9.	9999V99	0026̮54		26.54+
10.	9999V99	0038̮72		+38.72
11.	S999	00̄2̮	++++	
12.	S99		— — —	—4
13.	999V99	000̮00	$$$$.99	
14.	999V99	000̮00	$$$$.99 BLANK WHEN ZERO	
15.	9999V99	0238̮75	$$,$$$.99 BLANK WHEN ZERO	

*****

6. $.05

7. $.05

8. $.05—

9. ZZZZ.99+

10. +++++.99

11. —2

12. 0̄4

13. $.00

14. (blanks)

15. $238.75

REVIEW QUESTIONS

For Questions 1–22, fill in the missing column.

	Sending-Field PICTURE	Contents	Report-Item PICTURE	Contents
1.	99V99	04∧67	ZZ.99	
2.	9(4)V999	0086∧754	$Z,ZZZ.99	
3.	999	467	$ZZZ.99	
4.	S99V99	00∧98 (−)	+$ZZ.99	
5.	S99V99	00∧89 (+)	−$ZZ.99	
6.	S999	005 (+)	$ZZZ.99CR	
7.	S999	005 (+)	$ZZZ.99DB	
8.	S99V99	00∧06 (−)	$ZZ.99CR	
9.	S99V99	00∧05 (+)	$**.99—	
10.	9(4)	1357	$*,***.99	
11.	XXXX	CRDB	XXBBXX	
12.	9(4)	0170	99BB99	
13.	999V99	135∧79	$$$$.99	
14.	999V99	000∧09	$$$$.99	
15.	999V99	000∧00	$$$$.99	
16.	S9(5)	00567 (−)	++++++	
17.	S99V99	00∧34 (+)	$$$.99—	
18.	S99	00 (+)	+++	
19.	S99	00 (+)	+++ BLANK WHEN ZERO	
20.	9999V99	000∧988		$9.88
21.	9999V99	000∧988		$ 9.88
22.		87∧38		+$87.38

PROBLEMS

1. Write a program to print an output report from the following input card format:

   1–5   Product number
   6–8   Warehouse number
   9–11 Quantity (may be negative in case of credit)

14–18 Unit price xxx.xx
19–38 Product description
39–41 Discount percent .xxx
42–46 Customer number
47–80 Not used

Output: Print line

3–7	Product number	
10–29	Description	
32–38	Unit price	print decimal point; zero suppress; print dollar sign
40–44	Quantity	print minus sign, if present; zero suppress; print $
48–57	Gross	print minus sign, if present; zero suppress; print decimal point; print $
59–67	Discount amt	print decimal point; zeros suppress; print $
69–78	Net	zero suppress; decimal point, minus sign, if present; print $

Formulas

Gross = Quantity $\times$ Unit price
Discount amt = Gross $\times$ Discount Percent
Net = Gross — Discount amount

All three fields should be rounded to xxxxx.xx specification. Print heading **PRODUCT LISTING** on the top of the output page.

2. Write a program to print the total of the amount fields of every group of 100 tape records.

    Input: Standard labels, no blocking factor

    1–20 Name
    21–25 Amount xxx.xx

    Output: Print

    11–30 Name
    41–50 Total (edited with dollar sign, comma, decimal point, and check protection)

    (**Note.** The name is the same for each 100 records. The number of tape records is a multiple of 100.)

3. Consider the following input tape format.

    1–20 Customer name (1-initial 1, 2-initial 2)
    21–25 Transaction amount for week 1   xxx.xx
    26–30 Transaction amount for week 2   xxx.xx
    31–35 Transaction amount for week 3   xxx.xx
    36–40 Transaction amount for week 4   xxx.xx
    41–46 Amount of credit   xxxx.xx
    47–50 Not used

    Standard tape labels, no blocking factor

Problem Definition

1. Print heading MONTHLY TRANSACTIONS
2. Print each data field edited
   (a) Two spaces between initials of name.
   (b) Print decimal point, dollar sign, CR for negative transaction amount—dollar sign should float.
   (c) Print decimal point, comma, dollar sign and * for credit amount.
   (d) For each tape record, print a balance due (transaction amounts—credit), floating dollar sign, operational sign, decimal point.

Special Considerations for Printed Output

Thus far, we have discussed editing printed output. We have noted, however, that reports require additional programming. Let us consider first the spacing of forms.

A. SPACING OF FORMS

Issuing a WRITE (record-name) command, where the record indicated is in the file assigned to the printer, will cause **one line** of accumulated data to print. After the WRITE instruction, the paper will advance **one line;** that is, **single spacing** of forms will result.

Single spacing, however, is ordinarily not sufficient for most printing applications. Usually programs require special spacing features such as double spacing between some lines, and triple spacing between others. A simple WRITE command results in single spacing **only.**

We may achieve additional spacing of forms by issuing an AFTER or BEFORE ADVANCING option with every WRITE instruction for print operations:[1]

If a line is to print **after** the paper is spaced 1, 2, or 3 lines, the AFTER ADVANCING option is used. WRITE PRINT-REC AFTER ADVANCING 2 LINES will space two lines and **then** print. That is, after the paper advances two lines, printing will occur. If a line is to print **before** spacing occurs, the BEFORE ADVANCING option is used. WRITE HEADER-REC BEFORE ADVANCING 3 LINES will print and then advance the paper three lines.

Note that integers 1, 2, or 3 **only** may be used, with an ADVANCING option. If five spaces are desired between two print lines, the following routine may be used:

```
WRITE PRINT-REC AFTER ADVANCING 1
    LINES.
MOVE SPACES TO PRINT-REC.
WRITE PRINT-REC AFTER ADVANCING 3
    LINES.
MOVE NAME OF IN-REC TO NAME OF
    PRINT-REC.
    .
    .
WRITE PRINT-REC AFTER ADVANCING 3
    LINES.
```

WRITE (record-name) $\left[\begin{array}{c} \text{AFTER} \\ \hline \text{BEFORE} \end{array}\right]$ ADVANCING $\left[\begin{array}{c} 1 \\ 2 \\ 3 \end{array}\right]$ LINES

This instruction will indicate how many lines the paper is to advance. The form may be single, double, or triple spaced only. With a **single** WRITE statement, a maximum of triple spacing of forms may be achieved.

[1] The BEFORE ADVANCING option is **not** supported by some COBOL compilers. It is mentioned here because some manufacturers have incorporated the option. We will not, however, dwell on its use. We will restrict ourselves to the AFTER ADVANCING option which is common to all computers.

Suppose the paper were positioned on line 1 at the onset of this routine. After advancing one line, PRINT-REC will print on line 2. After advancing three lines to line 5, a blank line, or nothing, will print. After moving necessary data to the print area, the paper is advanced to line 8, where another line is printed. Thus **five** spaces occur between line 2, the first significant print line, and line 8, the next significant print line.

To space more than three lines, one point needs to be considered: writing a "dummy" record, with spaces on it, is the same as advancing the paper one line.

To advance the paper one line and then print, the following instruction is issued:

WRITE PRINT-1 AFTER ADVANCING 1
LINES.

Note that, even though the integer 1 denotes a **single** line, the plural LINES must be used. Although the English is not quite accurate, the notation **is** acceptable in COBOL.

Using the AFTER ADVANCING option will perform special spacing operations. The computer uses the **first position** in the print area for controlling the spacing of forms. Thus we must enlarge the print area to accommodate one **extra** position, which the computer will use for proper spacing of forms.

We specify 133 positions for print records, rather than 132. The first position of this area is used for **carriage** control. This first position should not be accessed in the program. The print area may be defined as follows:

FD   PRINT-FILE
      RECORDING MODE IS F
      LABEL RECORDS ARE OMITTED
      RECORD CONTAINS 133
          CHARACTERS
      DATA RECORD IS PRINTOUT.

01   PRINTOUT.
      02 FILLER   PICTURE X.
      02 REAL-REC.

.

.

.

When using an ADVANCING option with printed output, the record size must be 133 characters. The first position is not part of the actual print area, and should not be accessed by the programmer. If NAME, for example, is the first field in REAL-REC and is 20 positions, this field will print in the first 20 print positions. The initial FILLER is used for carriage control and is **not** printed.

You will recall that a WRITE command with 132 print positions designated will cause single spacing. This is generally acceptable when printed output is used for control purposes and is not the prime data created by the program. A card-to-tape program, for example, which prints several totals at the end of the job, may utilize a 132 print position record and may omit an ADVANCING clause. Since most applications require more advanced spacing features, henceforth we will denote our print area as 133 characters. A 133 position print record requires that the ADVANCING option be specified with **all** WRITE commands.

B. TESTING FOR THE END OF A PAGE AND SKIPPING TO A NEW PAGE

Computer generated reports are printed on **continuous forms.** All forms are connected, with perforations denoting the end of each page. After they are generated, these forms must be **burst,** or separated, into single sheets.

Unless the computer is instructed to do otherwise, it will write each line and advance the paper, printing from one form to another, ignoring the fact that each is really an individual page. At times, it may even print over the perforations which, at best, makes reading difficult.

Although printing is done from one continuous form to another, the computer must be instructed to observe page delineations. Each page should generally begin with a heading. Data lines follow and, when the end of a form is reached, we wish to skip to a new page and write the heading again.

The computer controls the sensing of various print lines by the use of a **carriage control tape.** This tape, which is attached to the printer, has designated holes corresponding to the first and last line of printing. With this tape, the computer can **sense** the last print line. When the form's end is sensed, the programmer must instruct the computer to advance to a new page. The tape will sense the start of a new page, as well as the end of the previous one.

Thus, through the use of the carriage control tape, the programmer can (1) test for the end of a form and (2) skip to a new page when necessary. First, we will consider the skipping to a new page.

To instruct the computer to skip to the beginning of a new page, the following instruction is issued:

WRITE (record-name) AFTER ADVANCING
  0 LINES.

The notation 0 LINES is the special format used for skipping to a new page. Thus the AFTER ADVANCING option may specify 0, 1, 2, or 3 lines. 1, 2, or 3 will advance the paper the corresponding number of lines, and 0 will advance the paper to a new page.

The first line of printing on each page is generally a heading, providing identifying data about the job. Thus, when skipping to a new page, the HEADING record is written:

. WRITE HEADING AFTER ADVANCING 0
  LINES.

HEADING, in the above case, is a record within the print file.

To test for the end of a form, or an OVERFLOW condition, a special paragraph in the ENVIRONMENT DIVISION is required. In the INPUT-OUTPUT section of the ENVIRONMENT DIVISION, after **all** files have been selected, the following entry is used to test for an overflow condition:

I-O-CONTROL.

APPLY (condition-name)
  TO FORM-OVERFLOW[2] ON (file-name).

The file name is the name assigned to the printer. The condition-name is a programmer-supplied name.

Example: APPLY END-OF-FORM TO
  FORM-OVERFLOW ON PRINT-FILE.

FORM-OVERFLOW is a special COBOL routine which tests for page overflow. PRINT-FILE is the name assigned in the SELECT clause. In the PROCEDURE DIVISION, we test to see if the end of the page has been reached by saying:

IF (condition-name)
                    (imperative-statement).

Example: IF END-OF-FORM GO TO
  NEW-PAGE-RTN.

FORM-OVERFLOW is a COBOL routine which tests for the end of a page. This routine is **called** into the program by the APPLY clause of the I-O-CONTROL paragraph. We say in the above example that if, by the test called FORM-OVERFLOW, the last line of printing has been reached, this condition will be called END-OF-FORM. We tell the computer what file we want this test performed upon by indicating the file name. The file name used must be the one assigned to the printer, in the SELECT clause.

By the I-O-CONTROL paragraph, then,

---

[2] FORM-OVERFLOW is the reserved name used with many computers. Check the appropriate computer manual for the specific name employed.

we call in a compiler-generated routine entitled **FORM-OVERFLOW**. This routine tests for the end of a page on a print file. If the end of the page has been reached, then such a condition will be called by whatever condition-name the programmer chooses (**END-OF-FORM** in the above example).

Each time a line is written in the **PROCEDURE DIVISION**, a test should be performed to determine if the end of the page has been reached. Generally, we wish to print headings on a new page when a form-overflow condition arises:

```
WRITE DETAIL-PRINT-REC.
IF END-OF-FORM WRITE HEADER-REC
    AFTER ADVANCING 0 LINES.
```

This end-of-form test should appear after each **WRITE** command.

Thus there are **two** parts to the test for the last print line: (1) The **APPLY** clause in the **I-O-CONTROL** paragraph of the **ENVIRONMENT DIVISION** calls the COBOL routine **FORM-OVERFLOW** into the program. (2) The condition-name is then tested in the **PROCEDURE DIVISION** to determine if, in fact, the last print line has been reached.

EXERCISES

1. To advance the paper a specified number of lines before or after printing is called _____.
*****
an **ADVANCING** option

2. To space the paper a designated number of lines and then to print a line, the _____ clause is used as part of the **WRITE** statement.
*****
AFTER ADVANCING

3. Within a single **WRITE** statement, the form may be advanced __, __ or _____ lines or _____.
*****
1, 2, or 3
to the top of a new page

4. Write a COBOL expression to advance the form two lines and then to print the record called **TOTAL**, which is part of the print file.
*****
WRITE TOTAL AFTER ADVANCING 2 LINES

What, if anything, is wrong with the following statements (5–7)?

5. **WRITE PRINT-REC AFTER ADVANCING TWO LINES.**
*****
Should be integer 2.

6. **WRITE PRINT-REC AFTER ADVANCING 1 LINE.**
*****
Plural **LINES** must be used.

7. WRITE PRINT-REC AFTER ADVANCING 5 LINES.
   *****
   Only 1, 2, or 3 may be specified.

8. To test for the last line of printing on a form, the _____-generated routine called _____ is accessed.
   *****
   compiler
   FORM-OVERFLOW

9. To access this routine, the _____ paragraph of the _____ SECTION of the _____ DIVISION is used.
   *****
   I-O-CONTROL
   INPUT-OUTPUT
   ENVIRONMENT

10. The statement to call this routine into the COBOL program begins with the word _____.
    *****
    APPLY

11. The word following APPLY is a programmer-supplied _____.
    *****
    condition-name

12. After APPLY NAME-1 TO FORM-OVERFLOW is written, the _____ must be specified.
    *****
    file name

13. This file name specified in the APPLY clause must also appear in the _____ DIVISION in a _____ clause.
    *****
    ENVIRONMENT
    SELECT

14. This file name must be assigned to the _____ device.
    *****
    print

15. APPLY END1 TO FORM-OVERFLOW ON PRINT-FILE appears in the ENVIRONMENT DIVISION. A statement in the PROCEDURE DIVISION to branch to HDR-RTN if the end of the form is sensed is _____.
    *****
    IF END1 GO TO HDR-RTN

16. The test for end of form should follow _____.
    *****
    each WRITE command

17. To write the record called HEADING-1 on a new page, the statement _____ is used.
    *****
    WRITE HEADING-1 AFTER ADVANCING 0 LINES

C. THE ALIGNMENT OF DATA AND THE PRINTING OF HEADER INFORMATION

The print area, you will recall, must contain 133 characters when the ADVANCING option is used for writing records. The first position of the area is used by the computer for proper spacing of forms, and should not be accessed by the programmer. Thus the second position denoted in the area is really the first print position. Positions 2 to 133 in the print area will be transmitted to the printer when a WRITE command is executed. Thus we set up our print area as follows:

```
01  PRINT-REC.
    02 FILLER     PICTURE X.
    02 REAL-REC.
       03 FLDA   PICTURE X.
           .
           .
           .
```

The first position is called FILLER to denote that it will not be accessed in the program. When a WRITE command is issued, whatever is in FLDA will appear in the first print position. The FILLER is not part of the print area and is used only for carriage control.

Thus 132 print positions are available. To produce clear and meaningful reports, information is ordinarily spaced on the line allowing adequate margins on each side of the paper and aligning the data so that fields are evenly distributed. In addition, headings are usually necessary to provide identifying information. Two types of headers generally appear on each page of a report.

1. Headings that identify the job, title, date, and specific application.

2. Headings that indicate field delineations.

Fig. 13-1 illustrates the two types of headers. Note that line 1 of the illustration supplies data about the job and its application and line 2 designates the fields to be printed. Notice that the headings and fields are neatly spaced across the form.

The headings are essential on each page, since continuous forms are burst, or separated, after they are generated. Each page, then, must have identifying information.

In preparing reports, the programmer often uses a print layout sheet (Fig. 13-2) to help in spacing data across the page. The print layout sheet is subdivided into 132 print positions. The heading or headings are placed evenly. From the numbered positions, the programmer can then determine in which print positions he should place the literals, and which positions should be left blank. Fig. 13-3 illustrates the print layout sheet for the report in Fig. 13-1. Note that print positions 1–56 will be left blank in the print area as will print positions 77–132 on the first line. The literal 'MONTHLY TRANSACTIONS' will be placed in the area between. On the print layout sheet, note that X's indicate where the actual data will be placed. Twenty X's under the field delineator NAME denote that the data field contains 20 characters.

If both detail and header information are required in the report, and they generally are, then several record formats must be specified. Thus the FD entry for the print file illustrated in Fig. 13-3 may be:

```
FD  PRINT-FILE
    RECORDING MODE IS F
```

MONTHLY TRANSACTIONS

CUSTOMER NAME   TRANSACTION NO   AMT OF TRANSACTION   DATE OF TRANS   SHIPPED TO   INVOICE NO

Fig. 13-1

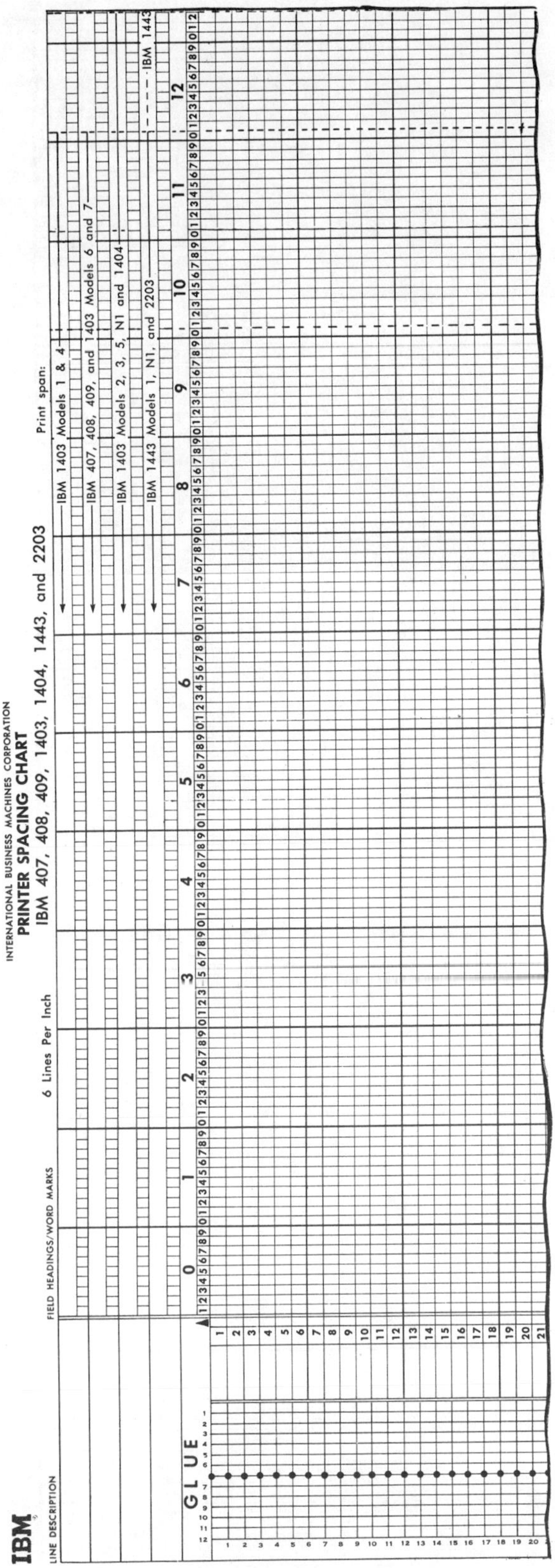
IBM
INTERNATIONAL BUSINESS MACHINES CORPORATION
PRINTER SPACING CHART
IBM 407, 408, 409, 1403, 1404, 1443, and 2203
6 Lines Per Inch
Print span:
IBM 1403 Models 1 & 4
IBM 407, 408, 409, and 1403 Models 6 and 7
IBM 1403 Models 2, 3, 5, N1 and 1404
IBM 1443 Models 1, N1, and 2203
IBM 1443
LINE DESCRIPTION
FIELD HEADINGS/WORD MARKS
GLUE
0 1 2 3 4 5 6 7 8 9 10 11 12

Fig. 13-2

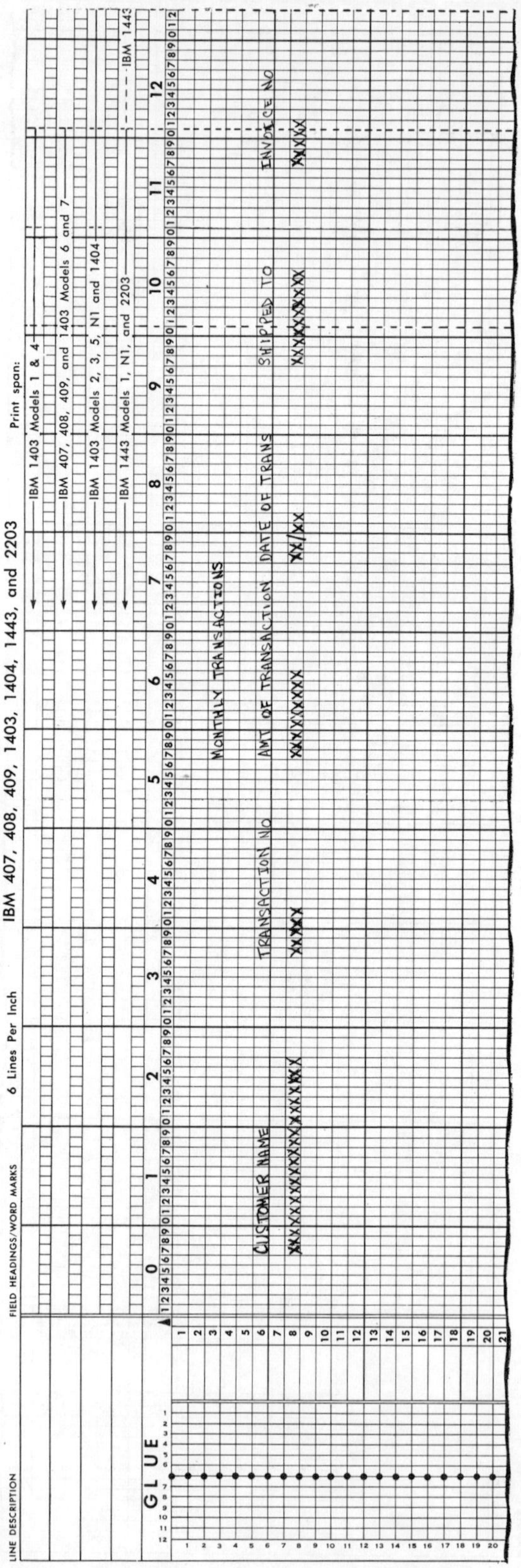

IBM
LINE DESCRIPTION
FIELD HEADINGS/WORD MARKS
INTERNATIONAL BUSINESS MACHINES CORPORATION
PRINTER SPACING CHART
IBM 407, 408, 409, 1403, 1404, 1443, and 2203
6 Lines Per Inch
Print span:
IBM 1403 Models 1 & 4
IBM 407, 408, 409, and 1403 Models 6 and 7
IBM 1403 Models 2, 3, 5, N1 and 1404
IBM 1443 Models 1, N1, and 2203
IBM 1443
GLUE
MONTHLY TRANSACTIONS
CUSTOMER NAME
TRANSACTION NO
AMT OF TRANSACTION
DATE OF TRANS
SHIPPED TO
INVOICE NO

Fig. 13-3

```
        LABEL RECORDS ARE OMITTED
        RECORD CONTAINS 133
            CHARACTERS
        DATA RECORDS ARE HEADER-1,
            HEADER-2, DETAIL-LINE.
```

Each record indicated above must be described by an 01 level entry and its corresponding fields. Let us look at the headings first.

```
01   HEADER-1.
     02 FILLER     PICTURE X.
     02 FILLER     PICTURE X(56).
     02 LITERAL1   PICTURE X(20).
     02 FILLER     PICTURE X(56).
01   HEADER-2.
     02 FILLER     PICTURE X.
     02 FILLER     PICTURE X(6).
     02 LITERAL2   PICTURE X(13).
     02 FILLER     PICTURE X(17).
     02 LITERAL3   PICTURE X(14).
     02 FILLER     PICTURE X(6).
     02 LITERAL4   PICTURE X(18).
     02 FILLER     PICTURE XX.
     02 LITERAL5   PICTURE X(13).
     02 FILLER     PICTURE X(7).
     02 LITERAL6   PICTURE X(10).
     02 FILLER     PICTURE X(10).
     02 LITERAL7   PICTURE X(10).
     02 FILLER     PICTURE X(6).
```

Note that the first position of each record is a one-position FILLER, since this is the area that is used by the computer for carriage control and should not be accessed by the programmer. The fields designated as LITERAL1,2, . . . will receive literals in the PROCEDURE DIVISION. Between each such field, there is a FILLER, since we wish spaces to appear on each side of a literal, thereby spacing the form. In the PROCEDURE DIVISION, then, we must first clear the print area and then move the corresponding literals into each data field:

```
HEADER-RTN.
    MOVE SPACES TO HEADER-1.
    MOVE 'MONTHLY TRANSACTIONS' TO
        LITERAL1.
```

```
    WRITE HEADER-1 AFTER ADVANCING 0
        LINES.
    MOVE SPACES TO HEADER-2.
    MOVE 'CUSTOMER NAME' TO LITERAL2.
    MOVE 'TRANSACTION NO' TO
        LITERAL3.
    MOVE 'AMT OF TRANSACTION' TO
        LITERAL4.
    MOVE 'DATE OF TRANS' TO LITERAL 5.
    MOVE 'SHIPPED TO' TO LITERAL6..
    MOVE 'INVOICE NO' TO LITERAL7.
    WRITE HEADER-2 AFTER ADVANCING 2
        LINES.
```

The print area must be initially cleared, since an output area has unpredictable contents at the onset of execution. The first heading information is moved to the print area, and the line is printed on a new page. The print area must **again** be cleared before HEADER-2 is written. Note that HEADER-1 and HEADER-2 occupy the **same** 133 position print area.[3] Thus this area must be cleared before additional information is moved in.

DETAIL-LINE, the third record of the PRINT-FILE, will also have FILLERS between each data field for proper alignment of information:

```
01   DETAIL-LINE.
     02 FILLER       PICTURE X.
     02 FILLER       PICTURE X(6).
     02 NAME         PICTURE X(20).
     02 FILLER       PICTURE X(10).
     02 TRANS-NO     PICTURE 9(5).
     02 FILLER       PICTURE X(15).
     02 AMT-OF-TRANS PICTURE
                         $$,$$$.99.
     02 FILLER       PICTURE X(11).
     02 DATE         PICTURE X(5).
     02 FILLER       PICTURE X(15).
     02 DESTINATION  PICTURE X(10).
     02 FILLER       PICTURE X(10).
     02 INV-NO       PICTURE 9(5).
     02 FILLER       PICTURE X(11).
```

The DETAIL-LINE contains editing symbols in the field called AMT-OF-TRANS.

---

[3] Through the use of **buffering,** it is possible to have two **separate** areas for a file.

Input data fields or intermediate work areas will be moved to the detail line:

```
DETAIL-RTN.
   MOVE SPACES TO DETAIL-LINE.
   MOVE NAME OF CARD-IN TO NAME
      OF DETAIL-LINE.
   MOVE TRANS-NO OF CARD-IN TO
      TRANS-NO OF DETAIL-LINE.
   MOVE AMT-OF-TRANS OF CARD-IN TO
      AMT-OF-TRANS OF DETAIL-LINE.
   MOVE DATE OF CARD-IN TO DATE OF
      DETAIL-LINE.
   MOVE DESTINATION OF CARD-IN TO
      DESTINATION OF DETAIL-LINE.
   MOVE INV-NO OF CARD-IN TO
      INV-NO OF DETAIL-LINE.
   WRITE DETAIL-LINE AFTER ADVANCING
      2 LINES.
   IF END-OF-PAGE GO TO HEADER-RTN
      ELSE GO TO START.
```

This method of creating output, although correct, is not considered very efficient. The two heading records and the detail line may be set up in the WORKING-STORAGE SECTION of the program. The chief reason for accumulating print information in the WORKING-STORAGE SECTION is that values may be assigned to the various fields in WORKING-STORAGE by VALUE clauses. This eliminates the neces-

sity of moving spaces and specific literals to each area in the PROCEDURE DIVISION. Since VALUE clauses may not be assigned in the FILE SECTION,[4] we accumulate data in WORKING-STORAGE, move the records to the FILE SECTION, and then WRITE the information.

Thus the FILE SECTION print area is 133 positions; data from the WORKING-STORAGE SECTION will be moved into this file area. Fields need not be denoted in the FILE SECTION, since the entire record in WORKING-STORAGE will be moved:

```
FD   PRINT-FILE
     RECORDING MODE IS F
     LABEL RECORDS ARE OMITTED
     RECORD CONTAINS 133
     CHARACTERS
     DATA RECORD IS PRINTOUT.
01   PRINTOUT PICTURE X(133).
```

In the PROCEDURE DIVISION, data from WORKING-STORAGE will be moved to PRINTOUT and WRITE PRINTOUT AFTER ADVANCING 2 LINES will then be executed.

The two heading records and the detail lines will be set up in the WORKING-STORAGE as group items, after any 77 level items used in the program:

[4] Except for condition-names.

```
WORKING-STORAGE SECTION.
77
   .
   .
   .
   01   HEADER-1.
        02 FILLER      PICTURE X, VALUE SPACES.
        02 FILLER      PICTURE X(56), VALUE SPACES.
        02 LITERAL1    PICTURE X(20), VALUE 'MONTHLY TRANSACTIONS'.
        02 FILLER      PICTURE X(56), VALUE SPACES.
   01   HEADER-2.
        02 FILLER      PICTURE X, VALUE SPACES.
        02 FILLER      PICTURE X(6), VALUE SPACES.
        02 LITERAL2    PICTURE X(13), VALUE 'CUSTOMER NAME'.
        02 FILLER      PICTURE X(7), VALUE SPACES.
        02 LITERAL3    PICTURE X(14), VALUE 'TRANSACTION NO'.
        02 FILLER      PICTURE X(6), VALUE SPACES.
        02 LITERAL4    PICTURE X(18), VALUE 'AMT OF TRANSACTION'.
        02 FILLER      PICTURE XX, VALUE SPACES.
```

```
    02 LITERAL5    PICTURE X(13), VALUE 'DATE OF TRANS'.
    02 FILLER      PICTURE X(7), VALUE SPACES.
    02 LITERAL6    PICTURE X(10), VALUE 'SHIPPED TO'.
    02 FILLER      PICTURE X(10), VALUE SPACES.
    02 LITERAL7    PICTURE X(10), VALUE 'INVOICE NO'.
    02 FILLER      PICTURE X(6), VALUE SPACES.
01  DETAIL-LINE.
```
(Same format as specified above.)

Note that, with the use of VALUE clauses in the WORKING-STORAGE SECTION, the movement of literals to the fields is unnecessary. All constants and blanks are preassigned. We must still, however, move these records to the print area before a line is to be written. Thus data is accumulated in WORKING-STORAGE and then transferred to the print area:

```
HEADER-RTN.
    MOVE HEADER-1 TO PRINTOUT.
    WRITE PRINTOUT AFTER ADVANCING 0
    LINES.
    MOVE HEADER-2 TO PRINTOUT.
    WRITE PRINTOUT AFTER ADVANCING 2
    LINES.
```

Note that it is unnecessary to clear PRINTOUT. The entire 133 positions called HEADER-1, which contain appropriate blank areas, are transmitted to the PRINTOUT area. Similarly, PRINTOUT need not be cleared before HEADER-2 is moved since HEADER-2 contains the necessary blanks. The DETAIL-RTN remains the same as above, since data must still be moved to the various fields from the input area.

Several shortcuts may be used in the WORKING-STORAGE SECTION to enhance the efficiency of the program. HEADER-1, for example, may be set up as follows:

```
01  HEADER-1.
    02 FILLER PICTURE X(57), VALUE
       SPACES.
    02 LITERAL1 PICTURE X(76), VALUE
       'MONTHLY TRANSACTIONS'.
```

The FILLER specified above will print 56 positions of blank since the first position of the record will be used for carriage control. It is unnecessary, therefore, to set up two filler areas, one containing a single blank and one containing 56 blanks. One FILLER will serve just as well. Recall that nonnumeric literals are left justified in a field. Thus LITERAL1 will contain, in its first 20 positions (which correspond to print positions 57–76), 'MONTHLY TRANS-ACTIONS'. The rest of the field will be replaced with blanks. The VALUE clause produces the same effect as moving 'MONTHLY TRANSACTIONS' TO LITERAL1.

Using the JUSTIFIED RIGHT clause, we may set up HEADER-1 slightly differently:

```
01  HEADER-1.
    02 LITERAL1  PICTURE X(77) VALUE
                 'MONTHLY TRANSACTIONS' JUSTIFIED RIGHT.
    02 FILLER    PICTURE X(56) VALUE SPACES.
```

This method may appear less efficient since it sets up three additional 133 position areas in WORKING-STORAGE, which are not specified in Method 1. Note, however, that the coding of the PROCEDURE DIVISION is simplified, since VALUE clauses in the WORKING-STORAGE SECTION are somewhat easier to supply than MOVE statements.

'MONTHLY TRANSACTIONS' will be placed in positions 58–77, which correspond to print positions 57–76. The rest of the field will be blank.

HEADER-2 may also be coded more efficiently. We may use two literals, each containing the proper number of spaces, to incorporate the entire record. Fig. 13-4 illustrates the necessary entries. Note that

IBM   COBOL Program Sheet   Form No. X28-1464-3 U/M 050
Printed in U. S. A.

| System | | Punching Instructions | | Sheet | of |

| Program | | Graphic | | | | | | Card | | * | Identification |
| Programmer | | Date | Punch | | | | | | Form # | | | 73⌐ | ⌐80 |

Fig. 13-4

the rules for continuation of literals, as indicated in Chapter 11, apply. Note also that 120 positions is the maximum size of a literal. Thus two fields, at least, must be designated for the entire print area, which is 133 positions long.

Often, when printing headers, a page number is required as part of each header record. Consider the following record described in **WORKING-STORAGE:**

```
01  HEAD-REC.
    02 FILLER    PICTURE X(61).
    02 LITERALX  PICTURE X(20) VALUE
                 'SALARY CHANGES'.
    02 LITERALY  PICTURE X(8) VALUE
                 'PAGE NO.'.
    02 PAGE-CT   PICTURE ZZZZ.
    02 FILLER    PICTURE X(40) VALUE
                 SPACES.
```

A 77 level item, called **CT1, PICTURE 9999, VALUE 0001,** is set up prior to the group items in **WORKING-STORAGE.** The following **HEADER-RTN** will print a page number on each page:

```
HEADER-RTN.
    MOVE CT1 TO PAGE-CT.
    MOVE HEAD-REC TO PRINTOUT.
    WRITE PRINTOUT AFTER ADVANCING 0
    LINES.
    ADD 1 TO CT1.
```

Each time through the routine **CT1** is incremented by 1. Before each record is printed, **CT1** is edited into **PAGE-CT.** Thus

a correct page number will appear on each form. Note that the following is **not** correct.

Invalid: ADD 1 TO PAGE-CT.

PAGE-CT is a **report-item** containing editing symbols which cause zero suppression. Only **numeric** items may be used in arithmetic operations. **PAGE-CT,** as a report-item, is not a numeric field.

A **MOVE** operation, in which data is transmitted to the output area, followed by a **WRITE** statement, may be replaced by a single **WRITE . . . FROM** instruction.

```
MOVE HEADING-1 TO PRINT-REC.
WRITE PRINT-REC AFTER ADVANCING 0
LINES.
```

may be replaced by

```
WRITE PRINT-REC FROM HEADING-1
AFTER ADVANCING 0 LINES.
```

At this point, it is probably quite clear that the printing of forms requires many programming considerations which are not necessary when producing other kinds of output. The following may provide a checklist of items that ought to be considered when printing data:

1. Record length must be defined as 133 characters when using an **ADVANCING** option. The first position should have initial contents of space or spaces, and should not be accessed in the program.

2. The **AFTER ADVANCING** option should be used with each **WRITE** command to indicate the spacing of the form. **AFTER ADVANCING 1, 2, 3 LINES** will cause one, two, or three blank lines, respectively, to appear before the next record is written. **AFTER ADVANCING 0 LINES** causes the paper to skip to a new page. Specify **AFTER ADVANCING 0 LINES** when printing the first header to insure that it appears on the first printing line of a form.

3. Print records, including headers and detail lines, should be established in **WORKING-STORAGE** to allow the use of **VALUE** clauses. These records must then be moved to the print area, and a **WRITE**, or a **WRITE . . . FROM . . .** command issued. Spacing of data on the line may be facilitated with the use of a print layout sheet.

4. After each record is printed, a test for the end of a form should be issued so that printing of headers on each page is insured.

5. The appropriate editing symbols should be specified in the **PICTURE** clauses of report-items within the detail record.

EXERCISES

1. The two types of headings that may appear on a printed report are _____ and _____.

   *****

   job headings
   field delineators

2. A form that is often used to facilitate the spacing of data across a page is called a _____.

   *****

   print layout sheet

3. To facilitate **PROCEDURE DIVISION** coding, print records are often specified in the _____ **SECTION**.

   *****

   WORKING-STORAGE

4. Records are described in the **WORKING-STORAGE SECTION** because this section allows the use of _____.

   *****

   VALUE clauses

5. If print records are **not** described with **VALUE** clauses in the **WORKING-STORAGE SECTION** then numerous _____ operations are required in the _____.

   *****

   MOVE
   PROCEDURE DIVISION

6. Assume print records are described in the **WORKING-STORAGE SECTION** with appropriate **VALUE** clauses. Give a sample record description entry in the **FILE SECTION** for the print file.

   *****

   01 PRINTOUT PICTURE X(133).

REVIEW QUESTIONS

1. Write a series of statements to print a line of data and then space the form 6 lines.

2. (T or F) With a single WRITE statement, a maximum of triple spacing may be achieved.

3. Indicate when 133 positions must be denoted for the print area. What is the function of the extra position?

4. Write the ENVIRONMENT DIVISION entry necessary to test for the end of a page.

5. Using the answer to Question 4, write the PROCEDURE DIVISION entry necessary to skip to a new page when the end of the previous page is sensed.

    What, if anything, is wrong with the following entries (6–8)?

6. WRITE PRINT-LINE AFTER ADVANCING 4 LINES.

7. WRITE PRINT-LINE AFTER ADVANCING 1 LINE.

8. IF FORM-OVERFLOW WRITE HEADER AFTER ADVANCING 0 LINES.

9. What is a carriage control tape?

10. What is the purpose of the I-O-CONTROL paragraph of the ENVIRONMENT DIVISION?

PROBLEMS

Code Problems 1–3 of the last chapter incorporating the following.

   (a) Print headings on each detail page.
   (b) Print page number on each page.
   (c) Double space between all detail lines.
   (d) Store output records in WORKING-STORAGE.

4. Using the following print layout sheet, write WORKING-STORAGE entries for the headers and detail line.

Print span:

LINE DESCRIPTION

FIELD HEADINGS/WORD MARKS   6 Lines Per Inch

◄──── IBM 1403 Models 1 & 4 ────►
◄──── IBM 407, 408, 409, and 1403 Models 6 and 7 ────►
◄──── IBM 1403 Models 2, 3, 5, N1 and 1404 ────►
◄──── IBM 1443 Models 1, N1, and 2203 ────► - - - - IBM 1443

GLUE	0	1	2	3	4	5	6	7	8	9	10	11	12

MONTHLY SALES REPORT

SALESMAN NO.	SALESMAN NAME	AMOUNT OF SALES FOR WEEK1	AMOUNT OF SALES FOR WEEK2	AMOUNT OF SALES FOR WEEK3	AMOUNT OF SALES FOR WEEK4	TOTAL CREDITS
XXXXX	XXXXXXXXXXXXXXXX	$XXX.XX	$XXX.XX	$XXX.XX	$XXX.XX	$XXXX.XX

Problem 4

Unit 4

Altering the Path of a Program

A. SIMPLE GO TO—REVIEW

COBOL statements are executed in the order in which they appear unless the computer is instructed to do otherwise.

Example 1

```
MOVE A TO B.
ADD C TO D.
SUBTRACT E FROM F.
```

Unless the computer is programmed to alter the sequence of execution, the **MOVE,** **ADD,** and **SUBTRACT** statements will be performed in that order.

This chapter will illustrate all the verbs that may be used to alter the path of a program. Thus far, we have discussed one method. By issuing a **GO TO** statement, we instruct the computer to change the sequence of instructions to be executed, and to proceed to another point in the program. We say: **GO TO** (paragraph name). This statement will alter the path of the program. After performing the **GO TO** (paragraph name) command, the next instruction to be executed is the one following the named paragraph:

Example 2

```
    MOVE A TO B.
    GO TO RTN-3.
```

```
RTN-2.
    ADD C TO D.
    SUBTRACT E FROM F.
RTN-3.
    WRITE OUT-REC.
```

After the **MOVE** statement is performed, a **branch** to **RTN-3** occurs. The next instruction to be executed is the **WRITE** statement, following **RTN-3**.

In the above illustration, **RTN-2** and **RTN-3** are paragraph names. They must be **uniquely** defined. The rules for forming paragraph names are the same as for data-names with one exception. A paragraph name may contain all digits. It may appear on the same line as an instruction or on a separate line, and it must end with a period.

RTN-2 and **RTN-3** are points that can be branched to in the program. Since **RTN-2** is a paragraph name, we expect **GO TO** **RTN-2** to be a coded statement. Paragraph names are usually not defined unless, at some point, the program is to branch there. Although specifying a paragraph name that is never used will not cause an error, we generally write such names for branch points only.

From the above illustration, we see that the program will always proceed **around** **RTN-2** and the statements indicated. We may assume that RTN-2 is branched to from some other point in the program. If **GO TO RTN-2** is **not** a coded statement, then the steps in RTN-2 will never be executed.

A simple **GO TO** (paragraph name) is called an **unconditional branch.** You will note that a **GO TO** statement corresponds to the flowcharting symbol (PARA-GRAPH NAME) , an unconditional branch connector. Whenever the unconditional branch connector appears in the flowchart, the COBOL statement **GO TO** (paragraph name) may be used in the program. Under **all** conditions, a branch will occur.

The conditional branch connector— (PARA-GAAPH NAME) indicates that the path of a program is to be altered only if a specific condition is met. The **GO TO** (paragraph

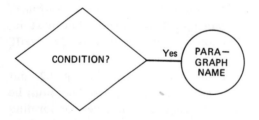

name) is, then, part of an **IF** statement:

IF (condition) **GO TO** (paragraph name), corresponds to the above figure.

A branch occurs only if the specific condition exists. If it does not, the program proceeds to the **ELSE** or **OTHERWISE** clause, if it is used, or to the next sequential step.

Besides the **GO TO** statement, which corresponds so exactly to the flowcharting branch symbols, there are other ways of altering the path of a program. The remainder of this chapter will discuss additional, more sophisticated, methods.

B. GO TO . . . DEPENDING ON . . . STATEMENT

Examine the following illustration:
Example 1

    IF CODE = 1 GO TO RTNA.
    IF CODE = 2 GO TO RTNB.
    IF CODE = 3 GO TO RTNC.
    GO TO ERR-RTN.

When the contents of a data field may be 1, 2, . . . n where n is any integer, and the program is to proceed to different points depending upon the data field, a "shortcut" use of the **GO TO** statement may be employed:

Example 2

    GO TO RTNA, RTNB, RTNC DEPENDING
    ON CODE.
    GO TO ERR-RTN.

The computer is instructed to branch to the first paragraph name, **RTNA,** if the data-name, **CODE,** has a one (1) as its contents. It will branch to the second specified paragraph name, **RTNB,** if **CODE** has a two. A branch to the third paragraph name, **RTNC,** will occur only if **CODE** equals three. If **CODE** does not equal 1, 2, or 3, a branch to **ERR-RTN** is performed.

In general, if there are n paragraph names specified in the **GO TO . . . DEPENDING ON . . .** statement, a branch to the first occurs if there is a 1 in the field, a branch to the second occurs if there is a 2 in the field, . . . a branch to the nth occurs if there is an n in the field. If the field consists of any number other than 1 to n (for example, -5, 0, $n + 1$), the program will proceed to the next sequential step. In other words, no branch within the **GO TO . . . DEPENDING ON . . .** will occur. In our example, the next sequential step was an unconditional branch to **ERR-RTN.** The format, then, for this statement is:

GO TO (paragraph-name-1, paragraph-name-2, . . . paragraph-name-n)

DEPENDING ON (data-name).

The GO TO . . . DEPENDING ON . . . statement may only be used for **numeric** fields. The statement GO TO PARA-1, PARA-2 DEPENDING ON FLDA will execute properly only if FLDA has a PICTURE of 9's.

Any number of paragraph names may be used within the GO TO . . . DEPENDING ON . . . statement. The only limitation is the size of the computer, which, in most cases, allows adequate flexibility.

Problem A

Branch to:

PARA-1 if FLDA = 3
PARA-2 if FLDA = 4
PARA-3 if FLDA = 5

otherwise branch to START.

On first inspection, it may appear that a GO TO . . . DEPENDING ON . . . statement is not applicable, since we want to proceed to different paragraphs depending on a 3, 4, or 5 in FLDA. Since the GO TO . . . DEPENDING ON . . . statement causes a branch to the first indicated paragraph if there is a 1, and not a 3, in the data field, it may seem that this statement is inappropriate.

Let us consider the conditions more closely, however. Suppose FLDA = 1. Since the field does not equal 3, 4, or 5, we wish to branch to START. Suppose FLDA = 2. Again, a branch to START is implied. Thus, if FLDA = 1, 2, 3, 4, or 5, we want to branch to START, START, PARA-1, PARA-2, PARA-3, respectively. The following would then be correct:

Solution 1 to Problem A

GO TO START, START, PARA-1, PARA-2, PARA-3 DEPENDING ON FLDA.
GO TO START.

Note that the same paragraph name may be used more than once in a GO TO . . . DEPENDING ON . . . statement. The only criterion for execution is that we wish to proceed to the first specified paragraph name if there is a one in the field, to the second paragraph name if there is a two in the field, and so on for all paragraph names indicated. If the field is not equal to any of these integers, the next sequential step will be executed. In our example, if FLDA is not equal to 1, 2, 3, 4, or 5, GO TO START is performed. Thus the GO TO . . . DEPENDING ON . . . statement is really only a "shortcut" method for writing a series of simple conditional statements.

The above use of the GO TO . . . DEPENDING ON . . . statement is not the only solution to the problem. Suppose we subtract two from FLDA. In that case, we wish to branch to PARA-1 if there is a one in FLDA, to PARA-2 if there is a two in FLDA, and to PARA-3 if there is a three in FLDA.

Solution 2 to Problem A

SUBTRACT 2 FROM FLDA.
GO TO PARA-1, PARA-2, PARA-3 DEPENDING ON FLDA.
GO TO START.

From the above illustration, it should be clear that a GO TO . . . DEPENDING ON . . . statement is easily derived from conditions where the paragraph names to be branched to are a function of a data field whose value increments by some constant. If the field has values of 15, 16, 17, 18, and branches to four different points occur accordingly, then merely subtract 14 from the field and proceed as if it had values 1, 2, 3, 4.

When dealing with a field that may have many values, each of which causes a specific branch, it is often advantageous to manipulate the data as above so that a GO TO . . . DEPENDING ON . . . command may be used. If not, a series of simple GO TO statements may prove tedious, time consuming, and inefficient. With manipulation of data, we can sometimes use this "shortcut" method even if the values in the field are not consecutive.

Problem B:

branch to:
   PARA-1 if FLDB = 2;
   PARA-2 if FLDB = 4;
   PARA-3 if FLDB = 6;
   PARA-4 if FLDB = 8;
   PARA-5 if FLDB = 10.

To set up five simple GO TO statements is one way to solve the problem. We can, however, use the shortcut method even though FLDB has values from 2 to 10 and is incremented by 2 instead of 1. We must first manipulate the data. Suppose we divide FLDB by 2. Then the values in the field vary from 1 to 5, incrementing by 1. This is the order we are seeking. Our statements then read as follows:

Solution 1 to Problem B

   DIVIDE 2 INTO FLDB.
   GO TO PARA-1, PARA-2, PARA-3, PARA-4, PARA-5 DEPENDING ON FLDB.

Note that, if the original contents of FLDB were required for future processing, the above solution would require an additional step. That is, we would multiply 2 by FLDB at the end of the routine to restore its original quantity.

C. STOP STATEMENT

The STOP statement alters the path of a program by halting the run. For an end of job halt, we say

   STOP RUN.

This instruction **permanently** halts execution of the program. It terminates the run. The program cannot be restarted after STOP RUN is executed.

We may also instruct the computer to (1) pause and (2) print a message by issuing the following instruction:

   STOP (literal).

This statement causes the computer to stop executing. The program **may be re-**started, however, by some form of operator intervention such as depressing the START key. Thus the STOP (literal) command causes a **pause** in execution. Unlike STOP RUN, STOP (literal) is **not** a permanent halt.

Thus the combined format for a STOP statement is:

The literal specified in a STOP statement will print on the printer as a message to the computer operator. The literal may be numeric or nonnumeric. Thus

   STOP 'NO DATE CARD'.
   STOP 111.

are valid instructions. In the first case, the message NO DATE CARD will print on the printer and the computer will pause. The message implies that a date card is required for execution and was not found. After the STOP instruction, a branch to the date card routine should follow to allow continuation of the program. A sample date card routine follows:

DATE-CARD-ROUTINE.
   READ CARD-IN AT END GO TO EOJ.
   IF CODE = 'D' GO TO INITIALIZE-RTN.
   STOP 'NO DATE CARD'.
   GO TO DATE-CARD-ROUTINE.
INITIALIZE-RTN.

   .

   .

   .

The date card contains a D in the field called CODE. If the date card is missing, no 'D' will be found. In that case, the computer will print a message, stop, and branch back to the date card routine after the operator inserts the correct card and depresses start.

A numeric literal is sometimes used in conjunction with a STOP statement when the computer operator is supplied with a list of numeric error codes. When STOP

111 is executed, for example, 111 will print and the computer will pause. The operator would then consult the list of codes to determine what error code 111 is, and what is to be done before the job is restarted.

Thus two forms of the **STOP** statement

exist. **STOP RUN** causes permanent termination of the job; the program may not be restarted. **STOP** (literal) causes the printing of the indicated literal and a pause in execution. The computer operator can restart the job by depressing the start key.

EXERCISES

1. The statement **GO TO** (paragraph name) is called an _____ branch.

*****

unconditional

2. The statement **IF A = B GO TO RTN-1** is called a _____ branch.

*****

conditional

3. What, if anything, is wrong with the following paragraph names?
   (a) **TOTAL-RTN**
   (b) **%-RTN**
   (c) **1**

*****

(a) Nothing wrong.
(b) No special characters permitted.
(c) Nothing wrong.

4. All paragraph names must be followed by a _____.

*****

period

5. What is wrong with the following statements?
   (a) **GO TO PARA-1 DEPENDING ON CODE.**
   (b) **GO TO RTN-1, RTN-2 DEPENDING UPON CODE.**
   (c) **GO TO PARA-1 DEPENDING ON CODE1, CODE2.**

*****

(a) Nothing wrong—a branch to **PARA-1** will occur if **CODE** = 1.
(b) **DEPENDING ON**, not **UPON**.
(c) Only **one** data-name may be specified.

6. **GO TO RTN-5, RTN-6, RTN-7 DEPENDING ON FLDA. GO TO RTN-8.** A branch to _____ will occur if there is a 0 in **FLDA**. A branch to **RTN-5** will occur if there is a _____ in **FLDA**.

*****

RTN-8
one

7. Write a statement or statements that will cause the following branches: RTN-1 if FLDB = 3; RTN-2 if FLDB = 6, RTN-3 if FLDB = 9; otherwise branch to START.
(**Note.** Use GO TO . . . DEPENDING ON option.)

*****

DIVIDE 3 INTO FLDB.
GO TO RTN-1, RTN-2, RTN-3 DEPENDING ON FLDB.
GO TO START.

8. To cause the program to terminate execution, the _____ instruction is indicated.

*****

STOP RUN

9. To cause the program to pause, the _____ format is used.

*****

STOP (literal)

10. The literal in a STOP (literal) command may be a _____ or a _____ literal.

*****

numeric
nonnumeric

11. _____ is required to continue execution after STOP (literal) has been performed.

*****

Operator intervention

D. ALTER STATEMENT

It is possible in COBOL to alter the path of a simple GO TO statement. That is, GO TO (paragraph-name-1) may be **altered** so that the instruction reads: GO TO (paragraph-name-2). ALTER statements change the path of unconditional branches, or simple GO TO statements. Consider the following instruction:

GO TO STEP-1.

We can change this statement so that it reads, instead, GO TO STEP-2. We must first **label** the GO TO statement, that is, assign it a paragraph name:

PARA-1. GO TO STEP-1.

To alter the above so that it proceeds instead to STEP-2, we say

ALTER PARA-1 TO PROCEED TO STEP-2.

The format, then, of the ALTER statement is as follows:

```
ALTER (paragraph-name-1)
      TO PROCEED TO
              (paragraph-name-2)
```

The ALTER statement changes the contents of the GO TO command at PARA-1. After the ALTER is executed, it is as if the GO TO statement now reads:

PARA-1. GO TO STEP-2.

Note that the ALTER statement changes the contents of the GO TO instruction **internally**, within the machine. The listing, or printout, of the program will not be changed.

Example 1

A4. GO TO A7.

To **ALTER** this instruction so that a branch to **A10**, instead of **A7** occurs, is performed by the following:

ALTER A4 TO PROCEED TO A10.

A4, the first paragraph name specified in the **ALTER** statement, is the name of the instruction to be changed. The statement **GO TO A7 must** have a paragraph-name associated with it. Paragraph **A4**, then, will no longer branch to **A7**, but will proceed to **A10**. It is as if the statement now reads, internally within the computer:

A4. GO TO A10.

Note that the paragraph being altered must have as its **only** entry a simple **GO TO** clause. To say: **ALTER RTN-1 TO PROCEED TO RTN-2** is valid if **RTN-1** contains only a **GO TO** statement. The following is **not** correct:

Invalid:

ALTER PATH1 TO PROCEED TO PATH10.

.
.
.

**PATH1. MOVE A TO B.
    GO TO PATH5.**

PATH1 has a **MOVE** statement as its first entry. To alter **PATH1** it must have only a **GO TO** associated with it.

The **GO TO** instruction which is accessed by an **ALTER** statement is permanently changed unless another **ALTER** is executed. In Example 1, the instruction at **A4** will remain **GO TO A10**, unless another instruction changes it back again.

ALTER statements change the path of simple **GO TO** statements; they do **not** cause branching. To say **ALTER PARA-1 TO PROCEED TO RTN-5** causes a change in the **GO TO** statement at **PARA-1;** it does not cause a branch to **PARA-1**. Consider the following illustration:

Example 2

**RTN-1. MOVE A TO B.
    ADD C TO D.
RTN-2. GO TO RTN-3.**

We wish to perform the **MOVE** and **ADD** instructions but to branch to **RTN-4** instead of **RTN-3**. The following two statements will accomplish this:

**ALTER RTN-2 TO PROCEED TO RTN-4.
GO TO RTN-1.**

The **ALTER** changes the **GO TO** statement at **RTN-2** so that it proceeds, instead, to **RTN-4**. A branch to **RTN-1** performs the **MOVE** and **ADD** operations. Since **RTN-2** now reads **GO TO RTN-4**, a branch to **RTN-4** will occur.

ALTER statements are issued when the programmer wishes to change the normal flow of the program to handle a special condition. The following example illustrates the use of these statements.

Example 3: Fig. 14-1 is the flowchart for the following program excerpt:

**START.
    READ CARD-FILE AT END GO TO EOJ.
    IF CARD-NO IS NOT EQUAL TO
    CARD-PREVIOUS GO TO TOTAL-RTN
    ELSE GO TO ADD-TO-TOTALS.
TOTAL-RTN.
    MOVE TOTAL-1 TO EDIT1.
    MOVE TOTAL-2 TO EDIT2.
    WRITE PRINT-REC AFTER
    ADVANCING 8 LINES.
    GO TO INITIALIZE-RTN.**

The above series of statements illustrates a program excerpt that will accumulate total information and print the totals when a change in card number occurs. If the card that is read has the same number as the previous card, information is added to the totals. If the numbers differ, the previous total data is printed. One of the advantages of COBOL is that a series of routines, such as those above, is readily understood without prior knowledge of the job.

Suppose there are no more cards to be read. The **AT END** clause of the **READ** statement is then executed and a branch to **EOJ** occurs. The first routine that should be performed at **EOJ** is the **TOTAL-**

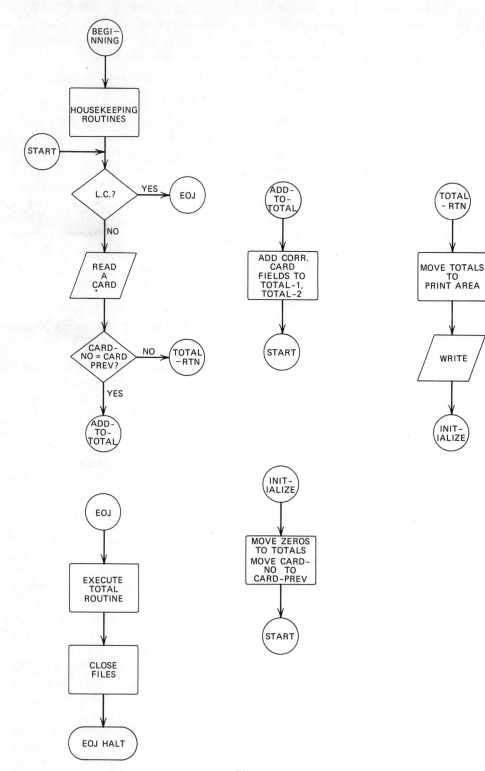

Fig. 14-1

RTN; the program must print out the previously accumulated totals before the files are closed. We cannot, however, issue a branch to **TOTAL-RTN**, since the last step in the paragraph transfers control to **INITIALIZE-RTN**.

We could duplicate all the statements of **TOTAL-RTN** at **EOJ**. This, however, is considered inefficient and unnecessary. Instead, we will **ALTER** the last step of **TOTAL-RTN** so that the program proceeds to the end of job functions:

```
TOTAL-RTN.
      MOVE TOTAL-1 TO EDIT1.
      MOVE TOTAL-2 TO EDIT2.
      WRITE PRINT-REC AFTER
      ADVANCING 0 LINES.
OUT1.
      GO TO INITIALIZE-RTN.
      .
      .
      .
EOJ.
      ALTER OUT1 TO PROCEED TO
      NEXT-STEP.
      GO TO TOTAL-RTN.
NEXT-STEP.
      CLOSE CARD-FILE, PRINT-FILE.
      STOP RUN.
```

Note that the **ALTER** statement is coded: **ALTER** (paragraph-name-1) **TO PROCEED TO** (paragraph-name-2). Paragraph-name-1 is the name of the statement that is changed. The original illustration did **not** have a paragraph name associated with **GO TO INITIALIZE-RTN**. To alter the flow of the statement, it was necessary to insert a paragraph name, called **OUT1**.

At **EOJ**, the **ALTER** statement changes the command at **OUT1** so that **GO TO INITIAL-IZE-RTN** will no longer be performed. After altering the path of **OUT1**, a branch to **TOTAL-RTN** occurs. When all statements are executed at **TOTAL-RTN**, the program branches to **NEXT-STEP** which continues the end of job functions.

Note that **OUT1** is **permanently** changed to proceed to **NEXT-STEP**. Since a branch to **TOTAL-RTN** will not occur again after

the end of job functions are performed, it is not necessary to alter **OUT1** back again to read **GO TO INITIALIZE-RTN**. If, however, the path of a program is changed by an **ALTER** statement during normal processing, it is sometimes necessary to issue a **second ALTER** statement in order to reset the program on its original course. The following illustration will clarify this point: (Fig. 14-2 is the flowchart for the following excerpt.)

Example 4

```
START.
      READ CARD-FILE AT END GO TO EOJ.
      IF CODE = 1 GO TO DEBIT-RTN ELSE
      GO TO CREDIT-RTN.
DEBIT-RTN.
      ADD AMT1, AMT2 GIVING TOTAL.
PRINT-RTN.
      MOVE NAME OF CARD-IN TO NAME
      OF PRINTOUT.
      MOVE TOTAL TO EDIT1.
      WRITE PRINTOUT AFTER ADVANCING 2
      LINES.
PATH1.
      GO TO STEP2.
STEP2.
      ADD 1 TO TOTAL-DEBITS.
      GO TO START.
CREDIT-RTN.
      SUBTRACT AMT2 FROM AMT1 GIVING
      TOTAL.
      ALTER PATH1 TO PROCEED TO STEP3.
      GO TO PRINT-RTN.
STEP3.
      ALTER PATH1 TO PROCEED TO STEP2.
      ADD 1 TO TOTAL-CREDITS.
      GO TO START.
```

Note that **PRINT-RTN** is performed both as credit and debit functions. **PRINT-RTN** is within the flow of **DEBIT-RTN**. To perform **PRINT-RTN** when operating on a credit card, we change the sequence of instructions. That is, we alter **PATH1** to proceed to **STEP3**. Note that it must be changed back again to proceed to its original destination. Unless this is done, a branch to **PRINT-RTN** when a debit card

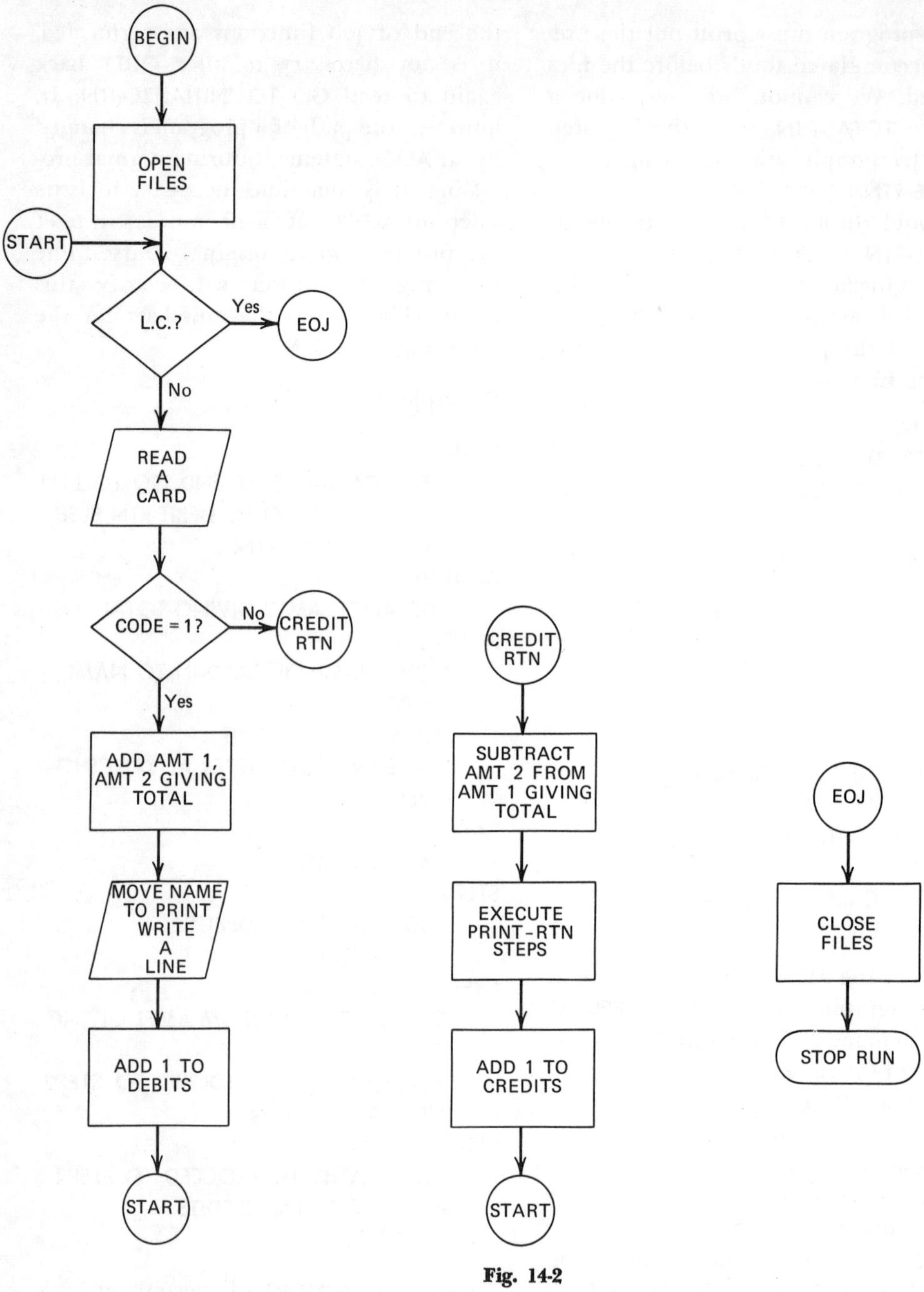

Fig. 14-2

is being processed will lead to **STEP3**, **permanently.**

Since the path of the program is altered for credit cards only, a second **ALTER** statement is necessary to set **PRINT-RTN** back on its original course.

E. PERFORM STATEMENT

From the last section, we see that it is sometimes necessary to perform a sequence of steps from two or more points in a program. In Example 4, the routine called PRINT-RTN was executed as part of the credit and debit card functions.

With the use of ALTER statements, the path of GO TO instructions may be changed. GO TO STEP2 was performed at PATH1 for debit cards and GO TO STEP3 was performed for credit cards by issuing ALTER commands.

The use of ALTER statements to facilitate branching out to specified routines is sometimes a cumbersome and difficult task. The programmer must: (1) ALTER the GO TO statement so that it proceeds to a different point; (2) branch to the specific routine; and (3) ALTER the GO TO statement back again to restore its original destination.

A simple PERFORM statement permits execution of a specified routine from several points in a program without altering the path of GO TO statements. The format is as follows:

```
PERFORM (paragraph-name)
```

The PERFORM statement will:

1. Execute all instructions in the named paragraph.
2. Transfer control to the next sequential step following the PERFORM statement.

Example 1

```
PERFORM TOTAL-RTN.
GO TO START.
      .
      .
      .
TOTAL-RTN.
      ADD AMT1 TO TOTAL1.
      ADD AMT2 TO TOTAL2.
```

The PERFORM statement will cause execution of the two ADD operations and then transfer control to the next sequential step following the PERFORM. Thus a branch to START will occur.

The following illustration replaces AL-TER statements in Example 4 of the last section with PERFORM statements:

```
START.
      READ CARD-FILE AT END GO TO EOJ.
      IF CODE = 1 GO TO DEBIT-RTN ELSE
         GO TO CREDIT-RTN.
DEBIT-RTN.
      ADD AMT1, AMT2 GIVING TOTAL.
      PERFORM PRINT-RTN.
      ADD 1 TO TOTAL-DEBITS.
      GO TO START.
PRINT-RTN.
      MOVE NAME OF CARD-IN TO NAME
         OF PRINTOUT.
      MOVE TOTAL TO EDIT1.
      WRITE PRINTOUT AFTER ADVANCING
         2 LINES.
CREDIT-RTN.
      SUBTRACT AMT2 FROM AMT1 GIVING
         TOTAL.
      PERFORM PRINT-RTN.
      ADD 1 TO TOTAL-CREDITS.
      GO TO START.
```

PERFORM PRINT-RTN causes execution of all instructions in that paragraph. The computer will execute all statements until it senses the next paragraph. When all statements in the paragraph are executed, control is transferred back to the instruction following the PERFORM.

Note that a PERFORM statement differs greatly from a GO TO statement which unconditionally and totally transfers control to another paragraph. The schematic in Fig. 14-3 illustrates the major difference between PERFORM and GO TO statements:

PERFORM and ALTER statements may be used interchangeably to branch into and out of specified routines. A PERFORM statement, however, is easier to understand and program than an ALTER instruction and, thus, is used more often.

A series of statements that will be executed by a PERFORM should not, generally, contain a GO TO statement. Consider the following illustration:

```
PERFORM PARA-1.
GO TO START.
PARA-1.
```

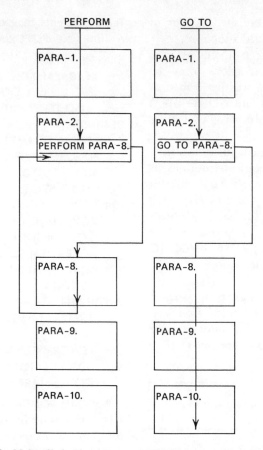

Fig. 14-3   Major distinction between PERFORM and GO TO statements.

MOVE A TO B.
ADD A TO C.
GO TO PARA-3.
PARA-2.

The **PERFORM** statement will execute all instructions within **PARA-1** and then proceed to the next sequential step after the **PERFORM**. **GO TO PARA-3**, the last step in **PARA-1**, transfers control to a **different** paragraph. Thus the statements following the **PERFORM** are **not** executed.

A **PERFORM** statement is the most sophisticated and widely used method of altering the path of a program. Its basic format was presented in this section. In the next chapter we will discuss the other formats of this statement and their various uses.

F. APPLICATION OF A SIMPLE PER-FORM STATEMENT IN AN UPDATE PROGRAM

The updating of files is an essential and widely used application of computers. Computer users concentrate much of their programming effort on this area. Because of its relative complexity and widespread use, we will discuss update programs at some length. We will see that **PERFORM** statements are often a necessary part of such programs.

An updating procedure is the process of making a file of data **current**. An update program consists of three files:

Input Master File. The input master file has all the data except that which is most current; that is, it contains master information that is current only up to the previous updating cycle. We will call this file **OLD-MASTER.**

Input Detail File. The input detail file contains data for the present updating cycle **only.** We will call this file **DETAIL.**

Output Master File.[1] The output master file incorporates the current detail data and the previous master information. That is, the output master file will combine data from **OLD-MASTER** and **DETAIL.** We will call this file **NEW-MASTER.**

For update programs, any form of input and output may be used. For purposes of illustration, we will assume that the input and output master files are on tape and that the detail information is on cards.

The following **systems** flowchart indicates the operations to be performed:

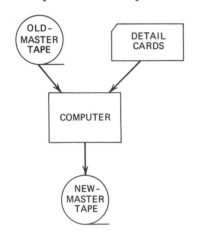

To update files, data must be read into the computer in a specific sequence. Since we wish to update each master record with a detail record, we must insure that each file is in the same sequence.

Let us assume that we are updating a master transaction file with detail transaction records. That is, **OLD-MASTER** contains all transaction data current through

the previous updating cycle; **DETAIL** contains transactions of the current period; and **NEW-MASTER** will incorporate both files of information.

Let us assume, in addition, that both input files are in sequence by account number. Consider both input files to have the following format:

OLD-MASTER		DETAIL	
1–5	ACCT-NO	1–5	ACCT-NO
6–11	AMOUNT-DUE xxxx.xx	6–10	AMT-TRANS-IN-CURRENT-PER
12–50	FILLER	11–80	FILLER

Since **NEW-MASTER** will be created to replace the **OLD-MASTER,** it will have the same format as **OLD-MASTER.**

The update program will read data from cards and tape, both of which are in **ACCT-NO** sequence. For each **ACCT-NO** that is both on the detail and old-master file, **AMT-TRANS-IN-CURRENT-PER** will be added to **AMOUNT-DUE** to obtain the current balance. For each **ACCT-NO** that is on the **OLD-MASTER** file but not on the **DETAIL** file, a record will be created on **NEW-MASTER** which merely duplicates the information of **OLD-MASTER.** In that case, we say that no updating of the record is necessary.

For each **ACCT-NO** that is on the **DETAIL** file but not on the **OLD-MASTER** file, a record is created on **NEW-MASTER** which is taken directly from the **DETAIL** file. When this occurs, we say that a **new account** is created.

Thus the control field on all files is **ACCT-NO.** The detail cards and the input master tape will both be in sequence by **ACCT-NO.** After reading a single card record and a tape record, we will test for three possible conditions.

(a) **ACCT-NO OF DETAIL = ACCT-NO OF OLD-MASTER**

When the account numbers are equal, the input master record is to be updated; that is, the card amount is added to the input tape amount to obtain the output

AMOUNT-DUE. When the new master record is created, new card and tape records are read and processing continues.

(b) ACCT-NO OF DETAIL IS GREATER THAN ACCT-NO OF OLD-MASTER

In this case, a master record exists with no corresponding card record. Since both files are in sequence, we may assume that no business has been transacted for the specific master record. Thus the new master record is created directly from OLD-MASTER, and a new input tape record is read. Note that another card is **not** read at this point. We have not yet processed the card that is in the input area. If, for example, a detail record has account number 00035 and the master record has account number 00034, we process the

master record and read the next master; account number 00035 of the card file remains to be processed.

(c) ACCT-NO OF DETAIL IS LESS THAN ACCT-NO OF OLD-MASTER

In this case, a detail card record exists for which there is no corresponding master record. We will consider this to be a new account. The new master tape record, then, will be created directly from the detail card. After it is created, another card is read. Note that we do not read a tape record at this point, since the previous record has not been processed.

The following are the PROCEDURE DIVISION entries for this update program. Examine them **carefully**:

```
PROCEDURE DIVISION.
    OPEN INPUT OLD-MASTER, DETAIL, OUTPUT NEW-MASTER.
    MOVE SPACES TO NEW-MASTER.
READ-DETAIL.
    READ DETAIL AT END GO TO EOJ1.
READ-MASTER.
    READ OLD-MASTER AT END GO TO EOJ2.
COMPARE-RTN.
    IF ACCT-NO OF DETAIL = ACCT-NO OF OLD-MASTER GO TO UPDATE-RTN.
    IF ACCT-NO OF DETAIL IS GREATER THAN ACCT-NO OF OLD-MASTER
    GO TO NO-UPDATE.
    IF ACCT-NO OF DETAIL IS LESS THAN ACCT-NO OF OLD-MASTER GO
    TO NEW-ACCT.
UPDATE-RTN.
    MOVE ACCT-NO OF OLD-MASTER TO ACCT-NO OF NEW-MASTER.
    ADD AMT-TRANS-IN-CURRENT-PER, AMOUNT-DUE OF OLD MASTER
    GIVING AMOUNT-DUE OF NEW-MASTER.
    PERFORM WRITE-RTN.
    GO TO READ-DETAIL.
NO-UPDATE.
    MOVE ACCT-NO OF OLD-MASTER TO ACCT-NO OF NEW-MASTER.
    MOVE AMOUNT-DUE OF OLD-MASTER TO AMOUNT-DUE OF NEW-MASTER.
    PERFORM WRITE-RTN.
X.      GO TO READ-MASTER.
NEW-ACCT.
    MOVE AMT-TRANS-IN-CURRENT-PER TO AMOUNT-DUE OF NEW-MASTER.
    MOVE ACCT-NO OF DETAIL TO ACCT-NO OF NEW-MASTER.
    PERFORM WRITE-RTN.
Y.      PERFORM READ-DETAIL.
    GO TO COMPARE-RTN.
WRITE-RTN.
    WRITE NEW-MASTER-REC.
```

Note that **EOJ1** and **EOJ2** have not been defined in the program. They, too, require special consideration. **EOJ1** is the routine that is branched to when there are no more detail cards. There may, however, still be **OLD-MASTER** records to be placed on the new file. Thus, if **EOJ1** is the **first** end of job routine that is branched to, old master tape records must still be processed.

Similarly, a branch to **EOJ2**, as the first end of job routine, implies that there may be **NEW-ACCT** detail cards to be processed.

At **EOJ1**, therefore, we must continue reading **OLD-MASTER** records until they are all processed. In the same way, at **EOJ2**, we must continue reading **DETAIL** records until they are all processed. After both files are completed, the program may be terminated:

```
EOJ1.
    READ OLD-MASTER AT END GO TO
        EOJ.
    PERFORM NO-UPDATE.
    GO TO EOJ1.
EOJ2.
    READ DETAIL AT END GO TO EOJ.
    PERFORM NEW-ACCT.
    GO TO EOJ2.
EOJ.
    CLOSE DETAIL, OLD-MASTER,
        NEW-MASTER.
    STOP RUN.
```

Note that the paragraph names **X** and **Y** are necessary to delineate the **NO-UPDATE** and **NEW-ACCT** routines.

In summary, this type of update program is a major programming function of many computer installations. Although the logic is somewhat complex, the programming elements are considered basic to COBOL.

EXERCISES

1. The purpose of **ALTER** statements is to _____.
   *****
   change the path of unconditional branch (**GO TO**) statements

2. If **GO TO RTN-X** is a statement which is to be altered, it must be supplied a _____.
   *****
   paragraph name

What, if anything, is wrong with the following statements (3–5)?

3. ALTER STEP-1 TO PROCEED TO STEP-2.
   .
   .
   .
   STEP-X. GO TO STEP-1.
   *****
   ALTER statement should read: ALTER STEP-X TO PROCEED TO STEP-2.

4. ALTER PATH-A TO PROCEED TO PATH-X.
   .
   .
   .
   PATH-A.   MOVE A TO B.
             GO TO PATH-Y.
   *****
   PATH-A must have a GO TO statement as its **only** entry.

5. ALTER RTN-X TO GO TO RTN-Z.

.

.

.

RTN-X.   GO TO RTN-Y.
*****

ALTER statement should read: **ALTER RTN-X TO PROCEED TO RTN-Z.**

6. Write a statement to change the path of **PARA-5** so that it will branch to **PARA-8** instead of **PARA-7**.
*****

ALTER PARA-5 TO PROCEED TO PARA-8.

.

.

.

PARA-5. GO TO PARA-7.

7. In the last example, to reset **PARA-5** so that it proceeds again to **PARA-8** requires _____.
*****

a second **ALTER** statement: **ALTER PARA-5 TO PROCEED TO PARA-8.**

8. A _____ statement may be used in place of **ALTER** statements to cause branching into and out of specified routines.
*****

simple **PERFORM**

9. **PERFORM** (paragraph-name) will cause _____.
*****

execution of all instructions in the named paragraph

10. After **PERFORM** (paragraph-name) is executed, control is transferred to _____.
*****

the next sequential step after the **PERFORM**

REVIEW QUESTIONS

1. Use a **GO TO** . . . **DEPENDING ON** statement to perform the following:

branch to: **START** if $A = 18$
                    RTN-X if $A = 19$
                    RTN-Y if $A = 20$
                    RTN-Z if $A = 21$
                    ERR-RTN otherwise

2. Use a **GO TO** . . . **DEPENDING ON** statement to perform the following:

branch to: PARA1 if B $= -20$
               PARA2 if B $= -15$
               PARA3 if B $= -10$
               PARA4 if B $= -5$
               ERR-RTN otherwise

3. **GO TO RTNA, RTNB, RTNC, RTND DEPENDING ON FIELDX. GO TO RTNE.**

   Using the above statement, indicate the branches that will occur if:

   (a) FIELDX $= 0$
   (b) FIELDX $= 4$
   (c) FIELDX $= -2$
   (d) FIELDX $= 5$
   (e) FIELDX $= 1$

4. Write a single statement to cause the computer to halt and to print the error code **999**.

5. Write a single statement to cause the computer to halt and to print the error message 'INVALID CARD CODE'.

6. (T or F) All **STOP** statements cause irreversible halts; that is, the computer may not be made to restart.

7. (T or F) An **ALTER** statement causes a branch to be executed.

8. (T or F) Unless a second **ALTER** statement is executed, a **GO TO** command that has been altered remains permanently changed.

9. (T or F) **PERFORM** statements cause the same sequence of instructions to be executed as **GO TO** commands.

10. Consider the following update program excerpt:

    READ CARD-IN AT END GO TO EOJ1.
    READ TAPE-IN AT END GO TO EOJ2.
    IF CARD-NO = TAPE-NO GO TO RECORD-UPDATE.
    IF CARD-NO IS LESS THAN TAPE-NO GO TO NEW-CARD-RTN.
    IF TAPE-NO IS LESS THAN CARD-NO GO TO NO-TAPE-UPDATE.

    If there are less card records than tape records, **EOJ1** will be executed first. In this case, we wish to read the remaining tape records, proceed to **NO-TAPE-UPDATE**, and stop the run at **EOJ2**, when all tape records have been processed. If there are less tape records than card records, **EOJ2** will be executed first. When this happens, we wish to read the remaining card records, proceed to **NEW-CARD-RTN**, and stop the run when there are no more card records.

    Write the routines to perform the end of job functions.

PROBLEMS

1. Write an update program using the following input files:

Detail Card File	Master Tape File
1–20 Employee name	1–20 Employee name
21–25 Annual salary	21–25 Annual salary
26–80 Not used	26–50 Other data
	standard labels
	blocking factor = 25

Both files are in sequence by Employee name.

Notes

(a) The output file has the same format as input master file.

(b) For master tape records with no corresponding detail records (no match on employee-name) create an output record from the input tape.

(c) For detail records with no corresponding tape records, create an output record from the input card.

(d) For master tape records with corresponding card records, take annual salary from card and all other data from tape.

(e) Use only ALTER . . . GO TO statements—not PERFORM statements.

2. Rewrite the program for Problem 1 using PERFORM statements in place of ALTER . . . GO TO commands.

3. Use GO TO . . . DEPENDING ON statement(s) to code Problem 4, Chapter 9.

4. Write a merge program using the following input files:

Detail Tape File

1–5   Transaction Number
6–10 Transaction Amount xxx.xx
11–70 Not used

Master Tape File

1–5   Transaction Number
6–10 Transaction Amount xxx.xx

All files are blocked 50 and have standard labels.

Notes

(a) Output file has the same format as the master tape file.

(b) Output file is to combine both input files into one file in transaction number sequence (both input files are in transaction number sequence).

(c) Transaction numbers for each file must be unique; that is, detail transaction number must **not** match master transaction numbers. If a match occurs, print an error message.

(d) Use **ALTER . . . GO TO** statements —and **not PERFORM** statements.

5. Rewrite the program for Problem 4 using **PERFORM** statements where **ALTER . . . GO TO** have been indicated above.

Perform Statements

A. THE BASIC FORMAT

In the last chapter, the basic form of the **PERFORM** statement was discussed. The format for a simple **PERFORM** is as follows:

I. <u>PERFORM</u> (paragraph-name).

A **PERFORM** statement causes execution of the series of instructions at the named paragraph. When all instructions at the indicated paragraph are executed, control is transferred to the statement directly following the **PERFORM**:

The computer executes all instructions at the named paragraph, **RTN-3**. When it senses the **next** paragraph name, **RTN-4**, control is transferred back to the statement following the **PERFORM**.

GO TO commands should **not** be included within paragraphs that are executed by **PERFORM** statements. To include **GO TO** statements transfers control to other paragraphs, outside the range of the **PERFORM**. This will then supersede the normal flow of a **PERFORM** statement. If **PERFORM STEP-5** is a coded statement, then **GO TO** (paragraph-name) should not be included within the paragraph called **STEP5**. The following illustrates a **violation** of this rule:

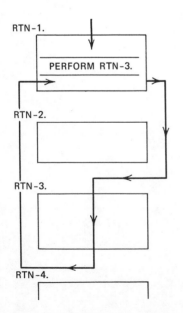

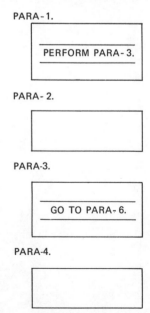

Consider the following routine:

    PERFORM PARA-8.
    GO TO START.
PARA-8.
    IF A < B GO TO PARA-9 ELSE ADD A
        TO TOTAL.
PARA-9.
    ADD B TO TOTAL.

If A is less than B, the statement directly following the PERFORM, (GO TO START) is never executed; a branch out of PARA-8 occurs, and control never returns to the instruction following the PERFORM.

In short, if PARAGRAPHX is executed by a PERFORM, do not transfer control out of PARAGRAPHX. To correct the preceding routine, we have

    PERFORM PARA-8.
    GO TO START.
PARA-8.
    IF A < B ADD B TO TOTAL ELSE ADD A
        TO TOTAL.

It is important to note that GO TO statements within the range of a PERFORM instruction do not cause the computer to stop or "hang-up." They transfer control out of the named paragraph, which implies that the range of the PERFORM has not been fully executed.

Observe that the following program excerpt causes addition of A to B twice.

    PERFORM PARA-2.
PARA-2.
    ADD A TO B.
PARA-3.
    SUBTRACT A FROM E.
    GO TO START.

PERFORM PARA-2 directly precedes PARA-2. Thus the ADD statement is executed and control then returns to the instruction following the PERFORM, which is again PARA-2.

To avoid confusion, PERFORM (paragraph-name-1) should not be followed by paragraph-name-1 and its instructions, unless execution is to occur twice. The purpose of a PERFORM statement is to transfer

control to some other paragraph that is not within the normal flow.

PERFORM statements are permitted within PERFORM statements. To say PERFORM PARA-1 is permissible if PARA-1 has a PERFORM statement as one of its instructions. The following is a valid routine:

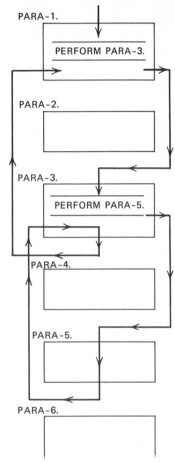

A simple PERFORM statement is used whenever a series of instructions at a particular paragraph is to be executed from different points in the program. Several paragraphs or routines may be executed using one PERFORM statement.

Extension of Format I:

    I. PERFORM (paragraph-name-1)
            {THRU (paragraph-name-n)}

All statements beginning at paragraph-name-1 and terminating at the **end of** paragraph-name-n are executed. Control is then transferred to the statement after the **PERFORM**. The following representation illustrates the complete form of Format I:

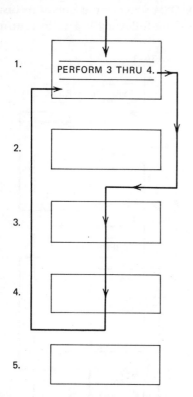

1. PERFORM 3 THRU 4.
2.
3.
4.
5.

Using the **THRU** option, **GO TO** statements may appear within the named paragraphs. Consider the following routines:

```
STEP1.   ADD A TO B.
         IF C = ZERO GO TO STEP3.
STEP2.   MULTIPLY C BY C.
STEP3.   MOVE B TO EDIT1.
STEP4.   WRITE PRINTOUT AFTER
         ADVANCING 2 LINES.
```

To say: **PERFORM STEP1 THRU STEP4** is permissible. Although a conditional branch in **STEP1** transfers control to another paragraph, **STEP3**, the latter is included within the range of the **PERFORM** and, thus, is acceptable.

When using the **THRU** option of the **PERFORM** statement, branches, or **GO TO** statements, are permitted **within the range of the named paragraphs**. Note,

however, that to say **PERFORM STEP 1 THRU STEP2** is **not** valid in the above illustration, since the conditional branch transfers control to **STEP3, outside** the **PERFORM** range. Thus control would not return to the statement directly following the **PERFORM**.

Consider the following example.

Problem

> If salary exceeds 100,000,
> employee is President.
> If salary exceeds 50,000,
> employee is Vice-President.
> If salary exceeds 40,000,
> employee is Asst-Vice-President.

The determination of an employee as **PRESIDENT, VICE-PRESIDENT,** or **ASST-VICE-PRESIDENT** is to be made from different points in the program. Thus the routine will be executed by a **PERFORM** statement. Note that the following is **not** a correct routine:

TITLE-RTN.

	IF SALARY > 100000 MOVE 'PRESIDENT' TO TITLE.
Not	IF SALARY > 50000 MOVE
correct	'VICE-PRESIDENT' TO TITLE.
logic:	IF SALARY > 40000 MOVE 'ASST-VICE-PRESIDENT' TO TITLE.

Suppose **EMPLOYEE-X** earns $110,000. Since the first condition is met, **'PRESIDENT'** is moved to **TITLE**. Note, however, that the last two conditions are **also** met. The last statement to be executed results in the literal **'ASST-VICE-PRESIDENT'** in the field called **TITLE**.

We must alter this routine so that, if the first condition is met, (**SALARY** greater than 100000), no other test is performed.

The following routine will be executed properly by coding **PERFORM TITLE-RTN THRU PARA-2:**

TITLE-RTN.

    IF SALARY > 100000 MOVE
       'PRESIDENT' TO TITLE, GO TO
       PARA-2.

```
IF SALARY > 50000 MOVE
    'VICE-PRESIDENT' TO TITLE, GO TO
    PARA-2.
IF SALARY > 40000 MOVE
    'ASST-VICE-PRESIDENT' TO TITLE.
PARA-2.
    EXIT.
```

EXIT is a COBOL reserved word. It is an instruction which performs **no operation.** It allows execution simply to pass over other statements in TITLE-RTN. It is used, when necessary, as an end point in paragraphs being performed.

EXERCISES

1. A **PERFORM** statement causes execution of instructions at _____.
   After the **PERFORM** is executed, control returns to _____.
   *****
   the indicated paragraph
   the statement directly following the **PERFORM**

2. _____ statements should not be included within paragraphs that are executed by **PERFORM** statements, when they _____.
   *****
   GO TO
   cause branches **outside** the range of the **PERFORM**

3. Indicate which of the following two routines is incorrect and why.

   (a) PERFORM RTN-1 THRU   (b) PERFORM RTN-1 THRU RTN-2.
        RTN-3.   .
        .   .
        .   .
        .   RTN-1. ADD A TO B.
   RTN-1. ADD A TO B.   IF B > 21 GO TO RTN-3.
           IF B > 21 GO TO   RTN-2. MULTIPLY B BY C.
           RTN-3.   RTN-3. MOVE C TO TOTAL.
           MULTIPLY B BY C.
   RTN-2. DIVIDE C INTO D.
   RTN-3. MOVE D TO TOTAL.
   *****
   a is correct. b transfers control outside the **PERFORM** range.

4. To execute several sequential paragraphs by a **PERFORM** statement, the _____ option is used. The format is _____.
   *****
   THRU
   PERFORM (paragraph-name-1) **THRU** (paragraph-name-n)

5. **GO TO** statements may be included within the named paragraphs using the **THRU** option as long as _____.
   *****
   control is not transferred outside the range of the indicated paragraphs

6. _____ is a COBOL reserved word which performs no operation and serves as an endpoint to paragraphs being performed.

*****

EXIT

B. ADDITIONAL FORMS OF THE PERFORM STATEMENT

A second format for the **PERFORM** statement enables a paragraph or paragraphs to be executed **several times**:

II. <u>PERFORM</u> (paragraph-name-1) $\left\{ \underline{\text{THRU}} \text{ (paragraph-name-n)} \right\}$ $\left[\begin{matrix} \text{(integer)} \\ \text{(data-name)} \end{matrix} \right]$ <u>TIMES</u>

Example 1: A program creates department store credit cards. Each customer is issued three cards:

PERFORM CREDIT-CARD-RTN 3 TIMES

Example 2: Each customer indicates the number of credit cards he desires. This information is punched into an input card in the field called **NO-OF-COPIES**. The card record is as follows:

01	CARD-REC.	
	02 NAME	PICTURE X(20).
	02 NO-OF-COPIES	PICTURE 9.
	02 FILLER	PICTURE X(59).

The routine is as follows:

PERFORM CREDIT-CARD-RTN

            NO-OF-COPIES TIMES

When using the format: **PERFORM** (paragraph-name) **data-name TIMES**, several rules are applicable. The data-name indicated must be specified in the **DATA DIVISION**, have a **numeric PICTURE** clause, and contain only integers or zeros. To say PERFORM RTN-1 X TIMES is valid if X has a numeric **PICTURE** clause and integer or zero contents. If X has a zero as its value, then RTN-1 will be performed 0, or **no**, times.

Note that X in the above example must be a data-name. It may not be an arithmetic expression. To say PERFORM PARA-1

B+1 TIMES is **invalid**. The word preceding TIMES may only be an integer or a data-name.

The **THRU** option in Format II is not required. We may say PERFORM RTN-1 THRU RTN-8 5 TIMES, or we may say PER-

FORM RTN-3 5 TIMES. Both are correct instructions.

Note that the following two instructions produce the same results.

1. PERFORM STEP-1 6 TIMES
2. PERFORM STEP-1 AAA TIMES

where **AAA** has the following description in the **WORKING-STORAGE SECTION**:

77 AAA PICTURE 9 VALUE 6.

When using the integer option for Format II, only the actual number is acceptable. We may **not** say: PERFORM RTN-1 FIVE TIMES. The integer itself must be used: PERFORM RTN-1 5 TIMES.

PERFORM statements, in their various formats, may be used in executing **loops**. A loop, as described in Chapter 9, is a repeated execution of a routine until a specific condition is met. In Chapter 9, looping was performed by utilizing conditional statements. In this chapter, we will execute loops with **PERFORM** statements, a more direct and less complicated method.

Consider the example on page 109 which performs multiplication of two data fields, **A** and **B**, with the use of only an **ADD** instruction:

Example 3

    MOVE ZEROS TO TOTAL.
RTN1. SUBTRACT 1 FROM B.

ADD A TO TOTAL.
IF B = ZEROS NEXT SENTENCE ELSE
GO TO RTN1.

Using a PERFORM statement to accomplish the same operation, we have:

MOVE ZEROS TO TOTAL.
PERFORM RTN1 B TIMES.
GO TO OUT.
RTN1. ADD A TO TOTAL.

Note that, when using a PERFORM statement, we do **not** decrement B. B remains constant. If B = 3 and A = 4, for example, RTN1 would be executed three times; that is, A would be added to TOTAL three times. Twelve would then be the correct result in TOTAL.

All loops may be executed with the use of either PERFORM or conditional statements.

Example 4: Write a routine to read a group of 10 cards and to print the total of the amount fields of all the cards.

Solution to Example 4

MOVE ZEROS TO TOTAL.
PERFORM READ-RTN 10 TIMES.
GO TO PRINT-RTN.
READ-RTN.
READ CARD-FILE AT END CLOSE
CARD-FILE, PRINT-FILE STOP RUN.
ADD AMT TO TOTAL.
PRINT-RTN.
MOVE TOTAL TO EDIT1.
WRITE PRINTOUT AFTER ADVANCING
2 LINES.

Note that the READ command does not have a conditional branch to EOJ. This would violate the rules which state that routines executed by PERFORM statements should not have GO TO instructions within them. Thus we have included the end of job functions within the READ statement itself.

The above routine is another example of a loop. READ-RTN is executed 10 times and then TOTAL is printed.

Suppose we wish to print **five** groups of ten totals. That is, we wish to execute the above routines five times and then proceed to some other point in the program. The following addition is correct:

PERFORM FIRST-RTN THRU PRINT-RTN 5
TIMES.
GO TO SECOND-RTN.

FIRST-RTN.
MOVE ZEROS TO TOTAL.
PERFORM READ-RTN 10 TIMES.
GO TO PRINT-RTN.
READ-RTN.
READ CARD-FILE AT END CLOSE
CARD-FILE, PRINT-FILE STOP RUN.
ADD AMT TO TOTAL.
PRINT-RTN.
MOVE TOTAL TO EDIT1.
WRITE-PRINTOUT AFTER ADVANCING
2 LINES.

SECOND-RTN.
.
.

The above is an illustration of a **double** loop. FIRST-RTN is performed five times. Within FIRST-RTN we read ten cards, accumulate the amounts, and then print the total. Since this is executed five times, **five** totals will print and **50** cards will be read. Double loops are efficiently coded with the use of PERFORM statements within PERFORM statements.

Format III of the PERFORM statement is as follows:

III. PERFORM (paragraph-name-1) {THRU (paragraph-name-n)} UNTIL (condition).

The condition that may be specified is any relational, simple, or compound.

Examples

(a) PERFORM PARA-1 THRU PARA-4 UNTIL
X = 2.

(b) PERFORM RTN-1 UNTIL X $>$ 7.

(c) PERFORM STEP-5 UNTIL A $=$ B OR A $=$ C.

(d) PERFORM PARA-X UNTIL A $>$ B AND A $>$ C.

It is implicit in this option that the data-name or data-names used in the UNTIL clause be altered within the paragraph(s) being performed. To say PERFORM PARA-1 THRU PARA-8 UNTIL X $=$ 5 implies that X will change somewhere within PARA-1 through PARA-8. If X remains as 3, for example, then these paragraphs will be performed indefinitely.

If the condition indicated in the UNTIL clause is met at the time of execution, then the named paragraph(s) will be executed 0, or no, times. If PERFORM RTN-5 UNTIL X $=$ 3 is executed and X equals 3 initially, then RTN-5 will not be performed at all. This condition does **not** imply that an error has occurred.

Format III may also be used to perform looping operations. Example 3, which performs multiplication of A and B using the ADD verb, may be coded using the UNTIL option:

```
    MOVE ZEROS TO TOTAL.
    PERFORM RTN1 UNTIL B = 0.
    GO TO OUT.
RTN1.
    ADD A TO TOTAL.
    SUBTRACT 1 FROM B.
```

Example 4 (the reading of ten cards, the summing of the amount fields, and the printing of a total) may be performed as follows:

```
    MOVE ZEROS TO TOTAL.
    MOVE ZEROS TO CTR.
    PERFORM READ-RTN UNTIL CTR = 10.
    GO TO PRINT-RTN.
READ-RTN.
    READ CARD-FILE AT END CLOSE
    CARD-FILE, PRINT-FILE STOP RUN.
    ADD AMT TO TOTAL.
    ADD 1 TO CTR.
PRINT-RTN.
    MOVE TOTAL TO EDIT1.
```

```
    WRITE PRINTOUT AFTER ADVANCING
    2 LINES.
```

CTR, a WORKING-STORAGE item, is initialized at zero. This may be accomplished in the PROCEDURE DIVISION or with a VALUE clause in WORKING-STORAGE. Each time a card is read, CTR is incremented by one. When CTR equals 10, ten cards have been read and totalled.

Suppose we wish to print five such totals instead of one. Again, we will perform the above operations **five** times. Note, however, that CTR must be initialized at zero each **time**:

```
    PERFORM FIRST-RTN THRU PRINT-RTN
    5 TIMES.
    GO TO SECOND-RTN.
```

```
FIRST-RTN.
    MOVE ZEROS TO TOTAL.
    MOVE ZEROS TO CTR.
    PERFORM READ-RTN UNTIL CTR = 10.
    GO TO PRINT-RTN.
READ-RTN.
    READ CARD-FILE AT END CLOSE
    CARD-FILE, PRINT-FILE STOP RUN.
    ADD AMT TO TOTAL.
    ADD 1 TO CTR.
PRINT-RTN.
    MOVE TOTAL TO EDIT1.
    WRITE PRINTOUT AFTER ADVANCING
    2 LINES.
```

Thus we see that all forms of the PERFORM statement are merely variations. They may be used alternatively to execute the same operations. The programmer may choose the one which is easiest for him.

Example 5: Find N! (N-FACTORIAL) where N is a data field. Note that N! $=$ N $\times$ N $-$ 1 $\times$ N $-$ 2 $\times$ .... 1; 5! $=$ 5 $\times$ 4 $\times$ 3 $\times$ 2 $\times$ 1 $=$ 120; 3! $=$ 3 $\times$ 2 $\times$ 1 $=$ 6:

```
    MOVE N TO M.
    PERFORM PARA-6 UNTIL M = 1.
    GO TO OUT.
```

PARA-6.

    SUBTRACT 1 FROM M.

    MULTIPLY M BY N.

The last format for a **PERFORM** statement is the most comprehensive and, thus, the most complicated:

VARYING DATE FROM 1900 BY 10 UNTIL DATE > 1950.

Using Format IV, the **PERFORM** statement itself will:

1. Set up a looping indicator or counter called date-name-1.

IV. <u>PERFORM</u> (paragraph-name-1) {<u>THRU</u> (paragraph-name-n)}

    <u>VARYING</u> (data-name-1) **<u>FROM</u>** $\begin{bmatrix} \text{(data-name-2)} \\ \text{(integer-1)} \end{bmatrix}$ **<u>BY</u>** $\begin{bmatrix} \text{(data-name-3)} \\ \text{(integer-2)} \end{bmatrix}$

        <u>UNTIL</u> (condition)

Examples

(1) PERFORM READ-RTN VARYING CTR FROM 0 BY 1 UNTIL CTR = 20

PERFORM READ-RTN VARYING CTR FROM 1 BY 1 UNTIL CTR IS GREATER THAN 20 (The two statements above perform the same functions.)

(2) **PERFORM RTN-1 THRU RTN-5**

2. Initialize this counter at data-name-2 or integer-1.

3. Increment the counter by integer-2 or the contents of data-name-3.

4. Test the looping indicator for the condition specified. If the condition is met, no further **PERFORM** is executed.

Fig. 15-1 illustrates the flowchart for this operation.

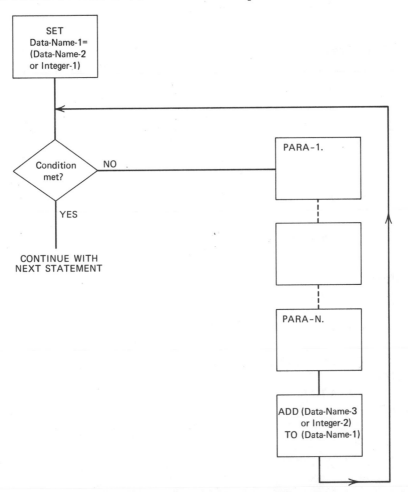

Suppose we wish to sum all odd-numbered integers from 1 to 1001. We could use Format IV of the PERFORM statement as follows:

PERFORM ADD-RTN VARYING XI FROM 1 BY 2 UNTIL X1 IS GREATER THAN 1001.

```
    GO TO NEXT-RTN.
ADD-RTN.
    ADD X1 TO ODD-CTR.
```

In the next chapter, which discusses subscripting and OCCURS clauses, we will make extensive use of PERFORM statements.

Exercises

1. After a PERFORM statement is executed, control returns to _____.
   *****
   the statement directly following the PERFORM

2. If PERFORM RTN-1 X TIMES is executed and X is equal to 0, RTN-1 will be performed _____ times.
   *****
   no

3. PERFORM PARA-1 ITEM TIMES is valid only if ITEM has contents of _____ or _____.
   *****
   0
   an integer

4. How many times will the paragraph named ROUTINE be executed by the following PERFORM statements?

   (a) PERFORM ROUTINE VARYING X FROM 1 BY 1 UNTIL X = 10.
   (b) PERFORM ROUTINE VARYING X FROM 1 BY 1 UNTIL X > 10.
   (c) PERFORM ROUTINE VARYING X FROM 0 BY 1 UNTIL X = 10.
   *****
   9 times.
   10 times.
   10 times.

5. Write a PERFORM routine to accomplish the following:

```
        MOVE 0 TO CTR.
START.
        ADD A TO B.
        ADD 1 TO CTR.
        IF CTR = 5 GO TO OUT ELSE GO TO START.
```
   *****
```
        PERFORM START 5 TIMES. GO TO OUT.
START.
        ADD A TO B.
OUT.
            .
            .
```

or

> MOVE 1 TO CTR.
> PERFORM START UNTIL CTR = 6. GO TO OUT.

START.

> ADD A TO B.
> ADD 1 TO CTR.

What, if anything, is wrong with the following routines (6–8)?

6.   PERFORM RTNX A TIMES.
> GO TO RTNZ.

RTNX.

> ADD C TO B.
> ADD 1 TO A.

> *****

A, the data-name in the **PERFORM** statement, may be accessed at
RTNX but may **not** be changed. To increment **A** will result in improper execution. In this case, **RTNX** will be performed indefinitely.

7.   PERFORM PARA-5 8 TIMES.
> STOP RUN.

PARA-5.

> IF A = B GO TO RTN3.
> ADD A TO B.

RTN3.

> ADD 5 TO B.

> *****

PARA-5, a paragraph executed by a **PERFORM** statement, should
not have a **GO TO** statement within its range. The following is
valid:

> PERFORM PARA-5 8 TIMES.
> STOP RUN.

PARA-5.

> IF A = B ADD 5 TO B, ELSE
> ADD A TO B.

8.   PERFORM RTNX UNTIL CTR = 8.
> STOP RUN.

RTNX.

> ADD A TO B.
> ADD 1 TO CTR.
> IF CTR = 8 STOP RUN.

> *****

PERFORM statement will internally compare **CTR** to 8; thus the last
conditional is redundant, unnecessary, and incorrect.

9. Using the **TIMES** option of the **PERFORM** statement, restate the
following:

> MOVE 0 TO X1.
> PERFORM RTN-X UNTIL X1 = 10.
> GO TO NEXT.

RTNX.

.

.

ADD 1 TO X1.
*****
PERFORM RTNX 10 TIMES.

10. Using the VARYING option of the PERFORM statement, write a routine to sum all even numbers from 2 to 100.
*****
PERFORM SUM-RTN VARYING X FROM 2 BY 2 UNTIL X IS GREATER THAN 100.
GO TO OUT.
SUM-RTN.
ADD X TO EVEN-SUM.

REVIEW QUESTIONS

1. Using a PERFORM statement with a TIMES option, write a routine to find N factorial where N is a data item. You will recall that N factorial $= N \times N - 1 \times N - 2 \times \ldots 1$; that is, 5 factorial $= 5 \times 4 \times 3 \times 2 \times 1 = 120$).

2. Assume the paragraphs in a program are called 1, 2, . . . 10 and appear in numerical sequence. Write a **single** statement to perform the following:

PERFORM 1.
PERFORM 2.
PERFORM 3.

3. Rewrite the following routine using a PERFORM statement with a TIMES option:

PERFORM RTN-X UNTIL COUNTER = 20.

.

.

.

.

.

RTN-X.
READ CARD-IN AT END CLOSE CARD-IN STOP RUN.
ADD QTY OF CARD-REC TO TOTAL.
ADD 1 TO COUNTER.
RTN-Y.

.

.

4. Rewrite the TITLE-RTN in this chapter **without** using EXIT.

5. (T or F) A GO TO statement may not be used in a paragraph that is executed by a PERFORM statement.

6. (T or F) To say PERFORM PARA-X XX TIMES is only valid if XX represents a numeric field.

7. (T or F) It is not valid to say PERFORM RTNX 0 TIMES.

8. Write a routine using the PERFORM statement with a TIMES option to sum all odd numbered integers from 1 to 1001.

9. Write a routine using the PERFORM statement with the UNTIL option to sum all odd-numbered integers from 1 to 1001.

10. Rewrite the solution to Question 3 using the PERFORM statement with a VARYING option.

PROBLEMS

1. Write a program to compute compound interest from the following formula:

$P_n = P_0 (1 + r)^n$
P_n = amount of principal after n periods of investment of P_0 at rate r/period

The input is a card file with the following format:

1–6 Principal P_0
7–8 Rate .xx r
9–80 Not used

Output is a printed report with compound interest calculated for periods 1 year to 10 years (n = 1, 2 .. 10):

PRINCIPAL — xxxxxx
RATE — .xx

PERIODS	AMOUNT
1	xxxxxx.xx
2	xxxxxx.xx
.	
.	
10	xxxxxx.xx

(**Hint.** $(1 + r)^5$ is the same as $1 + r$ multiplied by itself 5 times, i.e., PERFORM MULTIPLY-RTN 5 TIMES.)

2. Write a program to print one tape record from 20 card records. The input is as follows:

    1–20 Customer name (same for each group of 20 cards)
    21–25 Daily transaction amount xxx.xx
    26–80 Not used

The output is a tape file with each record containing customer name and a total field of the 20 daily transaction amounts. Output file has standard labels and 20 records/block.

3. Write a program to print one tape record from x number of cards, where x is denoted on the first card of each group:

Input

    1–2   Number of cards in group (only indicated on the first card for each group)
    3–22 Salesman Name—same for each card in group
    23–27 Amount xxx.xx
    28–80 Not used

The output is a tape file with each record consisting of salesman name and accumulated amount for x number of cards. Output file has standard labels and 50 records/block.

4. Each class in a school has exactly 20 students. The grade (0–100) for each student is punched into the first three columns of a card. Thus the first 20 cards are for the students in class 1, the second 20 cards are for students in class 2, etc. There are exactly 25 classes. Print a report with the class average for each class:

    CLASS 1   xxx.xx
    CLASS 2   xxx.xx
    .
    .
    .
    CLASS 25 xxx.xx

16

Occurs Clauses–Single Level

To indicate the **repeated occurrence** of an item having the same format, we use an **OCCURS** clause in COBOL.

Consider the following example. Each input data card has ten eight-position amount fields. Each card will be read, the amount fields summed, and a total printed. Since no "shortcut" methods are known at this time, we must define our card with ten independent fields:

```
01  CARD-REC.
    02  AMT1    PICTURE 9(8).
    02  AMT2    PICTURE 9(8).
            .
            .
    02  AMT10   PICTURE 9(8).
```

To perform the necessary addition, we write

ADD AMT1, AMT2, ... AMT10 GIVING TOTAL.[1]

Since each amount field is an eight-position integer field, they are said to have the same format. To indicate the repeated occurrence of amount fields with the same format, we may use an **OCCURS** clause. Using this clause, the ten fields may be defined as follows:

```
01  CARD-REC.
    02  AMT OCCURS 10 TIMES
        PICTURE 9(8).
```

[1] The series of dots indicates that each AMT must be repeated.

In this way, we have defined ten eight-position fields. All ten fields are called **AMT**. Thus we have described the 80-position card record with a single **02** level entry.

With an **OCCURS** clause, we indicate the repeated occurrence of items. **AMT** defines 10 items, each with a **PICTURE** of 9(8).

There are ten items called **AMT**. To access any one of these in the **PROCEDURE DIVISION**, we must use identifying numbers called **subscripts**. To denote repeated occurrences of items, we use an **OCCURS** clause in the **DATA DIVISION**. To access any of these items, we use subscripts in the **PROCEDURE DIVISION**. A subscript is enclosed in parentheses and refers to the data-name directly preceding it. To move the **first** eight-position amount field to a print area called **EDIT1**, for example, we say

MOVE AMT (1) TO EDIT1.

AMT contains ten eight-position fields. We are moving the **first** eight-position field to **EDIT1**.

We may operate on any of the ten amount fields by using the corresponding subscript. Since **AMT** contains ten fields, the subscript used may vary from 1 to 10. To say, however,

Invalid: MOVE AMT (0) TO EDIT2.
                MOVE AMT (11) TO EDIT3.

is obviously invalid. The subscript refers only to one of the ten amount fields. There is no eleventh amount nor is there a zeroth amount.

The data-name, which is specified with an **OCCURS** clause, will be accessed in the **PROCEDURE DIVISION** with a subscript. The data-name will be followed by a **space** and the corresponding subscript. The following serves to illustrate the proper spacing:

Thus far, we have discussed subscripts which are numeric literals. A subscript, however, may also be a data-name with a numeric **PICTURE** clause. If **X** were defined in the **WORKING-STORAGE SECTION** as follows:

77 X PICTURE 99 VALUE 1.

the first amount field may be moved to **EDIT1**:

MOVE AMT (X) TO EDIT1.

Subscripts, then, may be integers or data-names. If a data-name is used as a subscript, it must have a numeric **PICTURE** clause with an integer value. We use data-names as subscripts when we wish to access different items at different times.

Thus, to accumulate all ten amount fields, we may write

ADD AMT (1), AMT (2), . . . AMT (10) TO TOTAL

which is not any less tedious than the original method. Or we may use data-names as subscripts in conjunction with a **PERFORM** statement:

```
    MOVE 1 TO CTR.
    MOVE ZEROS TO TOTAL.
    PERFORM ADD-RTN 10 TIMES.
    GO TO WRITE-RTN.
ADD-RTN.
    ADD AMT (CTR) TO TOTAL.
    ADD 1 TO CTR.
```

This is another example of a **loop.** We are adding ten amount fields. **CTR,** the subscript, is initialized at 1. **AMT (CTR),** which is initially the same as **AMT (1)** is added to **TOTAL. CTR** is then incremented by 1. We then add **AMT (CTR),** or the second amount field, to **TOTAL.** This routine is performed ten times, until all ten amounts are added to **TOTAL.**

The **TIMES** option of the **PERFORM** statement was used in the above example. As indicated in the previous chapter, the **UNTIL** option may also be used to execute looping routines:

```
    MOVE 1 TO CTR.
    MOVE ZEROS TO TOTAL.
    PERFORM ADD-RTN UNTIL CTR = 11.
    GO TO WRITE-RTN.
ADD-RTN.
    ADD AMT (CTR) TO TOTAL.
    ADD 1 TO CTR.
```

The **VARYING** option of the **PERFORM** statement provides the most direct method for coding loops:

```
    MOVE ZEROS TO TOTAL.
    PERFORM ADD-RTN VARYING CTR
    FROM 1 BY 1 UNTIL CTR > 10.
    GO TO WRITE-RTN.
ADD-RTN.
    ADD AMT (CTR) TO TOTAL.
```

OCCURS clauses are used in the **DATA DIVISION** to denote the repeated occurrence of items with the same format. Subscripts are identifying numbers used in the **PROCEDURE DIVISION** to access fields specified with **OCCURS** clauses. Both are very often utilized in conjunction with **PERFORM** statements to code program loops. The **PERFORM** statement, or loop, executes the same series of operations repeatedly.

The format for an **OCCURS** clause is:

(level-number) (data-name) <u>OCCURS</u>
(integer) <u>TIMES</u>

An **OCCURS** clause may be written on any level **except 01, 77,** or **88.** That is, it may occur on levels **02–49.** This implies that an item specified with an **OCCURS** clause must be part of a record. It may **not** be an independent item.

Items may occur **integer** times only. We will use integers, not data-names, preceding the word **TIMES** in an **OCCURS** clause.

The data-name used with an **OCCURS** clause may be an elementary item, with a **PICTURE** clause, or it may be a group item, which is further subdivided:

```
02  ITEM OCCURS 20 TIMES.
    03 MONTH   PICTURE X(12).
    03 YEAR    PICTURE 9(4).
```

The above **OCCURS** clause reserves 320 positions of core storage. **ITEM** refers to 20 groupings, **each** divided into a 12-position **MONTH** field and a four-position **YEAR** field. To say **MOVE ITEM (3) TO HOLD** will result in a 16-position move operation. The third **MONTH** and the third **YEAR** will be moved. We may also move each individually:

```
MOVE MONTH (3) TO HOLD1.
MOVE YEAR (3) TO HOLD 2.
```

Thus any item subordinate to an **OCCURS** clause must also be referred to with a subscript. **MONTH** and **YEAR**, as fields subordinate to **ITEM**, must be accessed with the use of a subscript.

Example: Every input data card has five amount fields, each ten positions long. Print each amount and the total of all five amounts for each card on one line.

The input record has five amount fields:

```
01  CARD-REC.
    02 AMOUNT OCCURS 5 TIMES,
        PICTURE 9(10).
    02 FILLER PICTURE X(30).
```

The output area has **six** numeric amount fields. We will consider the **TOTAL** field to be the sixth amount. We will **not**, however, define these fields as follows:

```
01  PRINT-REC.
    02 FILLER PICTURE X.
```

```
    02 AMOUNT2 OCCURS 6 TIMES
        PICTURE 9(10).
    02 FILLER PICTURE X(72).
```

This would place all amount fields next to one another, with no spaces between them. For readability of reports, we wish to have a number of spaces between each output amount field:

```
01  PRINT-REC.
    02 FILLER         PICTURE X.
    02 ITEM OCCURS 6 TIMES.
       03 AMOUNT2   PICTURE 9(10).
       03 FILLER    PICTURE X(5).
    02 FILLER         PICTURE X(42).
```

In this way, each amount field has a five-position filler separating it from the next field. To perform the necessary operations, a data-name, to be used as a subscript, is defined in the **WORKING-STORAGE SECTION**:

```
77 SUB1 PICTURE 9, VALUE 1.
```

Subscripts are generally initialized at 1 rather than zero. The **PROCEDURE DIVISION** entries, then, for the above routine, are as follows:

```
START.
        MOVE SPACES TO PRINT-REC.
        MOVE ZEROS TO AMOUNT2 (6).
        READ CARD-FILE AT END CLOSE
        CARD-FILE, PRINT-FILE STOP RUN.
        PERFORM RTN-X 5 TIMES.
        WRITE PRINT-REC AFTER ADVANCING 2
        LINES. MOVE 1 TO SUB1. GO TO
        START.
RTN-X.
        ADD AMOUNT (SUB1) TO
        AMOUNT2 (6).
        MOVE AMOUNT (SUB1) TO
        AMOUNT2 (SUB1).
        ADD 1 TO SUB1.
```

A subscript may be an integer or a data-name. Integers are used as subscripts when the specific item is known and remains constant. **AMOUNT2 (6)** refers to the last output amount field, which is the **TOTAL**. Since all amounts from the card are to be added to the **TOTAL**, the receiving field in the addition is **AMOUNT2 (6)**.

When subscripts are meant to be variable, data-names are used. The data-name must be defined in the **DATA DIVISION**, have a numeric **PICTURE** clause, and contain only integers. We initialize the subscript at 1. In the above example, the subscript should only vary from 1 to 5, since the input area consists of five amount fields only.

OCCURS clauses denote the repeated occurrence of items with the same format. A widely used application of **OCCURS** clauses is in the defining of tables. A table is a series of items stored in core that is called upon to provide pertinent data throughout the execution of the program. A **TAX-TABLE** and a **DISCOUNT-RATE-TABLE** are examples of items that are stored during execution of a program.

Such table data is read into the computer. Since it is called upon at various points in the program, the data is usually stored in the **WORKING-STORAGE SECTION**. An area is **reserved** in **WORKING-STORAGE;** the data is then **read** and moved to this area.

Suppose a **POPULATION TABLE**, consisting of 50 state population figures, has been read into some area of **WORKING-STORAGE**. The table may be defined in **WORKING-STORAGE** as follows:

```
01   POPULATION-TABLE.
     02 STATE-POP OCCURS 50 TIMES,
        PICTURE 9(10).
```

Note that the **OCCURS** clause may not be used on the **01** level. **OCCURS** clauses may be written only on the **02–49** levels, subordinate to a record level.

The above table, in the **WORKING-STORAGE SECTION**, defines 50 ten-position figures. Five hundred core storage positions are reserved for this table.

To access any of the 50 figures, a subscript must be used in conjunction with the data-name **STATE-POP**. Since **STATE-POP** is a data-name defined by an **OCCURS** clause, it must **always** be accessed with a subscript.

Note that **POPULATION-TABLE** is the **record name** for these 50 fields; **POPULATION-TABLE** may **not** be accessed in the **PROCEDURE DIVISION**. Only the item containing the **OCCURS** clause or items subordinate to the **OCCURS** clause, if they exist, may be accessed in the **PROCEDURE DIVISION**. **STATE-POP** or any **03** level item subordinate to **STATE-POP**, if one existed, may be used.

The above entry defines the storage area for the table. Data must be **read** from an input device and **moved** into this area. Later in this section, we will discuss the routines necessary for reading and accumulating the table data. Let us assume, at this point, that **POPULATION-TABLE** contains all the data; that is, the information has been read and moved to this area. Thus 50 figures have been accumulated in this table and are now available for processing.

Problem 1: Write a routine to find the total population of all 50 states. The total population will be placed in a field called **USA-POP**. Assume **CTR**, a **77** level item, is the subscript.

We wish to add **STATE-POP (1)**, **STATE-POP (2)**, . . . **STATE-POP (50)** to **USA-POP**. The most efficient method to accomplish this is to use some variation of the **PERFORM** statement:

```
(a)  MOVE ZEROS TO USA-POP.
     MOVE 1 TO CTR.
     PERFORM RTN-1 50 TIMES.
     GO TO WRITE-RTN.
RTN-1.
     ADD STATE-POP (CTR) TO USA-POP.
     ADD 1 TO CTR.
```

```
(b)  MOVE ZEROS TO USA-POP.
     MOVE 1 TO CTR.
     PERFORM RTN-1 UNTIL CTR > 50.
     GO TO WRITE-RTN.
```

RTN-1.
ADD STATE-POP (CTR) TO USA-POP.
ADD 1 TO CTR.

(c) MOVE ZEROS TO USA-POP.
PERFORM RTN-1 VARYING CTR FROM
1 BY 1 UNTIL CTR > 50.
GO TO WRITE-RTN.
RTN-1.
ADD STATE-POP (CTR) TO USA-POP.

It is important to note that PERFORM statements execute looping operations, but simple conditionals may be used instead:

(d) MOVE ZEROS TO USA-POP.
MOVE 1 TO CTR.
RTN-1.
ADD STATE-POP (CTR) TO USA-POP.
ADD 1 TO CTR.
IF CTR = 51 GO TO WRITE-RTN ELSE
GO TO RTN-1.

In all cases, CTR is an independent numeric item defined in the WORKING-STORAGE SECTION. MOVE 1 TO CTR in routines a, b, and d could be replaced by a VALUE clause, where CTR is set equal to 1.

Problem 2: Suppose the population figures are in alphabetic order; that is, STATE-POP (1), the first entry on the table, refers to the population of ALABAMA. STATE-POP (2) corresponds to the population for ALASKA, . . . STATE-POP (50) corresponds to WYOMING's population. Write a routine to move CALIFORNIA's population to an output area called POP1. (CALIFORNIA is the fifth state in alphabetic order):

MOVE STATE-POP (5) TO POP1.

Problem 3: Write a routine to find the largest state population figure. Place this figure in an area called HOLD:

MOVE 1 TO CTR.
MOVE ZEROS TO HOLD.

PERFORM RTN-2 50 TIMES.
GO TO START.
RTN-2.
IF STATE-POP (CTR) > HOLD MOVE
STATE-POP (CTR) TO HOLD.
ADD 1 TO CTR.

Observe that each figure is compared to HOLD. If the population is greater than the one at HOLD, then that figure is placed in HOLD. Thus, after 50 comparisons, the largest population is the one accumulated at HOLD. CTR, the subscript, may be initialized in the WORKING-STORAGE SECTION by a VALUE clause. If, however, the same subscript is used repeatedly throughout the program, it must be initialized at every routine.

Problem 4: Find the **number** of the state with the largest population, and place this integer in HOLDX. If the 30th state has the largest population, for example, then 30 must be placed in HOLDX.

This is only a minor variation of PROBLEM3. In addition to storing the largest population, we must also store the **number of the state** with the largest population. The number of the state is the value of CTR. Using conditional statements rather than a PERFORM, we have:

MOVE 1 TO CTR.
MOVE ZEROS TO HOLD.
RTN-2.
IF STATE-POP (CTR) > HOLD MOVE
STATE-POP (CTR) TO HOLD MOVE
CTR TO HOLDX.
ADD 1 TO CTR.
IF CTR = 51 GO TO START ELSE GO
TO RTN-2.

Problem 5: Find the number of states that have population figures in excess of 1,000,000. Place this number in TOTAL.

MOVE 1 TO CTR.
MOVE ZEROS TO TOTAL.
RTN-Y.
IF STATE-POP (CTR) > 1000000 ADD 1
TO TOTAL.

ADD 1 TO CTR.
IF CTR < 51 GO TO RTN-Y.

In the five examples above, we have assumed that our population table has been read and accumulated in storage. Let us now consider the routine to perform the reading and accumulating of the data into the table.

Suppose there are 50 table cards, each having a ten-position population figure. We wish to accumulate these 50 figures in WORKING-STORAGE for future processing. Note that the table data is not read and immediately processed, as is the convention with other forms of input, but is read and **stored** for future processing.

Our card format is as follows:

```
01   CARD-REC.
     02 POP     PICTURE 9(10).
     02 FILLER  PICTURE X(70).
```

We will read 50 such cards and accumulate the data in the following WORKING-STORAGE area:

```
01   POPULATION-TABLE.
     02 STATE-POP OCCURS 50 TIMES,
        PICTURE 9(10).
```

Note that the card record does **not** have an OCCURS clause associated with it. Fields or items **within records** that have repeated occurrences are specified with OCCURS clauses. To indicate that the card record itself is read 50 times, we issue 50 READ instructions in the PROCEDURE DIVISION:

```
PROCEDURE DIVISION.
     OPEN INPUT CARD-FILE.
BEGIN.
     READ CARD-FILE AT END GO TO EOJ.
     MOVE POP TO STATE-POP (X).
     ADD 1 TO X.
     IF X = 51 NEXT SENTENCE ELSE GO
     TO BEGIN.
```

In the above routine, X, the subscript, is a **77** level numeric item initialized at 1. The routine reads 50 cards and places the population figure of each card in the table. The only item to be subscripted is STATE-POP, since this is the only item defined by an OCCURS clause.

Let us elaborate upon the read routine, slightly, by altering the card format. Suppose **each** card has five population figures instead of one. The first 50 positions of the card contain five population figures, each ten positions long. Thus only **ten** READ instructions will be performed, since each card has five figures. The card format contains an OCCURS clause for the five figures on **each** card:

```
01   CARD-REC.
     02 POP OCCURS 5 TIMES,
                PICTURE 9(10).
     02 FILLER  PICTURE X(30).
```

The routine to accumulate this data in the WORKING-STORAGE area, POPULATION-TABLE, is as follows:

```
PROCEDURE DIVISION.
     OPEN INPUT CARD-FILE. MOVE 1 TO X2.
BEGIN.
     READ CARD-FILE AT END GO TO EOJ.
     MOVE 1 TO X1.
     PERFORM RTN-Y 5 TIMES.
     IF X2 = 51 GO TO OUT ELSE GO TO
     BEGIN.
RTN-Y.
     MOVE POP (X1) TO STATE-POP (X2).
     ADD 1 TO X1.
     ADD 1 TO X2.
```

X1 and X2 are subscripts that are both initialized at 1 by VALUE clauses. X2, the subscript used with STATE-POP, is incremented from 1 to 51. X1, however, ranges from 1 to 5, since POP of the card file has only **five** figures associated with it.

Two PERFORM statements, one contained within the other, may be used to accomplish the same operations as above:

```
     PERFORM READ-RTN 10 TIMES.
     GO TO OUT.
READ-RTN.
     READ CARD-FILE AT END CLOSE
     CARD-FILE STOP RUN.
```

```
MOVE 1 TO X1.
PERFORM RTN-Y 5 TIMES.
RTN-Y.
MOVE POP (X1) TO STATE-POP (X2).
ADD 1 TO X1.
ADD 1 TO X2.
```

We wish to accumulate Table 16-1 in storage.

NO OF YRS EMPLOYED will **not** be an entry in the table. That is, the fifth grouping in the table, for example, will refer to five years of employment. The X's indicated above denote the number of posi-

```
01  CARD-REC.
    02  MAJOR.
        03  NO-OF-EMPLOYEES-IN
            PICTURE  9(4).
        03  WEEKS-VACATION-IN
            PICTURE 99.
        03  EXCUSED-DAYS-IN
            PICTURE  999.
    02  FILLER   PICTURE X(71).
```

To read 50 cards and accumulate the data in BENEFITS-TABLE, the following routine may be used, where SUB1 is a 77 level numeric item initialized at 1:

```
PERFORM READ-RTN 50 TIMES.
GO TO NEXT.
READ-RTN.
    READ CARD-FILE AT END CLOSE CARD-FILE STOP RUN.
    MOVE NO-OF-EXCUSED-DAYS-IN TO NO-OF-EXCUSED-DAYS (SUB1).
    MOVE WEEKS-VACATION-IN TO WEEKS-VACATION (SUB1).
    MOVE NO-OF-EMPLOYEES-IN TO NO-OF-EMPLOYEES (SUB1).
    ADD 1 TO SUB1.
```

tions in the field. WEEKS-VACATION, for example, is a two-position field.

Table 16-1   Benefits Table

NO OF YRS EMPLOYED	NO OF EMPLOYEES	WEEKS VACATION	EXCUSED DAYS
1	XXXX	XX	XXX
2	XXXX	.	.
3	.	.	.
.	.	.	.
.	.	.	.
50	XXXX	XX	XXX

The table is denoted in the WORKING-STORAGE SECTION as follows:

```
01  BENEFITS-TABLE.
    02  ITEM OCCURS 50 TIMES.
        03  NO-OF-EMPLOYEES
            PICTURE  9(4).
        03  WEEKS-VACATION
            PICTURE 99.
        03  EXCUSED DAYS
            PICTURE 999.
```

Let us assume that data for the table will be read in on cards with the following format:

With the use of a group MOVE operation, we may simplify the above:

```
PERFORM READ-RTN 50 TIMES.
GO TO NEXT.
READ-RTN.
    READ CARD-FILE AT END CLOSE
    CARD-FILE STOP RUN.
    MOVE MAJOR TO ITEM (SUB1).
    ADD 1 TO SUB1.
```

Problem 1: Find the number of weeks' vacation to which an employee with eight years of service is entitled. Place the result in a field called HOLD:

```
MOVE WEEKS-VACATION (8) TO HOLD.
```

Since the eighth entry in the table refers to eight years of service, the MOVE operation above will produce the desired results

Problem 2: Find the total number of employees. Place the result in a field called TOTAL.

```
MOVE ZEROS TO TOTAL.
MOVE 1 TO SUB1.
```

1. ADD NO-OF-EMPLOYEES (SUB1) TO
    TOTAL.
    ADD 1 TO SUB1.
    IF SUB1 = 51 NEXT SENTENCE ELSE
    GO TO 1.

Problem 3: Find the average number of excused days to which any employee is entitled. Place the result in **AVERAGE**.

    MOVE ZEROS TO AVERAGE.
    MOVE 1 TO SUB1.
1. ADD EXCUSED-DAYS (SUB1) TO
    AVERAGE.
    ADD 1 TO SUB1.
    IF SUB1 = 51 NEXT SENTENCE ELSE
    GO TO 1.
    DIVIDE 50 INTO AVERAGE.

Problem 4: Find the number of years an employee must be employed to accumulate more than 100 excused days. Place the result in **WORK**. Assume that the excused days' entries increment with each year of employment; that is, an employee with X number of years' employment is entitled to less excused days than an employee with $X + 1$ years of service:

    MOVE 1 TO SUB1.
RTN-X.
    IF EXCUSED-DAYS (SUB1) IS GREATER
    THAN 100 GO TO OUT.
    ADD 1 TO SUB1. GO TO RTN-X.
OUT.
    MOVE SUB1 TO WORK.

Exercises

1. An OCCURS clause is used to denote _____.
    *****
    the repeated occurrence of an item

2. An OCCURS clause is only used in the _____ DIVISION.
    *****
    DATA

3. (T or F) An OCCURS clause may be used in either the FILE SECTION or the WORKING-STORAGE SECTION of the DATA DIVISION.
    *****
    T

4. An OCCURS clause may not be used on the _____, _____, _____ levels.
    *****
    01
    77
    88

5. An item defined by an OCCURS clause or subordinate to another item defined by an OCCURS clause may be accessed in the PROCEDURE DIVISION with the use of a _____.
    *****
    subscript

6. Subscripts may be _____ or _____.

   *****

   integers
   data-names

7. If a subscript is a data-name, its **PICTURE** clause must indicate a _____ field.

   *****

   numeric (integer)

8. (T or F) **MOVE ITEM (A) TO HOLD,** where **A** has a value of zero, is a valid statement.

   *****

   F

9.   01   TABLE-X.
             02 ITEM-A OCCURS 120 TIMES.
                03 ITEM-A1 PICTURE 99.
                03 ITEM-A2 PICTURE XXX.

   The above entry reserves _____ positions of storage. **MOVE ITEM-A (6) TO HOLD** is a _____ -position **MOVE**.

   *****

   600
   5

10. Write a routine, **without using a PERFORM statement,** to read ten cards with the following format into the **TABLE** below:

                        1–5   SALARY
                        6–8   TAX
                        9–80   NOT USED
                  01   TABLE.
                       02 RATE OCCURS 10 TIMES.
                          03 SALX PICTURE 9(5).
                          03 TAXX PICTURE 9(3).

   *****

           MOVE 1 TO CTR.
   START.
           READ CARD-FILE AT END CLOSE CARD-FILE STOP RUN.
           MOVE SALARY TO SALX (CTR).
           MOVE TAX TO TAXX (CTR).
           ADD 1 TO CTR.
           IF CTR = 11 GO TO OUT ELSE GO TO START.

11. Write a routine for the above **using a PERFORM statement.**

    *****

            MOVE 1 TO CTR.
            PERFORM START 10 TIMES.
            GO TO OUT.
    START.
            READ CARD-FILE AT END CLOSE CARD-FILE STOP RUN.
            MOVE SALARY TO SALX (CTR).

```
MOVE TAX TO TAXX (CTR).
ADD 1 TO CTR.
```

12. Is the following routine the same as the routines in Questions 10 and 11?

```
        MOVE 1 TO CTR.
START.
        READ CARD-FILE AT END CLOSE CARD-FILE STOP RUN.
        MOVE SALARY TO SALX (CTR). MOVE TAX TO TAXX (CTR).
        IF CTR = 10 GO TO OUT.
        ADD 1 TO CTR.
        GO TO START.
        *****
```
Yes.

13. (T or F) Any loop executed by a **PERFORM** statement may also be accomplished with the use of a conditional.
    *****
    T

Review Questions

Correct the errors, if any, in each of the following (1-6):

1. 01 ITEM-X OCCURS 100 TIMES
    02 ITEM-1X PICTURE S99.

2. 01 ITEM-T.
    02 ITEM-T1 OCCURS 150 TIMES, PICTURE S999.

3. 77 ITEM-W OCCURS 20 TIMES, PICTURE 9999.

4. MOVE ITEM-XX (3) TO HOLD-1.
    MOVE ITEM-XX (0) TO HOLD-2.

5. 01 ITEM-Z.
    02 ITEM-ZZ OCCURS 10 TIMES, PICTURE S99.
    .
    .
    .
    MOVE ITEM-Z (X1) TO HOLD.

6. 77 X5 PICTURE XX VALUE '01'.
    .
    .
    MOVE ITEM-Z (X5) TO HOLD.

7. Using the following table in core storage, write a routine to print the state with the smallest population. Also print the smallest population figure.

```
01  POPULATION-TABLE.
02 STATE OCCURS 50 TIMES, PICTURE S9(10).
```

8. Using the table entry above, write a routine to print the number of states that have populations smaller than 250,000. Also print the number of each of these states.

9. Using the BENEFITS-TABLE described in the chapter, find the total number of employees who have been with the company more than 20 years.

10. Using the BENEFITS-TABLE described in this chapter, write a routine to print the number of employees who have been with the company an odd number of years and the number of employees who have been with the company an even number of years.

PROBLEMS

1. Monthly take-home pay is to be computed for each employee of Company ABC.

(a) A tax table must be read into core storage from 20 input cards:

1–5   Low bound salary
6–10 High bound salary
11–13 State tax percentage (.xxx)
14–16 Federal tax percentage (.xxx)
17–80 Not used

	Low bound	High bound	State tax	Federal tax

Example: 06700 |09800 |020 |100   denotes that state tax is 2% and federal tax is 10% for the salary range 6700–9800.

(b) Following the tax cards are detail employee cards containing the following information:

1–20 Employee name
21–25 Annual salary
  26 Number of dependents
27–80 Not used

(c) Monthly take-home pay is computed as follows:

(1) Standard deduction = 10% of annual salary up to $10,000
(2) Dependent deduction = 600 $\times$ number of dependents
(3) FICA (social security tax) = 4.8% of salary up to 7800
(4) Net salary = Annual salary — standard deduction — dependent deduction — FICA
(5) Find tax of net salary in tax table
 Annual take home pay = net — (state tax % $\times$ Net salary) — (federal tax % $\times$ Net salary)

(6) Monthly take home pay = Annual take home pay / 12

(d) Print employee name and monthly take home pay (edited).

2. Write a program to build a benefit table from the following input card format:

cc   1   Code
       2–3   Number of years of service
       4–5   Number of weeks vacation
       6–12 Life insurance policy xxxxx.xx
     13–14 Excused days
     15–80 Not used

All input cards should have a 1 in Column 1. If any input card does **not** have a 1, stop the run.

The program checks to see that the input cards are in sequence by number of years in service, with no missing numbers or duplicates, starting with 1 and ending with 50. If any record is out of sequence, stop the run.

The benefits table should have 50 records consisting of number of weeks' vacation, life insurance policy, and excused days—number of years of service is not part of the table.

Punch three output cards, the first indicating the average number of weeks' vacation, the second the average life insurance policy, and the third indicating the average number of excused days.

3. Input table entries have the following format:

      1–3   Warehouse number
      4–6   Product number
      7–11 Unit price xxx.xx

The above input is entered on tape, blocking factor is 50, and labels are standard. There are 250 of these table entries.
The detail card file is as follows:

      1–3   Product number
      4–7   Quantity
      8–20 Customer name
    21–80 Not used

Create an output tape containing product number, unit price, quantity, total amount, and customer name for each detail card. Total amount is equal to unit price multiplied by quantity.

Note that, for each detail card, the product number must be found on the table file to obtain the corresponding unit price.

4. There are 20 salesmen in Company XYZ. Each sale that they have made is punched into a card with the following format:

      1–5   Salesman No.
      6–20 Salesman name
    21–25 Amount of sale   xxx.xx
    26–80 Not used

The number of input cards is unknown. Salesman X may have ten sales, Salesman Y may have five sales, etc. The cards are **not** in sequence.

Write a program to print the total amount of sales for each salesman. Note that x number of input cards will be read and that 20 total amounts are to be printed, one for each salesman. All figures must be edited.

Print:

Salesman	Total Amount
1	xxxxx.xx
.	.
.	.
20	xxxxx.xx

5. Write a program to print 12 transaction amounts, one for each month of the year and, in addition, a grand yearly total. The input is as follows:

    1–5   Transaction amount   xxx.xx
    6–30 Not used
    31–32 Month number
    33–80 Not used

Note that an undetermined number of cards will serve as input, but only 12 totals are to be printed. All figures must be edited. NOTE: The cards are **not** in sequence.

6. Each input card will have the following format:

    1–5   Amount of sales — day x   xxx.xx
    6–10 Amount of sales — day x + 1   xxx.xx
    11–80 Not used

Twenty cards will serve as input, representing 40 daily figures. The first card will have sales amount for day 1 in cc1–5, the sales amount for day 2 in cc6–10. The second card will contain amount of sales for day 3 in cc1–5 and the amount of sales for day 4 in cc6–10, etc.

Write a program to create one block of 40 tape records, each five-positions long. The first tape record should contain sales amount for day 40, the second for day 39, etc.

17

Occurs Clauses–Double and Triple Levels

A. DOUBLE LEVEL OCCURS CLAUSE

When describing an area of storage, more than one level of **OCCURS** clauses may be used. Consider the following illustration. A population table for each state contains six population figures, one for each decade from 1900 to 1959. That is, each state contains six figures, one for 1900–1909, one for 1910–1919, and so on. Here is a pictorial representation of this table:

```
01  POPULATION-TABLE.
    02  STATE OCCURS 50 TIMES.
        03  DECADE1      PICTURE 9(10).
        03  DECADE2      PICTURE 9(10).
        03  DECADE3      PICTURE 9(10).
        03  DECADE4      PICTURE 9(10).
        03  DECADE5      PICTURE 9(10).
        03  DECADE6      PICTURE 9(10).
```

Each state is subdivided into six figures. To access the population for the first state, Alabama, for 1910–1919, we use **DECADE2 (1)**.

	1900–1909	1910–1919	1920–1929	1930–1939	1940–1949	1950–1959
Alabama						
Alaska						
. . .	.	.	.	.	.	.
Wyoming						

We may define this table in the **WORKING-STORAGE SECTION** with a **single** level **OCCURS** clause:

You will recall that an **OCCURS** clause may be used to denote the repeated occurrence of an item. Since each state is subdivided into six identical decade formats, the decades may be defined by an **OCCURS** clause.

is **not** valid, since the second subscript may not exceed 6. This is a pictorial representation of the table, with the appropriate subscripts:

	1900–1909	1910–1919	1920–1929	1930–1939	1940–1949	1950–1959
Alabama	(1, 1)	(1, 2)	(1, 3)	(1, 4)	(1, 5)	(1, 6)
Alaska	(2, 1)	(2, 2)	(2, 3)	(2, 4)	(2, 5)	(2, 6)
.	.	.	.	.	.	.
.	.	.	.	.	.	.
.	.	.	.	.	.	.
Wyoming	(50, 1)	(50, 2)	(50, 3)	(50, 4)	(50, 5)	(50, 6)

Example 1

```
01  POPULATION-TABLE.
   02  STATE OCCURS 50 TIMES.
      03  DECADE OCCURS 6 TIMES,
          PICTURE 9(10).
```

In this way, **each** state is subdivided into six decade figures. There are 300 decade fields in **POPULATION-TABLE**, each ten positions long.

To access any of these areas, the **lowest** level data-name must be used. We use the data-name **DECADE**, not **STATE**, to access any of the above areas.

DECADE is defined by **two OCCURS** clauses. Thus two subscripts must be used to access any of the decades within a state. The **first** subscript refers to the **major** level **OCCURS** clause, defining **STATE**. The **second** subscript refers to the **minor** level, defining the **DECADE**. Thus **DECADE** (5, 2) is a population figure for **STATE** 5, California, and **DECADE** 2, 1910–1919. To access the population figure for Arizona, the third state, for 1940–1949, we use **DECADE** (3, 5). The first subscript, **3**, refers to the major level item, **STATE**. The second subscript, **5**, refers to the minor level item, **DECADE**.

The first subscript, then, may vary from 1 to 50 since there are 50 **STATE** figures. The second subscript may vary from 1 to 6, since there are six **DECADE** figures within each state. To say MOVE DECADE (5, 51)

Note that we may **not** access six decade figures for Alabama, for example, by using **STATE** (1). Only the lowest level item may be accessed. The data-names **STATE** or **POPULATION-TABLE** may **not** be used in the **PROCEDURE DIVISION**. The data-name **DECADE**, or any item subordinate to **DECADE** (if one exists), must be employed.

If an item is defined by a double level **OCCURS** clause, it must be accessed by using **two** subscripts. The subscripts must be enclosed in parentheses. The left parenthesis must be preceded by a space. The first subscript within the parentheses is followed by a comma and a space.

Subscripts may be integers or data-names with integer contents. We may say:

DECADE (47, 6)

or

DECADE (CTR1, CTR2)

where **CTR1** has contents of 47 and **CTR2** has contents of 6.

Let us consider the following illustration of double level **OCCURS** clauses. Assume a table has been established in the **WORKING-STORAGE SECTION** and data has been read into the table. The **WORKING-STORAGE** entry is

```
01  TABLE-1.
   02  STATE OCCURS 50 TIMES.
      03  COUNTY OCCURS 10 TIMES,
          PICTURE 9(10).
```

The above table defines 500 fields of data. Each state is subdivided into 10 counties.

COUNTIES

States	1	2	3	4	5	6	7	8	9	10
Alabama										
. . .	.	.	.	.	.	.	.	.	.	.
Wyoming										

Let us write a routine to find the sum of all 500 fields. That is, we wish to accumulate a total USA population. We will add all ten counties for each of 50 states.

We must access a field by using the lowest level item, COUNTY. COUNTY must be described by **two** subscripts. The first will define the major level, STATE, and the second will define the minor level, COUNTY. COUNTY (5, 10) refers to STATE 5, COUNTY 10. The first subscript may vary from 1 to 50; the second may vary from 1 to 10.

To perform the required addition, we first accumulate all county figures for State 1. Thus the second subscript will vary from 1 to 10. After ten additions are performed, the ten county figures for State 2 must be accumulated. Thus we will add COUNTY (2, 1), COUNTY (2, 2), . . . COUNTY (2, 10) before we add the figures for State 3.

Note that **two** loops are implicit in this routine. The minor loop will increment the minor subscript from 1 to 10. The major loop will increment the major subscript from 1 to 50. A PERFORM statement within a PERFORM statement may be used to accumulate the TOTAL population:

```
        MOVE 1 TO SUB1.
        MOVE 1 TO SUB2.
        PERFORM PARA-2 50 TIMES.
        GO TO PRINT-TOTAL.
PARA-2.
        PERFORM PARA-3 10 TIMES.
        MOVE 1 TO SUB2.
        ADD 1 TO SUB1.
PARA-3.
        ADD COUNTY (SUB1, SUB2) TO TOTAL.
        ADD 1 TO SUB2.
```

Using the above routine, the following sequence of ADD statements are performed: COUNTY (1, 1), COUNTY (1, 2), ... COUNTY (1, 10), COUNTY (2, 1), COUNTY (2, 2), . . . COUNTY (2, 10), . . COUNTY (50, 1), . . . COUNTY (50, 10).

Any PERFORM option may be used to execute the above. The routine may also be performed, however, with the use of conditional statements:

```
        MOVE 1 TO SUB1.
        MOVE 1 TO SUB2.
X.      ADD COUNTY (SUB1, SUB2) TO
        TOTAL.
        IF SUB2 = 10 GO TO OUT.
        ADD 1 TO SUB2.
        GO TO X.
OUT.
        MOVE 1 TO SUB2.
        IF SUB1 = 50 GO TO PRINT-RTN.
        ADD 1 TO SUB1.
        GO TO X.
```

Using either of the routines above, we vary the minor subscript first, holding the major subscript constant. That is, when the major subscript is equal to 1, denoting State 1, all counties within that State are summed. We set SUB1 equal to 1 and increment SUB2 from 1 to 10. SUB1 is then set to 2, and we again increment SUB2 from 1 to 10, and so on.

Note that the sequence of additions may also be performed as follows: COUNTY (1, 1), COUNTY (2, 1), ... COUNTY (50, 1), COUNTY (1, 2), COUNTY (2, 2), . . . COUNTY (50, 2), ... COUNTY (50, 6). That is, we first add the population figures for all 50 states, first county. We vary the major subscript, holding the minor subscript constant. We set SUB2 equal to 1 and increment SUB1 from 1 to

50; we then set **SUB2** equal to 2 and increment **SUB1** again from 1 to 50 and so on. Using conditional statements to perform these operations, we have:

```
        MOVE ZEROS TO TOTAL.
        MOVE 1 TO SUB1.
        MOVE 1 TO SUB2.
  X.    ADD COUNTY (SUB1, SUB2) TO
        TOTAL.
        IF SUB1 = 50 GO TO Y.
        ADD 1 TO SUB1.
        GO TO X.
  Y.    MOVE 1 TO SUB1.
        IF SUB2 = 6 GO TO PRINT-RTN.
        ADD 1 TO SUB2.
        GO TO X.
```

Both sequences of operations result in the same accumulated population figure.

Example 2: We wish to store a table that will contain 12 monthly figures for each salesman in Company X. Each figure denotes the monthly sales amount credited to the salesman. Thus the first figure will be the sales amount for January, the second for February, etc. Company X has 25 salesmen, each having 12 monthly sales figures.

The **WORKING-STORAGE SECTION** entry to store this table is:

```
01  COMPANY-SALES-TABLE.
    02  SALESMAN OCCURS 25 TIMES.
        03  MONTH-AMT OCCURS 12
            TIMES, PICTURE 99V99.
```

The major level of **OCCURS** clause denotes that 25 salesmen are represented in the table. **Each** of the 25 has 12 monthly figures. Thus there are 300 fields, each four positions long, in the table.

The **WORKING-STORAGE** entry merely reserves storage for the table. Data must be read into storage before any processing may begin. Suppose 25 cards, each having 12 monthly figures, are to be read. We wish to perform several operations on the sales figures only after all the data has been accumulated in the **WORKING-STORAGE SECTION**.

The **FD** for the sales cards is:

```
FD  CARD-FILE
    RECORDING MODE IS F
    LABEL RECORDS ARE OMITTED
    RECORD CONTAINS 80 CHARACTERS
    DATA RECORD IS SALES-RECORD.
01  SALES-RECORD.
    02 AMOUNT OCCURS 12 TIMES,
                      PICTURE 99V99.
    02 FILLER PICTURE X(32).
```

Since each card contains 12 monthly figures, we use an **OCCURS** clause in the **FILE SECTION** to denote the repeated occurrence of the amount field. Note that the **FD** contains **no** indication that 25 sales cards will be read. This is indicated in the **PROCEDURE DIVISION**, by performing the **READ** operation 25 times.

The **PROCEDURE DIVISION** routines necessary to read data from the cards and store it in the table are:

```
        MOVE 1 TO X1.
        MOVE 1 TO X2.
        PERFORM READ-RTN 25 TIMES.
        GO TO NEXT-RTN.
READ-RTN.
        READ CARD-FILE AT END CLOSE
        CARD-FILE STOP RUN.
        PERFORM STORE-RTN 12 TIMES.
        MOVE 1 TO X2.
        ADD 1 TO X1.
STORE-RTN.
        MOVE AMOUNT (X2) TO
        MONTH-AMT (X1, X2).
        ADD 1 TO X2.
```

AMOUNT, a field within the card record, is described by a single level **OCCURS** clause. Thus it must be qualified by a single subscript in the **PROCEDURE DIVISION**. MONTH-AMT, an entry in the **WORKING-STORAGE SECTION**, is described by a double level **OCCURS** clause and must then be qualified by two subscripts in the **PROCEDURE DIVISION**. The subscript used to qualify **AMOUNT** is the same as the minor level subscript used to qualify MONTH-AMT. Since there are 12 **AMOUNT** figures, one for each month, and there are 12 MONTH-AMT figures for each salesman, the subscript will be the same for both items.

Using the above table now stored in the WORKING-STORAGE SECTION, we wish to print 12 lines of monthly data. Each line will contain 25 figures, one for each salesman. Line 1 will denote January data and contain 25 sales figures for January; line 2 will contain February data and have 25 sales figures; etc.

The print record is described this way:

```
FD   PRINT-FILE
     LABEL RECORDS ARE OMITTED
     RECORDING MODE IS F
     RECORD CONTAINS 133
     CHARACTERS
     DATA RECORD IS PRINT-REC.
01   PRINT-REC.
     02 FILLER          PICTURE X.
     02 ITEM OCCURS 25 TIMES.
        03 SALES-ITEM   PICTURE 99V99.
        03 FILLER       PICTURE X.
     02 FILLER          PICTURE X(7).
```

Note that we use a **single** level OCCURS clause to describe the print entry. Each line will contain 25 figures. Thus, only one level OCCURS clause is necessary. The fact that there will be 12 lines is **not** denoted by an OCCURS clause, but by repeating the print routine 12 times. As defined in the above illustration, ITEM OCCURS 25 TIMES. **Each** of these 25 items consists of **two** fields, SALES-ITEM and a FILLER. That is, a one-position filler will separate each amount field to make the line more "readable." If each sales item appeared next to another, it would be difficult to read the line.

The PROCEDURE DIVISION routine necessary to perform the required operation is:

```
     MOVE SPACES TO PRINT-REC.
     MOVE 1 TO X1.
     MOVE 1 TO X2.
     PERFORM WRITE-RTN 12 TIMES.
     GO TO EOJ.
WRITE-RTN.
     PERFORM MOVE-RTN 25 TIMES. WRITE
     PRINT-REC AFTER ADVANCING 2 LINES.
     MOVE 1 TO X1.
     ADD 1 TO X2.
```

```
MOVE-RTN.
     MOVE MONTH-AMT (X1, X2) TO
     SALES-ITEM (X1).
     ADD 1 TO X1.
```

B. TRIPLE LEVEL OCCURS CLAUSE

We have seen that OCCURS clauses may be written on one or two levels. We may also employ **triple** level OCCURS clauses. A **maximum** of three levels of OCCURS clauses may be used in a COBOL program.

Suppose we have a population table consisting of 50 state breakdowns. Each state is further subdivided into ten counties. Each county has five district figures. The following table may be established in the WORKING-STORAGE SECTION:

```
01   POPULATION-TABLE.
     02 STATE OCCURS 50 TIMES.
        03 COUNTY OCCURS 10 TIMES.
           04 DISTRICT OCCURS 5 TIMES,
              PICTURE 9(10).
```

In this way, we have defined 2500 fields ($50 \times 10 \times 5$) in core storage, each ten positions long. To access any field defined by several OCCURS clauses, we use the **lowest** level data-name. In the illustration above, the data-name DISTRICT must be used to access any of the 2500 fields of data.

Since DISTRICT is defined by a triple level OCCURS clause, **three** subscripts must be used to access the specific field desired. The **first** subscript refers to the **major** level item, STATE. The **second** subscript refers to the **intermediate** level item, COUNTY. The **third** subscript refers to the **minor** level, DISTRICT. Subscripts are always enclosed within parentheses. Each subscript is separated from the next by a comma and a space. Thus

```
DISTRICT (5, 4, 6)
```

refers to the population figure for:

STATE 5
COUNTY 4
DISTRICT 6

An item defined by a triple level OCCURS clause is accessed by utilizing three subscripts. Since no more than three levels of OCCURS clauses may be used to describe an item, we cannot have more than a triple level subscript.

Example 1: Write a routine to find the smallest population figure, in the above table. (We are assuming that data has already been placed in the table.) Place this smallest figure in HOLD.

Using three PERFORM statements, we have:

```
        MOVE 1 TO SUB1.
        MOVE 1 TO SUB2.
        MOVE 1 TO SUB3.
        MOVE DISTRICT (1, 1, 1) TO HOLD.
        PERFORM RTN-1 50 TIMES.
        GO TO NEXT-RTN.
RTN-1.
        PERFORM RTN-2 10 TIMES.
        MOVE 1 TO SUB2. ADD 1 TO SUB1.
RTN-2.
        PERFORM RTN-3 5 TIMES.
        MOVE 1 TO SUB3. ADD 1 TO SUB2.
RTN-3.
        IF DISTRICT (SUB1, SUB2, SUB3) IS LESS
        THAN HOLD MOVE
        DISTRICT (SUB1, SUB2, SUB3) TO HOLD.
        ADD 1 TO SUB3.
```

Using three conditional statements to execute the above looping, we have:

```
        MOVE 1 TO SUB1.
        MOVE 1 TO SUB2.
        MOVE 1 TO SUB3.
        MOVE DISTRICT (SUB1, SUB2, SUB3) TO
        HOLD.
RTN-A.
        IF DISTRICT (SUB1, SUB2, SUB3) IS LESS
        THAN HOLD MOVE
        DISTRICT (SUB1, SUB2, SUB3) TO HOLD.
        IF SUB3 = 5 GO TO RTN-B.
        ADD 1 TO SUB3.
        GO TO RTN-A.
RTN-B.
        MOVE 1 TO SUB3.
        IF SUB2 = 10 GO TO RTN-C.
        ADD 1 TO SUB2.
        GO TO RTN-A.
```

```
RTN-C.
        MOVE 1 TO SUB2.
        IF SUB1 = 50 GO TO NEXT-RTN.
        ADD 1 TO SUB1.
```

Some restrictions when using OCCURS clauses must be noted. VALUE clauses may **not** be used in conjunction with OCCURS clauses. Consider the following total areas:

```
01   TOTALS.
     02  SUM OCCURS 20 TIMES,
         PICTURE 999.
```

It is necessary to initialize each of the twenty SUM areas before any accumulations are performed. We may not, however, use a VALUE clause. Instead, each SUM must be set to zero in an initializing routine in the PROCEDURE DIVISION:

```
        MOVE 1 TO X1.
CLEAR.
        MOVE ZEROS TO SUM (X1).
        ADD 1 TO X1.
        IF X1 = 21 NEXT SENTENCE ELSE GO
        TO CLEAR.
```

A VALUE clause may not be used in conjunction with an OCCURS clause in the DATA DIVISION. We may **not** say:

```
            01   TOTALS VALUE ZEROS.
Invalid:         02  SUM OCCURS 20 TIMES,
                     PICTURE 999.
```

since only elementary items may contain VALUE statements and TOTALS is a group item, which is further subdivided. Similarly, we may **not** say:

```
            01   TOTALS.
Invalid:         02  SUM OCCURS 20 TIMES,
                     PICTURE 999 VALUE ZEROS.
```

since the computer is not able to determine which of the 20 occurrences of SUM is to be set to zero. Thus any attempt to initialize an area defined by an OCCURS clause must be performed in the PROCEDURE DIVISION in an initializing routine and not by a VALUE clause.

Areas defined by an **OCCURS** clause may not be redefined.

A **REDEFINES** clause may **not** follow an **OCCURS** clause. The following is **not** permissible:

Invalid:
```
01  TABLE-X.
    02  ITEM-A OCCURS 10 TIMES,
        PICTURE 99.
    02  ITEM-B REDEFINES ITEM-A
        PICTURE X(20).
```

Once an entry has been defined by an **OCCURS** clause, it may not be redefined. The converse, however, is acceptable. An item with an **OCCURS** clause may redefine another entry. The following **is** permissible:

Valid:
```
01  TABLE-X.
    02  ITEM-B PICTURE X(20).
    02  ITEM-AA REDEFINES ITEM-B.
        03  ITEM-A OCCURS 10 TIMES,
            PICTURE 99.
```

A **REDEFINES** clause may precede an **OCCURS** clause or they may be used in conjunction:

```
01  TABLE-X.
    02  ITEM-B PICTURE X(20).
    02  ITEM-A REDEFINES ITEM-B
        OCCURS 10 TIMES, PICTURE 99.
```

The point to remember when using an **OCCURS** clause in conjunction with a **REDEFINES** clause is that the **last** clause that may be used to describe an entry is an **OCCURS** clause.

The concept of **OCCURS** clauses, although difficult to understand fully, is a crucial part of COBOL programming. The use of **OCCURS** clauses requires precise, logical thinking on the part of the programmer. Most intermediate and high-level COBOL programs require knowledge of this concept.

EXERCISES

1. To access areas defined by double or triple level **OCCURS** clauses, we must use the _____ level item defined by an **OCCURS** clause.
*****
lowest

2. If MOVE ITEM (SUB1, SUB2) TO HOLD is a statement in the PROCEDURE DIVISION, then **SUB1** refers to the _____ level **OCCURS** clause and **SUB2** refers to the _____ level **OCCURS** clause.
*****
major
minor

3. Consider the following DATA DIVISION entry:

```
01  HOLD.
    02  FIELDX OCCURS 20 TIMES.
        03  FIELDXX OCCURS 50 TIMES.
            04  ITEM PICTURE S99.
```

The number of storage positions reserved for this area is _____. The data-name that may be accessed in the PROCEDURE DIVISION is _____. If ITEM (CTRA, CTRB) is used in the PROCEDURE DIVISION, then CTRA may vary from _____ to _____ and CTRB may vary from _____ to _____.

*****
2000
ITEM (or FIELDXX)
1 to 20
1 to 50

4. A maximum of _____ levels of OCCURS clauses may be used in the DATA DIVISION.
   *****
   three

5. If three levels of OCCURS clauses are used, then _____ subscripts must be used to access the specific field desired.
   *****
   three

6. If three subscripts are used to access an item, the first refers to the _____ level, the second to the _____ level, and the third to the _____ level.
   *****
   major
   intermediate
   minor

7. Each subscript within the parentheses is separated from the next by a _____ and a _____.
   *****
   comma
   space

8. A _____ clause may not be used in conjunction with an OCCURS clause in the DATA DIVISION.
   *****
   VALUE

9. Areas defined by an OCCURS clause may not be _____.
   *****
   redefined

10. An item with an OCCURS clause (may, may not) redefine another entry.
    *****
    may

Review Questions

1. There are 50 classes in College X. Each class has exactly 40 students. Each student has taken six exams. Write a **double** level OCCURS clause to define an area of storage that will hold these scores.

2. Write a **triple** level <u>OCCURS</u> clause for Question 1.

3. How many storage positions are reserved for the above **OCCURS** clause?

4. Write the File Description for a file of cards that will contain the students' test scores. Each card will contain six scores in the first 18 columns. The first card is for the first student in class 1, . . . the 40th card is for the 40th student in class 1, the 41st card is for the 1st student in class 2, etc.

5. Using the solutions to Questions 2 and 4, write the **PROCEDURE DIVISION** routines to read the test cards and to accumulate the data in the table area.

6. Write a routine to find the class with the highest class average.

7. Write a routine to find the student with the highest average.

8. If the following is a **WORKING-STORAGE** entry, write a routine to initialize the fields. Note that all areas to be used in arithmetic operations must first be cleared or set to zero:

```
01   TOTALS.
     02 MAJOR-TOTAL OCCURS 100 TIMES.
        03 INTERMEDIATE-TOTAL OCCURS 45 TIMES.
           04 MINOR-TOTAL OCCURS 25 TIMES, PICTURE S9(5).
```

Make necessary corrections to each of the following (9–10):

9. 01   ITEM OCCURS 20 TIMES, VALUE ZEROS.
   02 MINOR-ITEM OCCURS 15 TIMES, PICTURE S9.

10. 01   TABLE-A.
    02 FIELDX OCCURS 10 TIMES, PICTURE S99.
    02 FIELDY REDEFINES FIELDX PICTURE X(20).

PROBLEMS

1. Input tape records have the following format:

    1–2   Day number (01-07)
    3–5   Salesman number (001-025)
    6–10   Amount of transaction xxx.xx
    11–25 Not used

    Blocking factor-30
    Standard labels

Write a program to print **two** reports:

(a) The first report is a daily report giving seven daily figures, edited:

DAY	SALES-AMOUNT
1	$xx,xxx.xx
2	.
.	.
.	.
7	.
	$xx,xxx.xx

(b) The second report is a salesman report giving 25 salesmen figures, edited:

SALESMAN NUMBER	SALES-AMOUNT
001	$xx,xxx.xx
.	.
.	.
025	$xx,xxx.xx

For report (a), each daily figure consists of the addition of 25 salesmen figures for the corresponding day.

For report (b), each salesman figure consists of the addition of 7 daily figures for the corresponding salesman.

2. Write a program to tabulate the number of employees by area within department. The input card record has the following format:

                1–20 Employee name (not used)
                21–22 Department number
                23–24 Area number
                25–80 Not used

Notes

(a) There are 10 areas within each department; there are 50 departments.

(b) Cards are not in sequence.

(c) Output is a report with the following format:

TOTAL NUMBER OF EMPLOYEES BY AREA WITHIN DEPARTMENT

DEPARTMENT—01

AREA 1	AREA 2	. . .	AREA 10
xxx	xxx		xxx

DEPARTMENT—02

AREA 1	AREA 2	. . .	AREA 10
xxx	xxx		xxx

.
.
.

DEPARTMENT—50

AREA 1	AREA 2	. . .	AREA 10
xxx	xxx		xxx

All totals should be edited to suppress high order zeros.
Allow for page overflow.

3. Write a program to tabulate the number of employees by territory within area within department. The input tape record has the following format:

> 1–2   Territory number
> 3–4   Area number
> 5–6   Department number
> 7–50 Not used

Labels are Standard; blocking factor = 10.

Notes

(a) There are three territories within each area; there are 5 areas within each department; there are 10 departments.
(b) Tape records are not in sequence.
(c) Output is a report with the following format:

TOTAL NUMBER OF EMPLOYEES BY TERRITORY WITHIN AREA
WITHIN DEPT

DEPARTMENT—01

	AREA 1			AREA 2		. . .		AREA 5	
TERR-A	TERR-B	TERR-C	TERR-A	TERR-B	TERR-C		TERR-A	TERR-B	TERR-C
xxx	xxx	xxx	xxx	xxx	xxx		xxx	xxx	xxx

.
.
.

DEPARTMENT—10

	AREA 1		. . .		AREA 5	
TERR-A	TERR-B	TERR-C		TERR-A	TERR-B	TERR-C
xxx	xxx	xxx		xxx	xxx	xxx

4. Rewrite the program for Problem 3, assuming that tape records are in sequence by territory within area within depatrment.

5. The following card records are used to create a table in core storage:

> 1–5   Product number
> 6–10   Unit number
> 11–15 Price xxx.xx
> 16–80 Not used

There are 10 units for each product. There are 25 product numbers. The table, then, consists of 250 unit-prices.

The following is the format for the detail tape records:

> 1–20   Customer name
> 21–25 Product number
> 26–30 Unit number
> 31–33 Quantity sold

Labels are standard; blocking factor = 35.

Create output tape records with the following format:

> 1–20 Customer name
> 21–28 Amount xxxxxx.xx
> 29–30 Not used

Labels are standard; blocking factor = 50.

For each detail tape record, perform a table lookup of the price for the product number and unit number given. Amount of the output record = Quantity × Price. Note that Price is in the accumulated table.

Unit 5

Additional Input-Output Statements

A. DISPLAY STATEMENT

Thus far, we have discussed the WRITE command as the only method of producing output data. The format for a WRITE statement is:

```
WRITE (record-name)
```

The record is part of a file, assigned to a specific device in the ENVIRONMENT DIVISION, and described in the DATA DIVISION. An OPEN command must be issued before a record in the file can be written.

To produce most forms of output data, we use a WRITE statement. This is, however, not the only output operation available. The DISPLAY verb is also used to produce output. A DISPLAY statement, however, differs significantly from the WRITE operation. The format for a DISPLAY is as follows:

responding file need be defined in the ENVIRONMENT DIVISION. No OPEN statement is required. We may say DISPLAY FIELDA where FIELDA is any field defined in the DATA DIVISION. Any item defined in the FILE SECTION or the WORKING-STORAGE SECTION may be displayed. Similarly, we may say DISPLAY 'INVALID CODE', when the specific literal or message is required as output.

The DISPLAY verb, then, may be used in place of the WRITE statement. When only certain fields of information are required and no record format exists, the DISPLAY verb is used.

A DISPLAY statement is a method of producing output data that does not require the establishment of files. We DISPLAY data fields or literals; we WRITE records.

The DISPLAY verb has a very significant use in COBOL programs. It is used to produce a **low volume of output data.**

```
DISPLAY [ data-name ]  {UPON [device-name]}
        [ literal    ]
```

The UPON clause, which specifies the device, is optional. When omitted, data generally will be displayed on the printer. To say, for example, DISPLAY CODE prints the contents of CODE.

When using a DISPLAY verb, no cor-

For primary output from a program, we generally establish files and WRITE records. When a field or a literal is to be displayed depending on some condition such as an error condition, or when a message is to be relayed to the computer operator, it is too cumbersome to establish files and records for these special cases. For these output operations, we use DIS-PLAY statements.

Consider a card-to-tape program that performs arithmetic operations on the card data to produce tape records. The tape is the major form of output; it is established as a file with a specific record format. Data is created on tape by performing a WRITE operation. Let us suppose that all the arithmetic operations test for ON SIZE ERROR, or arithmetic overflow conditions. When an overflow condition exists, we wish to print the message INVALID CARD DATA. To use a WRITE statement would require the establishment of a print file and a record within the file for the message. Using a DISPLAY statement does not require files, and the message may be displayed as a literal:

```
PROCEDURE DIVISION.
    OPEN INPUT CARD-FILE, OUTPUT
    TAPE-FILE.
BEGIN.
    READ CARD-FILE AT END GO TO EOJ.
    ADD AMT1-IN, AMT2-IN GIVING
    AMT-OUT ON SIZE ERROR GO TO
    ERROR-RTN.
    MULTIPLY AMT-OUT BY .06 GIVING
    TAX-OUT ON SIZE ERROR GO TO
    ERROR-RTN.
    ADD TAX-OUT, AMT-OUT GIVING
    TOTAL ON SIZE ERROR GO TO
    ERROR-RTN.
    WRITE TAPE-REC.
    GO TO BEGIN.
ERROR-RTN.
    DISPLAY 'INVALID CARD DATA'.
    GO TO BEGIN.
```

Fields or literals may be displayed on specific devices. If a device name is not used in the DISPLAY statement, as in the above illustration, then the system logical output device is assumed. For most systems, the logical output device is the printer. Thus, to say DISPLAY TAX, where

no UPON clause is specified, prints the data in the TAX field. Data may also be displayed on the card punch; that is, a card may be punched by the computer with the use of a DISPLAY verb. We may also display data on the console. The console is a special typewriter that may serve as input to or output from the computer. The DISPLAY verb utilizes the console as an output device.

The device, then, used in the UPON clause may denote the console or the card punch. The names of these devices are assigned by the manufacturer, and are thus machine-dependent. For most computers, the device names CONSOLE and PUNCH are used.[1] Thus, to say

(1) DISPLAY $\begin{bmatrix} \text{data-name} \\ \text{literal} \end{bmatrix}$

prints the data on the printer

(2) DISPLAY $\begin{bmatrix} \text{data-name} \\ \text{literal} \end{bmatrix}$ UPON PUNCH

punches a card with the data

(3) DISPLAY $\begin{bmatrix} \text{data-name} \\ \text{literal} \end{bmatrix}$ UPON CONSOLE

prints the data on the typewriter or console

The size of the field or literal to be displayed is limited and depends upon the device used. When information is to be printed on the printer using a DISPLAY verb, the field or literal is limited to 120 positions. To say:

DISPLAY $\begin{bmatrix} \text{data-name} \\ \text{literal} \end{bmatrix}$

requires that the data be no more than 120 characters.

When a field or literal is displayed upon the console or card punch, the size of the data must not exceed 72 positions. Several fields or literals may be displayed with one statement. Modifying the format for a DISPLAY operation, we have:

[1] Consult the reference manual for specific computer device names.

```
┌─────────────────────────────────────────────────────────────────────┐
│         ┌ data-name-1 ┐   ┌ data-name-2 ┐                             │
│ DISPLAY │             │ , │             │ , . . . . . {UPON (device-name)} │
│         └ literal-1   ┘   └ literal-2   ┘                             │
└─────────────────────────────────────────────────────────────────────┘
```

Examples

(1) DISPLAY FIELDA, FIELDB UPON CONSOLE.

(2) DISPLAY 'THE MONTH OF', MONTH.

Note the difference between the following two routines.

(1) DISPLAY 'INCORRECT TAX AMOUNT', TAX.

will print:

INCORRECT TAX AMOUNT (contents of TAX).

(2) DISPLAY 'INCORRECT TAX AMOUNT'. DISPLAY TAX.

will print: INCORRECT TAX AMOUNT (contents of TAX).

Each DISPLAY verb prints one **line** of information.

One important point must be noted. We cannot WRITE and DISPLAY upon the same device. If a file is assigned to the card punch in the ENVIRONMENT DIVISION, then we may not display upon the punch.

Thus a WRITE statement is used to produce output **records.** For primary forms of output, we use the WRITE verb. A DISPLAY statement is used to produce a low volume of output on the printer, console, or punch. It does **not** require the establishment of files and records. Fields of data defined in the DATA DIVISION or literals may be displayed without opening files. A DISPLAY verb is most often used to give messages to the computer operator or the control supervisor.

B. ACCEPT STATEMENT

The ACCEPT statement performs an **input** operation. It results in the **reading** of **fields** of data into some area of core storage.

An ACCEPT verb is an input command that parallels the DISPLAY verb. The DISPLAY statement produces output data. It, unlike the WRITE command, does not require a device assigned in the ENVIRONMENT DIVISION, an output area defined in the DATA DIVISION, or an OPEN statement in the PROCEDURE DIVISION. It is used to produce a low volume of output data where record formats are not required.

An ACCEPT verb reads input data into the computer. It, unlike the READ command, does not require a device assigned in the ENVIRONMENT DIVISION, an input area defined in the DATA DIVISION, or an OPEN statement in the PROCEDURE DIVISION.

The format for an ACCEPT statement is:

```
┌─────────────────────────────────────────┐
│ ACCEPT (data-name)                        │
│                   {FROM device-name}      │
└─────────────────────────────────────────┘
```

The data-name may be any field defined in the DATA DIVISION. We may say ACCEPT data-name-1 where data-name-1 is a 77 level item in the WORKING-STORAGE SECTION or an 02 level item within the output record. It may be **any** field defined and described in the DATA DIVISION.

If the FROM option is not specified, data will be read from the card reader. To say ACCEPT data-name-1, where data-name-1 is a four-position numeric field, will result in the first four **card columns** of data being read.

We may not ACCEPT data from the reader if the reader is a device assigned in a SELECT clause. That is, we may not READ and ACCEPT from the same device.

The FROM option may be used with the

console. We may ACCEPT data FROM CONSOLE.

For the reading of primary input records, we always establish files and read them. For a small volume of secondary input data, the ACCEPT verb is often used. The ACCEPT statement is most often utilized to read **date** information or some form of control data into the computer. Consider the following two examples.

Example 1: A tape-to-print program is to be written. The major form of input is a tape, and thus a tape file is established in the FILE SECTION. The heading record of the output file is to contain the date of the run. The date is not part of the tape input, and will change with each monthly run.

We may read this date from a card. The card will contain month in cc 1–2, / in cc 3, and year in cc 4–5. Thus 03/70 denotes MARCH, 1970.

To use a READ statement for the card input requires a SELECT clause in the ENVIRONMENT DIVISION, an FD in the DATA DIVISION, and an OPEN statement in the PROCEDURE DIVISION. This is rather cumbersome programming for a single input card. Instead, an ACCEPT verb may be used. We may say:

ACCEPT DATE

where DATE is a five-position data field within the heading record:

```
01   HEADING.²
     02 FILLER   PICTURE X, VALUE SPACES.
     02 FILLER   PICTURE X(20) VALUE 'RUN DATE IS' JUSTIFIED RIGHT.
     02 DATE     PICTURE XXXXX.
     02 FILLER   PICTURE X(50) VALUE 'MONTHLY STATUS REPORT' JUSTIFIED RIGHT.
     02 FILLER   PICTURE X(57) VALUE SPACES.
```

Thus no file need be assigned to use the ACCEPT verb. The first five card columns of the date card are read into the field called DATE.

---

² This record must be a WORKING-STORAGE entry since it contains VALUE clauses.

Example 2: An input file consists of tape records. A single program is to be written to create an updated output tape biweekly and to create print records monthly. That is, with the use of some control data that denotes a biweekly or a monthly run, we will instruct the computer to create either print records or updated tape records. The routine is:

```
IF CODE = 1 GO TO TAPE-RTN.
IF CODE = 2 GO TO PRINT-RTN.
GO TO ERR-RTN.
```

CODE is a control field that is read into the computer during each run. It is not a **constant,** since it changes with each computer run. We may establish CODE as a WORKING-STORAGE item:

```
77   CODE PICTURE 9.
```

We may read a 1 or 2 into CODE by the following:

```
ACCEPT CODE FROM CONSOLE.
```

The computer operator will type a 1 on the biweekly run and a 2 on the monthly run. Thus we have:

```
ACCEPT CODE FROM CONSOLE.
IF CODE = 1 GO TO TAPE-RTN.
IF CODE = 2 GO TO PRINT-RTN.
GO TO ERR-RTN.
```

When **accepting** data from the console or the reader, a maximum of **72** characters of information may be transmitted.

Note that the computer will temporarily stop or pause after each use of the ACCEPT verb. After ACCEPT DATE is executed, the computer pauses. It is in the "wait state." The operator must press start before the machine will continue processing.

Thus, after **ACCEPT CODE FROM CON-SOLE** is executed, the computer is in the wait state. The operator must type the required data on the console and press start before execution continues.

The **ACCEPT** verb is an effective tool for transmitting a small amount of input data to the computer. It does not require the establishing of files. It should not be used, however, for large volumes of input since it is a time-consuming instruction. A **READ** statement transmits input data from the input device to the input area and continues with the next instruction. An **ACCEPT** verb causes a pause in execution before data is transmitted.

When the computer pauses after an **ACCEPT** statement is issued, the computer operator must perform some function. **No** message is given the operator except the standard entry, 'AWAITING REPLY'. He must be familiar with the program requirements and know what a halt in execution implies. If a card is required, for example, the operator must keypunch the correct data and press start. If console data is required, the operator must type the information and press start.

It is not always feasible to expect the computer operator to remember each program's requirements. For this reason, we generally **DISPLAY** a message to the operator before issuing an **ACCEPT** command. The message informs the operator of the necessary operations. It tells him what to do when the computer pauses.

Example 1

DISPLAY 'KEYPUNCH A CARD WITH MONTH IN CC1-2,
— '/IN CC 3, AND YEAR IN CC4-5 PLACE CARD IN
— 'READER AND PRESS START'. ACCEPT DATE.

The above literal prints on the printer. The **ACCEPT** statement follows and the computer stops. The operator reads the message, performs the required operations, and presses start. The first five columns of the card in the reader are then transmitted to the **DATE** field.

Example 2

START.
　　DISPLAY 'TYPE IN 1 FOR BIWEEKLY RUN
—　'OF PROGRAM' TYPE IN 2 FOR
—　'MONTHLY RUN OF PROGRAM' UPON
　　CONSOLE.
　　ACCEPT CODE FROM CONSOLE.
　　IF CODE = 1 GO TO TAPE-RTN.
　　IF CODE = 2 GO TO PRINT-RTN.
　　DISPLAY 'INCORRECT CODE TYPED'
　　UPON CONSOLE.
　　GO TO START.

The latter routine performs a check on the computer operator. A message of instruction is printed on the console. The operator is required to type a 1 or a 2. If a mistake has been made and a 1 or 2 has **not** been typed, an error message is printed and the routine is performed again.

Thus the **DISPLAY** and **ACCEPT** verbs perform input-output functions on a low volume of data. No files need be established nor records specified when using these verbs. The two commands are often used within the same routine. The **DIS-PLAY** verb prints a message of instruction to the operator before data is accepted.

EXERCISES

1. In addition to the **WRITE** statement, a _____ verb may also be used to produce output.
　　* * * * *
　　DISPLAY

2. If the **UPON** clause is omitted from a **DISPLAY** statement, then data will generally be displayed upon the _____.
*****
printer

3. We may **DISPLAY** _____ or _____.
*****
data-names
literals

4. When displaying a data-name, it (must, need not) be part of an output record.
*****
need not

5. The **DISPLAY** verb is used to produce a _____ volume of computer output.
*****
low

6. Besides the printer, data may be displayed upon the _____ or the _____.
*****
console typewriter
card punch

7. We (may, may not) **DISPLAY** and **WRITE** upon the same device.
*****
may not

8. In addition to the **READ** command, an _____ verb may also be used to access input data.
*****
ACCEPT

9. If a device name is not specified in an **ACCEPT** statement, the _____ is generally assumed.
*****
card reader.

10. When accepting data from the console or reader, a maximum of _____ characters is permitted.
*****
72

Review Questions

1. A control card is the only card data in a particular program. If it has an X in Column 1, then the **MONTHLY-UPDATE** routine is to be performed. If it has a Y in Column 1, then the **WEEKLY-UPDATE** routine is to be performed. Write the control card routine, with proper edit controls, to accept and process this card.

2. (T or F) An **ACCEPT** statement causes a temporary pause in execution.

3. (T or F) Several data fields may not be displayed with one **DISPLAY** statement.

4. (T or F) **WRITE** and **DISPLAY** statements may be used for the same device if the areas in question are cleared first.

5. When a particular error condition occurs, the program is to pause, print the message 'ERROR CONDITION X' on the console. If the operator types 'OK' in response, the program is to continue (branch to **START**). If the operator types 'NO GO' in response, a **STOP RUN** instruction is to be executed. Write the routine necessary to perform the above operations.

PROBLEMS

1. Rewrite the program for Problem 4, Chapter 14, using a **DISPLAY** verb to print the error message.

2. A control card is used to indicate the type of update to be performed. If the first column of the card is equal to '1', then the detail tape contains additions to the master file. The detail tape, then, contains Invoice numbers which do not match the master tape Invoice numbers. Both tapes are in Invoice number sequence. If a matching Invoice number exists, display the detail record with an appropriate error message. If the first column of the control card is to equal to '2', then the detail tape contains Invoice numbers which must match the Master tape entries for the updating of Quantity in stock (add **QUANTITY IN STOCK** from both files to obtain output). If a detail tape record does not match a master tape record, then display the detail record with a corresponding error message. Note that all master tape records need not be updated. The format of the detail and master tape and output is as follows:

   1–5   Invoice number
   6–9   Quantity on hand
   10–20 Item description

   Labels are standard; blocking factor is 100.

Additional Procedure Division Entries

A. COMPUTE STATEMENT

Many business applications of programming require a small number of arithmetic operations. Such applications operate on large volumes of input-output with little emphasis on numeric calculations. For this type of processing, the four arithmetic verbs discussed in Chapter 8 are adequate.

If, however, complex or extensive arithmetic operations are required in a program, the use of the four arithmetic statements may prove cumbersome. The COMPUTE verb provides a compact method of performing arithmetic operations.

The COMPUTE statement uses arithmetic **symbols** rather than arithmetic **verbs**. The following symbols may be utilized in a COMPUTE statement:

    + corresponds to ADD
    — corresponds to SUBTRACT
    * corresponds to MULTIPLY
    / corresponds to DIVIDE
    ** denotes EXPONENTIATION
       (no corresponding COBOL verb
       exists)

The following examples illustrate the use of the COMPUTE verb.

Examples

    (1) COMPUTE TAX = .05 * AMT
    (2) COMPUTE A   = B * C / D
    (3) COMPUTE NET = AMT — .05 * AMT

Note that the COMPUTE statement has a data-name to the left of, or preceding, the equal sign. The value computed from the arithmetic expression to the right of the equal sign **is made equal to** the data field.

Thus, if AMT = 200 in Example 1, TAX will equal $200 \times .05$, or 10, at the end of the operation. The original contents of TAX before the COMPUTE is executed is not retained. The fields specified to the right of the equal sign remain unchanged.

Example 4: COMPUTE A = B + C — D

	Contents before operation	Contents after operation
A	100	95
B	80	80
C	20	20
D	5	5

The fields employed in the arithmetic expression, B, C, and D, remain unchanged after the COMPUTE is performed. A is made equal to the result of B + C — D. The previous contents of A does not affect the operation. 95 is moved to A.

The fields specified after the equal sign in a COMPUTE statement may be literals or data-names. Literals need not be defined anywhere else in the program but data fields must be given specifications in the DATA DIVISION. All fields and literals in a COMPUTE statement must be numeric.

Note that the **COMPUTE** statement may call for more than one operation. In Example 2, both multiplication and division operations are performed. The following **two** statements are equivalent to the single **COMPUTE** statement in Example 2:

> **MULTIPLY B BY C GIVING A.**
> **DIVIDE D INTO A.**

Thus the **COMPUTE** statement has the advantage of performing more than one arithmetic operation with a single statement. For this reason, it is often less cumbersome to use **COMPUTE** statements to code complex arithmetic functions.

Thus **ADD**, **SUBTRACT**, **MULTIPLY**, and **DIVIDE** correspond to the arithmetic symbols, $+$, $-$, $*$, and $/$, respectively. We may exponentiate a number, or raise it to a power, with the use of the arithmetic symbol $**$. No COBOL verb corresponds to this operation. Thus **A ** 2** is identical to the mathematical expression A^2 or $A \times$

contents of **A** in the field called **B**. This is the same as saying **MOVE A TO B**. Thus, in a **COMPUTE** statement, we may have one of the three entries below following the equal sign.

1. An arithmetic expression
   e.g., **COMPUTE SALARY = HRS * RATE**

2. A literal
   e.g., **COMPUTE TAX = .05**

3. A data-name
   e.g., **COMPUTE FLDA = FLDB**

The **ROUNDED** and **ON SIZE ERROR** options may be used with the **COMPUTE** statement. The rules governing the use of these clauses in **ADD**, **SUBTRACT**, **MULTIPLY**, and **DIVIDE** operations apply to **COMPUTE** statements as well.

To round the results in a **COMPUTE** statement to the specifications of the receiving field, we use the **ROUNDED** option as follows:

$$\underline{\text{COMPUTE}} \text{ (data-name) } \underline{\text{ROUNDED}} = \begin{bmatrix} \text{arithmetic expression} \\ \text{literal} \\ \text{data-name} \end{bmatrix}$$

A. A ** 3 is the same as A^3 or $A \times A \times A$. To find B^4 and place the results in C, we have **COMPUTE C = B ** 4**.

COBOL rules for spacing are crucial when using the **COMPUTE** statement. All arithmetic symbols must be **preceded and followed** by a space. This rule applies to the equal sign as well. Thus the formula $A = B + C + D^2$ converts to the following **COMPUTE** statement:

C	O	M	P	U	T	E		A		=		B		+		C		+		D		*	*		2

Thus far, we have used arithmetic expressions to the right of the equal sign. We may also have literals or data-names as the **only** entry to the right of the equal sign. To say **COMPUTE A = 10.3** is the same as saying **MOVE 10.3 TO A**. We are placing the literal **10.3** in the field **A**. Similarly, to say **COMPUTE B = A** places the

Example 5

(a) **COMPUTE A = B + C + D**
(b) **COMPUTE A ROUNDED = B + C + D**

B		C		D	
P	C	P	C	P	C
9V99	105	9V99	210	9V99	684

Result in A
P   C

99V9

Example 5 (a)   099
Example 5 (b)   100

To test for an arithmetic overflow when the receiving field lacks enough integer positions for the result, we use an **ON SIZE ERROR** test. It is used in conjunction with a **COMPUTE** statement:

> COMPUTE (data-name) = $\begin{bmatrix} \text{literal} \\ \text{arithmetic expression} \\ \text{data-name} \end{bmatrix}$
>
> ON SIZE ERROR (imperative statement)

Example 6

COMPUTE A = 105 − 3

results in an overflow condition if **A** has a PICTURE of **99**. The computed result is 102. To place 102 in **A**, a two-position numeric field, results in the truncation of the most significant digit, the hundreds position. Thus 02 will be placed in **A**. To protect against truncation of high order integer positions, we use an **ON SIZE ERROR** test:

COMPUTE A = 105 − 3 ON SIZE ERROR
GO TO ERROR-RTN.

Thus the complete format for a COM-PUTE statement is:

any number is that number raised to the 1/2 or .5 power. Thus $\sqrt{25} = 25^{.5} = 5$.

Since we cannot use square root symbols in COBOL, the square root of any number will be represented as the number raised to the .5 power, or exponentiated by .5.

Formula: $C = \sqrt{A}$
COBOL Equivalent:
COMPUTE C = A ** .5

The order of evaluation of arithmetic operations is crucial in a **COMPUTE** statement. Consider the following example.

Example 7: COMPUTE D = A + B / C

> COMPUTE (data-name) $\{$ROUNDED$\}$ = $\begin{bmatrix} \text{literal} \\ \text{arithmetic expression} \\ \text{data-name} \end{bmatrix}$
>
> $\{$ON SIZE ERROR (imperative statement)$\}$

The primary advantage of a **COMPUTE** statement is that several arithmetic operations may be performed with one command.

The data-name preceding the equal sign is made equal to the literal, data field, or arithmetic expression to the right of the equal sign. Thus the following two arithmetic expressions are identical:

ADD 1 TO A.
COMPUTE A = A + 1

COMPUTE statements are easily written to express formulae. While the formula: $C = A^2 + B^2$ will result in several arithmetic operations, only one **COMPUTE** statement is required:

COMPUTE C = A ** 2 + B ** 2

There is no COBOL arithmetic symbol to perform a **square root** operation. Mathematically, however, the square root of

Depending upon the order of evaluation of arithmetic operations, one of the following is the mathematical equivalent of the above:

(a) $D = \dfrac{A + B}{C}$ (b) $D = A + \dfrac{B}{C}$

Note that (a) and (b) are **not** identical. If $A = 3$, $B = 6$, and $C = 3$, the results of the **COMPUTE** statement evaluated according to the formula in (a) is 3 and, according to the formula in (b), is 5.

The hierarchy of arithmetic operations is as follows:

1. **
2. * or /
3. + or −

Exponentiation operations are evaluated, or performed, first. Multiplication and division operations follow any exponentiation and precede addition or subtraction operations. If there is more than one multiplication or division operation, they are evaluated from left to right. Addition and subtraction are evaluated last, also reading from left to right.

Thus, **COMPUTE A = C + D ** 2** results in the following order of evaluation.

1. **D ** 2**   Exponentiation
2. **C + (D ** 2)**   Addition

The formula, then, is $A = C + D^2$, **not** $A = (C + D)^2$.

COMPUTE S = T * D + E / F results in the following order of evaluation:

1. **T * D**   Multiplication
2. **E / F**   Division
3. **(T * D) + (E /F)**   Addition

The formula, then, is $A = T \times D + \dfrac{E}{F}$.

Thus, in Example 7, **COMPUTE D = A + B / C** is calculated as follows.

1. **B / C**
2. **A + B / C**

The formula, then, is $D = A + \dfrac{B}{C}$ or formula (b).

To alter the order of evaluation in a **COMPUTE** statement, parentheses are used. Parentheses supersede all hierarchy rules.

To compute $C = \dfrac{A + B}{3}$ is **not** performed by

COMPUTE C = A + B / 3. The result of the latter operation is $C = A + \dfrac{B}{3}$. To divide the **sum** of A and B by 3, we must use parentheses:

COMPUTE C = (A + B) / 3

All operations within parentheses are evaluated first. Thus we have:

1. **A + B**
2. **(A + B) / 3**

Example 8: Suppose A, B, and C are three sides of a right triangle, C being the hypotenuse (side opposite the right angle). A and B have assigned values. We wish to compute C according to the Pythagorean Theorem as follows:

$$C = \sqrt{A^2 + B^2}$$

COMPUTE C ROUNDED =
      (A ** 2 + B ** 2) ** .5

Example 9: We wish to obtain **NET = GROSS — DISCOUNT** where **DISCOUNT = .03 × GROSS:**

COMPUTE NET = GROSS — .03 * GROSS

No parentheses are needed to alter the hierarchy, but including them for clarity is not incorrect:

COMPUTE NET =
      GROSS — (.03 * GROSS)

A simpler method of obtaining the correct result is:

COMPUTE NET = .97 * GROSS

EXERCISES

1. The **COMPUTE** statement uses arithmetic _____ rather than arithmetic verbs.
    *****
    symbols

2. The one symbol that may be used in a **COMPUTE** statement for which there is no corresponding arithmetic verb in COBOL is _____ which denotes the operation of _____.

*****

**

exponentiation

3. The word directly following the verb **COMPUTE** must be a _____.

*****

data-name

4. The result of the arithmetic expression to the right of the equal sign is _____ to the above data-name.

*****

made equal

5. The most important advantage of a **COMPUTE** statement is that it may _____.

*****

perform more than one arithmetic operation with a single command

6. What, if anything, is wrong with the following **COMPUTE** statements?

*****

   (a) **COMPUTE A = B + C ROUNDED**
   (b) **COMPUTE A = 10.5**
   (c) **COMPUTE OVERTIME-PAY = (HOURS — 40.) * 1.5**
   (d) **COMPUTE E = A * B / * C + D**
   (e) **COMPUTE X = (4 / 3) * PI * (R ** 3)**
   (f) **COMPUTE X + Y = A**
   (g) **COMPUTE 3.14 = PI**

   *****

   (a) **ROUNDED** follows the receiving field: **COMPUTE A ROUNDED = B + C**
   (b) Okay.
   (c) **40.** is not a valid numeric literal; numeric literals may not end with a decimal point.
   (d) **/*** may not appear together; each symbol must be preceded by and followed by a data field or a numeric literal.
   (e) Okay.
   (f) Arithmetic expressions must follow the equal sign and not precede it: **COMPUTE A = X + Y.**
   (g) Data-names, not literals, must follow the word **COMPUTE: COMPUTE PI = 3.14.**

7. Do the following pairs of operations perform the same function:

   (a) COMPUTE SUM = 0
       MOVE ZEROS TO SUM
   (b) COMPUTE A = A — 2
       SUBTRACT 2 FROM A.
   (c) COMPUTE X = A * B — C * D
       COMPUTE X = (A * B) — (C * D)
   (d) COMPUTE Y = A — B * C — D
       COMPUTE Y = (A — B) * (C — D)

   *****

   (a) Same.
   (b) Same.
   (c) Same.
   (d) First $= A - (B \times C) - D$
       Second $= (A - B) \times (C - D)$
       Not equivalent

8. Using a COMPUTE statement, find the average of A, B, and C.
   *****

   COMPUTE AVERAGE = (A + B + C) / 3

9. Using a COMPUTE statement, find total wages = rate × reg. hrs. + (1.5 × rate × overtime hours). Two fields are supplied: RATE and HRS-WORKED. Overtime hours is hours worked in excess of 40 hours. (Assume everyone works at least 40 hours.)
   *****

   COMPUTE WAGES = RATE * 40 + 1.5 * RATE * (HRS-WORKED — 40)

B. MOVE CORRESPONDING STATEMENT

The MOVE CORRESPONDING statement is an option of the simple MOVE command. The format is as follows:

```
MOVE CORRESPONDING (group-item-1)

              TO  (group-item-2)
```

You will recall that a group item is a data field or record that is further subdivided into elementary entries. In the format statement above, all items within group-item-1 that have the same names as corresponding items in group-item-2 are moved.

Example:

   MOVE CORRESPONDING RECORD-1 TO RECORD-2

With this option of the MOVE command, all data fields in RECORD-1 that have the same names as data fields in RECORD-2 are moved. The same named data fields in RECORD-2 need not be in any specific order. Any fields of the sending record, RECORD-1, not matched by the same named fields in the receiving record, RECORD-2, are ignored. Sending fields, as in all MOVE operations, remain unchanged.

Sending Field

			Contents before MOVE	Contents after MOVE
01	RECORD-1.			
	02 NAME	PICTURE X(6).	Arnold	Arnold
	02 AMT	PICTURE 999V99.	10000	10000
	02 TRANS	PICTURE X(5).	12345	12345
	02 DATE	PICTURE 9(4).	0670	0670

Receiving Field

			Contents before MOVE	Contents after MOVE
01	RECORD-2.			
	02 NAME	PICTURE X(6).	Peters	Arnold
	02 DATE	PICTURE 9(4).	0000	0670
	02 AMT	PICTURE 999V99.	00000	10000
	02 DISC	PICTURE V99.	10	10

Thus we see that the MOVE CORRESPOND-ING performs a series of simple moves. All fields in RECORD-1 that have the same name as fields in RECORD-2 are moved. The following MOVE instructions could be used in place of the MOVE CORRE-SPONDING statement to produce the same results:

> MOVE NAME OF RECORD-1 TO NAME
> OF RECORD-2.
> MOVE AMT OF RECORD-1 TO AMT OF
> RECORD-2.
> MOVE DATE OF RECORD-1 TO DATE OF
> RECORD-2.

NAME, AMT, and DATE of RECORD-2 are not in the same order as they appear in RECORD-1. The contents of these fields in RECORD-1 are, nevertheless, transmitted to RECORD-2, regardless of the order in which they appear.

Entries in RECORD-2 for which there are no corresponding items in RECORD-1 are unaffected by the MOVE CORRESPONDING statement. DISC, a field in RECORD-2, re-tains its original contents, since there is no corresponding DISC field in RECORD-1.

Entries in RECORD-1 for which there is no corresponding item in RECORD-2 are not transmitted. TRANS, a field in RECORD-1, is not moved, since there is no corre-sponding TRANS field in RECORD-2. In all cases, sending field items remain un-changed after the MOVE.

All rules for MOVE operations apply to MOVE CORRESPONDING statements. For numeric MOVE operations:

1. Data is right justified in the receiv-ing field; e.g., 075 moved to a two-position numeric field is transmitted as 75.

2. If the receiving field is larger than the sending field, high order positions are replaced with zeros; e.g., 524 moved to a four-position numeric field is transmitted as 0524.

For nonnumeric (alphabetic and alpha-numeric) MOVE operations:

1. Data is left-justified in the receiving field; e.g., ABC moved to a two-position nonnumeric field is transmitted as AB.

2. If the receiving field is larger than the sending field, low order positions are replaced with spaces; e.g., ABC moved to a four position nonnumeric field is trans-mitted as ABCb.

A numeric field may be moved to an alphanumeric field, but the reverse is not valid.

Example 2:

MOVE CORRESPONDING IN-REC TO OUT-REC.

Contents

```
01  IN-REC.
    02  DATE  PICTURE X(15).    JANUARY 15, 1971
    02  AMT   PICTURE 999.      023
    02  HRS   PICTURE 99.       40
```

Contents
after
MOVE

```
01  OUT-REC.
    02  DATE  PICTURE X(10).    JANUARY 15
    02  AMT   PICTURE 99.       23
    02  HRS   PICTURE 999.      040
```

The MOVE CORRESPONDING option is most often used to **edit** incoming fields. We edit input data by moving it to a report item in the receiving field.

Example 3:

```
MOVE  CORRESPONDING  REC-IN  TO
PRINT-OUT.
```

```
01  REC-IN.
    02  NAME PICTURE X(6).       JEADAMS
    02  AMT  PICTURE 999V99.     57524
```

Note that when using the MOVE CORRESPONDING option, all data-names which will be transmitted from the sending field must have the same name as corresponding items in the receiving field.

Consider the following input and output areas:

```
01  RECORD-B.
    02  NAME    PICTURE X(10).
    02  DB-AMT  PICTURE 99.
    02  CR-AMT  PICTURE 99.
```

In this case, it would be inefficient to use the MOVE CORRESPONDING option. It is more advantageous to say:

MOVE RECORD-A TO RECORD-B.

since **all** items in RECORD-A are identical in size and relative location to items in RECORD-B.

The MOVE CORRESPONDING option is used to replace a series of simple MOVE

```
01  PRINT-OUT.
    02  FILLER  PICTURE X.
    02  NAME    PICTURE XBXBXXXX.
    02  AMT     PICTURE $ZZZ.99.
```

instructions. All fields in the sending area are moved to the same named fields in the receiving area. All rules for MOVE operations hold when using the MOVE CORRESPONDING option. Note, however, that fields to be moved **must** have the same name in the sending and receiving areas.

```
01  RECORD-A.
    02  NAME    PICTURE X(10).
    02  DB-AMT  PICTURE 99.
    02  CR-AMT  PICTURE 99.
```

EXERCISES

1. With a **MOVE CORRESPONDING** statement, all fields in the sending area that _____ will be moved to the receiving area.
   *****
   have the same name as items in the receiving area

2. The items in both areas (need not, must) be in the same order.
   *****
   need not

3. Any item of the sending record or field that is not matched by the same named item in the receiving area is _____.
   *****
   ignored

4. The contents of the sending fields are _____ after the **MOVE** operation.
   *****
   unchanged

5. Fill in the missing entries:

MOVE CORRESPONDING RECORDA TO RECORDB.

		Contents before MOVE	Contents after MOVE					Contents after MOVE
01	RECORDA.				01	RECORDB.		
	02 FLDA PICTURE XX.	AB	_____			02 FLDA	PICTURE XXX.	_____
	02 AMT PICTURE 9(5).	02345	_____			02 DATE	PICTURE 99.	_____
	02 DATE PICTURE 9(4).	0171	_____			02 AMT	PICTURE 9(6).	_____
	02 NAME PICTURE X(5).	MARIE	_____			02 NAME	PICTURE XXX.	_____
*****								

Contents after MOVE	Contents after MOVE
AB	ABV
02345	45
0171	000171
MARIE	MAR

C. NESTED CONDITIONALS

You will recall that the format for a simple conditional is:

```
IF (condition) {THEN} (statement-1)

   { ELSE
     OTHERWISE  (statement-2) } .
```

In a simple conditional, statement-1 and statement-2 are **imperative.** That is, they are executable commands and do not themselves test conditions. In the conditional, IF A = B GO TO RTN-5 ELSE ADD 5 TO B, the statements GO TO RTN-5 and ADD 5 TO B are imperative. (Note that THEN is an optional word in a conditional.)

If, instead, statement-1 and statement-2 above are themselves conditional statements, we have a **nested conditional.**

Example 1

IF AMT = 6 THEN IF TAX = 10 GO TO Y ELSE GO TO Z ELSE GO TO W.

The above example conforms to the format statement. Statement-1, however, within the format, is a conditional:

$$\text{IF}\begin{Bmatrix} \text{condition} \\ \downarrow \\ \text{AMT} = 6 \end{Bmatrix}\text{THEN}\begin{Bmatrix} \text{(statement-1)} \\ \downarrow \\ \text{IF TAX} = 10\ \text{GO TO Y ELSE GO TO Z} \end{Bmatrix}\text{ELSE}\begin{Bmatrix} \text{(statement-2)} \\ \downarrow \\ \text{GO TO W.} \end{Bmatrix}$$

The clause (IF TAX = 10 GO TO Y ELSE GO TO Z) is considered statement-1 in the above. The nested conditional tests several conditions with a single statement:

1. If AMT is not equal to 6, a branch to W occurs.

If AMT equals 6, the second condition is tested.

2. If AMT = 6 and TAX = 10, a branch to Y occurs.

3. If AMT = 6 and TAX is not equal to 10, a branch to Z occurs.

A nested conditional is a shortcut method of writing a series of simple conditionals. The nested conditional in Example 1 may be written as follows:

IF AMT IS NOT EQUAL TO 6 GO TO W.
IF TAX = 10 GO TO Y ELSE GO TO Z.

It may also be written, using compound conditionals, as follows:

IF AMT = 6 AND TAX = 10 GO TO Y.
IF AMT = 6 AND TAX IS NOT EQUAL TO 10 GO TO Z.
GO TO W.

In addition to minimizing programming effort, nested conditionals have the added advantage of testing conditions just as they appear in a decision table or in an explanatory note.

Example 2

If A = B and C = D, branch to RTN-1.
If A = B and C is not equal to D, branch to RTN-2.
If A is not equal to B, branch to RTN-3.

Written as a nested conditional, we have:

IF A = B THEN IF C = D GO TO RTN-1 ELSE GO TO RTN-2 ELSE GO TO RTN-3.

Note that in a nested IF statement, the ELSE clause refers to the conditional statement directly preceding it. If an ELSE clause follows another ELSE clause, then the last one refers to the initial condition. The above statement is interpreted as follows:

IF A = B THEN (IF C = D GO TO RTN-1 ELSE GO TO RTN-2) ELSE GO TO RTN-3.

In the above, the initial condition, A = B, has the ELSE clause GO TO RTN-3 associated with it. Note, however, that ELSE clauses are optional in a conditional statement and need not be included.

Example 3

IF CREDIT-AMT = DEBIT-AMT THEN IF YEAR = 70 GO TO UPDATE-RTN ELSE GO TO INCORRECT-DATE-RTN.

Condition	Action
CREDIT-AMT IS NOT EQUAL TO DEBIT-AMT	NEXT SENTENCE
CREDIT-AMT = DEBIT-AMT and YEAR = 70	UPDATE-RTN
CREDIT-AMT = DEBIT-AMT AND YEAR IS NOT EQUAL TO 70	INCORRECT-DATE-RTN

The clause (ELSE GO TO INCORRECT-DATE-RTN) refers to the condition directly preceding it, IF YEAR = 70. Thus, if YEAR does not equal 70, the ELSE clause is executed and a branch to INCORRECT-DATE-RTN occurs.

Since there is only one ELSE clause, the condition IF A = B has no ELSE clause associated with it. If A is not equal to B, execution resumes with the next sentence.

Consider the following nested conditional:

IF (condition-1) THEN IF (condition-2) (statement-A) ELSE (statement-B) ELSE (statement-C).

The above performs the series of steps in the following flowchart:

Any number of conditions may be tested in a nested conditional. The only limitations are the size of the computer and the somewhat cumbersome nature of the statement. When too many conditions are specified in a nested conditional, it becomes difficult to follow. The programmer may use as many conditions in a NESTED IF statement as he considers feasible.

Example 4

IF MALE AND SINGLE ADD 1 TO SUM-1.
IF MALE AND MARRIED ADD 1 TO SUM-2.
IF FEMALE AND SINGLE ADD 1 TO SUM-3.
IF FEMALE AND MARRIED ADD 1 TO SUM-4.

MALE and FEMALE are condition-names referring to a sex field. SEX may contain only the codes for MALE and FEMALE.

SINGLE and MARRIED are condition-names referring to a marital status field. This field may contain only the codes for SINGLE and MARRIED.

Writing the above as a nested conditional, we have:

IF MALE THEN IF SINGLE ADD 1 TO SUM-1 ELSE ADD 1 TO SUM-2 ELSE IF SINGLE ADD 1 TO SUM-3 ELSE ADD 1 TO SUM-4.

Nested conditionals provide a method for writing a series of simple or compound conditions in a single statement. The programmer may represent tests with nested IF or simple IF statements. Observe that the following two routines perform identical functions:

(1) IF A = 1 AND B = 2 MOVE X TO Y.
    IF A = 1 AND B IS NOT EQUAL TO 2 MOVE X TO Z.
(2) IF A = 1 THEN IF B = 2 MOVE X TO Y ELSE MOVE X TO Z.

The nested conditional is a shortcut method for writing IF statements and is convenient for restating a series of conditions in a single statement. If not fully understood, however, it may lead to rampant logic errors. The programmer must note that any series of conditions may be represented by simple or compound conditionals, without the use of nested conditionals. If nested conditionals prove too cumbersome, he may use a series of simple statements.

EXERCISES

1. Using the following chart, write a nested conditional to perform the stated operations:

X	Y	Operation
1	1	ADD A TO B
1	Not = 1	GO TO RTN-2
Not = 1	A N Y T H I N G	SUBTRACT A FROM B

*****

IF X = 1 THEN IF Y = 1 ADD A TO B ELSE GO TO RTN-2 ELSE SUBTRACT A FROM B.

2. Using the following chart, write a nested conditional to perform the stated operations:

Y	Z	Operation
3	Not = 5	GO TO PATHA
3	5	GO TO PATHB
Not = 1	Anything	GO TO PATHC

*****

IF Y = 3 THEN IF Z IS NOT EQUAL TO 5 GO TO PATHA ELSE GO TO PATHB ELSE GO TO PATHC.

3. In the following statement, if FLDX = 3 and FLDY = 4, a branch to _____ will occur:

IF FLDX = 3 THEN IF FLDY = 5 GO TO Y ELSE GO TO Z ELSE GO TO W.

*****

Z

4. Using the above conditional, a branch to _____ will occur if FLDX = 4 and FLDY = 5.

*****

W

5. Using the above conditional, a branch to _____ will occur if FLDX = 3 and FLDY = 5.

*****

Y

D. EXAMINE STATEMENT

The **EXAMINE** statement performs two major functions.

(a) It is used to replace certain occurrences of a given character with another character.

Replacing blanks or spaces with zeros is a common application of the **EXAMINE** verb. Blanks, you will recall, are invalid in a numeric field but often are erroneously included to imply a zero balance or amount. Before performing an arithmetic operation on a field, an **EXAMINE** statement is often executed replacing all blanks with zeros.

(b) It is used to count the number of occurrences of a given character in a data item.

There are two formats of the **EXAMINE** statement. Format 1 may be used to perform **both** functions specified above. That is, Format 1 will replace a given character with another character while simultaneously counting the number of times such replacement is performed. In addition, Format 1 may be used to perform function b alone. That is, this option may perform just the counting function:

Format 1

```
EXAMINE (data-name) TALLYING
        ⎡ ALL         ⎤
        ⎢ LEADING     ⎥
        ⎣ UNTIL FIRST ⎦
'character-1' {REPLACING BY 'character-2'}.
```

Examples

(1) EXAMINE RECORD-1 TALLYING ALL
    '0'.
(2) EXAMINE ITEM-1 TALLYING LEADING
    '*' REPLACING BY '-'.
(3) EXAMINE ITEM-2 TALLYING UNTIL
    FIRST '1'.

This format of the **EXAMINE** statement will **always** count specified occurrences of character-1. Character-1 must be a single nonnumeric character enclosed in quotation marks, or a **figurative constant. ZERO, SPACE, '9', 'X'** are all valid entries for character-1.

As indicated, specified occurrences of character-1 will be counted using this format of the **EXAMINE** verb. The tallied count is placed in a five-position integer field called **TALLY**. **TALLY** is a COBOL reserved word and need not be defined in the **DATA DIVISION**. (If several **EXAMINE** statements are used in the same program it is not necessary to initialize **TALLY** at zero each time, since each **EXAMINE** command automatically clears its content.) **TALLY** may be accessed after an **EXAMINE** statement:

EXAMINE ITEM-A TALLYING ALL SPACES. IF TALLY IS GREATER THAN ZERO GO TO ERR-RTN.

The above routine will branch to an error routine if there are **any** spaces in **ITEM-A**.

The **REPLACING** clause in Format 1 is an optional entry. If included, a count will be taken as well as the replacement of given occurrences of character-1 with character-2. Character-2 must also be a single nonnumeric character or a figurative constant.

One of the three COBOL expressions, **ALL, LEADING,** or **UNTIL FIRST** is required when using **OPTION1:**

(a) If **ALL** is specified, **every** occurrence of character-1 in the data field will be counted and replaced, if the **REPLACING** clause is indicated.

Examples

	Item-B		Resulting Value of TALLY
	Before	After	
EXAMINE ITEM-B TALLYING ALL '0'.	102050	102050	3
EXAMINE ITEM-B TALLYING ALL '0' REPLACING BY ' '.	102050	1 2 5	3

(b) If **LEADING** is specified, all occurrences of character-1 **preceding any other character** will be tallied and replaced, if the **REPLACING** clause is indicated.

Examples

	Item-C		Resulting Value of TALLY
	Before	After	
EXAMINE ITEM-C TALLYING LEADING '9'.	99129	99129	2
EXAMINE ITEM-C TALLYING LEADING SPACES REPLACING BY ZERO.	⌿⌿120	00120	2

(c) If **UNTIL FIRST** is specified, **all characters preceding the first occurrence of character-1** will be tallied and replaced, if the **REPLACING** clause is indicated.

Examples

	Item-D		Resulting Value of TALLY
	Before	After	
EXAMINE ITEM-D TALLYING UNTIL FIRST '0'.	12300	12300	3
EXAMINE ITEM-D TALLYING UNTIL FIRST '9' REPLACING BY '0'.	12349	00009	4

Format 2 of the **EXAMINE** statement will replace specified occurrences of a given character with another character. It will **not** tally the occurrences of any character.

Format 2

```
EXAMINE (data-name) REPLACING
        ⎡ ALL         ⎤
        ⎢ LEADING     ⎥
        ⎢ UNTIL FIRST ⎥
        ⎣ FIRST       ⎦
        'character-1' BY 'character-2'.
```

Character-1 and character-2 must, as in Format 1, be single nonnumeric characters enclosed in quotation marks, or figurative constants.

ALL, LEADING, and **UNTIL FIRST** have the same meaning as previously noted. If **FIRST** is specified in Format 2, then the first occurrence of character-1 will be replaced by character-2. That is, a single character replacement will occur if character-1 is present in the data-field.

Examples

	Item-E	
	Before	After
EXAMINE ITEM-E REPLACING ALL '1' BY '2'.	112111	222222
EXAMINE ITEM-E REPLACING LEADING '1' BY '2'.	112111	222111
EXAMINE ITEM-E REPLACING UNTIL FIRST '2' BY '3'.	112111	332111
EXAMINE ITEM-E REPLACING FIRST 'X' BY 'Y'.	ABCXYZ	ABCYYZ

The COBOL reserved word, TALLY, is unaffected by this format of EXAMINE statement, since no counting operation is performed.

Note that when using either format, rules for inserting characters in data fields apply. We cannot, for example, replace an 'A' in an alphabetic data field that has a PICTURE of A's, with a '1'. A '1' is not a valid alphabetic character.

EXERCISES

1. The two major functions of the EXAMINE statement are _____ and _____.
*****
to replace certain characters with other characters
to count the number of occurrences of a given character in a data-item

2. The field that is used to count the number of occurrences of a character in an EXAMINE statement is called _____.
*****
TALLY

3. TALLY (must, need not) be defined in the DATA DIVISION.
*****
need not

4. TALLY is a _____ field.
*****
five-position numeric (integer)

In the following statements, fill in the missing columns, where applicable.

	Statement	FLDX Before	After	Value of TALLY
5.	EXAMINE FLDX TALLYING ALL '0'.	10050		
6.	EXAMINE FLDX TALLYING ALL ZEROS REPLACING BY SPACES.	10050		
7.	EXAMINE FLDX TALLYING LEADING ZEROS.	00057		
8.	EXAMINE FLDX TALLYING UNTIL FIRST '9'.	00579		

9.   EXAMINE FLDX TALLYING UNTIL   00579
      FIRST '9' REPLACING BY '8'.

10.   EXAMINE FLDX REPLACING UNTIL   ABCXY
      FIRST 'X' BY SPACE.

*****

	After	TALLY
5.	10050	3
6.	1ø ø5ø	3
7.	00057	3
8.	00579	4
9.	88889	4
10.	ø ø øXY	not applicable

E. LIBRARY STATEMENTS— AN OVERVIEW

It is possible to include prewritten source program entries in a COBOL program. A master transaction file, for example, with numerous field descriptions can be included in a **library** which may be accessed by the programmer. A COBOL program can incorporate any library file by **calling** for it. Similarly, a complex arithmetic routine may be included in a library. This routine may then be called for in any COBOL program.

Thus the COBOL programmer need not recode previously defined entries. A single File Description or a single COBOL routine may be utilized in many programs by placing it in a library and calling for it when needed. **Files** are accessed from the library by the **COPY** statement and **procedures** are accessed by the INCLUDE statement.

COPY Statement. The COPY clause permits the COBOL programmer to include prewritten **DATA DIVISION** or **ENVIRON-MENT DIVISION** entries in his source program. The format for copying files is as follows:

> FD (file-name) COPY (library-name)

The file-name is the programmer-supplied name of the file as it is known in the present program. It is the name defined in the **ENVIRONMENT DIVISION** of the current program. The library-name is the name of the file as it is known in the library.

Example:

> FD FILE-1 COPY FILE-X

All specifications, including File Descriptions (FD) and record descriptions for FILE-X are called for and printed on the COBOL listing of the current program.

INCLUDE Statement. The INCLUDE statement permits the COBOL programmer to utilize prewritten procedures in the **PROCEDURE DIVISION** of his source program. INCLUDE, itself, is a statement written in the **PROCEDURE DIVISION** as follows:

> INCLUDE (library-name)

The routine specified by the library-name will be accessed and printed on the COBOL listing of the current program. In effect, it is now part of the procedures of the current program.

EXERCISES

1. A single File Description or a single COBOL routine may be utilized in many programs by placing it in a _____ and _____ for it when needed.

   *****

   library
   calling

2. The _____ clause permits the COBOL programmer to include prewritten DATA DIVISION or ENVIRONMENT DIVISION entries in his programs.

   *****

   COPY

3. The format for copying files is _____.

   *****

   FD (file-name) COPY (library-name)

4. The _____ statement permits the COBOL programmer to utilize prewritten procedures in the PROCEDURE DIVISION of his source program.

   *****

   INCLUDE

5. To include a prewritten stacker-selection procedure called STACK-SELECT in a program, the PROCEDURE DIVISION entry _____ is used.

   *****

   INCLUDE STACK-SELECT

REVIEW QUESTIONS

Make necessary corrections to each of the following (1–5):

1. COMPUTE X = Y + Z ROUNDED.

2. COMPUTE Z ROUNDING = A + 7 ON SIZE ERROR GO TO ERR-RTN.

3. EXAMINE FLDA REPLACING ALL 8 BY 9.

4. EXAMINE FLDB REPLACING ALL 'X' WITH 'Y'.

5. MOVE GROUP-A CORRESPONDING TO GROUP-B.

6. Write a statement to calculate: $X = \dfrac{(M \times N)^2}{T}$.

7. Use a **COMPUTE** statement to add 1 to **A**.

8. Use a nested **IF** statement to perform the following:

A	B	Operation
Not = 7	Not = 3	GO TO RTNC.
Not = 7	= 3	GO TO RTND.
= 7	Anything	GO TO RTNE.

Rewrite the routine with a series of simple conditionals.

9. Write an **EXAMINE** statement to determine the number of J's in a data field, called **ITEM**. In the same statement, replace the J's with blanks. If the number of J's exceed ten, branch to **ERR-RTN**.

10. Write an **EXAMINE** statement to determine the number of characters that precede the first nine in a field called **AMOUNT**.

PROBLEMS

1. Write a program to compute compound interest from the following formula using the **COMPUTE** verb: (same as problem 1, Chapter 15).

$$P_n = P_0 (1 + r)^n$$

P_n = amount of principal after n periods of investment of P_0 at rate r/period

The input is a card file with the following format:

1–6   Principal P_0
7–8   Rate .xx   r
9–80 Not used

Output is a printed report with compound interest calculated from periods 1 year to 10 years (n = 1, 2, .. 10):

```
              PRINCIPAL—xxxxxx
                   RATE—.xx
          PERIODS            AMOUNT
             1             xxxxxx.xx
             2             xxxxxx.xx
             .
             .
            10             xxxxxx.xx
```

All amount fields must be edited; allow for form overflow.

2. Write an edit program using the following format for card input:

1–20 Name
21–35 Address
36–40 Quantity purchased
41–47 Amount owed xxxxx.xx
48–51 Date of purchase Mo/Yr
52–55 Transaction number
56–80 Not used

Output is a tape file with the following format:

1–4   Transaction number
5–9   Quantity purchased
10–16 Amount owed
17–36 Name
37–51 Address
52–55 Date

Labels are standard; blocking factor = 40.

Notes

1. Use **MOVE CORRESPONDING** statement to move input data to output.
2. For all numeric fields (quantity, amount owed, date of purchase, transaction number), replace blanks with zeros.

(**Hint.** Redefine fields as alphanumeric to test for blanks.)

3. Economic order quantity is used in inventory control to determine what is the most economical quantity of a product for the company to produce. Data cards with the following format will serve as input:

1–5   Product number
6–20 Product name
21–26 Total yearly production requirement   R
27–31 Inventory carrying cost/unit   I
32–36 Setup cost/order   S

The economic order quantity Q may be determined from the formula

$$Q = \sqrt{\frac{2RS}{I}}$$

Print the product name and the economic order quantity for each item. Also indicate the product with the **least** economic order quantity.

4. Write a program to create utility bills.

Charges: First 100 kilowatt hours (kwh) $.05/kwh
              Next 200 kwh   .04/kwh
              All other   .03/kwh

The input consists of a master tape and a detail card file.

Master Tape File	**Detail Card File**
1–20 Customer name	1–20 Customer name
21–25 Previous balance xxx.xx	21–40 Address
26 Credit rating	41–44 kwh used
	45–80 Not used

standard labels
blocking factor = 10

The two input files are used to create a utility punched card bill with the following format:

> 1–20 Name
> 21–40 Address
> 41–45 Amount owed
> 46–80 Message (if applicable)

Notes

There is one detail card for each tape record. For all matching tape and card records:

   (a) Calculate current charge from kwh on card.
   (b) Add to previous balance to obtain amount owed.
   (c) If credit rating is A, person may owe up to $50. If over $50, print REMINDER in message field.
   (d) If credit rating is B, person may owe up to $20.
       If person owes from $20–50, print REMINDER.
       If person owes over $50, print WARNING.
   (e) If credit rating is C, print REMINDER if person owes from $0–20 and WARNING if person owes over $20.

5. Rewrite program for Problem 1, Chapter 16, using the COMPUTE statement to handle all arithmetic operations.

6. Write a cost-of-item program using the following input tape format:

  1–20 Item description
21–24 Date purchased
25–29 Invoice number
30–34 Number of units bought
35–39 Cost of each item   xxx.xx
40–44 Labor   xxx.xx
45–49 Freight charges   xxx.xx
50–54 Sales tax   xxx.xx
55   Not used

Labels are standard; blocking factor = 50.

Print item description and unit price for each tape record.

$$\text{Unit price} = \text{Cost of item} + \frac{\text{Freight}}{\text{No. Units}} + \text{Labor} + \text{Overhead}$$

Overhead is equal to 20% of Labor.

Disk Operations

So far, we have discussed the use of magnetic tapes and punched cards to store information. Other common storage media include mass storage devices, such as magnetic disk, drum, and data cell. We will focus our discussion on the magnetic disk as a mass storage device.

The disk pack consists of several individual disks similar to phonograph records which rotate on a vertical shaft. The disks are made of metal and are coated on both sides with a magnetic oxide (see fig. 20-1).

Each surface of the disk is made of concentric tracks which are numbered. Each track is used to store information. A typical disk can store millions of characters of information. The actual capacity of any mass storage device varies among manufacturers.

A read-write head is used to read information from and record information onto any of the tracks on a given disk. Information can be located or accessed on a disk by specifying its "address." This is similar in concept to an "address" we can use to locate a given song on a phonograph record. By indicating the side of the record on which it appears and also what number it is on that side, we have specified an "address" by which we can access a particular song.

Because of some unique concepts employed in mass storage processing, a spe-cific kind of programming logic and terminology is required. Several factors, however, must be considered before we denote the COBOL programming specifications that are used with disk operations.

The ENVIRONMENT DIVISION will be altered somewhat in our discussion of disk. Since ENVIRONMENT DIVISION entries are not consistent among computers, the specifications denoted in this chapter may have to be altered for specific machines. The differences among computers are minor, however, and it should not be difficult to apply the disk concepts in the following pages to particular computers.[1]

This chapter will describe in detail the most widely used COBOL disk entries. In addition, illustrations of these entries will be provided which are specifically applicable to IBM S/360 Tape Operating System or Disk Operating System. Any computer with a similar configuration will employ the same concepts with only minor variations.

To simplify our discussion of disk, we will consider fixed length records only. Although variable length records may be created on a disk, the additional coding necessary is considered beyond the scope of this book.

[1] Appendix C lists sample ENVIRONMENT DIVI-SION entries for given computers.

Fig. 20-1   Magnetic disk drives (courtesy of IBM).

The following is the **SELECT** statement in its entirety, expanded to include **DIRECT-ACCESS** processing:

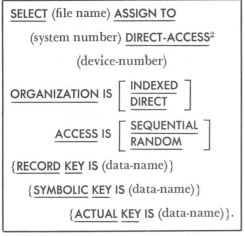

SELECT (file name) ASSIGN TO

(system number) DIRECT-ACCESS[2]

(device-number)

ORGANIZATION IS $\begin{bmatrix} \text{INDEXED} \\ \text{DIRECT} \end{bmatrix}$

ACCESS IS $\begin{bmatrix} \text{SEQUENTIAL} \\ \text{RANDOM} \end{bmatrix}$

{RECORD KEY IS (data-name)}

{SYMBOLIC KEY IS (data-name)}

{ACTUAL KEY IS (data-name)}.

You will recall that a disk is considered a DIRECT ACCESS file. The additional entries will be discussed below.

[2] Classification of devices as DIRECT-ACCESS and use of system numbers are not required for all computers.

A. ORGANIZATION OF DISK FILES

Information can be organized in several ways on a magnetic disk. The most common methods of organization are **STANDARD SEQUENTIAL, INDEXED SEQUENTIAL,**[3] and **DIRECT.**

A standard sequential file is one in which records that are placed on the disk in the order in which they are read are most often accessed in that order. Before creating a standard sequential disk file, we should first sort the input records into some meaningful sequence. Suppose, for example, a standard sequential disk file is to be established for all transactions of a given company. The input file should be sorted into some se-

[3] The standard COBOL compilers recognize only standard sequential and direct organization of files for mass storage devices. Since indexed sequential is used by some manufacturers and greatly adds to the organization capabilities of mass storage devices, we will include it in our discussion. Check the appropriate manual to determine if this option is applicable.

quence, such as transaction number or customer name, before creating the output file. In this way, it is relatively easy to locate a given record. We know, for example, that the record with transaction number 00345 is physically between transaction numbers 00344 and 00346.

You will recall that punched cards and magnetic tape **must** be processed in a sequential manner. We cannot easily access records on a tape, for example, in any order other than the one in which they appear. We must first read past 445 records to obtain the 446th. This method of access applies to standard sequential disk files as well.

When utilizing a standard sequential disk file, then, we are really using the disk as a high-speed tape. This is an efficient method of storage if there is a large number of records and all or most records are generally required for processing. If, instead, we process only isolated disk records, the access time of sequential processing is sometimes too great to make this method efficient.

The two other methods of disk file organization, indexed sequential and direct, may not be used with magnetic tape and punched cards. These methods can utilize the disk pack's ability to access records directly. By specifying the address of the records, information may be immediately accessed. That is, we need not pass the first 678 records to obtain the 679th; by specifying the actual disk address of the record, the read-write head can access it directly.

An **indexed sequential file** is one in which the control system of the computer establishes a table with a **key** field within the disk record equated to an actual disk address. This key field is defined by the programmer as a unique field within the record.

This concept is not unlike that of an index in the back of a book which has unique subjects (keys) and their corresponding page numbers (actual addresses).

The programmer states, for example, that the social security number of each record within the Employee File is to serve as a key field. This is appropriate, since all social security numbers are unique. The computer's control system establishes a table with each social security number and the address to which it is assigned on the disk. To access a particular record, then, the programmer specifies the social security number of the desired record, and the computer "looks up" its address and accesses it immediately. Thus, access time for indexed sequential files is significantly less than for standard sequential files when records are processed in a sequence other than the one in which they appear on the disk.

Another method of disk organization is called **DIRECT** organization. In this type of file, records are accessed by a key field which, through some arithmetic calculation, reduces to the actual address. Suppose, for example, the programmer states that **FIELDX**, when multiplied by 356 and then added to 89, produces the surface number of a record, and that **FIELDX**, when added to 15, produces the track number. Thus no table (which would have to be searched) is used for the actual address; rather, a simple mathematical calculation produces the actual address. This method of organization results in even less access time when records are processed randomly.

One disadvantage, however, of direct files is that it requires more programming effort than indexed sequential files. It is necessary for the programmer to supply the routine for converting the key fields into actual addresses. Similarly, the programmer must be aware of each address used on the disk. These problems are handled by the control system when indexed sequential files are processed.

The **ORGANIZATION** clause of a **SELECT** statement is used for disk processing. If the clause is omitted, organization is considered to be standard sequential. If **OR-**

GANIZATION **IS** INDEXED is used, an indexed sequential file is assumed. **ORGA-NIZATION IS DIRECT** applies to direct files.

B. METHOD OF ACCESS

For standard sequential disk files, no further entries are required in a **SELECT** clause. That is, processing is performed in exactly the same manner as was previously discussed with tape operations. Thus we will continue our discussion of disk files by denoting entries for random processing only. That is, our discussion will include indexed sequential and direct files only.

We may access indexed sequential files and direct files either **randomly** or **sequentially**.

Suppose, for example, we wish to create an indexed sequential or direct transaction file. The creation of this file will generally be performed by reading each input record and writing an output record. That is, output records are written sequentially (they are placed on the unit in the order in which they are read). In that case, we say **ACCESS IS SEQUENTIAL**. To create indexed sequential or direct files, access is always sequential.

Let us assume that this transaction file is created in transaction number sequence. If we wish to **read** records from this file, we may do so randomly or sequentially. To read records in some sequence other than the one in which they are written is called **random access**. Suppose transaction numbers that are multiples of ten denote special customers; to access only these records would be performed more efficiently by a **random** method. To access the transaction records in their original sequence of transaction numbers would be handled best by sequential access.

Thus indexed sequential or direct **input** files may be **accessed** or read sequentially or randomly. Indexed sequential or direct **output** files, however, must be **created** sequentially.

Example 1: Suppose we wish to read from a tax table file on disk. Detail employee card records have salary amount as a data field. For each of these records, we wish to find the corresponding tax amount from the table. The **SELECT** clauses in the **ENVIRONMENT DIVISION** would contain the following entries:

```
SELECT CARDS ASSIGN TO 'SYS001'
    UNIT-RECORD 2540R UNIT.
SELECT TAX-TABLE ASSIGN TO 'SYS008'
    DIRECT-ACCESS 2311 UNIT
    ORGANIZATION IS INDEXED ACCESS
    IS RANDOM.
```

Since the detail data cards are not in sequence by salary, the tax table file must be accessed randomly. In the above case, the tax table file is used only for input and is so defined in the **PROCEDURE DIVISION**.

Example 2: A group of input transaction tape records are used to create an indexed sequential disk file. The **ENVIRONMENT DIVISION SELECT** clause entries are as follows:

```
SELECT IN-TAPE ASSIGN TO TAPE 1.
SELECT MASTER-FILE ASSIGN TO MASS
    STORAGE ORGANIZATION IS INDEXED
    ACCESS IS SEQUENTIAL.
```

Keep in mind that the device specification is dependent upon the computer manufacturer.

Example 3: An update program will use detail cards to update every record on a master disk file. The detail cards are in the same sequence as the master disk file. The **ENVIRONMENT DIVISION SELECT** clause entries are as follows:

```
SELECT CARD-FILE ASSIGN TO 'SYS009'
    UNIT-RECORD 2540R UNIT.
SELECT MASTER-FILE ASSIGN TO 'SYS020'
    DIRECT ACCESS 2011 UNIT
    ORGANIZATION IS INDEXED ACCESS
    IS SEQUENTIAL.
```

Since the card data is in the same order as the disk records, each disk record will be accessed in sequence. Thus the access method of the disk file is sequential.

C. KEYS

You will recall that key fields are utilized in creating indexed sequential and direct files.

For an indexed sequential file, a unique nonblank key is necessary for establishing the index. You will recall that the key and actual address of each record is placed on a table or index. In this way records can be accessed randomly by specifying the key.

The key field of an indexed sequential file is part of the record. It is called a **RECORD KEY**.[4] The **RECORD KEY** clause must be specified for all indexed sequential files.

For a direct file, a unique nonblank key is also needed. This key, you will recall, can be directly converted into the actual address of the record on the disk. It is called an **ACTUAL KEY**.[4] The **ACTUAL KEY** clause must be specified for all direct files.

Thus we have a **RECORD KEY** for every indexed sequential file and an **ACTUAL KEY** for every direct file. Suppose we wish to access a record on either of these files. We must set up a field in storage with the key information. This field is used to compare against the **RECORD KEY** of indexed sequential files and the **ACTUAL KEY** of direct files to obtain the appropriate rec-

---

[4] The **ACTUAL KEY** is the **only** key field which is universal for all COBOL compilers. The discussion of **RECORD KEY** and **SYMBOLIC KEY** is applicable to many compilers and is included here because it is felt that they add clarity to the concept of keys. Check the appropriate computer manual to determine if these options are available.

ord. That is, we establish a key field in storage to indicate the desired record. This field is called a **SYMBOLIC KEY**. The **SYMBOLIC KEY** clause is required for all **input** indexed sequential or direct files which are processed randomly. When we wish to read a specific record randomly, we place the key information in **SYMBOLIC KEY**. This field is **not** part of the disk record but may be part of another record (card, for example) or a data field in **WORKING-STORAGE**. This field contains the key of the record to be accessed or read.

We will see in the next section that a **SYMBOLIC KEY** is sometimes used for **output** indexed sequential files also. A **SYMBOLIC KEY** field may be used for an output file to perform a check on the **RECORD KEY**.

Example: Suppose we wish to create an indexed sequential output file which has invoice number as its only unique field. The **ENVIRONMENT DIVISION SELECT** clause for this file is:

SELECT INV-FILE ASSIGN TO MASS
    STORAGE ORGANIZATION IS INDEXED,
    ACCESS IS SEQUENTIAL, RECORD KEY
    IS INVOICE-NO.

Note that, in this case, **INVOICE-NO** is a data item within the record.

Example: Suppose we read a disk **TABLE-FILE** as input which has as its key field **CITY**. This file contains each city and its corresponding sales tax. We also read an indexed sequential disk file which is in transaction-number sequence. The program will read the transaction file, process it, look up the **CITY** of each transaction record on the **TABLE-FILE** to obtain **CITY-TAX**, and print a report. The **SELECT** clauses for the two disk input files are:

SELECT TABLE-FILE ASSIGN TO 'SYS004' DIRECT-ACCESS 2311 UNIT
    ORGANIZATION IS INDEXED, ACCESS IS RANDOM, RECORD KEY IS
    CITY-ON-TABLE-FILE, SYMBOLIC KEY IS CITY-ON-TRANS-FILE.
SELECT TRANS-FILE ASSIGN TO 'SYS003' DIRECT-ACCESS 2311 UNIT
    ORGANIZATION IS INDEXED, ACCESS IS SEQUENTIAL, RECORD KEY IS
    TRANS-NO.

Table 20-1

	ORGANIZATION	ACCESS	KEY
OUTPUT	INDEXED	SEQUENTIAL	RECORD KEY (SYMBOLIC KEY OPTIONAL)[a]
OUTPUT	DIRECT	SEQUENTIAL	ACTUAL KEY (SYMBOLIC KEY OPTIONAL)[a]
INPUT	INDEXED	SEQUENTIAL	RECORD KEY (SYMBOLIC KEY OPTIONAL)[a]
INPUT	INDEXED	RANDOM	RECORD KEY SYMBOLIC KEY
INPUT	DIRECT	SEQUENTIAL	ACTUAL KEY
INPUT	DIRECT	RANDOM	ACTUAL KEY SYMBOLIC KEY

[a] Where an optional SYMBOLIC KEY is noted, the programmer may incude it to check for INVALID KEY. The INVALID KEY test is performed in the PROCEDURE DIVISION and requires a key field different from RECORD KEY. This will be discussed fully in the next section.

Note that a **SYMBOLIC KEY** is not necessary when reading records **sequentially** from an indexed sequential file. In that case, we need not indicate to the computer which record we are seeking, since we are reading them in the order in which they appear.

Table 20-1 summarizes the entries discussed above.

EXERCISES

1. If the **ORGANIZATION** clause is omitted from the **SELECT** statement in the **ENVIRONMENT DIVISION**, then _____ organization is assumed.
   *****
   sequential

2. To use a direct access device sequentially is the same as using a _____.
   *****
   high-speed tape

3. When using indexed sequential files, we say that **ORGANIZATION IS** _____.
   *****
   INDEXED

4. The initial creation of an indexed sequential file is performed _____.
   *****
   sequentially

5. Addressing of records in indexed sequential files is performed by _____ while addressing of direct files is performed by _____.
   *****
   the input-output control system
   the programmer

6. When **creating** an indexed sequential file **ACCESS IS** _____. When using an indexed sequential file as input, **ACCESS IS** either _____ or _____.
   *****
   SEQUENTIAL
   SEQUENTIAL
   RANDOM

7. **ACTUAL KEY** may not be used with _____ files.
   *****
   indexed sequential

D. PROCEDURE DIVISION ENTRIES FOR DISK PROCESSING

The OPEN Statement. You will recall that all files must be opened before they may be read or written. As previously defined, an OPEN statement indicates whether the file is input or output. The format is as follows:

A specific disk file, however, may be used as **both** input and output. That is, the same disk file may be read from and written onto in one program. In this case, we call it an input-output or I-O file. The format of the OPEN statement must be expanded to include such disk files:

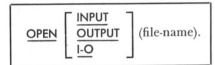

Note that a disk may be used as input to a computer, as output from a computer, or as both. All sequential access media such as cards and magnetic tape may only serve as **either** input or output. One cannot, for example, write onto an input tape. If TAPE-A contains 10,000 records and a single addition is to be made to the file, a new tape must be created with the 10,001 entries. With disk, however, we can add onto the same pack by labeling it as an I-O device. This is a significant advantage for all **updating** procedures.

INVALID KEY Option. When dealing with indexed sequential or direct files, key fields are extremely significant. The specific key or keys that are used to locate a disk record are specified in the ENVIRONMENT DIVISION. The key or keys that are used, however, must be unique, nonblank fields. That is, two records within a disk file may not have the same RECORD or ACTUAL KEY.

The INVALID KEY option may be used in conjunction with the READ or WRITE verb

to insure that a duplication of keys or a blank key is not found. The format for these operations is:

```
READ  (file-name)
   INVALID KEY (imperative statement(s))

WRITE  (record-name)
   INVALID KEY (imperative statement(s))
```

Examples

    READ FILE-A INVALID KEY GO TO
    ERR-RTN.
    WRITE REC-B INVALID KEY DISPLAY
    REC-B STOP RUN.

In each case, the program will perform the operations following the INVALID KEY clause only if an improper key field is found.

The INVALID KEY option will test for the validity of a SYMBOLIC KEY or ACTUAL KEY only. It will not perform any operation on the RECORD KEY.

Thus, if SYMBOLIC or ACTUAL KEY is defined in the ENVIRONMENT DIVISION, the INVALID KEY option may be used in the PROCEDURE DIVISION to insure that a duplication of keys does not exist. Thus, we sometimes use a SYMBOLIC KEY for indexed sequential **output** files, when we wish to use an INVALID KEY option.

Let us consider an illustration. Suppose a disk file is to be **created** from payroll card records. Since each employee has a unique social security number, this field as part of the output record will be used as a RECORD KEY. Thus, in the ENVIRONMENT DIVISION, we specify that the output social security number is to be used as the RECORD KEY. We also set aside the input area with the social security number as a SYMBOLIC KEY so that an INVALID KEY test may be performed for each output record processed.

Note that the SYMBOLIC KEY is part of the input card record. Suppose an error occurs and the first two input cards have the same social security number. The SYMBOLIC KEY, then, is not unique. The following routine is used to create the output:

```
OPEN INPUT CARD-IN, OUTPUT DISK-OUT.
READ CARD-IN AT END GO TO EOJ.
MOVE CARD-IN TO DISK-REC-OUT.
WRITE DISK-REC-OUT INVALID KEY GO
    TO ERR-RTN.
GO TO A.
```

The first record will be placed on the disk. The second time the WRITE command is executed, however, a branch to ERR-RTN will occur. Since two records have the same SYMBOLIC KEY or social security number, the second is said to have an IN-VALID KEY.

REWRITE Statement.[5] After an input disk record has been read, a REWRITE statement may be issued to recreate the record with some variations. That is, a REWRITE command does not create a new record, but, in effect, writes over a previously defined input record.

Note that the REWRITE verb may only be used after a file has been opened as I-O and a specific record has been read. The REWRITE verb applies to the record which has been accessed by the last READ command. Consider the following illustration:

```
OPEN I-O FILE-A.
READ FILE-A INVALID KEY GO TO
    ERR-RTN.
ADD TAX TO TOTAL OF FILE-A.
REWRITE REC-A INVALID KEY GO TO
    ERR-RTN.
```

The REWRITE statement results in the recreating of the disk file, FILE-A, with the addition of a TAX to the TOTAL field of the file. Note that the INVALID KEY option is used with the READ statement. This implies that a SYMBOLIC KEY for indexed sequential files or an ACTUAL KEY for direct files has been defined in the ENVIRON-MENT DIVISION. The INVALID KEY option

_____
[5] The REWRITE statement is not universal to all COBOL compilers. Check the specific manual to determine if it is applicable.

is used with the REWRITE statement to insure that a duplication of keys does not occur.

REWRITE statements are most often used with input-output files in update programs. An update, you will recall, is the process of making a master file current with new detail information.

Suppose, for example, we have a payroll file which is used to write weekly employee salary checks. This payroll file must be periodically updated with detail data containing promotions, raises, transfers, resignations, and new hire information to make it current.

To perform an update operation on a master tape file, for example, it is necessary to read as input the detail data and the master tape. A new master tape must be created incorporating old master data and the current detail data.

To perform an update operation on a master disk file, however, is somewhat less complex. Since it is possible to use a disk for both input and output, a new disk file need not be created. We can add to and change the one disk file to make it current; that is, we can update the same disk file without creating a new one.

When defining a disk as an I-O file, it is possible to perform all three of the following update procedures:

1. Creation of new records, i.e., new hires must be added to a payroll file. A simple WRITE command may be used to create new records.

2. Deletion of some old records, i.e., resignations must be deleted from a payroll file. Special delete codes must be placed in the key.

3. Changes to specific records, i.e., promotions, raises, and transfers must be incorporated in existing records. The RE-WRITE verb may be used to alter existing records.

Example: Consider an update program where card data will be used to change existing records or to create new records.

The cards are **not** in the same sequence as the disk. The card format is as follows:

   1–9   Social Security number
 10–79 Payroll data
    80 Code (1-New employee, 2-update)

The disk format is as follows:

   1–9   Social Security number
 10–79 Payroll data

The program reads as follows:

```
IDENTIFICATION DIVISION.
PROGRAM-ID. 'SAMPLEX'.
ENVIRONMENT DIVISION.
CONFIGURATION SECTION.
SOURCE-COMPUTER.   IBM-360 F40.
OBJECT-COMPUTER.   IBM-360 F40.
INPUT-OUTPUT SECTION.
FILE-CONTROL. SELECT CARDS ASSIGN TO
    'SYS004' UNIT-RECORD 2540R UNIT.
    SELECT DISK-A ASSIGN TO 'SYS007'
    DIRECT-ACCESS 2311 UNIT
    ORGANIZATION IS INDEXED ACCESS IS
    RANDOM SYMBOLIC KEY IS SOC-SEC-NO
    RECORD KEY IS DISK-SSNO.
DATA DIVISION.
FILE SECTION.
FD   CARDS RECORDING MODE F LABEL
     RECORDS ARE OMITTED DATA RECORD
     IS REC-A.
01   REC-A.
     02  SOC-SEC-NO     PICTURE X(9).
     02  PAYROLL-DATA   PICTURE X(70).
     02  CODE           PICTURE X.
         88  NEW-EMPL     VALUE '1'.
FD   DISK-A RECORDING MODE F LABEL
     RECORDS ARE STANDARD DATA
     RECORD IS R-2.
01   R-2.
     02  FILLER        PICTURE X.
     02  DISK-SSNO     PICTURE X(9).
     02  DISK-DATA     PICTURE X(70).
PROCEDURE-DIVISION.
     OPEN INPUT CARDS, I-O DISK-A.
```

```
START. READ CARDS AT END GO TO EOJ.
    IF NEW-EMPL MOVE SOC-SEC-NO TO
    DISK-SSNO MOVE PAYROLL-DATA TO
    DISK-DATA WRITE R-2 GO TO START.
UPDATE.
    MOVE SOC-SEC-NO TO DISK-SSNO.
    READ DISK-A INVALID KEY STOP RUN.
    MOVE PAYROLL-DATA TO DISK-DATA.
    REWRITE R-2 INVALID KEY STOP RUN.
    GO TO START.
EOJ. CLOSE CARDS, DISK-A.
    STOP RUN.
```

The IDENTIFICATION DIVISION of programs utilizing disk is the same as previously described. The ENVIRONMENT DIVISION merely incorporates the specified disk options. Since the disk file is indexed sequential and the records are not accessed in sequence, ORGANIZATION IS INDEXED and ACCESS IS RANDOM. According to the supplied chart, both SYMBOLIC KEY and RECORD KEY are required for randomly accessed indexed sequential files.

The DATA DIVISION is basically the same as when describing standard sequential files. Note that the SYMBOLIC KEY, SOC-SEC-NO, is part of the **input** record. Note also that disk records generally utilize standard labels unless the programmer wishes to supply his own labels. The first position of the disk record is a FILLER, since it must not be accessed by the programmer. The first data field within the disk file is the RECORD KEY.

The PROCEDURE DIVISION entries indicate the format of an update routine. Note, however, that the SYMBOLIC KEY field, SOC-SEC-NO, must be moved to the RECORD KEY, DISK-SSNO, before a DISK record may be accessed. SYMBOLIC KEY and RECORD KEY must be the same for such records.

With these basic rules, the beginning programmer should be able to process disk files with little or no difficulty.

EXERCISES

1. A disk file may be opened as _____, _____, or _____.
   *****
   INPUT
   OUTPUT
   I-O

2. If OPEN I-O FILE-X is a coded statement, then FILE-X must be a _____ file.
   *****
   disk

3. (T or F) If one record is to be added to a tape file, it can be added to the same tape.
   *****
   F

4. (T or F) If one record is to be added to a disk file, it can be added to the same disk.
   *****
   T

5. A unique field within an indexed sequential file that is used to locate records on a disk pack is called a _____ _____.
   *****
   RECORD KEY

6. A unique field not part of an indexed sequential or direct file that is used to locate records on the indexed sequential or direct disk file is called a _____ _____.
   *****
   SYMBOLIC KEY

7. A unique field used to indicate the exact address of records within a direct file is called a(n) _____ _____.
   *****
   ACTUAL KEY

8. A key field, when specified, must be _____ and _____.
   *****
   unique
   nonblank

9. A PROCEDURE DIVISION test for the duplication of a KEY field is called the _____ _____ option.
   *****
   INVALID KEY

10. The **INVALID KEY** option is part of a _____ or _____ statement for disk files.
    *****
    READ
    WRITE (REWRITE)

11. The **INVALID KEY** option tests the validity of the _____ or _____ **KEY**.
    *****
    SYMBOLIC
    ACTUAL

12. If **READ FILE-X INVALID KEY GO TO ERROR-1** is executed, a branch to **ERROR-1** will occur if _____.
    *****
    two records on the file have the same **SYMBOLIC** or **ACTUAL KEY**

13. The specific key used to locate a record is specified in the _____ **DIVISION**.
    *****
    ENVIRONMENT

14. A **REWRITE** statement is used to _____.
    *****
    alter previously existing disk records

15. If a record is to be added to a disk file, a (**WRITE, REWRITE**) statement is used.
    *****
    WRITE

16. If **REWRITE REC-X** is executed, and **REC-X** is part of **FILE-X**, then **FILE-X** must have been opened as _____ and a _____ command must have preceded the **REWRITE**.
    *****
    I-O
    READ

17. The **REWRITE** statement is most often used as part of _____ programs.
    *****
    update

18. An update is _____.
    *****
    the process of making a file current with new detail data

19. The three steps generally necessary to update a file are _____, _____, and _____.
    *****
    creation of new records
    deletion of some old records
    additions to some existing records

20. To change or add to an existing record requires the use of the _____ verb for disk files.

*****

REWRITE

21. Consider the following input card record:

cc 1–   Code (1-New account; 2-update of old account)
   2–5   Transaction No.
   6–80   Transaction data

Consider the following master disk record:

   1–   Code 2
   2–5   Transaction No.
   6–80   Transaction data

Write a **PROCEDURE DIVISION** routine to update the master file with input data.

*****

```
    OPEN INPUT TRANS-CARDS, I-O DISK-FILE.
A.  READ DISK-FILE AT END GO TO EOJ.
BEGIN. READ TRANS-CARDS AT END GO TO EOJ.
    IF CODE = 1 WRITE DISK-REC FROM TRANS-REC INVALID KEY
    STOP RUN, GO TO BEGIN.
    IF CODE = 2 MOVE TRANS-REC TO DISK-REC.
    REWRITE DISK-REC INVALID KEY GO TO ERR. GO TO A.
```

REVIEW QUESTIONS

1. Write the **ENVIRONMENT DIVISION** entries for the creation of an indexed sequential file called **DISK-FILE**.

2. Write the **ENVIRONMENT DIVISION** entries for an indexed sequential file called **IN-FILE** which is in transaction number sequence but which will be accessed by invoice number.

3. Explain the purpose of the **REWRITE** statement in a COBOL program.

4. Explain the use of the **INVALID KEY** option.

5. When is a file opened as **I-O**?

PROBLEMS

1. Write a program to update a master disk file. The format of the disk file is:

    1–20 Customer name
    21–25 Mailing address
    26–29 Date of last purchase   month/year
    30–35 Amount owed xxxx.xx
    Labels are standard.
    Customer name is key field.

    The disk file is to be updated with card records with the following format:

    1–20 Customer name
    21–24 Date of purchase   month/year
    25–29 Amount of purchase xxx.xx
    30–80 Not used

    Notes

    (1) Create a disk record for any card that does not have a corresponding master record (compare on Customer Name).
    (2) For all cards with corresponding master records (these are master records to be updated), add amount of purchase from card to amount owed on disk and update the date of last purchase.
    (3) There need not be a card record for each master record.
    (4) Master file is indexed sequential; cards are not in sequence.

2. Write a program to update a master transaction disk file. The format of the disk file is as follows:

    1–5   Transaction number
    6–10 Amount xxx.xx
    Labels are standard.
    Transaction number is key field.

    The disk file is to be updated with tape records having the following format:

    1–5   Transaction number
    6–10 Amount xxx.xx
    11–25 Not used
    Labels are standard; blocking factor = 12.

    Notes

    (1) Tape records are to update amount fields on disk file. If a tape record has the same transaction number as a disk record, process; if not, display the tape record as an error.
    (2) Disk records are indexed sequential; tape records are not in sequence by transaction number.

3. A table is to be created in core storage from the following card records:

   1–5   Product number
   6–10 Unit price xxx.xx
   11–80 Not used
   Product number is key field.

   There are 150 product numbers with independent unit prices. Create an indexed sequential disk file from the following tape records:

   1–5   Customer number
   6–20 Customer name
   21–23 Quantity sold
   24–28 Product number
   29–30 Not used
   Labels are standard; blocking factor is 100.

   The disk file is to have the following format:

   1–5   Customer number
   6–13 Amount owed xxxxxx.xx
   14–18 Product number
   19–20 Not used
   Labels are standard.
   Customer number is key field.

   Amount owed = Quantity sold × Unit price (from table).

   Perform a table lookup using Product No. from tape to find unit price on the table.

4. 3 disk files contain the following table records:

   File 1

   1–3   Man number
   4–20 Employee name

   File 2

   1–3   Title number
   4–6   Job number
   7–20 Job name

   File 3

   1–   Level number
   2–8   Salary xxxxx.xx
   9–20 Not used
   Labels are standard.
   First field of each file represents key field.

   Write a program to create an indexed sequential disk file from the following card records:

   1–3   Man number
   4–6   Title number
   7–9   Job number
   10–   Level number
   11–80 Not used

The format for the output disk records is as follows:

    1-3 Man number
    4-20 Employee name
    21-23 Title number
    24-26 Job number
    27-40 Job name
    41- Level number
    42-48 Salary
    49-50 Not used
Labels are standard.

Employee name, Job name, and Salary are obtained from the three table files on disk.

(**Hint.** Define three I|P disk files. Use man number on card as symbolic key to look up employee name, etc.)

5. A disk file contains the following table records:

    1-2 State number
    3-4 County number
    5-7 Tax rate .xxx
    8-10 Not used
Labels are standard.
State number is key field.

Write a program to create an indexed sequential disk file from the following tape records:

    1-20 Customer name
    21-25 Quantity
    26-30 Price/unit xxx.xx
    31-32 State number
    33-34 County number
    35- Not used
Labels are standard; blocking factor = 50.

The format for the output disk records is as follows:

    1-34 Same as tape
    35-44 Amount owed
    45- Not used
Labels are standard.

Amount Owed = Quantity × Price/Unit − Tax Rate ×
(Quantity × Price)
Tax Rate is obtained from table.

Appendix

A

All Characters in the Cobol Character Set

Letters—A–Z

Digits—0–9

and the following special characters:

Name	Symbol
Blank or space	(written ⊬ in the text)
Plus sign	+
Minus sign or hyphen	—
Asterisk or multiplication sign	*
Slash or division sign	/
Equal sign	=
Period or decimal point	.
Semicolon	;
Comma	,
Quotation mark	'
Left parenthesis	(
Right parenthesis	)
Dollar sign	$
"Greater than" symbol	>
"Less than" symbol	<

Cobol Reserved Words

The following is a list of COBOL reserved words—words that have special significance to the COBOL compiler. Such words **cannot** be used as data or paragraph names.

Some of the words below may not be reserved for specific computers. It is advisable, however, not to use any of the ones on the list in forming programmer-supplied words.

This list denotes only the singular of reserved words. Note, however, that the plural of any noun specified below also must not be used to define data or paragraph names.

ABOUT	CHARACTERS	EQUAL
ACCEPT	CHECK	ERROR
ACCESS	CLASS	EVERY
ACTUAL	CLOCK-UNITS	EXAMINE
ADD	CLOSE	EXIT
ADVANCING	COBOL	
AFTER	COMPUTATIONAL	FD
ALL	COMPUTE	FILE
ALPHABETIC	CONFIGURATION	FILE-CONTROL
ALPHANUMERIC	CONSOLE	FILLER
ALTER	CONSTANT	FIRST
ALTERNATE	CONTAINS	FLOAT
AN	CONTROL	FOR
AND	COPY	FROM
APPLY	CORRESPONDING	
ARE		GIVING
AREA	DATA	GO
ASSIGN	DATE-COMPILED	GREATER
AT	DATE-WRITTEN	GROUP
AUTHOR	DECLARATIVES	
	DEFINE	HASHED
BEFORE	DEPENDING	HIGH-VALUE
BEGINNING	DISPLAY	
BITS	DIVIDE	I-O
BLANK	DIVISION	I-O-CONTROL
BLOCK		IDENTIFICATION
BY	ELSE	IF
	END	IN
CF	ENTER	INCLUDE
CH	ENVIRONMENT	INDEX

300

INPUT	PAGE	SIGNED
INPUT-OUTPUT	PAGE-COUNTER	SIZE
INSTALLATION	PERFORM	SORT
INTO	PICTURE	SOURCE-COMPUTER
INVALID	PLACE	SPACE
IS	PLUS	SPECIAL-NAMES
	POINT	STANDARD
JUSTIFIED	POSITIVE	STATUS
	PRIORITY	STOP
KEY	PROCEDURE	SUBTRACT
	PROCEED	SUM
LABEL	PROGRAM-ID	SUPERVISOR
LAST	PROTECT	SUPPRESS
LEADING		SYMBOLIC
LEFT	QUOTE	SYNCHRONIZED
LESS		
LIBRARY	RANDOM	TALLY
LINE	RANGE	TALLYING
LOCATION	READ	TAPE
LOCK	RECORD	TERMINATE
LOW-VALUE	RECORDING	THAN
	REDEFINES	THEN
MEMORY	REEL	THROUGH or THRU
MINUS	RELEASE	TIMES
MODE	REMARKS	TO
MODULES	RENAMES	TRACK
MOVE	RENAMING	TRANSFORM
MULTIPLY	REPLACING	TYPE
	REPORT	
NEGATIVE	REPORTING	UNEQUAL
NEXT	RERUN	UNIT
NO	RESET	UNTIL
NOT	RESERVE	UPON
NOTE	RETURN	UPPER-BOUND
NUMBER	REVERSED	USAGE
NUMERIC	REWIND	USE
	RIGHT	USING
OBJECT-COMPUTER	ROUNDED	
OBJECT-PROGRAM	RUN	VALUE
OCCURS		VARYING
OF	SAME	
OFF	SEARCH	WHEN
OMITTED	SECTION	WITH
ON	SECURITY	WORD
OPEN	SEEK	WORKING-STORAGE
OPTIONAL	SELECT	WRITE
OR	SENTENCE	
OTHERWISE	SEQUENCED	ZERO
OUTPUT	SEQUENTIAL	ZEROES
OVERFLOW	SIGN	ZEROS

Basic Elements of Flowcharting

A useful tool for analyzing the logic necessary in a program is called a **flowchart.** A flowchart is a diagram, or pictorial representation, of the logic flow of a program; it is drawn **before** the problem is coded. It is like the blueprint an architect prepares before a house is built. Through the use of a flowchart, the programmer can organize and verify the logic he must employ.

This section is designed to illustrate the **elements** of program flowcharting. It does not presume to teach the beginner how to **write** such diagrams. It will, however, indicate the method used to **read** flowcharts since they will be employed throughout the text to denote program logic. It is hoped that the ability to write flowcharts will come with constant exposure to their use.

Consider the program flowchart indicated in Fig. B-1.

This flowchart depicts the logic flow used to print salary checks for all salesmen in a company. If a salesman has made $100 or more in sales, his commission is 10% of his sales, which is added to his salary. Similarly, if a salesman has made $50 or more (but not more than $100), his commission is 5% of his sales, which is added to his salary. The unfortunate salesman who has made less than $50 receives his salary with no commission.

The logic flow, as denoted in a flowchart, is fairly easy to read. In addition, we will see later that it is relatively simple to code the program from a flowchart.

Several important points may be noted from the above illustration.

1. A logic flow is read from top to bottom unless a specific condition alters the path.
2. Different symbols are used to denote different functions. See Fig. B-2 for an explanation of the symbols and their use.
3. All symbols have explanatory notes indicating the specific operations.

Since a symbol denotes a major class of function such as input-output or processing, a note is required within the symbol to describe the specific operation to be performed.

Observe that the flowchart illustrated in Fig. B-1 reads salesmen cards as input. Note, however, that there is no indication of when the job is terminated. All flowcharts must indicate under what conditions a job is considered to be completed. Unless this is done, the flowchart seems to indicate an **infinite loop;** that is, it appears as if the program will read cards indefinitely and the flow will never end.

Symbol	Name	Use
(parallelogram)	Input-Output	Used for all I-O operations. For example, the reading of a card, the writing of a line, and the writing of a magnetic tape are considered I-O functions.
(rectangle)	Processing	Used for all arithmetic and data transfer operations. For example, moving of data from one area of storage (input) to another area (output), and multiplying percentage by total sales are processing functions.
(diamond)	Decision	Used to test all conditions. For example, testing whether one field is larger than another, and testing whether a given field has specific contents (zeros, blanks) are considered decision functions.
(circle)	Connectors	Used to change the normal path of a flowchart. There are two kinds of branches:

(a) **Unconditional branch connector:**

(circle with line entering top)

When an unconditional branch connector is indicated, control is transferred to another point. For example, (START) . When this symbol is reached, a transfer to START always occurs.

(b) **Conditional branch connector:**

(circle with line on left)

denotes that if a specific condition exists, then a transfer or branch will occur. Conditional branches are always the result of a decision.

(decision diamond: IS SALES GREATER THAN 100.00? — YES → (PATH X)) If sales exceed $100 a conditional branch to PATH-X occurs.

The symbol *(connector symbols)* or *(connector symbol)* is called an **entry connector** and denotes entry points into the logic flow.

INPUT

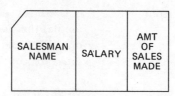

OUTPUT

SALESMEN
CHECKS

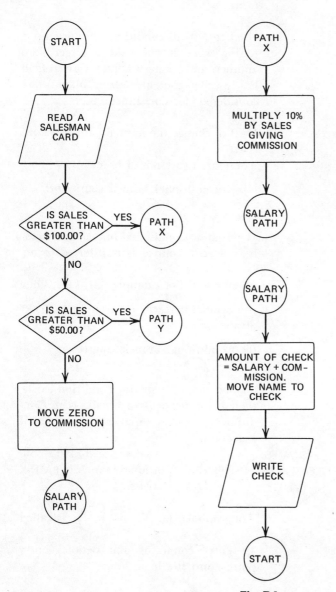

Fig. B-1.

Thus we must modify the flowchart to indicate an end of job, **EOJ**. The logical ending of the flowchart above is reached when there are no more cards to be read. Fig. B-3 illustrates the completed program.

The symbol ⬭ is called a **terminal** symbol and is used to denote a halt.

Note that we test a card to determine if it is the last one **after** it has been processed. The usual place for testing for the last card is prior to the next **READ** command, as in Fig. B-4.

Placing the last card test before a **READ** command is exactly the same as placing it after all processing. Note, also, that in the above variation several flowcharting steps are combined.

Let us consider a second illustration. From the following card format, we wish to print the names of all blue-eyed, blonde males and all brown-eyed, brunette females.

Card format

card cols:
  1–20 NAME
  21   SEX (M-male, F-female)
  22   COLOR OF EYES.
        (1-Blue, 2-Brown, 3-Other)
  23   COLOR OF HAIR
        (1-Brown, 2-Blonde, 3-Other)
  24–80 Not used

The flowchart for this problem is illustrated in Fig. B-5.

Note that the writing of flowcharts is a difficult task for the beginner in data processing. One advantage of COBOL is that the elementary level programs are relatively simple to code and a flowchart is therefore unnecessary. For intermediate level programs, where the logic flow is often complex, a flowchart can be quite helpful. At this stage, however, it is hoped that the student will be familiar enough with data processing to be able to write adequate flowcharts.

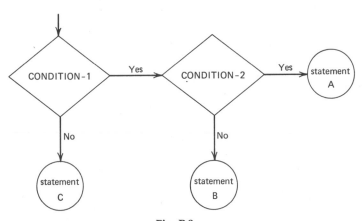

Fig. B-2.

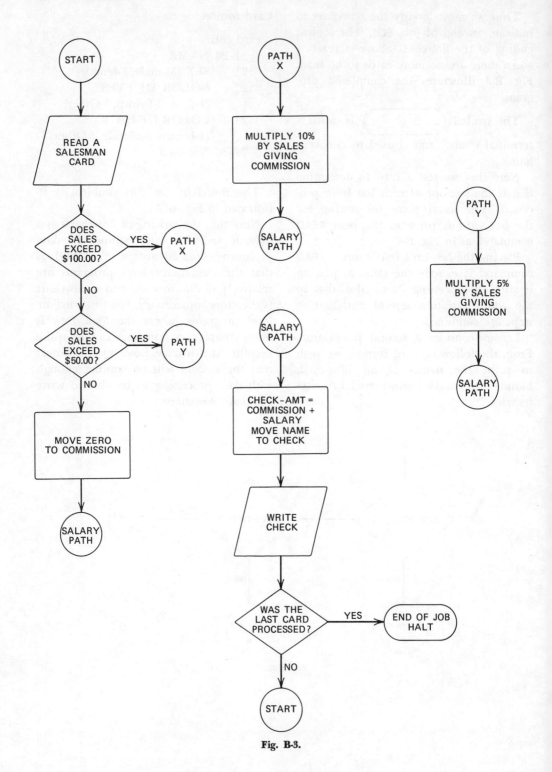

Fig. B-3.

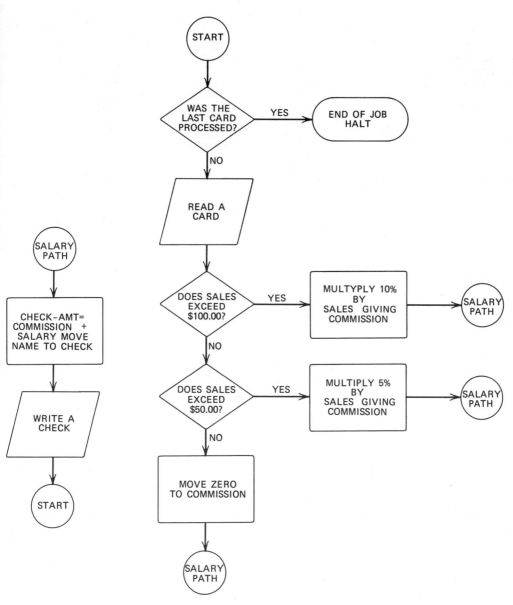

Fig. B-4.

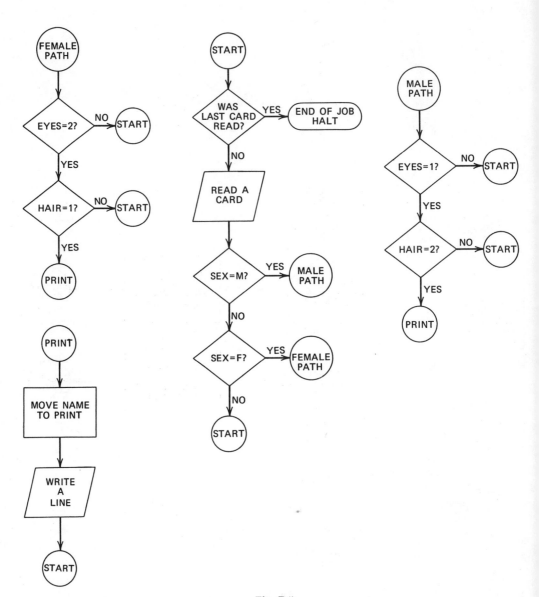

Fig. B-5.

EXERCISES

1. A flowchart is used for analyzing the _____ necessary in a program.
   *****
   logic

2. A flowchart is drawn (before, after) the problem is coded.
   *****
   before

3. A program flowchart is read from _____ to _____.
   *****
   top
   bottom

4. Different _____ are used to denote different functions.
   *****
   symbols

5. The input-output symbol is coded as _____.
   *****

6. A processing symbol is coded as _____.
   *****

7. [diamond shape] is called a _____ symbol.
   *****
   decision

8. The three kinds of connector symbols are _____, _____, and _____.
   *****
   unconditional branch connector
   conditional branch connector
   entry connector

9. A conditional branch connector always accompanies a _____ symbol.

*****

decision

10. All symbols have _____ indicating the specific operations.

*****

explanatory notes

11. A last card test usually _____ the READ command.

*****

precedes

REVIEW QUESTIONS

1. Give four examples of input-output functions.

2. Give four examples of processing functions.

3. Give two examples of decision functions.

4. (T or F) A program flowchart is required before any programs are written.

5. What is the purpose of a last card test?

PROBLEMS

1. Consider the flowchart on the following page:
With the following input cards, what will be the contents of TOTAL at the end of all operations?

Card No.	Contents of Column 18	Contents of Column 19
1	1	2
2	1	3
3	1	2
4	1	0
5	(blank)	(blank)
6	(blank)	1
7	1	(blank)
8	1	2
9	1	2
10	(blank)	2

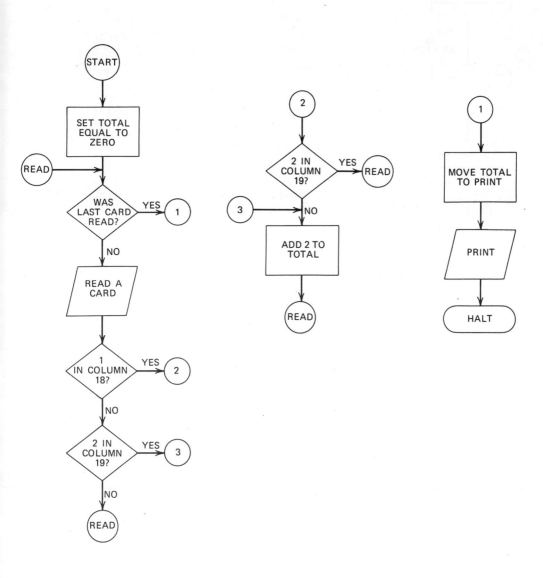

2. Given the following flowchart:

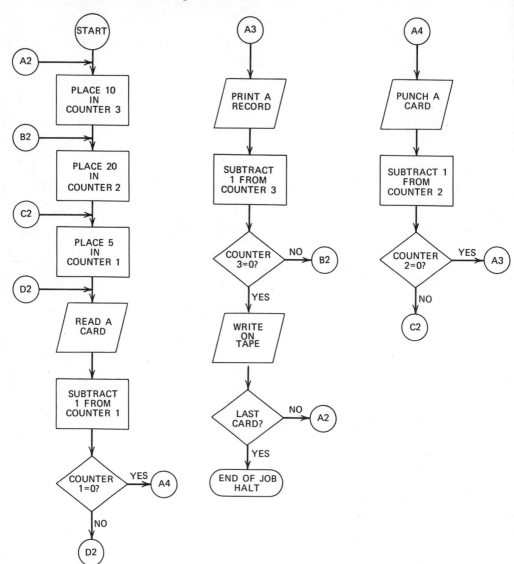

(a) In the above system, a record is punched after reading how many cards? Explain.
(b) The system is printing a record after reading how many cards? Explain.
(c) The system is writing on tape after reading how many cards? Explain.

3. Questions a-d refer to the following flowchart:

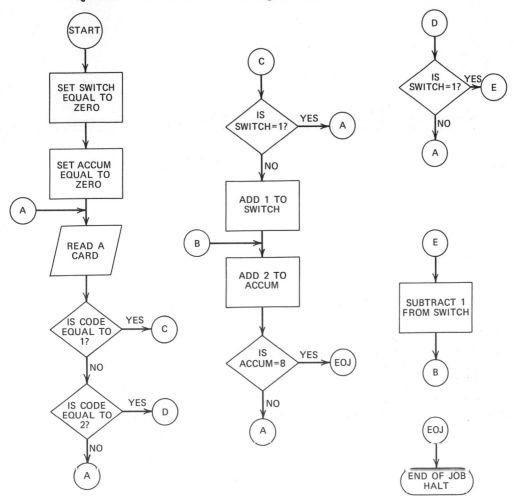

Input used is on 15 cards.
Codes on 15 cards (in Column 1) are:

1, 2, 3, 2, 1, 1, 2, 2, 3, 3, 1, 2, 3, 1, 2

(a) How many cards will be read?
(b) What is the value of switch when a branch to **EOJ** occurs?
(c) What is the value of **ACCUM** when a branch to **EOJ** occurs?
(d) How many cards would have been read if **ACCUM** were originally set to 1 instead of 0?

Sample Environment Division Entries for Specific Computers

SAMPLE BURROUGHS 5500 ENTRIES

ENVIRONMENT DIVISION.
CONFIGURATION SECTION.
SOURCE-COMPUTER.   B-5500.
OBJECT-COMPUTER.   B-5500.
INPUT-OUTPUT SECTION.
FILE-CONTROL. SELECT (file-name) **ASSIGN TO** (integer)

```
READER
READERS
CARD-READERS
PRINTER
PRINTERS
TAPE
TAPES
SORT-TAPES
PUNCH
CARD-PUNCH
KEYBOARD
MESSAGE-PRINTER
DISK
PAPER-TAPE-READER
PAPER-TAPE-PUNCH
DATA
SORT DISK
MERGE
```

**SAMPLE HONEYWELL 200 ENTRIES-
COMPILER C (MASS STORAGE
RESIDENT)**

ENVIRONMENT DIVISION.
CONFIGURATION SECTION.

SOURCE-COMPUTER.   SERIES-200
$\begin{bmatrix} \text{MODEL-120} \\ \text{MODEL-200} \\ \text{MODEL-1200} \\ \text{MODEL-2200} \end{bmatrix}$

OBJECT-COMPUTER. (same as above).
INPUT-OUTPUT SECTION.

FILE-CONTROL. SELECT (file-name) ASSIGN TO
$\begin{bmatrix} \text{INPUT} \\ \text{OUTPUT} \\ \text{INPUT-OUTPUT} \\ \text{I-O} \end{bmatrix}$

$\begin{bmatrix} \text{INPUT-TAPE n} \\ \text{OUTPUT-TAPE n} \\ \text{CARD-READER} \\ \text{CARD-PUNCH} \\ \text{PRINTER} \\ \text{MASS-STORAGE-DEVICE mmm} \\ \text{MSD mmm} \end{bmatrix}$

$\left\{ \text{ACCESS MODE IS} \begin{bmatrix} \text{SEQUENTIAL} \\ \text{PARTITIONED} \\ \text{RANDOM} \\ \text{INDEXED SEQUENTIAL} \end{bmatrix} \text{[PROCESSING MODE IS SEQUENTIAL]} \right\}$.

[ACTUAL KEY IS (data-name)] [RELATIVE KEY IS (data-name)]

[RECORD KEY IS (data-name)] [SYMBOLIC KEY IS data-name]

**SAMPLE HONEYWELL 200 ENTRIES-
COMPILERS D & H (TAPE RESIDENT)**

ENVIRONMENT DIVISION.
CONFIGURATION SECTION.

SOURCE-COMPUTER. $\begin{bmatrix} \text{H-200} \\ \text{HONEYWELL-200} \\ \text{H-200-SPECIAL} \end{bmatrix}$.

OBJECT-COMPUTER. $\begin{bmatrix} \text{HONEYWELL-200} \\ \text{H-200} \end{bmatrix}$.

INPUT-OUTPUT SECTION.

FILE-CONTROL. SELECT (file-name) ASSIGN TO $\begin{bmatrix} \text{TAPE-UNIT (no.)} \\ \text{CARD-READER (no.)} \\ \text{CARD-PUNCH (no.)} \\ \text{PRINTER (no.)} \end{bmatrix}$.

SAMPLE IBM 1401

```
ENVIRONMENT  DIVISION.
CONFIGURATION  SECTION.
SOURCE-COMPUTER.        IBM-1401.
OBJECT-COMPUTER.        IBM-1401.
INPUT-OUTPUT  SECTION.
```

FILE-CONTROL. SELECT (file-name) ASSIGN TO $\begin{bmatrix} \text{1402-R} \\ \text{1402-P} \\ \text{1403} \\ \text{TAPE n} \end{bmatrix}$.

SAMPLE IBM S/360 ENTRIES

```
ENVIRONMENT  DIVISION.
CONFIGURATION  SECTION.
```

SOURCE-COMPUTER. IBM-360 $\begin{bmatrix} \text{C} \\ \text{D} \\ \text{E} \\ \text{F} \\ \text{G} \\ \text{H} \\ \text{I} \end{bmatrix}$ * (model-number).

```
OBJECT-COMPUTER. (same as above).
INPUT-OUTPUT  SECTION.
FILE-CONTROL. SELECT (file-name) ASSIGN TO (external-name)
```

$\begin{bmatrix} \text{DIRECT-ACCESS} \\ \text{UTILITY} \\ \text{UNIT-RECORD} \end{bmatrix}$ (device-number) UNIT (s)

$\left\{ \begin{array}{l} \text{ACCESS IS} \begin{bmatrix} \text{SEQUENTIAL} \\ \text{RANDOM} \end{bmatrix} \text{ORGANIZATION IS} \begin{bmatrix} \text{INDEXED} \\ \text{DIRECT} \end{bmatrix} \\ \qquad \text{SYMBOLIC KEY IS (data-name)} \\ \qquad\quad \text{ACTUAL KEY IS (data-name)} \\ \qquad\qquad \text{RECORD KEY IS (data-name).} \end{array} \right\}$

*C = 8, 192 bytes	G = 131, 072 bytes
D = 16, 384 bytes	H = 262, 144 bytes
E = 32, 768 bytes	I = 524, 288 bytes
F = 65, 536 bytes	

SAMPLE NCR 315 ENTRIES

ENVIRONMENT DIVISION.
CONFIGURATION SECTION.
SOURCE-COMPUTER.
$\begin{bmatrix} 315 \\ \text{NCR-315} \end{bmatrix}$.

OBJECT-COMPUTER.
$\begin{bmatrix} 315 \\ \text{NCR-315} \end{bmatrix}$.

INPUT-OUTPUT SECTION.

FILE-CONTROL. SELECT (file-name) ASSIGN TO
$\begin{bmatrix} \text{HANDLER} \\ \text{CRAM} \\ \text{CARD-PUNCH} \\ \text{CARD-READER} \\ \text{CARD-READER-HS} \\ \text{PT-READER} \\ \text{PT-PUNCH} \\ \text{READER-PUNCH} \\ \text{PRINTER} \end{bmatrix}$

$\left\{\begin{array}{l} \text{ACCESS MODE IS} \begin{bmatrix} \text{SEQUENTIAL} \\ \text{RANDOM} \end{bmatrix} \\ \text{PROCESSING MODE IS SEQUENTIAL} \\ \text{ACTUAL KEY IS (data-name)} \end{array}\right\}$.

SAMPLE UNIVAC 1108 ENTRIES

ENVIRONMENT DIVISION.
CONFIGURATION SECTION.
SOURCE-COMPUTER. UNIVAC-1108.
OBJECT-COMPUTER. UNIVAC-1108.

INPUT-OUTPUT SECTION.
FILE-CONTROL. SELECT (file-name) ASSIGN TO
$\begin{bmatrix} \text{CARD-READER-EIGHTY} \\ \text{CARD-PUNCH-EIGHTY} \\ \text{PRINTER} \\ \text{UNISERVO}[1] \\ \text{MASS-STORAGE} \end{bmatrix}$

$\left\{\begin{array}{l} \text{ACCESS MODE IS} \begin{bmatrix} \text{SEQUENTIAL} \\ \text{RANDOM} \\ \text{MIXED} \end{bmatrix} \\ \text{ACTUAL KEY IS (data-name)} \\ \text{SYMBOLIC KEY IS (data-name)} \end{array}\right\}$.

[1] Trademark of Sperry Rand Corporation—name for tape unit.

D

Compiler Generated Messages

Thus far, we have provided all the rules and most of the options necessary for writing COBOL programs. With knowledge of these rules and options, the reader should be able to code fairly complex COBOL programs.

The writing of such programs, however, represents only a segment of the programmer's task. Programs must be **tested** after they are written. Most programs, regardless of the computer language in which they are written, contain minor errors or "bugs" which must be corrected before these programs are considered complete. Thus, the second task of a programmer's job, after the coding is completed, is to **debug** the program. This section will discuss, in detail, this second task.

After a COBOL program is written, the coded statements are then punched into cards. The program deck is called the COBOL **source deck.**

This source deck must be read into the computer and converted to actual machine language before it can be tested, or executed, with test data. This conversion of a COBOL source deck into actual machine language is called a **compilation.**

A COBOL compilation is, in effect, the processing of the COBOL program. All COBOL source statements are converted, by this **compiler program,** into actual machine language instructions. In so doing,

the compiler program **edits** the source deck and prints any violations of COBOL rules that are encountered.

Thus, before execution may occur, COBOL programs must be compiled. A compilation requires the COBOL source deck as input. The output from this compilation is the converted actual machine language program, a listing of all COBOL source statements, and a list of **diagnostics,** or error messages. The compilation phase, then, does not **test** a program, but prepares it for execution.

Any violations of COBOL rules encountered during the compilation are indicated on this list of diagnostics which may appear together at the end of the COBOL listing, or individually, directly following each erroneous statement. Note that logic errors are **not** detected during this phase, but may only be determined during the actual execution of the program. The compilation, or conversion, of the COBOL source deck into actual machine language lists the program and also any violations of rules. Major violations must be corrected before execution of the program can occur.

The format of diagnostics varies significantly among computers. This discussion is designed merely to familiarize the reader with the kinds of error messages that may be encountered when compiling a COBOL program and will not indicate

318

any one format for denoting diagnostics.

Each diagnostic message generally provides three basic points of information:

Identification of Error. If the diagnostics appear at the end of the COBOL listing, each message will contain a page and line number reference, indicating which COBOL source statement is in error. In addition, an error code or classification will accompany the diagnostic, which may be cross-referenced in the COBOL manual for the specific computer manufacturer.

Classification of Error. Errors generally fall into three categories.

(a) **Minor** level errors, sometimes called observation, or W-level, messages, will **not** cause termination of the program. They are merely warnings to the programmer. To attempt to place a five-position alphanumeric field into a three-position alphanumeric field, for example, may result in the following warning message:

DESTINATION FIELD DOES NOT ACCEPT THE WHOLE SENDING FIELD IN MOVE.

To perform the above operation is **not** incorrect. The compiler is merely indicating that truncation will occur. If truncation occurs as a result of a programming oversight, it should be corrected. If, however, the programmer **chooses** to truncate a field, no changes are necessary. That is, the program will execute with such diagnostics.

(b) **Intermediate** level errors are **conditional** errors, usually called C-level, where the compiler makes an adjustment for the error. If the correction is what the programmer intended to do, execution will proceed normally. If, however, the correction is **not** the desired one, execution must be terminated and the error corrected. Consider the following C-level diagnostic:

> 007020 C-QUALIFICATION—NAME
> REQUIRES MORE QUALIFICATION
> FIRST NAME DEFINED IS ASSUMED

which applies to the following statement (page 007, line 020):

007020 MOVE NAME TO NAME OF
        REC-OUT.

The first **NAME** field in the statement is not properly qualified. The diagnostic indicates that the first **NAME** field encountered in the **DATA DIVISION** is considered to be the desired one. If, in fact, the first **NAME** field designated in the **DATA DIVISION** is the required one, the statement need not be corrected for execution to continue properly. If, however, the **NAME** field required is **not** the first one, then the program must be corrected before execution can begin. In any case, all C-level diagnostics should eventually be corrected.

(c) **Major** level errors, called **execution-level,** or **fatal,** diagnostics by some compilers, will terminate execution. The compiler deems these errors of such magnitude that it will not permit execution to occur. The following are examples of major level errors:

> FILE SECTION OUT OF SEQUENCE
> ENVIRONMENT DIVISION MISSING
> UNDEFINED DATA-NAME
> INVALID LITERAL: $100.00
> INVALID DATA-NAME: DISCOUNT-%

A list of all possible diagnostics is **not** feasible, since they vary among compilers and are generally provided in a reference manual for specific computers. Keep in mind that familiarity with these messages comes with exposure. Do not become discouraged by large numbers of diagnostics. Even the most experienced programmer forgets some of the basic rules of COBOL and finds many diagnostics.

Rules for Efficient Coding

The following is a list of programming considerations that can result in the conserving of core storage. This does not mean that the less efficient techniques are invalid.

1. Numeric fields should be decimally aligned. When performing a **MOVE** or arithmetic operation on fields of data, it is more efficient to specify the **same** number of decimal positions for all such fields.

Example

    02 AMT-1 PICTURE 99V99.
    02 AMT-2 PICTURE 99V99.

Operation:

    MOVE AMT-1 TO AMT-2.

Similarly, to increase efficiency, **AMT-1** and **AMT-2** should have the same **PICTURE** clause, if possible.

2. Include an **S** in the **PICTURE** clause of all numeric fields.

Example:

    02 AMT PICTURE S99.

rather than:

    02 AMT PICTURE 99.

3. Use integers, rather than data-names, as subscripts where possible.

Example:

    MOVE FLDA (4) TO FLDB.

rather than:

    MOVE FLDA (SUB1) TO FLDB.

4. Use one **OPEN** statement to open all files rather than multiple **OPEN** statements.

Example:

    OPEN INPUT FILE-X OUTPUT FILE-Y

rather than:

    OPEN INPUT FILE-X
    OPEN OUTPUT FILE-Y

5. Avoid the use of the **BLANK WHEN ZERO** option when the report-item **PICTURE** clause implies blank results for a zero filled sending field.

Example:

    02 EDIT1 PICTURE ZZZ.ZZ.

rather than:

    02 EDIT1 PICTURE ZZZ.ZZ BLANK WHEN ZERO.

6. Avoid complex arithmetic expressions in a **COMPUTE** statement.

Example:

MULTIPLY D BY E GIVING B.
COMPUTE C = A ** B

rather than:

COMPUTE C = A ** (D * E).

7. Avoid the use of arithmetic expressions in conditional statements.

Example:

ADD C TO D.
IF D = E GO TO ERR-RTN.

rather than:

IF D + C = E GO TO ERR-RTN.

8. Avoid exponentiation to a fractional power, where possible.

9. Group MOVE operations should not exceed 256 characters.

F

Solutions to Selected Problems

A solution to Problem 2 of every chapter beginning with Chapter 6 is provided. Note that the solutions represent suggested methods for solving the problems and are not the only answers possible.

Chapter 6

```
IDENTIFICATION DIVISION.
PROGRAM-ID. 'CHAPT6'.
ENVIRONMENT DIVISION.
CONFIGURATION SECTION.
SOURCE-COMPUTER. (name).
OBJECT-COMPUTER. (name).
INPUT-OUTPUT SECTION.
FILE-CONTROL.   SELECT EMPLOYEE-CARDS ASSIGN TO READER.
                SELECT SALARY-CARDS ASSIGN TO PUNCH.
DATA DIVISION.
FILE SECTION.
FD   EMPLOYEE-CARDS,
     RECORDING MODE IS F,
     LABEL RECORDS ARE OMITTED,
     RECORD CONTAINS 80 CHARACTERS,
     DATA RECORD IS EMPLOYEE-REC.
01   EMPLOYEE-REC.
     02 EMPLOYEE-NAME-IN    PICTURE X(20).
     02 SALARY-IN           PICTURE 9(5).
     02 NO-OF-DEPENDENTS    PICTURE 9.
     02 FICA                PICTURE 999V99.
     02 STATE-TAX           PICTURE 9(4)V99.
     02 FED-TAX             PICTURE 9(4)V99.
     02 FILLER              PICTURE X(37).
FD   SALARY-CARDS,
     RECORDING MODE IS F,
     LABEL RECORDS ARE OMITTED,
     RECORD CONTAINS 80 CHARACTERS,
     DATA RECORD IS SALARY-REC.
```

```
01  SALARY-REC.
    02 EMPLOYEE-NAME-OUT   PICTURE X(20).
    02 SALARY-OUT          PICTURE 9(5).
    02 FILLER              PICTURE X(55).
PROCEDURE DIVISION.
    OPEN INPUT EMPLOYEE-CARDS, OUTPUT SALARY-CARDS. MOVE
    SPACES TO SALARY-REC.
START.
    READ EMPLOYEE-CARDS AT END GO TO END-OF-JOB.
    MOVE EMPLOYEE-NAME-IN TO EMPLOYEE-NAME-OUT.
    MOVE SALARY-IN TO SALARY-OUT.
    WRITE SALARY-REC.
    GO TO START.
END-OF-JOB.
    CLOSE EMPLOYEE-CARDS, SALARY-CARDS.
    STOP RUN.
```

Chapter 7

```
IDENTIFICATION DIVISION.
PROGRAM-ID. 'CHAPT7'.
ENVIRONMENT DIVISION.
CONFIGURATION SECTION.
SOURCE-COMPUTER. (name).
OBJECT-COMPUTER. (name).
INPUT-OUTPUT SECTION.
FILE-CONTROL.   SELECT CARD-FILE ASSIGN TO READER.
                SELECT PRINT-FILE ASSIGN TO PRINTER.
DATA DIVISION.
FILE SECTION.
FD   CARD-FILE,
     RECORDING MODE IS F,
     LABEL RECORDS ARE OMITTED,
     RECORD CONTAINS 80 CHARACTERS,
     DATA RECORD IS CARD-REC.
01   CARD-REC.
     02 CUSTOMER-NAME.
        03 INITIAL-1                 PICTURE X.
        03 INITIAL-2                 PICTURE X.
        03 LAST-NAME                 PICTURE X(18).
     02 DATE-OF-TRANSACTION.
        03 MONTH                     PICTURE 99.
        03 YEAR                      PICTURE 99.
     02 AMOUNT-OF-TRANSACTION        PICTURE 9(6).
     02 FILLER                       PICTURE X(50).
FD   PRINT-FILE,
     RECORDING MODE IS F,
     LABEL RECORDS ARE OMITTED,
     RECORD CONTAINS 132 CHARACTERS,
     DATA RECORDS ARE HEADING, DETAIL-LINE.
01   HEADING.
     02 FILLER                       PICTURE X(20).
     02 LITERAL1                     PICTURE X(4).
     02 FILLER                       PICTURE X(25).
     02 LITERAL2                     PICTURE X(19).
     02 FILLER                       PICTURE X(25).
     02 LITERAL3                     PICTURE X(21).
     02 FILLER                       PICTURE X(18).
01   DETAIL-LINE.
     02 FILLER                       PICTURE X(15).
     02 INIT1-OUT                    PICTURE X.
     02 POINT1                       PICTURE X.
     02 INIT2-OUT                    PICTURE X.
     02 POINT2                       PICTURE X.
     02 LAST-NAME-OUT                PICTURE X(18).
     02 FILLER                       PICTURE X(19).
     02 MONTH-OUT                    PICTURE 99.
```

```
          02  DASH                    PICTURE X.
          02  YEAR-OUT                PICTURE 99.
          02  FILLER                  PICTURE X(39).
          02  AMOUNT-OUT              PICTURE 9(6).
          02  FILLER                  PICTURE X(26).
PROCEDURE DIVISION.
     OPEN INPUT CARD-FILE, OUTPUT PRINT-FILE.
     MOVE SPACES TO HEADING.
     MOVE 'NAME' TO LITERAL1.
     MOVE 'DATE OF TRANSACTION' TO LITERAL2.
     MOVE 'AMOUNT OF TRANSACTION' TO LITERAL3.
     WRITE HEADING.
     MOVE SPACES TO DETAIL-LINE.
     MOVE '.' TO POINT1.
     MOVE '.' TO POINT2.
     MOVE '/' TO DASH.
START.
     READ CARD-FILE AT END GO TO EOJ.
     MOVE INITIAL-1 TO INIT1-OUT.
     MOVE INITIAL-2 TO INIT2-OUT.
     MOVE LAST-NAME TO LAST-NAME-OUT.
     MOVE MONTH TO MONTH-OUT.
     MOVE YEAR TO YEAR-OUT.
     MOVE AMOUNT-OF-TRANSACTION TO AMOUNT-OUT.
     WRITE DETAIL-LINE.
     GO TO START.
EOJ.
     CLOSE CARD-FILE, PRINT-FILE.
     STOP RUN.
```

Chapter 8

```
IDENTIFICATION DIVISION.
PROGRAM-ID. 'CHAPT8'.
ENVIRONMENT DIVISION.
CONFIGURATION SECTION.
SOURCE-COMPUTER. (name).
OBJECT-COMPUTER. (name).
INPUT-OUTPUT SECTION.
FILE-CONTROL.   SELECT EMPLOYEE-CARDS ASSIGN TO READER.
                SELECT SALARY-FILE ASSIGN TO TAPE 1.
DATA DIVISION.
FILE SECTION.
FD   EMPLOYEE-CARDS
     RECORDING MODE IS F,
     LABEL RECORDS ARE OMITTED,
     RECORD CONTAINS 80 CHARACTERS,
     DATA RECORD IS EMPLOYEE-REC.
01   EMPLOYEE-REC.
     02 NAME           PICTURE X(15).
     02 HOURS          PICTURE 999.
     02 RATE           PICTURE 9V99.
     02 FILLER         PICTURE X(59).
FD   SALARY-FILE
     RECORDING MODE IS F,
     LABEL RECORDS ARE STANDARD,
     RECORD CONTAINS 75 CHARACTERS,
     BLOCK CONTAINS 15 RECORDS,
     DATA RECORD IS SALARY-REC.
01   SALARY-REC.
     02 FILLER         PICTURE X(5).
     02 NAME-OUT       PICTURE X(15).
     02 FILLER         PICTURE X(10).
     02 GROSS-PAY      PICTURE 9(4)V99.
     02 FILLER         PICTURE XXXX.
     02 SOC-SEC-TAX    PICTURE 999V99.
     02 FILLER         PICTURE X(5).
     02 NET-PAY        PICTURE 9(4)V99.
     02 FILLER         PICTURE X(19).
PROCEDURE DIVISION.
     OPEN INPUT EMPLOYEE-CARDS, OUTPUT SALARY-FILE.
     MOVE SPACES TO SALARY-REC.
START.
     READ EMPLOYEE-CARDS AT END GO TO EOJ.
     MOVE NAME TO NAME-OUT.
     MULTIPLY HOURS BY RATE GIVING GROSS-PAY.
     MULTIPLY .048 BY GROSS-PAY GIVING SOC-SEC-TAX.
     SUBTRACT SOC-SEC-TAX FROM GROSS-PAY GIVING NET-PAY.
     WRITE SALARY-REC.
     GO TO START.
```

```
EOJ.
    CLOSE EMPLOYEE-CARDS, SALARY-FILE.
    STOP RUN.
```

Chapter 9

```
IDENTIFICATION DIVISION.
PROGRAM-ID. 'CHAPT9'.
ENVIRONMENT DIVISION.
CONFIGURATION SECTION.
SOURCE-COMPUTER. (name).
OBJECT-COMPUTER. (name).
INPUT-OUTPUT SECTION.
FILE-CONTROL.  SELECT MEDICAL-FILE ASSIGN TO READER.
               SELECT DIAGNOSIS-REPORT ASSIGN TO PRINTER.
DATA DIVISION.
FILE SECTION.
FD   MEDICAL-FILE
     RECORDING MODE IS F,
     LABEL RECORDS ARE OMITTED,
     RECORD CONTAINS 80 CHARACTERS,
     DATA RECORD IS REC-IN.
01   REC-IN.
     02 PATIENT-NAME      PICTURE X(20).
     02 LUNG INFECTION    PICTURE 9.
     02 TEMPERATURE       PICTURE 9.
     02 SNIFFLES          PICTURE 9.
     02 SORE-THROAT       PICTURE 9.
     02 FILLER            PICTURE X(56).
FD   DIAGNOSIS-REPORT
     RECORDING MODE IS F,
     LABEL RECORDS ARE OMITTED,
     RECORD CONTAINS 132 CHARACTERS,
     DATA RECORDS ARE HEADER, DETAIL-LINE.
01   HEADER.
     02 FILLER            PICTURE X(58).
     02 LITERAL1          PICTURE X(16).
     02 FILLER            PICTURE X(58).
01   DETAIL-LINE.
     02 FILLER            PICTURE X(25).
     02 NAME              PICTURE X(20).
     02 FILLER            PICTURE X(20).
     02 DIAGNOSIS         PICTURE X(20).
     02 FILLER            PICTURE X(47).
PROCEDURE DIVISION.
     OPEN INPUT MEDICAL-FILE, OUTPUT DIAGNOSIS-REPORT.
     MOVE SPACES TO HEADER.
     MOVE 'DIAGNOSIS REPORT' TO LITERAL1.
     WRITE HEADER.
     MOVE SPACES TO DETAIL-LINE.
BEGIN.
     READ MEDICAL-FILE AT END GO TO EOJ.
     IF TEMPERATURE = 1 AND LUNG-INFECTION = 1 MOVE
        'PNEUMONIA' TO DIAGNOSIS GO TO WRITE-RTN.
```

```
    IF (LUNG-INFECTION = 1 AND SNIFFLES = 1) OR
        (LUNG-INFECTION = 1 AND SORE-THROAT = 1) OR
        (TEMPERATURE = 1 AND SNIFFLES = 1) OR (TEMPERATURE =
        1 AND SORE-THROAT = 1) OR (SNIFFLES = 1 AND
        SORE-THROAT = 1) MOVE 'COLD' TO DIAGNOSIS GO TO
        WRITE-RTN.        ·
    MOVE 'PHONY' TO DIAGNOSIS.
WRITE-RTN.
    MOVE PATIENT-NAME TO NAME.
    WRITE DETAIL-LINE.
    GO TO BEGIN.
EOJ.
    CLOSE MEDICAL-FILE, DIAGNOSIS-REPORT.
    STOP RUN.
```

Note. The routine for determining if diagnosis is a **cold** could be simplified as follows:

```
    ADD LUNG-INFECTION, TEMPERATURES, SNIFFLES, TO
        SORE-THROAT.
    IF SORE-THROAT IS GREATER THAN 1 MOVE 'COLD' TO
        DIAGNOSIS GO TO WRITE-RTN.
```

Chapter 10

```
IDENTIFICATION DIVISION.
PROGRAM-ID. 'CHAPT10'.
ENVIRONMENT DIVISION.
CONFIGURATION SECTION.
SOURCE-COMPUTER. (name).
OBJECT-COMPUTER. (name).
INPUT-OUTPUT SECTION.
FILE-CONTROL.  SELECT ACCIDENT-FILE ASSIGN TO TAPE 1.
               SELECT REPORT-OUT ASSIGN TO PRINTER.
DATA DIVISION.
FILE SECTION.
FD   ACCIDENT-FILE
     RECORDING MODE IS F,
     LABEL RECORDS ARE STANDARD,
     RECORD CONTAINS 10 CHARACTERS,
     BLOCK CONTAINS 50 RECORDS,
     DATA RECORD IS REC-IN.
01   REC-IN.
     02 DRIVER-NO       PICTURE 9(4).
     02 STATE-CODE      PICTURE 9.
     02 BIRTH-DATE.
        03 MONTH        PICTURE 99.
        03 YEAR         PICTURE 99.
     02 SEX             PICTURE X.
FD   REPORT-OUT
     RECORDING MODE IS F,
     LABEL RECORDS ARE OMITTED,
     RECORD CONTAINS 132 CHARACTERS,
     DATA RECORD IS REC-OUT.
01   REC-OUT.
     02 FILLER          PICTURE X(20).
     02 LITERAL1        PICTURE X(21).
     02 FILLER          PICTURE X(5).
     02 RESULT          PICTURE V999.
     02 FILLER          PICTURE X(83).
WORKING-STORAGE SECTION.
77   NO-OF-DRIVERS      PICTURE 9(5), VALUE ZERO.
77   NY-DRIVERS         PICTURE 9(5), VALUE ZERO.
77   FEMALE-DRIVERS     PICTURE 9(5), VALUE ZERO.
77   DRIVERS-UNDER-25   PICTURE 9(5), VALUE ZERO.
PROCEDURE DIVISION.
     OPEN INPUT ACCIDENT-FILE, OUTPUT REPORT-OUT.
     MOVE SPACES TO REC-OUT.
BEGIN.
     READ ACCIDENT-FILE AT END GO TO EOJ.
     ADD 1 TO NO-OF-DRIVERS.
     IF YEAR IS GREATER THAN 44[1] ADD 1 TO DRIVERS-UNDER-25.
```

_____

[1] Assuming that present year is 1970.

```
        IF STATE-CODE = 1 ADD 1 TO NY-DRIVERS.
        IF SEX = 'F' ADD 1 TO FEMALE-DRIVERS.
        GO TO BEGIN.
EOJ.
        DIVIDE NO-OF-DRIVERS INTO DRIVERS-UNDER-25 GIVING RESULT.
        MOVE '% OF DRIVERS UNDER 25' TO LITERAL1.
        WRITE REC-OUT.
        DIVIDE NO-OF-DRIVERS INTO FEMALE-DRIVERS GIVING RESULT.
        MOVE '% OF DRIVERS FEMALE' TO LITERAL1.
        WRITE REC-OUT.
        DIVIDE NO-OF-DRIVERS INTO NY-DRIVERS GIVING RESULT.
        MOVE '% OF DRIVERS FROM NY' TO LITERAL1.
        WRITE REC-OUT.
        CLOSE ACCIDENT-FILE, REPORT-OUT.
        STOP RUN.
```

Chapter 11

```
IDENTIFICATION DIVISION.
PROGRAM-ID. 'CHAPT11'.
ENVIRONMENT DIVISION.
CONFIGURATION SECTION.
SOURCE-COMPUTER. (name).
OBJECT-COMPUTER. (name).
INPUT-OUTPUT SECTION.
FILE-CONTROL. SELECT EMPLOYEE-CARDS ASSIGN TO READER.
              SELECT FEMALE-TAPE ASSIGN TO TAPE 1.
              SELECT MALE-TAPE ASSIGN TO TAPE 2.
DATA DIVISION.
FILE SECTION.
FD  EMPLOYEE-CARDS
    RECORDING MODE IS F,
    LABEL RECORDS ARE OMITTED,
    RECORD CONTAINS 80 CHARACTERS,
    DATA RECORD IS CARD-REC.
01  CARD-REC.
    02 MAJOR.
    03 NAME      PICTURE X(15).
    03 SEX       PICTURE X.
        88 MALE                VALUE 'M'.
        88 FEMALE              VALUE 'F'.
    03 AGE       PICTURE X.
        88 AGE-20              VALUE 'Y'.
        88 AGE-30              VALUE 'M'.
        88 AGE-50              VALUE 'G'.
        88 AGE-OVER-50         VALUE 'E'.
    03 HEIGHT    PICTURE X.
        88 OVER-6-FT           VALUE 'X'.
        88 BET-66-72           VALUE 'M'.
        88 BET-60-66           VALUE 'A'.
    03 WEIGHT    PICTURE X.
        88 OVER-185            VALUE 'H'.
        88 BET-120-185         VALUE 'M'.
        88 UNDER-120           VALUE 'N'.
    03 HAIR      PICTURE X.
        88 BALD                VALUE 'B'.
        88 NOT-BALD            VALUE 'N'.
    02 FILLER    PICTURE X(60).
FD  FEMALE-TAPE
    RECORDING MODE IS F
    LABEL RECORDS ARE STANDARD
    RECORD CONTAINS 20 CHARACTERS
    BLOCK CONTAINS 20 RECORDS
    DATA RECORD IS FEMALE-REC.
01  FEMALE-REC PICTURE X(20).
```

```
FD   MALE-TAPE
     RECORDING MODE IS F
     LABEL RECORDS ARE STANDARD
     RECORD CONTAINS 20 CHARACTERS
     BLOCK CONTAINS 20 RECORDS
     DATA RECORD IS MALE-REC.
01   MALE-REC   PICTURE X(20).
PROCEDURE DIVISION.
     OPEN INPUT EMPLOYEE-CARDS, OUTPUT MALE-TAPE, FEMALE-TAPE.
BEGIN.
     READ EMPLOYEE-CARDS AT END GO TO FINISH.
     IF FEMALE AND AGE-30 AND BET-60-66 AND UNDER-120 MOVE
     MAJOR TO FEMALE-REC WRITE FEMALE-REC GO TO BEGIN.
     IF MALE AND AGE-OVER-50 AND BET-66-72 AND OVER-185 AND
     BALD MOVE MAJOR TO MALE-REC WRITE MALE-REC. GO TO BEGIN.
FINISH.
     CLOSE EMPLOYEE-CARDS, MALE-TAPE, FEMALE-TAPE.
     STOP RUN.
```

Chapter 12

```
IDENTIFICATION DIVISION.
PROGRAM-ID. 'CHAPT12'.
ENVIRONMENT DIVISION.
CONFIGURATION SECTION.
SOURCE-COMPUTER. (name).
OBJECT-COMPUTER. (name).
INPUT-OUTPUT SECTION.
FILE-CONTROL. SELECT TAPE-FILE ASSIGN TO TAPE 1.
               SELECT PRINT-FILE ASSIGN TO PRINTER.
DATA DIVISION.
FILE SECTION.
FD   TAPE-FILE
     RECORDING MODE IS F
     LABEL RECORDS ARE STANDARD
     RECORD CONTAINS 25 CHARACTERS
     DATA RECORD IS TAPE-REC.
01   TAPE-REC.
     02 NAME          PICTURE X(20).
     02 AMOUNT        PICTURE 999V99.
FD   PRINT-FILE
     RECORDING MODE IS F
     LABEL RECORDS ARE OMITTED
     RECORD CONTAINS 132 CHARACTERS
     DATA RECORD IS PRINT-REC.
01   PRINT-REC.
     02 FILLER        PICTURE X(10).
     02 NAME          PICTURE X(20).
     02 FILLER        PICTURE X(10).
     02 TOTAL         PICTURE $**,***.99.
     02 FILLER        PICTURE X(82).
WORKING-STORAGE SECTION.
77   TOTAL-AMOUNT   PICTURE 9(5)V99,  VALUE ZEROS.
77   CTR            PICTURE 9(3),     VALUE ZEROS.
PROCEDURE DIVISION.
     OPEN INPUT TAPE-FILE, OUTPUT PRINT-FILE. MOVE SPACES TO
     PRINT-REC.
START.
     READ TAPE-FILE AT END GO TO FINISH.
     ADD 1 TO CTR.
     ADD AMOUNT TO TOTAL-AMOUNT.
     IF CTR = 100 NEXT SENTENCE ELSE GO TO START.
     MOVE NAME OF TAPE-REC TO NAME OF PRINT-REC.
     MOVE TOTAL-AMOUNT TO TOTAL.
     WRITE PRINT-REC.
     MOVE ZEROS TO CTR.
     MOVE ZEROS TO TOTAL-AMOUNT.
     GO TO START.
FINISH.
     CLOSE TAPE-FILE, PRINT-FILE.
     STOP RUN.
```

Chapter 13

```
IDENTIFICATION DIVISION.
PROGRAM-ID. 'CHAPT13'.
ENVIRONMENT DIVISION.
CONFIGURATION SECTION.
SOURCE-COMPUTER. (name).
OBJECT-COMPUTER. (name).
INPUT-OUTPUT SECTION.
FILE-CONTROL. SELECT TAPE-FILE ASSIGN TO TAPE 1.
              SELECT PRINT-FILE ASSIGN TO PRINTER.
I-O-CONTROL.
    APPLY END-OF-FORM TO FORM-OVERFLOW ON PRINT-FILE.
DATA DIVISION.
FILE SECTION.
FD   TAPE-FILE
     RECORDING MODE IS F
     LABEL RECORDS ARE STANDARD
     RECORD CONTAINS 25 CHARACTERS
     DATA RECORD IS TAPE-REC.
01   TAPE-REC.
     02 NAME      PICTURE X(20).
     02 AMOUNT    PICTURE 999V99.
FD   PRINT-FILE
     RECORDING MODE IS F
     LABEL RECORDS ARE OMITTED
     RECORD CONTAINS 133 CHARACTERS
     DATA RECORD IS PRINT-REC.
01   PRINT-REC    PICTURE X(133).
WORKING-STORAGE SECTION.
77   TOTAL-AMOUNT PICTURE 9(5)V99,  VALUE ZEROS.
77   CTR          PICTURE 999,      VALUE ZEROS.
77   PAGE-NO      PICTURE 9(4),     VALUE 1.
01   HEADER-1.
     02 FILLER    PICTURE X(50),    VALUE SPACES.
     02 HDR-A     PICTURE X(25),    VALUE '100 CA
-    'RD TOTALS'.
     02 HDR-B     PICTURE X(9),     VALUE 'PAGE N
-    '0. '.
     02 PAGE-CT   PICTURE ZZZ9.
     02 FILLER    PICTURE X(45),    VALUE SPACES.
01   DETAIL-LINE.
     02 FILLER    PICTURE X(11),    VALUE SPACES.
     02 NAME      PICTURE X(20).
     02 FILLER    PICTURE X(10),    VALUE SPACES.
     02 TOTAL     PICTURE $**,***.99.
     02 FILLER    PICTURE X(82),    VALUE SPACES.
PROCEDURE DIVISION.
     OPEN INPUT TAPE-FILE, OUTPUT PRINT-FILE.
```

```
HDR-RTN.
     MOVE PAGE-NO TO PAGE-CT.
     ADD 1 TO PAGE-NO.
     WRITE PRINT-REC FROM HEADER-1 AFTER ADVANCING 0 LINES.
START.
     READ TAPE-FILE AT END GO TO EOJ.
     ADD 1 TO CTR.
     ADD AMOUNT TO TOTAL-AMOUNT.
     IF CTR = 100 NEXT SENTENCE ELSE GO TO START.
     MOVE NAME OF TAPE-REC TO NAME OF DETAIL-LINE.
     MOVE TOTAL-AMOUNT TO TOTAL.
     WRITE PRINT-REC FROM DETAIL-LINE AFTER ADVANCING 2 LINES.
     MOVE ZEROS TO CTR.
     MOVE ZEROS TO TOTAL-AMOUNT.
     IF END-OF-FORM GO TO HDR-RTN ELSE GO TO START.
EOJ.
     CLOSE TAPE-FILE, PRINT-FILE.
     STOP RUN.
```

Chapter 14

```
IDENTIFICATION DIVISION.
PROGRAM-ID. 'CHAPT14'.
ENVIRONMENT DIVISION.
CONFIGURATION SECTION.
SOURCE-COMPUTER. (name).
OBJECT-COMPUTER. (name).
INPUT-OUTPUT SECTION.
FILE-CONTROL. SELECT DETAIL-FILE ASSIGN TO READER.
               SELECT MASTER-FILE ASSIGN TO TAPE 1.
               SELECT MASTER-OUT ASSIGN TO TAPE 2.
DATA DIVISION.
FILE SECTION.
FD   DETAIL-FILE
     RECORDING MODE IS F,
     LABEL RECORDS ARE OMITTED,
     RECORD CONTAINS 80 CHARACTERS,
     DATA RECORD IS DETAIL-REC.
01   DETAIL-REC.
     02 EMPLOYEE-NAME   PICTURE X(20).
     02 SALARY          PICTURE 9(5).
     02 FILLER          PICTURE X(55).
FD   MASTER-FILE
     RECORDING MODE IS F,
     LABEL RECORDS ARE STANDARD,
     RECORD CONTAINS 50 CHARACTERS,
     BLOCK CONTAINS 25 RECORDS,
     DATA RECORD IS MASTER-REC.
01   MASTER-REC.
     02 EMPLOYEE-NAME   PICTURE X(20).
     02 SALARY          PICTURE 9(5).
     02 FILLER          PICTURE X(25).
FD   MASTER-OUT
     RECORDING MODE IS F,
     LABEL RECORDS ARE STANDARD,
     RECORD CONTAINS 50 CHARACTERS,
     BLOCK CONTAINS 25 RECORDS,
     DATA RECORD IS REC-OUT.
01   REC-OUT.
     02 EMPLOYEE-NAME   PICTURE X(20).
     02 SALARY          PICTURE 9(5).
     02 FILLER          PICTURE X(25).
WORKING-STORAGE SECTION.
77   SWITCH-A           PICTURE 9, VALUE ZERO.
77   SWITCH-B           PICTURE 9, VALUE ZERO.
PROCEDURE DIVISION.
     OPEN INPUT DETAIL-FILE, MASTER-FILE, OUTPUT MASTER-OUT.
     MOVE SPACES TO REC-OUT.
READ-CARD.
     READ DETAIL-FILE AT END GO TO EOJ1.
```

```
READ-TAPE.
    READ MASTER-FILE AT END GO TO EOJ2.
COMPARE-RTN.
    IF EMPLOYEE-NAME OF DETAIL-REC = EMPLOYEE-NAME OF
    MASTER-REC MOVE SALARY OF DETAIL-REC TO SALARY OF
    REC-OUT, MOVE EMPLOYEE-NAME OF DETAIL-REC TO
    EMPLOYEE-NAME OF REC-OUT, WRITE REC-OUT GO TO READ-CARD.
    IF EMPLOYEE-NAME OF DETAIL-REC IS LESS THAN EMPLOYEE-NAME
    OF MASTER-REC GO TO NEW-CARD ELSE GO TO TAPE-UPDATE.
NEW-CARD.
    MOVE EMPLOYEE-NAME OF DETAIL-REC TO EMPLOYEE-NAME OF
    REC-OUT.
    MOVE SALARY OF DETAIL-REC TO SALARY OF REC-OUT.
    WRITE REC-OUT.
X.  PERFORM READ-CARD.
    GO TO COMPARE-RTN.
TAPE-UPDATE.
    MOVE EMPLOYEE-NAME OF MASTER-REC TO EMPLOYEE-NAME
    OF REC-OUT.
    MOVE SALARY OF MASTER-REC TO SALARY OF REC-OUT.
    WRITE REC-OUT.
Y.  GO TO READ-TAPE.
EOJ1.
    MOVE 1 TO SWITCH-A. IF SWITCH-B = 1 GO TO EOJ.
    PERFORM READ-TAPE.
    PERFORM TAPE-UPDATE.
    GO TO EOJ1.
EOJ2.
    MOVE 1 TO SWITCH-B. IF SWITCH-A = 1 GO TO EOJ.
    PERFORM READ-CARD.
    PERFORM NEW-CARD.
    GO TO EOJ2.
EOJ.
    CLOSE DETAIL-FILE, MASTER-FILE, MASTER-OUT.
    STOP RUN.
```

Note. SWITCH-A and SWITCH-B may be employed in place of the end
of job functions discussed in the chapter. The advantage of the above
is that a single READ command is used for each file.

Chapter 15

```
IDENTIFICATION DIVISION.
PROGRAM-ID. 'CHAPT15'.
ENVIRONMENT DIVISION.
CONFIGURATION SECTION.
SOURCE-COMPUTER. (name).
OBJECT-COMPUTER. (name).
INPUT-OUTPUT SECTION.
FILE-CONTROL. SELECT CARD-IN ASSIGN TO READER.
             SELECT TAPE-OUT ASSIGN TO TAPE 1.
DATA DIVISION.
FILE SECTION.
FD  CARD-IN
    RECORDING MODE IS F,
    LABEL RECORDS ARE OMITTED,
    RECORD CONTAINS 80 CHARACTERS,
    DATA RECORD IS CARD-REC.
01  CARD-REC.
    02 CUSTOMER-NAME      PICTURE X(20).
    02 TRANSACTION-AMT    PICTURE 999V99.
    02 FILLER             PICTURE X(55).
FD  TAPE-OUT
    RECORDING MODE IS F
    LABEL RECORDS ARE STANDARD
    RECORD CONTAINS 27 CHARACTERS
    BLOCK CONTAINS 20 RECORDS
    DATA RECORD IS TAPE-REC.
01  TAPE-REC.
    02 CUSTOMER-NAME      PICTURE X(20).
    02 TOTAL              PICTURE 9(5)V99.
PROCEDURE DIVISION.
    OPEN INPUT CARD-IN, OUTPUT TAPE-OUT.
BEGIN.
    MOVE ZEROS TO TOTAL.
    PERFORM READ-RTN 20 TIMES. MOVE CUSTOMER-NAME OF
    CARD-REC TO CUSTOMER-NAME OF TAPE-REC.
    WRITE TAPE-REC.
    GO TO BEGIN.
READ-RTN.
    READ CARD-IN AT END GO TO EOJ.
    ADD TRANSACTION-AMT TO TOTAL.
EOJ.
    CLOSE CARD-IN, TAPE-OUT.
    STOP RUN.
```

Chapter 16

```
IDENTIFICATION DIVISION.
PROGRAM-ID. 'CHAPT16'.
ENVIRONMENT DIVISION.
CONFIGURATION SECTION.
SOURCE-COMPUTER. (name).
OBJECT-COMPUTER. (name).
INPUT-OUTPUT SECTION.
FILE-CONTROL. SELECT TABLE-FILE ASSIGN TO READER.
               SELECT PUNCH-FILE ASSIGN TO PUNCH.
DATA DIVISION.
FILE SECTION.
FD  TABLE-FILE
     RECORDING MODE IS F,
     LABEL RECORDS ARE OMITTED,
     RECORD CONTAINS 80 CHARACTERS,
     DATA RECORD IS REC-IN.
01  REC-IN.
     02 CODE              PICTURE X.
     02 YRS-SERVICE       PICTURE 99.
     02 MAJOR.
        03 WKS-VACATION   PICTURE 99.
        03 LIFE-INSUR     PICTURE 9(5)V99.
        03 EXCUSED-DAYS   PICTURE 99.
     02 FILLER            PICTURE X(66).
FD  PUNCH-FILE
     RECORDING MODE IS F,
     LABEL RECORDS ARE OMITTED,
     RECORD CONTAINS 80 CHARACTERS,
     DATA RECORD IS REC-OUT.
01  REC-OUT.
     02 MESSAGE           PICTURE X(30).
     02 AVERAGE           PICTURE 999.99.
     02 FILLER            PICTURE X(44).
WORKING-STORAGE SECTION.
77  CTR                   PICTURE 999,     VALUE ZEROS.
77  AVERAGE-A             PICTURE 999V99,  VALUE ZEROS.
01  TABLE.
     02 ITEM OCCURS 50 TIMES.
        03 VACATION       PICTURE 99.
        03 INSURANCE      PICTURE 9(5)V99.
        03 DAYS           PICTURE 99.
PROCEDURE DIVISION.
     OPEN INPUT TABLE-FILE, OUTPUT PUNCH-FILE.
START.
     READ TABLE-FILE AT END GO TO PROCESS.
     ADD 1 TO CTR.
     IF CTR IS GREATER THAN 50 STOP RUN.
     IF CTR IS NOT EQUAL TO YRS-SERVICE STOP RUN.
```

```
        IF CODE = 1 NEXT SENTENCE ELSE STOP RUN.
        MOVE MAJOR TO ITEM (CTR).
        GO TO START.
PROCESS.
        MOVE ZEROS TO CTR.
        PERFORM VACATION-RTN 5O TIMES.
        MOVE 'AVERAGE NO OF WEEKS VACATION' TO MESSAGE.
        PERFORM PUNCH-RIN.
        PERFORM INSURANCE-RTN 50 TIMES.
        MOVE 'AVERAGE AMT OF INSURANCE' TO MESSAGE.
        PERFORM PUNCH-RTN.
        PERFORM DAYS-RTN 50 TIMES.
        MOVE 'AVERAGE NO EXCUSED DAYS' TO MESSAGE.
        PERFORM PUNCH-RTN.
        CLOSE TABLE-FILE, PUNCH-FILE.
        STOP RUN.
PUNCH-RTN.
        DIVIDE 50 INTO AVERAGE-A. MOVE AVERAGE-A TO AVERAGE.
        WRITE REC-OUT.
        MOVE ZEROS TO CTR. MOVE ZEROS TO AVERAGE-A.
VACATION-RTN.
        ADD 1 TO CTR.
        ADD VACATION (CTR) TO AVERAGE-A.
INSURANCE-RTN.
        ADD 1 TO CTR.
        ADD INSURANCE (CTR) TO AVERAGE-A.
DAYS-RTN.
        ADD 1 TO CTR.
        ADD DAYS (CTR) TO AVERAGE-A.
```

Chapter 17

```
IDENTIFICATION DIVISION.
PROGRAM-ID. 'CHAPT17'.
ENVIRONMENT DIVISION.
CONFIGURATION SECTION.
SOURCE-COMPUTER. (name).
OBJECT-COMPUTER. (name).
INPUT-OUTPUT SECTION.
FILE-CONTROL. SELECT CARD-FILE ASSIGN TO READER.
               SELECT PRINT-FILE ASSIGN TO PRINTER.
I-O-CONTROL. APPLY END-OF-PAGE TO FORM-OVERFLOW ON
               PRINT-FILE.
DATA DIVISION.
FILE SECTION.
FD   CARD-FILE
     RECORDING MODE IS F,
     LABEL RECORDS ARE OMITTED,
     RECORD CONTAINS 80 CHARACTERS,
     DATA RECORD IS CARD-REC.
01   CARD-REC.
     02 FILLER      PICTURE X(20).
     02 DEPT        PICTURE 99.
     02 AREA        PICTURE 99.
     02 FILLER      PICTURE X(56).
FD   PRINT-FILE
     RECORDING MODE IS F,
     LABEL RECORDS ARE OMITTED,
     RECORD CONTAINS 133 CHARACTERS,
     DATA RECORD IS PRINT-REC.
01   PRINT-REC      PICTURE X(133).
WORKING-STORAGE SECTION.
77   CTR1           PICTURE 99      VALUE 1.
77   CTR2           PICTURE 99      VALUE 1.
01   TOTALS.
     02 DEPTX OCCURS 50 TIMES.
          03 AREAX OCCURS 10 TIMES,   PICTURE 9(3).
01   HEADER-1.
     02 FILLER      PICTURE X(91)    VALUE 'TOTAL N
-    '0 OF EMPLOYEES BY AREA WITHIN DEPARTMENT' JUSTIFIED
          RIGHT.
     02 FILLER      PICTURE X(42)    VALUE SPACES.
01   HEADER-2.
     02 FILLER      PICTURE X(25)    VALUE 'DEPARTM
-    'ENT — ' JUSTIFIED RIGHT.
     02 DEPT-NO     PICTURE 99,      VALUE 00.
     02 FILLER      PICTURE X(106)   VALUE SPACES.
01   HEADER-3.
     02 FILLER      PICTURE X(30),   VALUE SPACES.
     02 FILLER      PICTURE X(103),  VALUE 'AREA 1
-    '   AREA 2      AREA 3      AREA 4      AREA 5      AREA 6
-    '   AREA 7      AREA 8      AREA 9      AREA 10
```

```
01   DETAIL-LINE.
     02 FILLER       PICTURE X(30)      VALUE SPACES.
     02 ITEM OCCURS 10 TIMES.
        03 FILLER   PICTURE XX.
        03 AREAY   PICTURE 999.
        03 FILLER   PICTURE X(5).
     02 FILLER       PICTURE XXX.
PROCEDURE DIVISION.
     OPEN INPUT CARD-FILE, OUTPUT PRINT-FILE.
     MOVE SPACES TO DETAIL-LINE.
INITIALIZE-RTN.
     MOVE ZEROS TO AREAX (CTR1, CTR2).
     ADD 1 TO CTR2.
     IF CTR2 = 11 NEXT SENTENCE ELSE GO TO INITIALIZE-RTN.
     ADD 1 TO CTR1.
     MOVE 1 TO CTR2.
     IF CTR1 = 51 NEXT SENTENCE ELSE GO TO INITIALIZE-RTN.
HEADER-RTN.
     WRITE PRINT-REC FROM HEADER-1 AFTER ADVANCING 0 LINES.
READ-RTN.
     READ CARD-FILE AT END GO TO EOJ.
     ADD 1 TO AREAX (DEPT, AREA).
     GO TO READ-RTN.
RTN-X.
     ADD 1 TO DEPT-NO.
     WRITE PRINT-REC FROM HEADER-2 AFTER ADVANCING 2 LINES.
     IF END-OF-PAGE PERFORM HEADER-RTN.
     WRITE PRINT-REC FROM HEADER-3 AFTER ADVANCING 2 LINES.
     IF END-OF-PAGE PERFORM HEADER-RTN.
A.   MOVE AREAX (CTR1, CTR2) TO AREAY (CTR2).
     ADD 1 TO CTR2.
     IF CTR = 11 NEXT SENTENCE ELSE GO TO A.
     WRITE PRINT-REC FROM DETAIL-LINE AFTER ADVANCING 2 LINES.
     IF END-OF-PAGE PERFORM HEADER-RTN.
     MOVE 1 TO CTR2.
     ADD 1 TO CTR1.
EOJ.
     MOVE 1 TO CTR1. MOVE 1 TO CTR2.
     PERFORM RTN-X THRU A 50 TIMES.
     CLOSE CARD-FILE, PRINT-FILE.
     STOP RUN.
```

Chapter 18

```
IDENTIFICATION DIVISION.
PROGRAM-ID. 'CHAPT18'.
ENVIRONMENT DIVISION.
CONFIGURATION SECTION.
SOURCE-COMPUTER. (name).
OBJECT-COMPUTER. (name).
INPUT-OUTPUT SECTION.
FILE-CONTROL. SELECT DETAIL-TAPE ASSIGN TO TAPE 1.
              SELECT MASTER-IN ASSIGN TO TAPE 2.
              SELECT MASTER-OUT ASSIGN TO TAPE 3.
DATA DIVISION.
FILE SECTION.
FD    DETAIL-TAPE
      RECORDING MODE IS F,
      LABEL RECORDS ARE STANDARD,
      RECORD CONTAINS 20 CHARACTERS,
      BLOCK CONTAINS 100 RECORDS,
      DATA RECORD IS DETAIL-REC.
01    DETAIL-REC.
      02 INV-NO              PICTURE 9(5).
      02 QTY-ON-HAND         PICTURE 9(4).
      02 ITEM-DESCRIPTION    PICTURE X(11).
FD    MASTER-IN
      RECORDING MODE IS F,
      LABEL RECORDS ARE STANDARD,
      RECORD CONTAINS 20 CHARACTERS,
      BLOCK CONTAINS 100 RECORDS,
      DATA RECORD IS MASTER-REC-IN.
01    MASTER-REC-IN.
      02 INV-NO              PICTURE 9(5).
      02 QTY-ON-HAND         PICTURE 9(4).
      02 ITEM-DESCRIPTION    PICTURE X(11).
FD    MASTER-OUT
      RECORDING MODE IS F,
      LABEL RECORDS ARE STANDARD,
      RECORD CONTAINS 20 CHARACTERS,
      BLOCK CONTAINS 100 RECORDS,
      DATA RECORD IS MASTER-REC-OUT.
01    MASTER-REC-OUT.
      02 INV-NO              PICTURE 9(5).
      02 QTY-ON-HAND         PICTURE 9(4).
      02 ITEM-DESCRIPTION    PICTURE X(11).
WORKING-STORAGE SECTION.
77    CODE                   PICTURE 9.
77    A                      PICTURE 9,   VALUE ZERO.
77    B                      PICTURE 9,   VALUE ZERO.
PROCEDURE DIVISION.
      OPEN INPUT DETAIL-TAPE, MASTER-IN, OUTPUT MASTER-OUT.
```

1.   DISPLAY 'KEYPUNCH A CARD WITH A 1 OR A 2 IN CC-1; 1 DENOTES
—   'ADDITIONS TO MASTER TAPE, 2 DENOTES UPDATE OF MASTER TAPE
—   'RECORDS'.
      ACCEPT CODE.
      IF CODE = 1 GO TO ADDITIONS.
      IF CODE = 2 GO TO UPDATE.
      DISPLAY 'INCORRECT CODE PUNCHED-REPUNCH CARD'.
      GO TO 1.
ADDITIONS.
      PERFORM READ-DETAIL.
BB.
      PERFORM READ-MASTER.
C.   IF A = 1 AND B = 1 GO TO EOJ. IF A = 1 WRITE MASTER-REC-OUT
      FROM MASTER-REC-IN GO TO BB.
      IF B = 1 WRITE MASTER-REC-OUT FROM DETAIL-REC, PERFORM
      READ-DETAIL GO TO C.
      IF INV-NO OF DETAIL-REC IS LESS THAN INV-NO OF MASTER-REC-IN
      WRITE MASTER-REC-OUT FROM DETAIL-REC PERFORM READ-DETAIL
      GO TO C.
      IF INV-NO OF DETAIL-REC IS GREATER THAN INV-NO OF
      MASTER-REC-IN WRITE MASTER-REC-OUT FROM MASTER-REC-IN GO
      TO BB.
Z.   DISPLAY 'DETAIL RECORD AND MASTER RECORD HAVE THE SAME
—   'INVOICE NO', DETAIL-REC, MASTER-REC-IN.
      GO TO ADDITIONS.
UPDATE.
      PERFORM READ-DETAIL.
D.
      PERFORM READ-MASTER.
E.   IF A = 1 AND B = 1 GO TO EOJ. IF A = 1
      WRITE MASTER-REC-OUT FROM MASTER-REC-IN GO TO D.
      IF B = 1 GO TO Y.
      IF INV-NO OF DETAIL-REC IS GREATER THAN INV-NO OF
      MASTER-REC-IN WRITE MASTER-REC-OUT FROM MASTER-REC-IN
      GO TO D.
      IF INV-NO OF DETAIL-REC IS EQUAL TO INV-NO OF MASTER-REC-IN
      ADD QTY-ON-HAND OF DETAIL-REC TO QTY-ON-HAND OF
      MASTER-REC-IN WRITE MASTER-REC-OUT FROM MASTER-REC-IN
      GO TO UPDATE.
Y.   DISPLAY 'DETAIL RECORD WITH NO CORRESPONDING MASTER
—   'RECORD', DETAIL-REC.
      PERFORM READ-DETAIL.
      GO TO E.
READ-DETAIL.
      READ DETAIL-TAPE AT END MOVE 1 TO A.
READ-MASTER.
      READ MASTER-IN AT END MOVE 1 TO B.
EOJ.
      CLOSE DETAIL-TAPE, MASTER-IN, MASTER-OUT.
      STOP RUN.

Chapter 19

```
IDENTIFICATION DIVISION.
PROGRAM-ID. 'CHAPT19'.
ENVIRONMENT DIVISION.
CONFIGURATION SECTION.
SOURCE-COMPUTER.    (name).
OBJECT-COMPUTER.    (name).
INPUT-OUTPUT SECTION.
FILE-CONTROL.   SELECT CARDS ASSIGN TO READER.
                SELECT TAPE-OUT ASSIGN TO TAPE 1.
DATA DIVISION.
FILE SECTION.
FD   CARDS
     RECORDING MODE IS F,
     LABEL RECORDS ARE OMITTED,
     RECORD CONTAINS 80 CHARACTERS,
     DATA RECORD IS CARD-REC.
01   CARD-REC.
     02 NAME              PICTURE  X(20).
     02 ADDRESS           PICTURE  X(15).
     02 NUMERIC-FIELDS.
        03  QTY           PICTURE  9(5)
        03  AMT           PICTURE  9(5)V99.
        03  DATE          PICTURE  9(4).
        03  TRANS-NO      PICTURE  9(4).
     02 FILLER            PICTURE  X(25).
FD   TAPE-OUT
     RECORDING MODE IS F,
     LABEL RECORDS ARE STANDARD,
     RECORD CONTAINS 55 CHARACTERS,
     BLOCK CONTAINS 40 RECORDS,
     DATA RECORD IS TAPE-REC.
01   TAPE-REC.
     02 TRANS-NO          PICTURE  9(4).
     02 QTY               PICTURE  9(5).
     02 AMT               PICTURE  9(5)V99.
     02 NAME              PICTURE  X(20).
     02 ADDRESS           PICTURE  X(15).
     02 DATE              PICTURE  9(4).
PROCEDURE DIVISION.
     OPEN INPUT CARDS, OUTPUT TAPE-OUT.
START.
     READ CARDS AT END GO TO EOJ.
     EXAMINE NUMERIC-FIELDS REPLACING ALL ' ' BY ZEROS.
     MOVE CORRESPONDING CARD-REC TO TAPE-REC.
     WRITE TAPE-REC.
     GO TO START.
EOJ.
     CLOSE CARDS, TAPE-OUT.
     STOP RUN.
```

Chapter 20

```
IDENTIFICATION DIVISION.
PROGRAM-ID. 'CHAPT20'.
ENVIRONMENT DIVISION.
CONFIGURATION SECTION.
SOURCE-COMPUTER.   (name).
OBJECT-COMPUTER.   (name).
INPUT-OUTPUT SECTION.
FILE-CONTROL. SELECT MASTER-DISK ASSIGN TO 'SYS005' DIRECT-ACCESS
      2311 UNIT, ORGANIZATION IS INDEXED, ACCESS IS SEQUENTIAL,
      RECORD KEY IS TRAN-NO-DISK, SYMBOLIC KEY IS KEY-A.
      SELECT DETAIL ASSIGN TO 'SYS004' UTILITY 2400 UNITS.
DATA DIVISION.
FILE SECTION.
FD   MASTER-DISK
     RECORDING MODE IS F
     LABEL RECORDS ARE STANDARD
     RECORD CONTAINS 10 CHARACTERS
     DATA RECORD IS DISK-REC.
01   DISK-REC.
     02 TRAN-NO-DISK   PICTURE 9(5).
     02 AMT            PICTURE 999V99.
FD   DETAIL
     RECORDING MODE IS F
     LABEL RECORDS ARE STANDARD
     RECORD CONTAINS 25 CHARACTERS
     BLOCK CONTAINS 12 RECORDS
     DATA RECORD IS TAPE-REC.
01   TAPE-REC.
     02 TRAN-NO-TAPE   PICTURE 9(5).
     02 AMT            PICTURE 999V99.
     02 FILLER         PICTURE X(15).
WORKING-STORAGE SECTION.
77   KEY-A            PICTURE 9(5).
PROCEDURE DIVISION.
     OPEN INPUT DETAIL, I-O MASTER-DISK.
START
     READ DETAIL AT END GO TO EOJ.
     MOVE TRAN-NO-TAPE TO KEY-A.
     MOVE TRAN-NO-TAPE TO TRAN-NO-DISK.
     READ MASTER-DISK INVALID KEY DISPLAY 'INVALID TAPE RECORD',
     TAPE-REC, GO TO START.
     MOVE AMT OF TAPE-REC TO AMT OF DISK-REC.
     REWRITE DISK-REC
     GO TO START.
EOJ.
     CLOSE DETAIL, MASTER-DISK.
     STOP RUN.
```

Index

BLUE CDS   RUN CD
WHITE CD   COB

   SOURCE DK.

RED   FIN CD